NOWHERE NEAR GREENLAND

A PERSONAL MEMOIR

BARRY WEIGHTMAN

Manples (BFoV) Publishing

http://www.british-friends-of-vanuatu.com

Manples (BFOV) Publishing
20A Pear Tree Road, Ashford, Middlesex, TW15 1PW

First published in the UK by Manples (BFoV) Publishing in 2008

Copyright © 2008 by Barry Weightman

The moral rights of the author have been asserted.

All rights reserved

Without limiting the rights under copyright reserved above, no part of this publication may be reproduced, stored or introduced into a retrieval system, or transmitted, in any form or by any means (electronic, mechanical, photocopying, recording or otherwise), without the prior written permission of both the copyright owner and the above publisher of this book.

ISBN 978-0-9560985-3-5

Printed in Great Britain by Manples (BFoV) Publishing

By the Same Author

Agriculture in Vanuatu (1989) ISBN 0 9514377 04
(Reprinted 2009)

Introduction and Acknowledgements

In the 1950s, during my first leave in Britain following five years in East Africa, I remember standing at the top of an escalator in one of London's largest department stores watching the serried ranks of faces floating up towards me and being struck that not only were they almost all white, but that I did not know any of them. I had by then been well conditioned to living in small, remote and close knit expatriate communities, but with the opportunity in my job of frequently interacting with the wider population of the local people. I knew then that I would not willingly return to live en masse among strangers, maintaining and respecting anonymity with averted gaze, or today with ipods and cell phones staving off a self imposed isolation that is, sadly, a practical necessity. Only in deepest rural Britain may I succumb to my impulse to wave to passing motorists or greet passers by, without, I hope, being mistaken for a crank or suffering from extreme myopia. (My very beautiful younger sister, who once worked in the field of high fashion in London, was very short-sighted and for reasons of vanity would remove her glasses in restaurants, and having briefly absented herself would sometimes return to sit down at a table of complete strangers).

So I must first acknowledge the great good fortune I have had to live much of my life in such places where I knew everyone in the community. We cooperated in creating our own entertainment, defying geographic and ethnic isolation and enhancing the daily enjoyment of our lives. We knew one-another in the round, and there could be no divide between our social and working personas. This book largely celebrates the lives of those who shared this with me.

My grateful thanks go to Norman Shackley of the British Friends of Vanuatu who almost single-handed prepared this book for publication; to Nathan Shackley for his help in preparing the maps; to Don and Sue Mallick who undertook the arduous task of proof reading, with the many essential corrections that entailed, and for their several constructive suggestions; to Tessa Fowler for reading an intermediate draft of the manuscript and providing the photo of my cyclone-wrecked house; to the Mallicks again, and Richard and Toni Cozens for the reproduction, respectively, of the drawing and pastel by Lesley Weightman; to Shaun and Wendy Quayle for the photo of me dancing on the Spitzkoppe; to Christy Gavitt for her photo of the Avenue des Etats-Unis d'Amérique in the Comores; to Francesca Sullivan for the cover-photograph of the author as well as her photo of Jimmy Jones on the Crocodile river; and to my cousin Denise Groves for the family wedding photo in which I appear plastered.

Barry Weightman
St Sulpice de Mareuil
Mareuil 24340, Perigord
F R A N C E

FOREWORD

I wish I had known Barry Weightman better and for longer. He is clearly someone worth knowing, not just in a pub over a beer, but as a professional agriculturalist, administrator, adviser, organiser, prankster, adventurer, raconteur, friend and colleague. He had worked in Tanganyika and I in Uganda, and though the Colonial Service in East Africa tended to specialise and one seldom crossed paths with colleagues even from just across the border, it seems that in 1954 we met briefly in my office in Fort Portal when he and a fellow climber came to seek my advice on their proposed climb in the Ruwenzori.

Briefly, however, from 1978 to 1980, we found ourselves in the same little South Pacific islands of the New Hebrides. But those were fraught times, trying to get that absurd Anglo-French so-called Condominium, (but more popularly known as "The Pandemonium") to independence. Moreover for some of that time Barry was in a sort of limbo, after he had been elbowed by the French out of his task of developing the agriculture of the condominium and before he was, with great enthusiasm, given a new job as Director of Agriculture by the independent government of what now became called the Republic of Vanuatu.

For my part too, those were whirlwind years, having been sent as the British Resident Commissioner to help the Condominium to independence, but finding my French colleagues markedly unenthusiastic about losing one of their colonies, even a colony which had to be shared with the pesky British.

At one point I even had to ask Mrs Thatcher to send me the Royal Marines, to prevent the largest of the New Hebrides islands, Santo, from being detached and retained as French territory. I never had any indication that Paris was behind this secessionist movement, but there were plenty of French nationals on Santo ready to do the job for them, not to mention a half-mad, half Scottish bulldozer driver, who was the selfproclaimed leader of the local "Kastom" movement of fantasists, most of them so high on the national drink of Kava (a mild anaesthetic) that they were fortunately unable to move with any great purpose or speed.

I can relate most closely with the hundred and fifty pages of Barry's book that describe his time in the New Hebrides and thereafter. I greatly relish his descriptions of island life in the ten years before I arrived. In those years the New Hebrides, despite the absurd condominium system, from which Barry suffered as much as anyone, was at least still delivering a semblance of orderly administration and steady if unspectacular growth.

Island life in the South Pacific has to be experienced to be fully understood and Barry's descriptions of bizarre relationships, chaotic journeys and considerable hardships, but in a fascinating setting and, above all, an inextinguishable determination to do the job fully and well, make for fascinating reading. They could well be an account of colonialist life anywhere in the world. But above all they are firmly based in the ultimate madness ofthe New Hebrides, hot, humid, unhealthy, cyclone and fly-ridden, cursed with four incomprehensible and mutually incompatible governments, British, French, Condominium and fledgling Independent, but blessed with an extraordinary beauty and with a people who had (and have) a courtesy and gentility that often put their colonialist masters to shame.

It is Barry's account of what to him may have been a humdrum life, but to most people would seem almost impossibly exotic, that fills me with regret. I wish I had had the time and opportunity to live like that in the New Hebrides. It was the way I started my own career in Africa. But there was never time or opportunity to tour the islands, to know the people, the country, the history or to learn the language properly. That language alone was a source of endless pleasure, mixed with hilarity. An amalgam of local dialects, English, French and bits of Chinese stirred with a portion of soaring imagination and known as Bislama, I discovered when, with great pride, I donned my colonial governor's uniform, topped with soaring ostrich plumes above a ridiculous white topee, that the local description of those plumes was "Grass blong arse blong chicken". It is impossible to remain too pompous when you are walking around with grass blong arse blong chicken on your head.

But nor is it possible to be patronising towards people of such wit and imagination. The pleasure of Barry's book is that he is never patronising. Again and again he refers to some local politician as "my good friend" or "a new and dynamic minister". Virtually the only time he refers disparagingly to anyone is when his (French) preindependence superior and some unnamed functionary in my (British) office indulge in the sort of national chauvinism that was, sadly, all too common in those hectic last days of the condominium.

Undoubtedly Barry's book will appeal principally to those who already know something of the New Hebrides or Vanuatu and its tangled history. There's not much in it about the condominium system and how it operated (or did not operate). Early on in his account things like Kava, the Nambas and the Pentecost jump are mentioned but not, at that stage, very clearly explained to those who do not know what he is talking about. This is probably because he modestly imagines that his story will appeal only to those of us who, at least in part, have shared his experiences. That may be so, but I doubt it.

Prefaces are written to help sell you the book. Whoever you may be and whatever your experience, I hope you will do so. You will find it a vivid account of an experience that is past and of a man whom most of us would wish to know.

Andrew Stuart 2008

NOWHERE NEAR GREENLAND

Contents

The Crocodile Tree	1
Into Africa	31
Under Rubber	93
Kiwis and Canaries	123
A Sad Chapter	141
To Coral Strands	165
The Comores, Coffee and Kava	323
Sir, the Hippo	353
Terraces, Toad Soup and Atoll Gods	373

In memory of VWV and JW who loved to travel

Cover photo: Makalani palms in Namibia

NOWHERE NEAR GREENLAND

THE CROCODILE TREE

The Oxford House nursing home where I was born, an elegant early Victorian building in Clarendon Road, Watford, was demolished in the 1950s to make way for an ugly income tax office, which I hope has in its turn been reduced to rubble for something better. I was carried back to Shady Firs, a corner detached house in the nearby village of Abbots Langley; the village is known to some of its residents and to a few historians as the birthplace of England's only pope, Nicholas Breakspeare, who as Pope Adrian IV pontificated for five years in the twelfth century. Surprising, perhaps, that someone with so English a surname should have gained such pre-eminence in a Norman-dominated century. By the early 1930s, and thirty years before it became a satellite town for London commuters, this village was set amidst a patchwork of small woods and fields threaded here and there by narrow lanes, frequently sunken with age between high hedges and amply shaded by oak and chestnut.

Abbot's Langley then comprised a single street of shops that included Kemp the dairy, Mr Aves (invariably pronounced Misstraves) the butcher, Fenton the chemist with large, long-necked bottles of clear red, green, blue and orange fluid as the sole display in his window, Kingman the hardware shop whose brightly patterned rolls of oil-redolent linoleum stood tall on the pavement, Audrey's whose shop smelled of sugared buns and vanilla, and my bête noire Dobson the barber whose frosted corner-shop window screened from all compassionate sight the submission of his customers beneath scissors and clippers, for me his chosen instruments of torment. The charge for a small child's haircut was sixpence, with a penny back to buy an ice cream if you behaved.

The Crocodile Tree

That was indeed a concessionary rate for me, for I made the barber's task as hard as possible, twisting and turning from the waist and neck, arching back in the chair, fighting the firmness of his splayed fingers on the top of my head, hating the sound and feel of snip snipping and my ears being touched. I recall throwing a tantrum on the floor behind his frosted glass entrance door, and I never, ever got my penny back. My sister always, always did. She had started school in the village at Mr. and Mrs. Moon's kindergarten. Beside his unquestioned vocation for teaching, Mr Moon demonstrated a whimsical inventiveness at the village fetes, for which he custom-built a sort of green garden shed which was turned over and over on an axle with screaming adults strapped inside. And there was his stuffed rat on wheels, that skittered down a wooden chute and you had to whack it with a stick it before it shot through a hole into a box at the bottom.

Ignoring the Dog - Abbotts Langley, 1933

Once a week, a muffin man came round the village, one hand clanging a bell, the other clutching a large flat tray on his head, upon which his wares were heaped under a white cloth. Hauling long drays, their slow, huge hoofed, hollow clopping echoing through the village, great Shire horses delivered barrels of beer from Benskins Brewery, or assorted goods in boxes and parcels of all shapes and sizes from Kings Langley railway station, and coal in ranks of blackened, pungent sacks from

NOWHERE NEAR GREENLAND

the local merchants. A single brown pony pulled the baker's and dairy vans laden with loaves or jingling, cardboard-capped milk bottles. On mornings of indeterminate weather, the milkman's invariable greeting was "What's it going to do today, rain or shine?" and we children skipped gleefully around the house chanting this to one another. A long narrow field bounded our house on one side, and I would squat, peering though the laurel hedge, as a pair of huge horses leaning into their traces hauled a plough or harrow up and down, the flinty brown soil curling and breaking behind them, brasses tinkling when they tossed their heads, the ploughman plodding behind in tall brown boots, softly calling his coded orders. Once, when I had been missing long enough for my parents to initiate a search throughout the village, I was discovered under a hedge silently observing chickens.

My father was the chief accountant for a large paper-making company, and travelled about Britain by rail, and by steamer ferries to Ireland. Sometimes my mother or Alice the maid would take me and my elder sister to stand beside the London Midland and Scottish railway line near Hunton Bridge. Thrilled with anticipation, we would crane and watch for a tiny dot to appear at the end of the long straight, silently growing larger and larger, and then as the rails began to sing and the ground tremble, a deep rhythmic throbbing grew in volume until suddenly this mighty contraption was upon us in a blast of wind, sound, steam, stinging smuts, and the smell of soot as we watched the Royal Scot or Mallard thunder past, the fastest locomotives in the world heading north, my father's white handkerchief flatly streaming from one of the carriage windows, all too soon reduced again to a silent, dwindling dot in the distance.

In the countryside outside Hemel Hempstead lived my Uncle John, Aunty Rosa and their son Baby John. They were no relation, and he was probably a soldier friend of my father's from the First World War. He was a small balding, wiry Scot and she was seriously and motherly large. They lived in the house of an abandoned and derelict chicken farm, probably a victim of the Great Depression of that time. There were several long sheds of grey, unpainted wood, with mouldering straw in dusty nesting boxes, and the full length of the sheds along one side was screened with wire netting. Baby John and I enjoyed running through them, the wooden planks drumming, the dust and smell of chickens past erupting under our feet. I was a compulsive climber, and once there was a garden bonfire while I was on the roof of one of the sheds. Somehow the smoke penetrated my eyes and I suffered a 'white out', I couldn't see anything, just white, I was blind, and had to be helped

The Crocodile Tree

down from the roof. It was a strange experience. In compensation, Uncle John promised to show me a crocodile the next time we visited, probably with the added conditionality 'if you're a good boy'. I had not yet seen a real live crocodile, as our annual visits to the London Zoo in Regents Park, where I would be photographed in their 'children's corner' with a lion cub in a wicker basket, and my sister standing next to a llama, had not yet begun. So I built up quite a head of impatience and expectation until the great day came, which was probably brought forward in response to constant pestering. So we set off, not for some pen or cage in a town, but striding across a meadow, down into a valley and across another field. A real live crocodile loose in a Hertfordshire field; that was really something to see! My expectation knew no bounds, as I skipped around and tugged at my uncle John's hand. Eventually we came to an overgrown hedge and stopped. "Do you see it?" said Uncle John. "Where?" I whispered, crouching low. "There," he said, pointing to a gnarled and knobbly root protruding from the foot of a tree, "See, it looks just like a crocodile". I couldn't believe it. The expression 'you can not be serious' was not yet in vogue, and being 'gobsmacked' was even then confined to the vulgar vernacular, but I was definitely 'devastated'.

When I was four, we moved to the nearby village of Hunton Bridge, through which ran the London, Midland and Scottish railway's main line from Euston to the north, and here the Grand Union canal threaded the valley to link London with Birmingham. The village boasted, perhaps literally, four public houses, Benskins brewery and a single shop, Robinson's. At the weekends, when the trades horses had clopped by with their deliveries, my father was in keen competition with Mr. Boatwright, another avid gardener who lived in the house opposite, to shovel up the fresh horse manure from the road.

Our house had been newly painted when we moved in, and the workmen left behind high trestles and a long plank, iron-bound at the ends and excellent material for a spectacular seesaw. When one end was down on the ground, the other was way up in the air, and one day my sister suggested she stand on one end while I walk up to the other. Just as I reached the top and was piping "Taraa!", or similar, she stepped off and down I came and broke my left arm.

We were shortly to go down to the sea for a holiday at Dymchurch, where, with my arm in plaster, I entertained myself by jumping from the sea wall, progressing along the top as it rose higher and higher above the sand below, until the growing

NOWHERE NEAR GREENLAND

disquiet this was creating among the elderly seeking stress-free relaxation in deck chairs, and to the parents of children admiring and itching to imitate my antics, was brought to the attention of my mother, who was probably deep in a book

We were staying at a private hotel, and the owner, a thin man with round glasses and red hair, grew his prize geraniums in a great shallow bowl of marble set on a pedestal. Presumably with nothing better to do, now that the wall was off limits, I commenced with my good arm to rock this floral edifice, gradually building up a momentum until the whole thing came crashing down in a turbulent shower of earth and flowers. Fortunately the bowl was well secured to the pedestal, so that I lay quite unharmed in the angle between them and the ground.

A Family wedding, 1936 - me, front centre with arm in plaster

From my prone position, I observed the owner marching across the lawn, shouting and seemingly upset, so I piped up that he was not to worry, I was quite all right. When he was right above me, all I could see were his brown shoes and grey flannel turn-ups, hopping and stamping in a most curious manner. Then he gave one of his newly recumbent geraniums a terrific kick, though I suspect it was merely proxy for myself.

The Crocodile Tree

The next morning, I was first into the dining room and sifted ample sugar onto my porridge - only it proved to be salt and I threw up all over the table. I recall no expressions of thanks from the other guests for having saved them all from similar embarrassment, for a new maid had filled all the silver sugar sifters with salt, and was summarily dismissed, poor girl. I believe we returned home rather earlier than planned, where I immediately resumed my acquaintance with the 'great plank', this time struggling one handed to stand it upright; but my grip slipped, and failing

Stepping Out - with mother, sister and aunt
Swanage, 1937

to outrun its fall the ironbound end bashed me on the head. I trotted into the scullery and clambered onto a chair to admire the blood in the mirror, and as Alice the maid came through from the kitchen, I turned and said "Look, a Red Indian" and she screamed and fainted. With my plastered arm, I then wore, with more theatrical than wounded pride, a white turban of bandages over my six stitches. Although around this time I was quite unnecessarily 'rescued' from window ledges

NOWHERE NEAR GREENLAND

and other high places, I was not particularly accident prone.

Two years later I was six, it was 1938 and my mother, elder sister and I went on holiday to Belgium. For the first week, father stayed behind to work and a young French friend of my mother's, who later became a nun, looked after Sally, our new baby sister, at home. We stayed first at the Hotel Bellevue on the sea front at Westende, near Ostend. Sand yachts skimmed at speed across the wide sands, yellow trams rumbled and clanged their bells and I learned to ride a bicycle with a little balancing wheel on the back. Just behind the beach was a fenced-off derelict lunar park with a scenic railway, or big dipper, swooping up and down, rusting and sadly abandoned. Once through the broken fence, I scrambled through tall weeds to the far end where the ride began, and started up the rails. Some of the wooden cross-ties were missing, and here and there I had to make a little jump to clear the gaps, but I made good progress to the top; then down and up again to the highest point, from where the people down below looked very small, only they seemed to be gathering in a crowd, their little white faces staring up at me.

They were very quiet except when I had to jump a gap, when squeaks, oohs, ahs and shushes came floating up to me. They need not have worried, for I had excellent balance, and positively scampered down the final incline of the track. At the bottom, dodging hands thrust out to grab me and, ducking under outspread arms, I ran back down the beach and hid behind my mother. Two or three people came stomping along the beach looking for me, including a large, scary lady in a dark red bathing costume, but I was not discovered. I then joined my sister who was busy collecting small, almost transparent pink shells that resembled painted fingernails, putting them into the red and gold hexagonal chocolate tins we had been given when we went to the Royal Tournament earlier that year, on the same night as the king and queen and the princesses Elizabeth and Margaret Rose, and we saw them all come down in a lift. Unfortunately, some of the shells we had collected were alive, but when we opened the tins back in Hunton Bridge, they were quite evidently no longer alive and there was a terrible smell.

Father joined us for our second week, and he took me off in a charabanc filled with fellow World War One veterans to look at old battlefields, cemeteries, the city of Bruges and the battered town of Ypres. One extensive section of the trenches had been preserved, or possibly just left untouched. There were duck boards, redoubts and bunkers, lots of rusted barbed wire and a massive gun sunk in a concrete cais-

The Crocodile Tree

son. Father said it was a German gun that could shoot a shell many miles. Hating loud bangs, I began to whimper, fearing that it was about to be fired, but he showed me the split in the huge barrel where the retreating Germans had put in a charge and burst it. The orderly ranks of white crosses in the many cemeteries seemed to stretch for miles, and at the Menin gate, father stood a while reading the inscribed names of lost comrades. A private infantryman in the 7th London battalion, he was one of a very few who survived in his company. Before he was wounded in the battle of Messines, also known as the 3rd battle of Ypres, he had survived entombment in a tunnel that was being dug under the enemy lines, and a gas attack at the onset of which he discovered his gas mask had been stolen, and the only one available was lying in a pool of whale oil, with which the men treated themselves to fend off trench foot. He nearly suffocated. Then during the attack on Messines Ridge, he was struck in the right thigh by a large chunk and many fragments of shrapnel from a bursting shell, and lay overnight in a flooded crater between the lines, until rescued by a stretcher party. By the age of twenty he was already a talented golf and tennis player, and first at the field hospital, and then back at Roehampton in England, he rejected advice to have his leg amputated. But between 1917 and 1944, he had seventeen operations on his leg to remove shell fragments, some of them lodged in the bone, finally dying when a blood clot lodged in his heart. Fifty years later, I wept when I read Sebastian Faulks 'Birdsong', which so vividly described the similar and common experiences of soldiers in the hell of those trenches, and his own which he had recounted to me just months before he died.

At Ypres, we climbed the high Cloth Tower, then still isolated among ruins, in which each floor on the way up had been made into a museum of war medals and the insignia of the units that had fought in that sector, and from the very top, the people in the square far below seemed tiny. Something about heights I really found thrilling, the very opposite of vertigo, whatever that might be. On the way back to Westende we stopped at Bruges. We looked over a bridge into the river, sat outside a café, and father despatched me to order in French two coffees. This was also the first time I used a public urinal. The surface against which we peed was made of grey slate.

When we left for Belgium I was in the second year of the kindergarten section of Northfield school near Watford, whose teaching methods followed the Montessori system. Thus, I quickly learned to knit (a dishcloth), weave (two woollen place mats and a tea cosy), and craft a two-shelf bookcase. When father's car was unavailable,

NOWHERE NEAR GREENLAND

which was often, we were taken to school in Mr Quelch's taxi. He had worked first as coachman and then chauffeur to a lord, who when he died left him his Rolls Royce, a huge affair of early 1920s vintage which then became our village taxi, though at the age of five I hardly appreciated the grandeur of our arrivals and departures. My teacher there was a remarkable Miss Harris, who crossed to New York and back on the maiden voyage of the Queen Mary, and sent every child in the class a picture postcard of that great liner.

One summer night in 1939, my mother called us children to her bedroom whose windows faced towards London some seventeen miles to the south. This was to see a trial of the searchlights that ringed the city. Their great white beams silently swept the black night in all directions across the starlit sky, criss-crossed each other and groped the high, scattered clouds. Remembering the coloured spotlights of the Royal Tournament, I was disappointed that these lights were all the same boring white. Later we would learn to identify the different pitch and patterns of the air raid sirens as they started up in the far distance, and gradually advanced towards us across the northern suburbs of London to Bushey and Watford, and then to the nearest siren at Kings Langley. Deep wails, high wails, low honking, slow warbles, all out of time and out of tune with one another, and then as they died away the stark contrast of ensuing silence, listening for the drone of planes, the uneven, unsynchronised throb that characterised the Hun, the sharp bangs of anti-aircraft guns and sometimes the whistle and whoosh of falling bombs.

That same summer, we travelled down to Devon in my father's green and black Austin 7, and stopped at midday for cold drinks in the garden of a roadside pub near Sidmouth. There we heard Mr. Chamberlain intoning over the wireless, that because he had not received a reply from Herr Hitler, we were now at war with Germany. We continued on to the hamlet of North Bovey on the edge of Dartmoor, where we rented a mill cottage next-door to a golfing friend of my father, who was the 'pro' at Morton Hampstead - which was where Germany's then ambassador von Ribbentrop often played. While I explored the moor with Reggie, the young son of my father's friend, seeing my first snake in the wild - an adder in a hedgerow - and learning to pee from an upstairs window into the millstream, my father hurried back to Hertfordshire to dig an air-raid shelter in the garden. Very much modelled on his experience of dugouts in the Ypres trenches, this was put to use during the first raids over London. But we were pestered sleepless by mosquitoes, and our family of five was very uncomfortable on camp beds, so while we were all away at

The Crocodile Tree

Swanage the following summer he built mark 2, a far more sophisticated affair. The entrance was down a sloping tunnel that turned at right-angles before a steel reinforced door. This opened into a vaulted asbestos-lined chamber equipped with six double bunk beds, electric light and fire, and an emergency exit fronted by a thick, reinforced concrete wall. Over the top was a high mound of earth and clay, surmounted by a rockery planted with flowers, and the two mature apple trees that the excavations had carefully spared. The one spare top bunk was used for storing apples over the winter, so the shelter soon welcomed us with a fruity aroma, which at times was akin to cider when the odd, bruised apple decayed within its newspaper wrappings. Our household's preparations for total war included sticky brown paper criss-crossing all our windows, which my father soon replaced with a glued-on fine mesh which covered all the glass and you could not see through the windows for five years. A luggage label with all our names was tied to the letter-box on the front door because, we were told, the door would be blown clear of the general rubble of a destroyed house and the rescue team would know how many to look for. Mother and Alice sewed and hung heavy blackout curtains at every window, and the newspapers and wireless advertised the hours between which not a light must be shown, and cars' headlights were reduced by a visor to a narrow slit. Air raid wardens patrolled the streets of the village and yelled, banged on the door or blew their whistle if they could spot a chink of light. They carried a rattle to be whirled round in the event of a gas attack. We each had our gas masks, first issued in a cardboard box threaded on string, but soon weatherproof containers could be bought in the shops and mine was a grey metal canister. Soon after the beginning of the war, we were issued with a metallic green filter which was taped to the snout of the mask, presumably to neutralise some new gas the Germans had devised for us. To arrive at school without a gas mask was to be sent straight back home again to get it. In the wider scheme of things, church bells were silenced for the duration and only to be rung as a warning of invasion, cast-iron railings were cut down to make Spitfires, and all signposts on roads throughout the country were removed so that strangers, particularly enemy strangers, would quickly lose their way in the maze of rural lanes. (Many years later, my stepfather, who was a general during the war, told me that once travelling in his staff car with a driver, both in full uniform, they became hopelessly lost somewhere in the home counties. They stopped to ask the way from a pedestrian who was quite obviously local. "Oi baint be telling yer" he replied, eying them balefully.)

But returning from Devon in the late summer of 1939, I was enrolled in the prepara-

NOWHERE NEAR GREENLAND

tory section of Berkhamsted public school some ten miles up the road, and to that destination, from the age of seven to twelve when my father died, I commuted on a double-decker bus every day with my elder sister who was attending the girls' school in the same town - where Winston Churchill's wife Clementine had been educated a couple of generations before. Boys and girls of both schools boarded the bus at stops along the way, all of us always travelling upstairs where we spent a jolly half an hour or more. We invented a game whereby it was lucky if the four numbers on your bus ticket added up to twenty one - there was no prize, you were just lucky and waved your ticket around in triumph. Two regular travellers to my sister's school were Ann Powell and Judith Neal, both about my age and on whom I developed a deep crush, and I ingratiated myself by giving them small, hot peppermints which I called 'killem-quicks' that my father had somehow obtained off the ration. One of the stops along the way was called Two Waters where my great, great grandfather had owned an inn called the Spotted Bull, and just opposite the road in a field, was the grave of a hanged highwayman. We also passed through Boxmoor, where nearby the Americans created a great airbase called Bovingdon for their massed Flying Fortress raids over Germany. At Apsley, near Hemel Hempstead, my father had his office, and here the basic products of the two paper mills in the valley, Croxley and Nash mills (where my uncle Albert was manager), were manufactured into envelopes, writing paper and other stationery. It was to Apsley that my father's own great great grandfather had moved from South Scarle in Nottinghamshire at the beginning of the 19th century, and where he was employed as a wire weaver.

At Berkhamsted, separate from the rest of the school in the centre of town, one climbed a steep hill past the forbidding edifices of the upper school houses of Incents and St. Johns to reach the preparatory school. This consisted of a single storey building accommodating three classrooms, and some distance away, at the top of a long lawn, the large Edwardian house where the senior master lived, the boys boarded, and where we 'dayboys' took our lunches with the rest of them. Mr. Hilliard, one of the masters, presided at my table of some eighteen boys. Whereas tales of 'Mrs. Giddlehouse', the little old lady who lived at the bottom of my bed, had been appropriate and quite likely credible fare for my audience at kindergarten, sterner stuff was now required for my now more mature and all male listeners at the lunch table, so I regaled them with daily reports of the lion I kept in the garden. There was a high level of interest among my fellows, and never any shortage of questions requiring detailed answers regarding all aspects of lion hus-

The Crocodile Tree

bandry, but one day, without preamble, Mr. Hilliard, perhaps long grown bored with my flagging talent for new invention, announced "Weightman, you are a liar". Shocking words indeed, and a shot that killed that lion stone dead. At least, maybe, those yarns served to distract somewhat from the truly horrible food, the brown, stinking mounds of slushy lentils, the unpeeled and poorly washed boiled potatoes, from whose dirty eyes grey squiggles grew into their middle. From such fare, the inevitable rice puddings provided blessed relief.

Miss Bartlett, who lived to be a hundred, taught English grammar in the first form and underlined the parts of speech on the blackboard. Nouns were underlined with green chalk, verbs with red, adjectives with yellow, adverbs with mauve and conjunctions with blue. Mr. Johnstone taught French. He would come up behind you, seize you by the hair and then slowly wind your head round and round; and between saying "Ouch sir, ouch" you were expected to correct whatever error you had made. He was also pretty mean with the ruler and a good shot with a piece of chalk, so his lessons could be said to have been quite physical. Mr. Davis, the elderly and kindly senior master, was a great fan of early Walt Disney and he regularly showed us some of the first films made of Mickey and Minnie Mouse, Donald Duck and their supporting animated cast.

In the winter of 1940, I contracted bovine tuberculosis on my right lung, most likely from one of 'Misstraves' cows that supplied our milk; the routine tuberculin testing of herds had probably become lax with the departure of so many men to the war. Having developed a soaring night temperature, my parents thought I might have meningitis and I was taken to the West Herts hospital. However, after a few tests, I was diagnosed with TB. The Great Ormond Street Children's Hospital had been evacuated here from London, so I had the very best of care, remembering among my fellow patients children who had come in to have their tonsils removed and spat dark blood into white enamel bowls, and a senior boy from my school in whose hand a 'thunderflash' had exploded and seriously injured it. After three weeks there, I was sent home to spend nearly six months in bed; bed rest and a good diet being the only remedies for TB in those days before antibiotics, and the clean, high air and sun of Switzerland sanatoriums had been put out of reach by the war. My mother must have been particularly anxious, because her father had died of 'galloping consumption' in 1907 when she was eleven years old, and I had evidently inherited the predisposition to this disease. The bed rest was largely spent clambering in and out of it, maintaining some schooling and melting father's

NOWHERE NEAR GREENLAND

peppermints on the blue enamel top of the electric fire.

During the 1941 blitz on London, a number of stray or jettisoned bombs and land mines fell on neighbourhood fields, and at weekends with Torben, my Danish friend who lived next door, we cycled out to locate craters and scavenge bits of bomb, of which we amassed quite a collection, together with spent bullets, cannon shells and German insignia from various sources. Torben's father was a Danish civil engineer who worked for the company that before the war had built the white hump-backed bridge over the Grand Union canal between Watford and Hunton Bridge, and the brief, near-weightlessness experienced crossing over it on the bus never failed to raise a cheer. The family had escaped Denmark just before the Germans invaded, but were thence dogged by ill-luck. First the mother died of cancer, then the eldest son training for the RAF crashed into power lines and was killed. Ivor the second son, then at medical college, died of a combination of asthma and pneumonia, and my friend Torben died of a heat stroke while doing his national service on a route march near Colchester in the summer of 1947. (Three died that day from the same cause, which gave rise to questions in the House of Commons). Torben, Michael, Richard and I played elaborate war games of invasion and defence with our combined collections of toy ships, planes and soldiers, battling across the green oceans of lawn, to the harbours, islands and continents of flowerbeds in our respective gardens, sometimes beneath the high condensation trails of real air battles raging somewhere between the horizon and zenith.

In 1942, I progressed from the preparatory school to one of the junior houses, St. George's, which catered for the boys who came in by bus, train or bicycle, and on foot if they lived nearby. The 'house' as such consisted of no more than somewhat temporary buildings down near the fives courts, and included a dining room, kitchen and changing rooms. Mr Edge was the housemaster, a pleasant, good-looking man who for some reason gave all his boys a passport-size photograph of himself. My mother was so taken with it she kept it for years in her handbag.

The summer of 1944 brought overshoots of the V1 flying bomb, a.k.a. doodlebug, into Hertfordshire, and one of the worst in the war fell near Watford Junction railway station, exploding the gas mains and killing my mother's hairdresser, Mr. Harris, and all his family, as well as some sixty others. Two or three V1s came roaring and clattering like old motorbikes up our valley and crashed into fields killing a few livestock. The harsh noise of one on a summer weekend afternoon brought

The Crocodile Tree

everyone out into their gardens to watch this speeding jet-black object, with flaming horizontal stovepipe, fly past until its engine cut out and it angled down in a sudden, shocking silence behind distant trees and blew up. Then, just a few nights later, my father died, crying out when he was hit by a massive heart attack. My 'uncles', really business associates of my father, decided I should board at Berkhamsted, and one of them had a wooden, iron-bound tuck box made for me in the Nash Mills workshop.

So I moved into Overton house on the main street of Berkhamsted town and was initially treated rather snobbishly as a latecomer and former dayboy. Mr. Gulland the housemaster was a gruff and kindly family man, and Mr. Manning, bald as a coot, was also resident there and taught either Latin or maths, or perhaps both. A fellow schoolmate was Barry Oakely who was to become a parson. His father at that time was the editor of the Baghdad Times and sent him a banana in the post. Since no-one since 1939 had seen a banana - and I believe the following year the Queen auctioned one for the Red Cross - the opening of the parcel attracted considerable interest, and we all crowded round Oakely for the event. The banana was of course completely black, having spent several weeks in un-refrigerated, compost-promoting transit, but it had at least retained the shape of a banana, which duly informed us. It was Oakley who introduced me to a Christian organisation for young boys called the Crusaders, who wore a small shield on a lapel as a badge of membership. They met every Sunday afternoon in one of the classrooms and sang hymns. During one of the hymns, the adult in charge of the proceedings came right up to me and, whispering in my right ear, asked if I had seen the light. I do not recall my reply, and though I very much enjoyed singing hymns I did not become a Crusader, preferring not to miss my pleasant and exploratory Sunday afternoon walks in the countryside around Berkhamsted.

From the top attic window of Overton house, where I shared a dormitory with boys named Pringle and Wynne-Wilson, we leaned out to watch the spontaneous celebrations in the High Street below when VE Day, for victory in Europe, was proclaimed. My mother took me and my sisters up to London for the big parade, and from a good first floor vantage point, and later from outside Buckingham Palace, we saw Churchill, the Royal Family, and many heroes of the war, the splendour of uniforms, carriages and horses in a seemingly endless procession, and then planes roaring over. At a thanksgiving service in Westminster Abbey, by great coincidence I stood next to the matron of my school's Incents house. My promotion

NOWHERE NEAR GREENLAND

to the senior school when I was thirteen heralded my adoption of long trousers, and a visit was made to the school's second-hand clothes shop housed in a wooden shed next to the music school. At this time, clothes were still rationed and the coupons to buy them scarce, and I bought for a few shillings a pair of formal black-striped trousers and a black jacket; these presumably reflected the standard pre-war uniform, but was still largely adopted for Sunday wear, when those of us who had been confirmed were expected to attend the school chapel three times, for holy communion, matins and evensong. I had been allocated to School House, which was divided into Uppers and Lowers, depending on the level of your dormitory, which were housed in one of the early Victorian buildings on either side of the mid-16th century Old Hall with its fine oak beams, complete with gargoyles, a massive Elizabethan outer door and dark wooden panelling. This was both our common room where we ate or hurled one-currant buns during morning break, and did our prep in the evenings. We were seated in four rows at desks stretching the length of the hall. Small boys were seated at the front and senior boys along the back nearest to the fat heating pipes along the base of the wall, though in the immediate post-war years of shortages and privation they were rarely warm, let alone hot. Facing us on three raised dais spaced along the hall, and seated in massive oak arm-chairs were invigilating prefects, one of whose duties was to call out the name of the boy whose once a week bath time was due, for which the immediate cue was the reappearance through a door in the hall of his now squeaky clean predecessor. Somehow, at least, the hot water extended to the bathrooms, but not to our Edwardian indoor swimming pool, redolent with the odour of chlorine, and its flanking rows of cubicles smelling of sweaty, wet towels.

During the summer term, a couple of lengths swum naked in the unheated pool before breakfast were de rigueur, but gave me earache and conditioned me to a lifelong hatred of bathing or showering in cold water.

During the war, several of the masters had returned to teaching from retirement, some of them continuing to prefix their name with their First World War officer's rank, and most of them were majors. One was reputed to have had his bottom shot off and wear a cork replacement, so there were recurrent stories of boys putting a drawing pin on his classroom chair to test this hypothesis, but none of him either leaping to his feet or leaving the class with the pin stuck in the back of his trousers. If there was any truth to the story, perhaps his eyes were sharper than the pin. And there was old sergeant-major Bunker with a pronounced hobble, one of whose du-

The Crocodile Tree

ties was to ring the school bell. He also taught shooting in the indoor rifle range - for which the school won many prizes, but was too infirm to participate in the weekly parades of the school's Officer Training Corps. At the end of the war he was replaced by a real terror, a newly demobbed sergeant-major White who yelled at us as though we were real soldiers and generally behaved like that rank's martinet stereotype, as depicted in the cinema. At an outdoor firing range, awaiting the order to fire, and not appreciating the delicacy of the trigger, I prematurely let off a burst of three shots from a Bren gun. S.M. White then simulated apoplexy and accused me of sticking out my tongue at him, when I was simply gripping it between my teeth in fright.

Many Jewish boys whose families had fled Germany came to the school. One of them, a great friend of mine, was Thomas Glaser whose family lived in a big house on the outskirts of Watford. Before I became a boarder at school I often went there to play. They were a very talented family, whose other members during my visits would sometimes form a trio or quartet to play classical music. But Thomas and I, with higher things in mind, took to exploring the attics. There among the boxes we discovered two fencing swords. What better invitation to a duel could there be! It was dark in the attic, and we had already lit a candle and stuck it on top of one of the boxes. A furious duel by candlelight ensued, and the candle was, predictably, knocked into an open box, on the top of which was packed Mrs. Glaser's fur coat, fur side up. The flame flashed instantly across the fur, and as the attic filled with very expensive, choking smoke, we flailed away at the fire with tennis racquets. Though I visited the house many times afterwards, this episode was never mentioned, however I remember the whole family in tears just after they received the news from Germany that all their relatives there had fallen victim to Hitler's final solution. Another friend who was in my boarding house was Kempner, a heavy, studious and short-sighted boy with whom I took long walks around Berkhamsted on Sunday afternoons. A refugee from Germany, his father was a toy maker and had set up a factory in Aylesbury. Moseiwitch, son of the famous concert pianist at that time, was in the same class as me, and Goehr, son of a well-known conductor, was in my house and later became professor of music at Cambridge and a composer; my mother, a fine pianist, would have included his creations in her broad category for contemporary composition, as 'stomach-ache music'.

At one end of the Old Hall was a door lined on the far side with green baize. This led into an almost pitch dark corridor, on the right side of which was matron's room

NOWHERE NEAR GREENLAND

and the study of the deputy headmaster. At the end was a door leading into the headmaster's house whose fine drawing room had a wide view of the parish church and churchyard. All the boys in my first year in School House were called in, one by one, for a quiet chat in the drawing room with the headmaster, who was then in his last year before retirement. Large, avuncular and owlish, he sat me on a sofa, and in fatherly tones described the awakening temptations of puberty, and then asked me if I had been touching myself. Not quite sure of what he was talking about I brightly replied "Oh no sir". So that was all right then. A few years later I realised I had lied, but was thankful I had not asked him to explain. Our new headmaster had a young family, and a nanny who lived just through a door opposite our dormitory. One day, my head of house disappeared, never to be seen again, and it was said that he had been caught trysting with the nanny.

Once, returning from holiday, I brought back with me, and foolishly put in my locker in the house changing room, a book that had been handed down in the family for generations. Printed in the 17th century, it was entitled 'The Life and Death of Sir Matthew Hale, Lord Chief Justice of England' and on the front end paper were the names of my mother's forebears, the Leeson-Prices of Packington Hall in Leicestershire. This was fairly swiftly stolen and I never confessed the loss to my mother, though I have considered from time to time putting a notice in the 'Old Berkhamstedian' asking the boy who had removed this book from my locker to return it anonymously to me as he had now had it for long enough. The boy whom I suspected of this later became a barrister. Very many years later I would visit the village of Packington, the first in my family to do so since my mother was taken there as a small child at the very beginning of the 20th century. She recalled seeing in the parish church the monument to a Leeson who had two wives, and I found it there, a finely sculpted and coloured Elizabethan memorial of the recumbent husband with two kneeling helpmates at his feet.

There were three serving girls in the dining room of School House, not very flatteringly called Redbush, Blackbush and Blondie, and they were presided over by a very dignified butler type named Mr. Jones. Blondie was stunning and no doubt the object of much pubescent fantasising, and boys would claim to have arranged meetings with her on the common, though by all accounts she never showed up. Under the rationing system, we each had a pot of jam marked with our personal number to last us a month, and similarly two much smaller pots containing butter and sugar to last a week. The jam always ran out well before its time and I took to

The Crocodile Tree

spreading my bread with Coleman's mustard. It was said that in pre-rationing winters, boys would flick up pats of butter with their table-knives to stick to the dining room ceiling, which in the summer would melt and drip rancidly down; so the war had brought hidden blessings.

Possibly through chewing a packet of twenty Players Navy Cut cigarettes that had been left lying around when I was about one year old, I was very early on sensitised to the effects of nicotine. And this sensitisation was to be reinforced when Popple, a boy in my house, suggested that we each buy a pipe and some tobacco and smoke them during the lunch hour. Having obtained written permission from our housemaster to visit town to buy a bottle of ink, we proceeded to purchase at a tobacconists two 'Montgomery' pipes – so called after the general of that name had recently promoted them for his soldiers' use in north Africa, and being very short in the stem they were easily stowed in a kit bag – and a packet of dark, coarse tobacco labelled Black Shag. After lunch, we carried our spoils to a place where White Hill passes through a deep cutting, scrambled up one side through undergrowth and, since time was limited, each rapidly smoked a pipeful of Black Shag, even experimenting with inhaling. That afternoon's double period of German awaited me, and Popple had to report for Greek, and we ran all the way back to the school. About ten minutes into my lesson, Herr Hieber enquired after my health since my complexion had turned distinctly green. And moments after I had replied "perfectly alright sir", just made it outside in time to regurgitate my nicotine contaminated lunch. I then used up copious amounts of toothpaste before reporting sick to matron, and subsequently spent two days in bed with what had been diagnosed as an acute attack of gastric flu.

The Bourne End rail crash, at the time cited as the worst British rail disaster since the Tay bridge collapsed under a train in the 19th century, occurred a few miles south of Berkhamsted on the main line to Euston. Apparently, the express train from Scotland, while on a long fast straight, was abruptly switched to the slow line and at high speed leapt off the tracks and plunged into a turnip field. Aboard were many members of the royal household travelling from Balmoral for seasonal redeployment at Buckingham palace. On the morning after the crash, I accompanied some of the boys from my house, walking along the line to the site of the wreck. The massive engine lay on its side, largely buried in the earth, and behind it a chaos of carriages, some piled one upon another. More than eighty people had died, and there were piles of bloody clothing and scattered belongings. Airmen from the

NOWHERE NEAR GREENLAND

American base at nearby Bovingdon answered the alarm, and arrived in force shortly after the crash to assist with rescue work and the evacuation of the dead and injured. Some of us boys took mementoes from the scene, and I left with a long length of bright red communication cord.

The school had magnificent playing fields opposite the Thomas Coram School, though in my day it was still called the Foundling Hospital, with which George Frederick Handel had had much to do in its creation and support. Here fine old chestnut trees lined the road on either side, and under these, near to the pitch where the big matches were played, we would sit and watch the cricket. Hoare and I were thus engaged one Saturday summer afternoon, when we were joined by an imposing, white-bristle-moustached, red-faced gent who introduced himself as Colonel Scott. At the end of the game he asked us to join him at the Mill House for tea. Knowing the mouth-watering reputation of teas at that establishment, we very regretfully informed him that to accept we would first need the written permission of our housemaster, 'Streaky' Wraith. This was duly obtained for the next weekend, and we enjoyed the mother of all teas. The following summer holiday, Colonel Scott turned up at our door in Branksome Park near Bournemouth, where my mother at that time ran a holiday home for children. Could he take me out for the day and give me lunch? This was agreed, and we crossed over on the ferry to Studland Bay where the colonel proposed we skinny dip. This was declined, I swam in my costume and we crossed back to Poole to have a lobster lunch at the 'Dolphin'. After the meal he said he wanted to show me a book that was in his room. Opening this on his bed, this turned out to be a book of photographs of naked children. I fled the room, slammed the door, raced down the stairs and the high street of Poole, and took a bus home, never to see the colonel again. "Did you have a nice time dear?", asked my mother.

My papermaking uncles were keen to see me through university, after which they would find me a place in their John Dickinson's branch in Johannesburg. However, I was against the idea of an office-orientated career, and resisted their argument to the effect that any other young man would give his right arm for the opportunity, etcetera. That may have been true, but I was not prepared to sacrifice any part of my anatomy for such advancement. My friend Hoare was set to enter naval college when he left school, and I was more attracted to that choice of occupation, and so were my mother and her sister. They had a relative who was head of the Cunard White Star Line in New York, and this connection persuaded them that perhaps I

The Crocodile Tree

should train to be an officer in the merchant navy, and I was duly enrolled for the Warsash Naval College near Southampton. My mother had me kitted out by 'Gieves' in the work and dress uniforms of an officer cadet, and very smart I looked. However, I had early misgivings about this choice of career, particularly after several days hammering and prizing off asbestos lagging from pipes in a derelict ship's engine room (and sixty years later count myself lucky for not having developed asbestosis). Moreover, I was the only cadet at that college who had had a public school education and was subjected to persistent inverted snobbery, so after a few weeks I decamped to consider my future.

In the winter of 1949 I answered an advertisement in the personal column of 'The Times', seeking a personal assistant to the owner of a hotel in the Cotswolds. Following a telephone conversation, I was provisionally accepted and took a Black and White bus to Cheltenham. I was met at the bus station by a tall, bespectacled, stout, middle-aged gentleman in a tweed suit and flat cap, with a round face of somewhat fleshy-pink blandness. He then donned goggles and gauntlets, as though we were about to set off in a large open tourer of two decades earlier, and we drove in his small, black Standard saloon car to Stow-on-the-Wold, which, as his low key publicity boasted, stood 800 feet above sea level. His hotel was the Old Red Lion, which fronted a small patch of greenery and ancient stocks in the imposingly large square of this small town. Effectively, his establishment comprised a terrace of three Cotswold stone Elizabethan houses linked together by communicating doors. The owner was the Reverend Alan Edgar Lucius Burr, MA Cantab. After the First World War he had studied music and theology at Cambridge and had been the organist at Jesus College, and some years before buying the hotel he had owned and operated a preparatory school for boys, and previous to that had been a private tutor to minor royalty.

Mr. Burr was a discerning collector of antiques. The entire hotel was furnished in period furniture, more than twenty clocks from the late 17th and 18th centuries bonged, pinged and chimed the hours in all but the bedrooms, and an even greater number of original oil paintings up to the early 19th century decorated the walls. These were landscapes and seascapes by artists such as Richard Wilson, William Shayer, Vickers and David Teniers. I was entrusted with the weekly duty of winding the clocks and adjusting their time.

Hanging on the wall of the hotel's entrance hall was an original music score of the

NOWHERE NEAR GREENLAND

composer Delius, and two cricket bats separately signed with the names of the Australian and English cricketers who had comprised the teams in the 1948 test match series. His study and office, adjoining the hall with a clear view of the front door, was largely taken up by a Steinway grand piano, and on shelves above his desk were arranged three Elizabethan silver chalices and pattens, a Queen Anne coffee pot, several early Georgian silver salvers and a cream jug. At his feet by the desk were large glass jars of toffee, which he made in the top pantry and doled out at the rate of one lump an evening after supper.

Mr. Burr had introduced a system for afternoon teas whereby non-residents, that is people not staying at the hotel, could eat as much as they liked for one shilling and ninepence in one of the hotel lounges, and this attracted lots of students from Oxford who tried their physical utmost to make their visit to Stow gastronomically worthwhile. From the top pantry I would arrange a considerable array of small cakes on antique Spode plates, regularly replenishing these and maintaining a relay of large brown pots of tea. A recurring problem with the top pantry was that at night it became infested with black beetles, apparently coming up for a feed from the long disused cellars beneath the house. So, every evening before retiring, we liberally sprinkled the floor with a grey-green product called Keatings Powder. While this killed the beetles in the pantry, it did not address the source of the problem. One could descend into one of the cellars on a rickety flight of wooden steps, which I once did though Mr. Burr never had. The floor was strewn with shards of Spode pottery, presumably from breakages unreported by my predecessors.

Every bedroom in the hotel bore the name of a musical composer, inscribed in gold on a small black plaque above the door. The principal bedrooms bore the names of major composers, such as Bach, Beethoven, Brahms, Mozart, Haydn and Handel, and for the smaller, single rooms tucked under the roof, such as the one I occupied, those of Quilter, Delius, Purcell and Field. Properly speaking, there were twenty-one bedrooms, though the last of these, Holst, was furnished with two paraffin-fuelled brooders for sexed, day old chicks. Confining to room 21 the warm, humid and malodorous mix of burning paraffin and the natural waste of a hundred chicks, required the swift opening and closing of its door. These birds were reared to occupy the four movable chicken arks parked in the lane at the end of the back garden, from which the hotel obtained a regular supply of eggs, then still on ration in the shops.

One very ancient hen, by name of Dorothy, was quite a pet of Mr. Burr, and he

The Crocodile Tree

claimed she was about twenty years old; she probably had not laid an egg for at least a decade. Mrs.Wilkins, a former Wimbledon tennis player but now in late middle age, was the cook, and was escorted everywhere by her two Scottish terriers. The cleaning ladies, Mrs Williams, Mrs. Harris and Norah each looked after one of the houses, and Phillips, whose wooden leg replaced the one lost in WW1, was the gardener, cleaned the guests' shoes and moved the chicken arks around. John, a lame Irish boy with a built-up boot, assisted the cook in the kitchen and helped at table, and another lad - whose father was on the staff of Buckingham Palace, and would be the one to discover that King George VI had died in his sleep - was delegated various duties by the cook and also served at table. He and John were expected to accompany the cook and terriers on their regular afternoon walks. At busy times, a large village woman with a spectacular wall eye did the washing up and pot cleaning.

Antithetic villain, second left, in Shakespeare's Tempest
Bournemouth 1950.

Mr. Burr and I took our meals alone and in some style in the back dining-room adjoining the kitchen. We ate with Georgian silver cutlery off separate antique dropside tables. One of Mr. Burr's more curious habits was always to eat with his right leg on the table, which he explained at the earliest opportunity was the legacy of falling down a shell hole in the First World War. Less curious but more impressive,

NOWHERE NEAR GREENLAND

perhaps, was his propensity for loudly breaking wind several times during a meal. Of this he would take absolutely no notice, and continue talking and eating as though there had been no audible punctuation to these activities. I was thankful for the decent distance between our tables.

Despite its name, the hotel was not licensed, and this was such a disappointment to some arriving guests that they departed immediately. Mr. Burr would wear his dog collar only on Sundays, which was always a mild shock and surprise to guests who had already been staying for some days, possibly questioning themselves as to whether their language and general deportment had been altogether blameless in the presence of this man of the cloth. He acted in a locum capacity for Cotswold churches when the substantive vicar was sick, on holiday, or the living was vacant. This was effectively every Sunday, and I was taken along to read the lessons and if necessary pump the organ, which, of course, he played brilliantly. I calculated that if he played pieces that incorporated the big base pipes - and he was always driven to explore the utmost limits of even modest instruments, demonstrate his skill with hands and feet, and otherwise hugely enjoy himself, leaning back, gazing at the roof beams - I had to pump that much harder to feed them the breeze they needed, especially for the sustained crescendos, such as in Bach's great toccata and fugue in D minor, which would shake the very fabric and the congregation. These churches, built with fortunes from the wool trade between the 12th and 15th centuries, were truly gems of their kind, of great dignity and modest adornment: Naunton down in the valley, Upper and Lower Swell, Guiting Power, Upper and Lower Slaughter. I sat in the choir, at hand for organ duty and lessons, and developed a lingering eye contact crush for one of the Naunton choir girls on the opposite side of the aisle. The attending congregation was sometimes less than a dozen during the winter months, and the sermon the Reverend Burr had rummaged from the heap in his desk drawer the previous Saturday evening, dated from decades before and seemed always to deal with arcane points of theology, bearing neither relation to the season nor addressing the simple concerns of village folk, and was way above their heads and mine. Seated where I was, I was well placed to observe their incomprehension, manifested equally by closed eyes and open mouth, or seriously enquiring looks between the pews expressing "what's he on about?"

For our daily afternoon walks, Mr Burr habitually wore a long grey cotton housecoat, of the kind worn by assistants in hardware shops, and if the sunlight was bright, his heavily tinted goggles; and I habitually carried a hatchet and trowel.

The Crocodile Tree

There are many hills around Stow-on-the-Wold, such is the nature of the Cotswolds, and I have walked up all of them backwards. As Mr. Burr had explained, to get the benefit of the sweeping views and not see just the road before one's feet, hills should be tackled backwards. Fortunately, in those days and in that part of the country there was very little traffic. He hated ivy, and I was despatched through hedges and over barbed wire fences to hack this parasite from the trunks of creeper-festooned oak trees. While we progressed backwards, he read all the mail for the hotel, his private mail, share prospectuses and what today would be termed junk, and for whatever might immediately be discarded I dug a hole with the trowel and buried it.

Mr. Burr's eyes were apparently very sensitive. He never wore his goggles in the hotel, but if I were to switch on an electric light in his presence, I had to warn him first, whereupon he would shield his eyes with both hands. Once the light was on he would remove his hands and, if such a thing is possible, slowly open his eyes and gaze around blinking, as though only now fully apprehending where he was. Failure by me to observe this ritual would evoke a cry of pain, a deeply bowed head with scrunched up eyes, and a scolding. Such extreme sensitivity extended to instantly catching a cold from the great draught I created by walking past him at speed in the hotel. Thus I would learn when he hove into sight, to slow right down and then accelerate once I had passed him. I habitually moved at speed and he was always concerned I might collide with and damage his antique furniture. When very occasionally such minor collisions occurred, he would rush to his study for his large magnifying glass to examine minutely the supposed point of impact. He also frequently adopted bizarre, even ludicrous, behaviour when meeting people. This ranged from a an entirely bogus attack of acute shyness, stuttering and rolling his head around, to a highly exaggerated gallantry which he reserved for women, manifested by repeated bowing and lofty and grandiloquent expressions of admiration and eternal obedience. Often I would be despatched to pluck a rose from the hotel's garden, which he would then, with even greater ceremony, present to the lady on a silver salver. Their reaction was naturally one of surprise and a degree of alarm, and this was Mr. Burr's means of thereafter keeping these hapless women at a safe distance, for they would do their best to avoid him after such an unsettling encounter.

We would drive into Cheltenham once a week to buy provisions for the hotel, specifically to the grocery department of Cavendish House where a Mr.Gumble

NOWHERE NEAR GREENLAND

was in charge. In his grey housecoat, flat cap and goggles, his reverence would deliberately elbow provisions off the shelves if he did not get almost immediate attention. "Coming Mr. Burr, coming" Mr. Gumble would cry despairingly, and make haste to follow up his words as a pot of Tiptree's raspberry jam crashed to the floor. While in town we would pay a visit to Mr. Carter-Bowles the clockmaker and Mr. Ward the picture restorer, both from whom Mr. Burr had obtained restored antique clocks and paintings, and with required ceremony I would present them with a couple of eggs in a paper bag. We would also sometimes visit a seller of antique furniture, who once showed us a massive Elizabethan dining table he said had belonged to Sir Francis Drake.

We would also trawl the windows of the jewellers that sold antique silver. The standard routine was that having spotted something of interest in the window, I would be despatched inside to ask the price. Mr. Burr was quite convinced that if he himself made the enquiry, an absolutely exorbitant sum would be quoted. Meanwhile Mr. Burr would have flattened himself against the wall to one side of the shop window to await developments. If, as sometimes happened, a shop assistant came outside for me to point to the item of interest, his reverence would turn away, and head bowed slink furtively off down the street. If finally the reported price was to his satisfaction, he would then burst into the shop and laughingly seal the deal, with the air of someone who had caught them out and cunningly finessed this satisfactory outcome, and he would chortle about it on the way home. He repeated this embarrassing routine far afield, at silver shops in Oxford and Gloucester, and in London when we went to the Antique Dealers Fair at Grosvenor House. Mr Burr was a keen follower of cricket, and in the summer if there was county or a test match to listen to, we would stop the car in a lay-by halfway back to Stow, eat Cavendish House cakes from a tin, drink thermos tea, and tune in to the game on his portable radio. At this time, petrol was rationed, and that sold for strictly commercial purposes was coloured red, so we always carried a mop in the back of the car as incontestable proof of pursuing hotel business.

Visitors to the Old Red Lion represented a general cross-section of the middle classes and included many recently demobbed servicemen and their wives and girlfriends. Perhaps, for the lack of strong drink, there was never an occasion of unruly behaviour on the premises, though mild eccentricities were very much in keeping with the establishment. One long-staying elderly lady had the habit of whispering to her fellow guests that she wished she were dead. There were few

The Crocodile Tree

celebrities but one was Kingsley Martin, at that time the editor of the 'New Statesman'. Of course, his political views were diametrically opposed to those of Mr. Burr who was staunchly Conservative and a great admirer of Winston Churchill. Kingsley Martin accompanied us on one of our country walks and even walked backwards up at least one hill; but apparently mindful either of the unaccustomed muscular effort or his public image, he then followed behind, but in front of, that is to say facing, Mr. Burr during which he recounted a little anecdote. Churchill, then out of office, was informed that Sir Stafford Cripps was ill. "Nothing trivial I trust" responded Winston. The heroine of a popular BBC radio drama series came with a woman friend to stay at the hotel. This was Marjory Westbury who had the most beautiful voice and played the part of Steve, the woman partner of Paul Temple the detective, though in life she was a rather plain, dumpy little, utterly charming, middle-aged lady.

At the very height of the summer season when the hotel was full of guests, including the death wish whisperer, Mr. Burr was felled by acute appendicitis. He was carted off to Cheltenham hospital and I was thrown into the deep end of hotel management. However, all went well during his two weeks at the hospital and subsequent convalescence. But once he returned, I took a holiday back home in Bournemouth, following this period of unique but sometimes stressful work experience, and in discussions with my mother I decided I would like to go overseas to farm. She was also keen to escape the drabness of post-war Britain, and we had the notion that we might buy a farm in the highlands of Kenya. We contacted the Crown Agents in London with the view to my being accepted to study tropical agriculture at the Egerton Agricultural College at Njoro. However, as I did not have a farming background, they stipulated that I would first have to work on a farm in the UK for a year. Early in 1950 I found a placement as a farm student - essentially a labourer in return for my keep - at New Park Farm near Brockenhurst in the New Forest. Thus, I said goodbye to the Old Red Lion and the Reverend Alan Burr, though not to my lifelong interest he had awakened in antique paintings, silver and furniture - not to mention toffee and chickens, and an abiding dislike of ivy.

Before I commenced working at the farm, I joined the Bournemouth Shakespeare Players, as I was keen to retain some element of drama in my life. I was soon rehearsing for the part of Antonio the villain in The Tempest, and we put on three performances in Bournemouth, Christchurch and Swanage. In this thespian group I met Revell de Valda, son of an explorer and writer, who had recently returned

NOWHERE NEAR GREENLAND

from a visit to Kenya, about which he was encouragingly enthusiastic. He would soon depart to plant rubber in Malaya, and eight years later I was to follow him there. Then after another six years he followed me to New Zealand. On our way by car to Swanage, to give our final performance of the Bard's last play, one of us read out the Bournemouth Echo's review of the previous night's performance, which included, 'Barry Weightman as Antonio was the antithesis of a villain'. Not too clear as to the meaning of antithesis, I sought enlightenment. "It means you were jolly good" said Olive Crocker our director, sitting in the back. Thus I was able to give a confident, if still anodyne, performance that night in Swanage.

I cycled from Bournemouth to New Park Farm to start work there. The farm belonged to the Forestry Commission and Mr. Gossling had been the tenant farmer there for many years. A flat meadow near the farmhouse was the Rhinefield Club polo ground, and while I was there Prince Philip accompanied by Princess Elizabeth came to play and I carried buckets of water for the ponies. I was lodged in a cottage next to the cow sheds with the family of a man who worked for the Post Office. The manure heap for the straw and dung was against the wall directly beneath my first floor bedroom window, and one of my jobs after morning milking was to add to it, though I admit that in self interest I made some effort to extend its breadth rather than height. Shortly after my arrival, Mr. Gossling demolished the roofs of the milking sheds in anticipation of a swift follow-up by Gascoigne Ltd. to install a modern milking parlour. However, this did not eventuate during my time there, and twice a day we milked the cows in sixty open-air standings in rain, sleet, snow, frost, fog, wind and occasionally the sun. In the most inclement of these conditions, it was comforting to lean one's forehead against cow's warm flank and regain circulation in one's hands on their teats. At that time we did a combination of machine and hand milking, since some cows did not accept the former and persistently kicked off the cluster holding the cups.

Very early into my education pertaining to the body language of cows, I continued to stand close behind one of them in my nice Harris tweed sports jacket after she had raised her tail. The consequence of this was the cause of considerable rustic hilarity among my milking colleagues, Sylvia, a Land Army girl, and the old cowman Joe Fripp. Old Joe would set off across the fields in the pitch dark at five in the morning to call in the cattle for milking: "Coo ah yip, coo ah yip", he would holler, having first given me a shout beneath my window - or as near as he could get to it. I was intrigued to see how, unguided, the cows would all file quietly to their ac-

The Crocodile Tree

customed individual standings. Joe had never been to London, and while I was there made his first trip to Southampton, a full twelve miles away.

Though I had not driven a tractor before, I was soon entrusted with the orange-coloured Allis Chalmers, which was allocated the lighter duties of hauling carts, harrowing and hay raking. Combine harvesters had not yet been introduced, and the wheat, barley and oats were cut and tied into sheaves by a reaper and binder. This was followed up by our manual labour collecting six or more sheaves, and standing them in stooks at intervals up and down the field, which was sore on the hands as there were many thistles in the field. These stooks in turn would be collected and built into cottage-shaped ricks in the corner of the field, where the massive steam engine and threshing machine would come in the winter to separate the grain from the straw. Mr. Gossling was avant-garde in having an Allis Chalmers Roto-baler for baling the hay, and the sausage-roll shaped bales were of a size that with some strength and knack, which I soon acquired, could be heaved or pitched onto a cart. Twice, members of the cast from the Archers BBC radio series came for working holidays on the farm and assisted with this work, so that they would know, I suppose, what they were on about.

One day a cow fell sick, having ingested a length of fencing wire. The vet detected that it was lodged in her rumen, the largest of a cow's four stomachs, and I was called upon to assist him in an operation to remove it. He made a long incision in her flank and I was required to hold it open with silk tapes while he rummaged around up to his shoulder in the digesting mess of grass inside. The incision was about level with my face and venting a lot of methane gas. To my surprise and embarrassment I returned to consciousness lying on the cool stone floor of the dairy.

As Christmas of 1950 approached, and my time drew near for departure for Africa, I received my call-up papers to do two years National Service. However, farming and coal mining were reserved occupations, and I was also able to produce my boat ticket to prove that my departure overseas was imminent.

EAST AFRICA

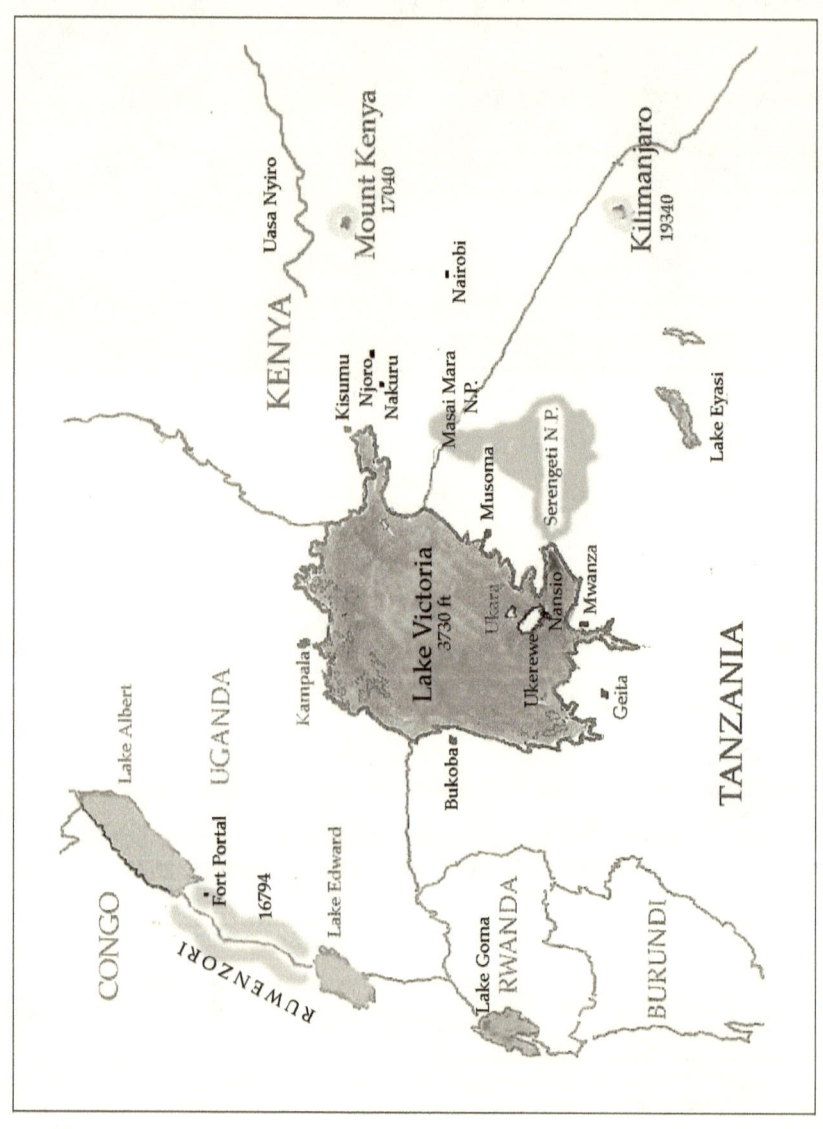

NOWHERE NEAR GREENLAND

INTO AFRICA

On the morning of 2nd January 1951, I took a train up to London from the Bournemouth West station, accompanied by my elder sister Jill, a black tin trunk bearing my initials and a tantalizing blue and red label of the Union Castle Steamship Company inscribed 'Not Wanted On Voyage', plus a leather suitcase to take to my cabin. The drab, green carriage of the Southern Railway clattered through the chill countryside and into the London suburbs with its enduring stark scars of bombed and blackened buildings, bereft by winter of the wildflowers which in their season would again create ragged memorial gardens among the ruined walls. Then, slowing by the blitz-cropped, red-banded church spire, the train pulled into the long curve of Waterloo station with its black tarred concourse and long, heavy wooden benches for tired travellers under the high glass and cast-iron roof. We took a cab to Liverpool Street station and a coffee on its concourse; then I bid farewell to my sister and boarded the boat train for King George V dock where the mauve-hulled Warwick Castle with a single red funnel awaited on the Pool of London. Aboard, and having made acquaintance with my small two berth cabin low down on the port side, I presented myself for tea in the dining room and rather absentmindedly sought someone to pay.

The next morning, we were in a force nine gale in the Bay of Biscay and heading into the greatest sea swells I have ever encountered. I stood quite alone, gripping the rail at the very stern of the ship, one moment high above the ocean as a great rolling sea passed beneath me, then right down into the trough so that the wave that had just passed was now a retreating grey, green wall of water high above me,

Into Africa

with the boiling wake of the ship now rising almost to my feet. Thus I spent all that first morning at sea, my back to the wind in a dark blue three piece suit, soaring up and plummeting down, hour after hour over that surging sea. When I eventually went below for lunch, the dining room was all but deserted, wooden fiddles fixed around the table edges to prevent plates from sliding onto laps, and the waiters heroically serving the sparse but hardiest of hungry passengers, leaning forwards with bowls of hot soup into the steep ascent of the floor, and then leaning back and braking flat-footed against the descent.

From the passenger list and information given me by the Crown Agents, I identified the four fellow passengers who were also bound for Mombasa and the Egerton Agricultural College, two of whom, newly-married David and Elizabeth were travelling first class and George, a taciturn Scot, and Tommy, a genial English lad, and me in second class. By the time we reached our first port of call at Gibraltar, we had met up and went to photograph the grey-uniformed Spanish guards in their curiously cornered hats outside the sentry boxes at the Algeciras frontier. At Marseilles I went ashore alone with the express purpose of buying a ping pong bat and discovered exactly what I wanted in a minor street far from the port; a bat with a hard cork surface on both sides,. We were to be in Genoa a couple of days, and with two young South African girls, blonde and brunette, I went up by train to Milan where we saw a performance of the ballet Giselle at La Scala opera house, and toured the richly decorated roof of the cathedral.

Two decades later, I would again visit La Scala to see an opera by Verdi. This time, during an interval, I was in one of the splendid refreshment rooms that are found on every tier of this great theatre. It was divided from the immediate bar area by a series of arches along one wall. As I went to enter the bar, I saw someone coming towards me through the same archway and I politely stood aside. Whereupon he also stood aside, so we remained face to face. There then followed a series of prances from left to right and it seemed we had reached something of an impasse. I then made a deep bow, making a theatrical circular motion with the hand of my extended right arm, as though holding a kerchief, and then looked up directly at my opposite number with an expression of wry humour and apology to denote how silly all this was. It was silly indeed, for it was me, no doubt quite unaccustomed to seeing myself in a suit, for the arches were alternate doors and full length mirrors. I wondered how many in the now crowded foyer had been entertained by this extempore performance.

NOWHERE NEAR GREENLAND

A night on the town in Genoa included a visit to a sleazy nightclub where girls were selling themselves for cigarettes and dancing with their partner's manhood in their left hands. At Port Said, a 'gully gully' man came aboard and performed magical acts with eggs and chickens. I bought a cotton shirt at Simon Artz and went up by bus to Cairo where the day tour included a visit to the Blue Mosque, the museum, to see the treasures of ancient Egypt, and with another blond, pigtailed South African girl I careered twice around the pyramids cross-legged on a camel. At Aden I was whispered and beckoned into the back of a shop on the Crescent where I paid to see a 'mermaid' in a glass case, but was instead shown a propped-erect, shrivelled-up sea cow. At Port Sudan we took a taxi inland along an earth track that ran in shimmering heat between frequent encampments of very black Sudanese and their herds of goats, sheep and donkeys that filled the air with shouts, bleating, braying and dust pungent with the nose-tickling snuff of dried dung. A few days later we arrived at Mombasa and a disagreeable, white customs officer demanded I pay eighteen shillings duty on my maiden aunt's battery radio. I never managed to find the right batteries for it in Kenya. And some months later a fellow student claimed to have a 'high resistance wire' that converted mains electricity to just a few volts. It didn't, and when before a crowd of interested spectators a switch was thrown, there was a loud bang and some laughter as the radio caught fire.

With our tickets to Nakuru in the Kenya highlands, George, Tommy and I boarded the train, sharing a compartment with a pale young missionary bound for Kampala. The train made a slow, rumbling, overnight climb into the hinterland, past the junction at Voi where a branch line ran west to Mount Kilimanjaro, and then over the bridge at Tsavo river whose construction had been held up for weeks by man-eating lion less than fifty years before. The light of dawn revealed a landscape of red-earthed savannah, over which the pair of powerful diesel locomotives were slowly hauling us up a steep incline. Children running alongside reached up and we bought a large pineapple and put it in the washbasin whose lid formed a small table under the window.

In the still early morning, we pulled into Nairobi station where we were told our train onwards to Nakuru would not be leaving until after midday, so we left on foot to explore the city. Two-storey Indian shop-houses lined a busy street thronged with African pedestrians, bicycles, battered buses belching black diesel smoke and cars dusted red by roads beyond the city. Our stroll took us to Delamere Avenue

Into Africa

lined with jacaranda trees, and the New Stanley hotel's immense ground floor cafeteria and meeting place, where black African waiters in long white kanzus, red fez and cummerbunds served an exclusively white clientele with tea, coffee and every kind of drink.

After sampling Imperial Pale Ale dispensed in large brown bottles, we made our way back to the station and boarded the same train still standing at the platform. On reaching our compartment we discovered it jam-packed with Indians, their copious luggage and a jumble of household items including several charpoys and a wind-up gramophone. I ran back along the platform to complain to the European station master, who on discovering where we were bound informed me that this train was now bound for Nanyuki, that we should have changed trains and it was leaving immediately. I clambered back into the compartment where I was kindly but over-enthusiastically assisted by the interlopers in locating our now buried and scattered items of luggage. Once identified, I heaved these through the corridor window into the uplifted arms of Tommy and George jogging alongside the train as it left the station and slowly gathered speed. When I eventually leaped from the train we were some distance beyond the station, moving faster than my compatriots could run so that lately discovered items lay scattered beside the track. One of these was a new shaving brush which none of us recognised and we decided must have belonged to the missionary of whom there had been no sign. We later lamented the loss of the ripe pineapple in the washbasin.

From the green shambas and shade of trees on either side of the track, our train emerged an hour later at the edge of the escarpment, and as a sudden bright light flooded the carriage, our first sight of the Great Rift Valley burst upon our senses like a clash of cymbals. Far below, at the bottom of this sudden gulf of air, a tawny plain painted with cloud shadows and the dark mirrors of lakes stretched across thirty miles to the far side of the valley where the land rose again to ten thousand feet. Winding and doubling down to the base of this two thousand foot drop, we passed near the stone-built church constructed some seven years previously by Italian prisoners of war, captured during the WW2 Ethiopian campaign, to commemorate the completion of the vastly improved road they had made up the escarpment to Nairobi. Then past the lakes of Naivasha and Elementaita, pink-fringed with flamingos and glittering in the late afternoon sun. We made a brief halt at Gilgil where a dark-haired, slim young woman who called herself Anisette, a fellow passenger on the Warwick Castle, was later reported lying naked

NOWHERE NEAR GREENLAND

on the bar of the Gilgil Club where gentlemen members, presumably reliving the Happy Valley set's halcyon days of the previous decade, were playing poker on her tummy. Then westward we went across the valley floor's savannah and scattered farms to the country town of Nakuru, lying between its lake and the quiescent Menengai volcano. We were met here at the station by Patterson, a second-year student at the agricultural college who drove us in its old wooden-bodied Bedford mini-bus through the road's billowing dust up the less steep western side of the Rift Valley to Njoro. We arrived just in time for dinner in the college's grey stone and shingle-roofed dining-room where we were introduced to the Kenya settlers' idiosyncrasy of dining out in nightwear, which here at above 7,000 feet meant a warm dressing-gown over pyjamas or nightdress.

Slouching in gumboots with gun
Kenya, 1951

All but a half dozen or so of the forty students were the sons and daughters of first or second generation Kenya settlers, now undertaking one and two year courses in tropical agriculture which largely related to conditions of farming in the highlands. The few of us who had come out from Britain aspired to owning or managing farms here, or related employment. The tropical crops studied included sisal, maize, coffee and tea, and many temperate crops that can be grown in the tropics at a high elevation, such as wheat, barley, oats, and pyrethrum of the chrysanthemum family grown for organic insecticide. Work oxen were still widely used for ploughing and general haulage and we learned to 'in-span' and 'out-span' teams of up to sixteen animals, and the husbandry of pigs, poultry and horses was also included in the tuition.

It was six years since the end of the WW2, but still the fashion in Kenya for anyone

Into Africa

who had held a rank above that of lieutenant to retain their military title. At the college, the manager of the farm was a Colonel Thornton, one lecturer a major and several students bore similar ranks . One of the high areas on the flank of the Aberdare mountains was nicknamed blood pressure ridge for all the high-ranking former officers who farmed there, and during one vacation I harvested a field of barley for a General Smallwood, late of the Ethiopian campaign, who at the end of the day, while I sat still covered in dust and sweat on the combine, would present me a glass of sherry on a salver. It was said, perhaps with some truth, that after the war the officer class emigrated to Kenya while other ranks went to Rhodesia.

Our lecturer in botany, a Scotsman, flogged handguns to the students, and since it was the fashion of my peers to pack a pistol I purchased a little Mauser .22 automatic, complete with shoulder holster which I wore beneath my Harris tweed sports jacket. My friend George bought a larger .32 calibre Biretta automatic and we went out to a field of sunflowers to test them and our aim. The large round blooms with their clearly marked centres made ideal targets, though even at close range we entirely failed to hit any. Another popular target was the roadside triangular yellow and red cattle crossing signs that bore the silhouette of a cow. Passing these, students would blaze away at them through the car windows and many of these signs bore dents and holes in evidence of success. All the Kenya-born students knew how to drive, and had probably acquired the skill at a young age on their farms, and some had their own cars at the college.

We went to the car races at the Langa Langa circuit on the site of the former Italian prisoner-of-war camp near Gilgil. There were XK Jaguars and a number of souped-up supercharged saloon cars including a Skoda loaded with lead ballast in the lower part of the door panels to prevent overturning. A madcap English driver named Sasserthwaite, recently celebrated for firing his revolver through the ceiling of the ground floor bar at the Stag hotel in Nakuru and into the bedroom above, was killed when his Jaguar ran out of track. Charley Stonewig, a fellow student had a large khaki-coloured 1930s Chrysler saloon and entered an improvised race for spectators' cars down a straight kilometre of track. His running-boards were crowded with cheering students and he came in last. (Almost exactly fifty years later he was hacked to death in his bed by disgruntled labour on his Kenya farm, and his wife Anne who had also been a fellow student was maimed). Spectators with us at one of these races were Major James, who held an administrative position at the college, and his very beautiful wife. Driving back to Njoro he drove over the

NOWHERE NEAR GREENLAND

parapet of a railway bridge onto the track below and she was killed instantly against the door pillar. Seat belts were yet to be invented.

As with the landed gentry of England, the independent lifestyle of the settlers allowed and even encouraged the development of eccentricity. "It's the altitude" was the common and generally accepted excuse for strange behaviour, and examples of this were always forthcoming from those living at a very high elevation. One group of settlers high on the flanks of the Aberdares was held to be potty, and the highest of these, Old Ma Trent at over ten thousand feet, was said to see off her neighbours with a shotgun - perhaps because they were potty. Once when walking in Nakuru town I was confronted by a young and clearly distraught European who asked me wildly where he could buy a violin. Years later my wife and I stayed at Naru Moru with an elderly Irish lady whose house was full of donkeys. Its long corridors were exceptionally narrow, but coming face to muzzle it was always the donkey who respectfully backed up.

I worked my college vacations on highland farms, twice at an altitude of over 9,000 feet on the very edge of the Great Rift Valley's eastern escarpment. The settler's name was Platt, whose daughter was by coincidence engaged to a boy three years my senior in my house at Berkhamsted. On the first occasion, the family was away at the coast and I was collected from Nakuru by a pair of elderly bachelor brothers named Jones, much decorated officers from WW1. One was nicknamed 'Mad Bomber Jones' for his heroic exploits with grenades in that conflict. With me and a number of farm labourers in the covered back of their pick-up, we were driven over an appalling road for miles at breakneck speed, which for me almost proved literally true since with one hand trying to prevent my suitcase from becoming repeatedly airborne, I was more than once hurled upwards against the wooden roof and practically knocked unconscious. Perhaps the other brother was the Mad Driver. My fellow travellers held on grimly with both hands as best they could and I sensed that they were well accustomed to being driven in this manner, those up front presumably oblivious of our violent treatment. On the Platt's farm, the Kikuyu labour walked barefoot over thickly frosted grass to the movable bail where I supervised the early morning milking, in sight of the distant, snowy twin peaks of Mount Kenya silhouetted against a still lightening eastern sky. And later in the day I supervised the harvesting and weighing of pyrethrum flowers by their womenfolk who wore baskets strapped across their foreheads, and often a length of calico across their backs holding an infant. There was an old European lady living in a

Into Africa

bungalow near the farmstead, but I only saw her once. A donkey had been braying nearby during the night, with the customary anguished heaving sobs, and she called round to tell me that she was sure someone was being tortured.

I spent one vacation on the maize research station at Njoro, and used to cycle there and back every day from my temporary lodging at the farm of Mrs. Prothero, a portly widow living alone whose daughter was studying nursing in Scotland. Maize is highly sensitive to altitude change, and since in Kenya it is grown from sea level to ten thousand feet, it is important to have seed of the appropriate variety available to farmers. This involved much varietal crossing for the production of hybrids, and my work on the station consisted largely of harvesting the tassels, or the male part of the plant bearing pollen, putting them separately in coded, brown paper bags and then upending, tying and shaking them over the silk, or female part of the plants selected for breeding. This was extremely boring work, and being out in the field all day in the sun gave me sunstroke. On another vacation I went with fellow student Tony Swain to work on the farm of a woman whom I never met as she was away at the coast, but apparently she had only one arm, as evidenced by the large wooden knob on the steering wheel of her International pick-up truck. On the wall of her sitting room was an original oil painting of a horse by Alfred Munnings, and her cook's pièce de resistance was a fabulous combination of corn and cheese baked in a small glass dish, the equal of which I have never since encountered.

Tony and I soon decided that there was really only enough work for one of us, and I spent the rest of the vacation near Ol Joro Orok on the farm of John Armitage, who had been a fellow passenger in the Warwick Castle. John was a pioneer of underwater photography and had adapted the controls of his 9mm Bolex movie camera so that he could manipulate them through the thickness of a car's inner-tube. At either end of the tube he fastened an oval piece of plate glass clamped tight with a large hose-clip. John showed me how he shaped the glass into an oval with a pair of scissors by holding it under water, which dampened the vibrations and prevented the glass from breaking. Though the cut was always somewhat ragged and did the scissors absolutely no good at all, this was a useful trick which I subsequently employed many times, particularly for reshaping sunglass lenses to make up a pair in frames where one had been broken.

John's elderly aunt came out from Lancashire and we drove up to Buffalo Springs

NOWHERE NEAR GREENLAND

near Archers Post in the Northern Frontier Province. We swam in the clear waters of a volcanic pool that we shared with turtles, and so dry was the air and so rapid the evaporation of water from our skin, that for a few moments after we emerged we felt quite frozen. We continued to the Samburu National Park where we stayed in a thatched rondavel hired for ten shillings a night from the forestry and wildlife department. Then in the morning we drove to the Uaso Nyiro river which flowed broad and shallow in streamlets over pale sand, and between stands of massive, wide-canopied acacia trees along its banks. One the far side from us, a large herd of elephants splashed and played with their young in the shallow pools. John started filming them with his Bolex while his aunt and I watched them through binoculars. Thus preoccupied, we failed to notice a large bull elephant making his way alone and silently towards us along our bank of the river. That is, until he started feeding from the far side of canopy of the very tree beneath which we stood, reaching up with his trunk and tearing off small branches and foliage. John stopped shooting with his whirring Bolex and we stood absolutely still as the elephant came even closer, and I was certain he would hear the thumping of my heart. Then facing us he began feeling and sniffing the air with his sinuous trunk; and suddenly raising his massive cape-like ears, he squealed, spun round and lumbered off. When John was able to speak, he assured us the elephant could not charge because immediately behind where we stood was a perpendicular three feet drop to the bed of the river. Very reassuring after the event! We continued north into an area of stony hills where John believed there were rhino, and I sat on the roof rack of his Peugeot ready to film with the Bolex. Rhino there were in plenty; in fact we came around a corner to find a female and her calf right in the middle of the track. John did a quick gear change and we proceeded rapidly in the opposite direction. Other rhino we saw at a more comfortable distance browsing among the scrubby vegetation.

One day back at the farm, John took me goose hunting on Ol Bolossit lake at the far end of his property. With shotguns we waded through reeds up to our waist and eventually put up a flight of spurwing of which we bagged a pair. I had neglected to tuck the cuffs of my trousers into my boots, and when later I stood in a bath to remove my wet clothes, I discovered a great squiggling cluster of gorged leaches hanging like small, fat, black sausages where they had floated to the surface around my private parts and waist. Quel horreur! I sprinkled them liberally with detergent powder and they promptly dropped off - preferable to employing the tip of a lighted cigarette, I thought.

Into Africa

During my second year at the college a separate hostel was built for the women students. One evening I heard piercing screams coming from their common-room. Propelling myself at speed to the source of the commotion, I found an agitated group standing back from the wide stone fireplace within which two of my own sex were pounding a yard long snake with pieces of firewood. It was patternless, burnished brown along its length; I recognised it as a harmless mole snake, though its principal prey is rats. I quickly grabbed it close behind the head and carried it, cool, dry and coiled around my bare arm, and released it in a nearby field. Almost all the students there were Kenya born and would have known the snake was not venomous, but perhaps they were motivated by our species' atavistic hatred of snakes. Moreover, the girls were able to demonstrate their female vulnerability, the boys a courageous and masculine protective role; and I with my compassion for the snake, a certain and somewhat priggish disdain for them both.

That same year, in October 1952, the Mau Mau 'emergency' was declared to counter the rebellion of members of the Kikuyu tribe, pent up in their progressively overcrowded reserves around Nairobi, and scattered throughout the 'white highlands' where they provided the majority of the workforce on the farms and estates of European settlers. This was an area that traditionally and for many hundreds of years had provided hunting grounds for the nomadic Masai, and seasonal grazing for their huge herds of cattle, and except where renamed by the white farmers all the natural features of this landscape bear Masai names.

At the onset of the emergency, two bachelors, Ferguson and Bingley, were murdered one evening on their property on the Kinankop where there was a cluster of white farms high on the western flank of the Aberdare mountains. Serving at table, their cook dashed hot soup in their faces and was closely followed into the house by a number of Mau Mau adherents who then killed them. Egerton College offered to provide night shifts of students to man the police station at Njoro, thus freeing the police to patrol the farms in the area. I was selected to be on the shift from midnight to six and needed to drive myself to Njoro in the college's ancient Bedford bus. Surrounded by students who had all driven cars from an early age, I had been too shy to declare my ignorance of driving, with the exception of the small Alice Chalmers tractor in which one had to come a full stop in order to change gear, so I had had no practice of synchronising a gear change with the clutch and accelerator. Thus I awoke the whole college with horrible roaring and grinding noises while I attempted to get the old bus into gear while depressing the accelerator.

NOWHERE NEAR GREENLAND

Eventually I got the hang of it, and possibly leap-frogging off in the wrong gear, departed for Njoro where by the time I had driven the few miles there I was a passing proficient gear changer.

At the end of that November, I went to work my Christmas vacation on John Armitage's Manyatta farm near Ol Joro Orok. We were harvesting a thousand acres of wheat and barley and my crew on the combine were all Kikuyu. I had applied to the police station at Thompsons Falls (now Nyahururu) for a more substantial weapon than my .22 Mauser and was issued with a relic of World War 1, a massive .45 Colt automatic in a leather holster to wear on my belt. However, large areas of the standing crop were infested with a weed called Mexican Marigold whose green, wet and strongly pungent stems frequently jammed the drum of the combine and clogged the straw-walkers which carry the straw to the rear of the machine. This problem frequently required me to crawl deep inside the combine to free the blockage, but I found it impossible to do this with the heavy Colt strapped to my waist which snagged on the many protrusions within the machine, and though loath to do so I was thus obliged to take it off. With an all Kikuyu crew, this was certainly foolhardy, and it would also have been highly irresponsible, and probably deemed criminal to have had my weapon captured, but it did not occur to me to ask one of my fellow workers to crawl inside the machine in my place.

On alternate Sunday mornings an Anglican service for neighbourhood settlers was held in John's large living room, but that Christmas morning we attended a matins service in the church at Thompsons Falls. It was packed with the wives and children of white farmers whose colourful best dresses and hats belied the menace outside, but was confirmed however by the hand guns, rifles and shotguns that every man carried with him into the church, and the vicar laid down his arms by the altar steps. The traditional Christmas hymns and carols were sung with great voice, and there was a great sense of unity in defying the horrors of the Mau Mau. Leaving town after the service, we passed by a crowd of Africaaners outside their own Dutch Reform church, more soberly dressed in subdued colours and the men all wearing hats.

John then departed for the west of Kenya to recruit labour as replacements for the Kikuyu, whom it was said were soon to be relocated or interned, and I was left by myself. Following the earlier attacks on homesteads, we had already adopted certain commonsense precautions, such as having the house staff bring in the evening

Into Africa

meal well before dusk and leaving it beside the log fire which, at seven or more thousand feet above sea level was essential for comfort. Then, securely locked inside the house, one took care not to throw a silhouette on the curtains and took the advice not always to sleep in the same bedroom. At about this time the Ruck family living at nearby Ol Kalau were murdered on their farm. He was called out of the house in the evening on the pretext that recently dipped cattle were suffering from arsenic poisoning, and he was killed. The Mau Mau gang then entered the house and killed his doctor wife, and finally their very young son who was slaughtered in his cot. Commander Meikeljohn and his wife, who was also a doctor, were then attacked in their home near Thompsons Falls. He died attempting to assemble his shotgun and she escaped the house having had a hand severed at the wrist but managed to drive to Thompsons Falls for help. Both of these doctors regularly tended to the Kikuyu and spoke their language. As a security measure, Manyatta farm was now linked to a party telephone line serving nearby farms, and I was invited to join a vigilante group, the majority of which was made up of Africaans farmers from the immediate neighbourhood, to hunt down the Meikeljohns' attackers. We drove at night to a property to which the gang was thought to have fled, and members of the group proceeded to beat the two Africans they found there with heavy lengths of firewood in order to extract information as to the present whereabouts of the gang. They said nothing and certainly would have been clubbed to death had not a British farmer in the group intervened.

A few nights later we received news that the gang of the notorious terrorist, Dedan Kamathi (who now has a street in Nairobi named after him) was going to attack homesteads in the area of Ol Joro Orok. I set out with a farmer in his old Ford van, and by the light of the full moon we drove around to a number of farms that had no telephone and hence had received no warning, and by prearrangement told them to come in to Jocelyn's farm. Jocelyn grew barley for the brewery in Nairobi and had a fine singing voice. On occasions I had met his car on the road and observed and heard him with his head thrown back singing at full volume. Now we were all to meet at his stone-built farmhouse, the only one in the area not built of inflammable cedar with a wood shingle roof. It was soon crowded with the women and children of outlying farms, their men crouched at the windows on all sides of the house, hand guns and rifles at the ready, reminiscent of the Alamo, but the night passed slowly without incident.

For the settlers, this was very much a time of self-defence in a situation of siege and terror on their widely scattered and isolated farms, small islands in a hostile

NOWHERE NEAR GREENLAND

sea. There had been no strengthening of police numbers or capacity, the British army had yet to be called in, and none of the young men of Kenya had been conscripted to fight the Mau Mau. Hence the ad hoc formation of vigilante groups, the ready distribution by the police of previously confiscated firearms, and the linking of farms by telephone. Many of the farms bordered extensive forest on steep terrain, which in some cases rose above the tree and bamboo line to 12,000 feet, and it was here in this relative security that the Mau Mau established their camps from which they launched their raids on the farms below.

Driving back to Manyatta farm one afternoon from the post office at Ol Joro Orok, there was a very loud bang. Since the steering was not affected, I decided I had been shot at and accelerated back to the farm where I telephoned neighbours on the party line We converged in our cars to where I believed I had been ambushed, and a search of the deep ditch on the upper side of the road where a culvert passed under it discovered a single cartridge case. John returned from his recruitment drive in the tribal areas of the Kipsigis and Luo people and not long afterwards we went up into the forest with a tractor and trailer, and with a chain pulled down all the huts of a small village where many of John's Kikuyu labour lived, and from which they were now to be relocated.

Headhigh in Elephant Grass
Musoma, Tanganyika, 1953

We carried the old, infirm and very young, and many of the people's belongings including chickens and some cats, back with us in the trailer to the farm. The able-bodied followed us on foot with their dogs and goats, and it was a very sad and dejected scene.

Into Africa

By the end of the last term at college, those who were not returning to family farms were seeking employment on the large estates of tea and sisal companies or with the Kenya department of agriculture. Though when departing for Kenya I had held the hope of buying a farm there, it was now clearly evident that with the Mau Mau rebellion and other winds of change already blowing strongly across Africa it was already a generation too late to emulate the 'Out of Africa' scenario, so I applied for the post of an agricultural extension officer in Tanganyika.

Meanwhile, back in England my mother, now in her mid-fifties and who had obtained a teaching diploma at Birmingham University during the First World War, had sold our house in Dorset and was working as a private tutor to children, successively in Greece, Colombia, Switzerland and Burma. One day she was at a writing desk in the reading room of an hotel in Gstaad, quite possibly penning me an aerogram, when the only other occupants were Humphrey Bogart and Lauren Bacall in quiet conversation. As they left the room, Bogart said to my mother "You're a lovely lady", a gallantry that quite made her day. (Star-struck in her teens, she once wrote to Mary Pickford wanting to know how she might pursue a career in films. She received a reply to the effect that she should ask her mother.)

Thus an invitation came to me at Manyatta farm to attend an interview with the regional director of agriculture in Arusha. I boarded the train at Gilgil for the overnight trip, and at Voi where the line divided, one heading west to Tanganyika and the other continuing east to Mombasa, the all-white first class passengers alighted for dinner in the station restaurant. The next morning, having skirted around the southern foothills of Mount Kilimanjaro - a generous birthday gift from Queen Victoria to her grandson Kaiser Wilhelm, which put a considerable kink in the formerly arrow-straight border between British Kenya and German Tanganyika - the train pulled into Arusha station. After the interview, a beer and lunch at the Arusha hotel, I was told I had the job and would be posted to Lake Victoria province, starting in late January.

Back at Manyatta farm, John was asked if he would feed the animals that had recently starred in the film 'Where No Vultures Fly' as they passed through Ol Joro Orok railway station. So, armed with quantities of fresh meat for the lions and hay for the hippos, giraffe, elephants and rhinos, we dished out the rations from one end of the long train to the other and filled up troughs with water. The tall necks of the giraffe protruding at steep angles high above the wagons, presented a bizarre

NOWHERE NEAR GREENLAND

sight as the train pulled away down the track. An American named Carl Hartley, based at Rumuruti in the Northern Frontier Province, hunted and trapped animals to supply zoos and star in films. He provided them for 'King Solomon's Mines', 'Mogambo', 'The African Queen' and 'Where No Vultures Fly', big Hollywood epics with their top superstars filmed in East Africa during the 1950s. At New Year in 1953, I visited Carl Hartley's animal holding area where his captured herbivores were held in stout wooden stockades and the big cats in cages. I passed close to a cage holding a leopard which, still totally wild, in a flash crashed snarling against the bars close to my head and I nearly fell over in fright. I joined New Year celebrations at the Rumuruti club, and as midnight approached an unruly and inebriated game of rugby got underway on its moonlit football ground.

I took the train to Kisumu, Kenya's busy port in the north east corner of Lake Victoria. Second largest fresh water lake in the world, with a surface area and shape similar to that of Ireland, it stands at over 3,700 feet above sea level. It is shallow and nowhere more than 250 feet deep, which with its extent can contribute in a storm to very rough conditions. I boarded the steamship Rusinga, which with its sister-ship Usoga was prefabricated in Liverpool at the beginning of the twentieth century, and the sections were then transported on the newly completed railway line from Mombasa and assembled at Kisumu. The two ships ran regularly in opposite directions around the periphery of the lake - the Rusinga clockwise and the Usoga counter-clockwise - taking exactly a week to complete the circuit, calling at Musoma, Mwanza, Bukoba, Port Bell and Kisumu. The ships had a dozen or so first class cabins and a fine dining-room where meals were served by uniformed Goan stewards, and at the stern of the upper deck were wicker armchairs under an awning where one could have drinks and observe the foaming wake and passing shore. These steamboats crossed in their circuit at Musoma every Sunday morning, providing its small white community with a shipboard bar and restaurant, the chance to meet passing travellers and indulge the fantasy of steaming off to far away places. During our call at Musoma the regional director of agriculture came aboard to meet me and asked if I would choose between working with a farm mechanisation scheme or working in the field as an advisor to African farmers. For me, this was what today would be termed a 'no brainer'. Having said that I had absolutely no patience with things mechanical, the director made the choice for me; I was to proceed on south down the lake to Mwanza where the department of agriculture had its regional headquarters and I was again to meet its director. This was Norman Rounce, a long-time expert in the farming systems of the area. I met him

Into Africa

again briefly just that once when his terse advice to me was "keep your mouth shut and your bowels open", for soon after that he departed for England and died of cancer, leaving behind him a large, black American saloon car. He despatched me back to Musoma on the next steamer going north, the Usoga, where I was to understudy an assistant agricultural officer for six months.

On the rock above Musoma
Tanganyika, 1953

I had not thought much of Musoma on my way south to Mwanza, though I had seen it only from the wharf at the broad mouth of the Mara river, but exploring it on my return it seemed not such a bad place at all. The houses occupied by the dozen or so white population stretched along the pale sand shoreline of the lake. I had been assigned to share a house with a bachelor livestock officer, and further up the line lived the two district officers, assistants to the district commissioner who lived in a much larger house with a fine lawn sloping down to the edge of the lake; beyond that was the officer commanding the police and the single-storied Musoma hotel, whose ten bedroom ceilings sagged under the weight of bat droppings, the acrid odour commingled with that of regularly applied 'flit' insecticide. The medical officer lived next to the small whitewashed hospital on the inland side of town. A granite outcrop of massive rocks rose through greenery to a height of some two hundred feet above the little town, at the base of which was the fortress-like stone building constructed by the Germans at the beginning of the 20th century as the 'boma', or offices of the district commissioner and his administrative staff, near to which were the modest two rooms of the agricultural department. A small, thatched, fly-screened mud and wattle structure on the edge of the airstrip served

NOWHERE NEAR GREENLAND

as the Musoma club. The commercial part of the town comprised a dozen or so Indian 'dukas', along a single wide street, just one of which stocked groceries for European needs. The cinema was named the Musoma Diamond Talkies, and here on Saturday evenings the few Europeans would sit in a line in the back row to watch the show. It was then customary for every performance to commence with a playing of 'God Save the King' for which the audience was expected to rise to its feet. Once, when we were graced by the presence of the district commissioner and his wife, a number of Africans failed to stand for the national anthem. He called up to stop the projection and then strode down to the front to announce, in Swahili of course, that unless and until everyone stood up when the anthem was repeated there would be no show that night. Everyone stood.

The man with whom I was initially to work was a Seychellois named John Savy, a small, spare and light brown francophone who habitually wore a pith helmet. On my first trip with him we drove inland to Ikoma near the district border with the Serengeti National Park. On the way there we passed through Maji Moto where an elderly half-caste German gold miner appeared suddenly from a deep hole near the road and passed the time of day with us. I peered into the narrow shaft and saw only rickety wooden ladders disappearing down into the darkness. I had earlier noticed that Ikoma was writ large on the map of Tanganyika, but now there was only one small Indian duka and the ruin of a large fort built half a century before by the Germans, though from its design and present condition it could well have been built by the Normans. It was now entirely abandoned to weeds and wandering goats, and we walked atop its high crenulated walls and around the broad courtyard and derelict well they enclosed. (When I visited here again exactly fifty years later, the fort had been converted into a hotel and yet again abandoned, though some huts built for staff just outside the castle walls were still occupied). We camped there in a tent by a dried up river, but by digging a hole in the riverbed sand we obtained enough water for our needs. A few months later the district commissioner, Brian Hodgson, an Oxford rowing blue, despatched me to the area to investigate a land dispute between the Wa-Ikoma and the Wa-Nata, two of the twelve tribes in Musoma district, and to draw a map showing the distribution of planted crops and disputed claims. I was driven there and back in a government Bedford lorry and along the way picked up a number of footsore pedestrians. On arriving back in Musoma all alighted, leaving me with a solitary large goat. I enquired as to whom it belonged and was told it was mine! No doubt one of the tribal chiefs had attempted to curry favour, but I immediately donated it to the driver. The Wa-Ikoma had several times complained to the district commissioner that

Into Africa

neighbouring Masai from the Serengeti were rustling their cattle and could they please have a police post established at Ikoma. Brian Hodgson was not convinced by the argument for their request until a small but weighty bag was placed on his desk. It contained the head of a Masai, and Ikoma got its police post.

Agricultural extension officers such as myself were expected to spend at least a dozen nights a month in the field, and I had been issued with a splendid tent made by Black's of Greenock in Scotland. Of heavy green canvas, its outer fly extended to create a veranda in front of the sleeping area, and at the rear was a semicircular bathroom. The tent was supported by three stout wooden, brass-socketed poles, and on the iron spike at their top was placed a wooden ball from which radiated the heavy guy ropes. This issue came complete with a canvas folding bath and wash basin, and a folding table and chairs. (My immediate superior there, David Brewin, went one better with his safari kit; he owned an oval tin bath with a leather strap-on lid which also served as a container for his clothes.)

While I was still in Kenya, King George VI died and Elizabeth became queen while up a tree, either asleep or viewing game. (The Treetops Hotel was later burned down by the Mau Mau.) Now, six months later in Musoma, plans to celebrate the coronation had been completed, and these included the creation and opening of a commemorative garden in the town, a football match between the Africans and resident Europeans, and in the evening a drinks party on the district commissioner's lawn attended by ourselves and the twelve local chiefs and their sub-chiefs. The opening of the Coronation Garden was not without unforeseen drama. Brian Hodgson in his splendid white uniform and pith helmet stood with his beautiful wife Pat beside an ornate new fountain, closely surrounded by a great crowd. Pat, holding a pair of scissors, was to cut a ribbon simultaneously with water being turned on to the fountain, and Eddie Ratzburg of the public works department had retreated to a distant hydrant to effect this. Pat cut the ribbon and Eddie turned the wheel. Nothing. Then with a bang the fountain's pedestal was blown into the air as it was hit by water under high pressure and a geyser descended upon the crowd. The Africans loved it, for surely it was meant to be.

Afterwards at the Musoma hotel we listened through whistling static to the coronation service broadcast by the BBC and then, after a number of drinks, we went to play the football match which the African side won seven-nil. Our boots and tennis shoes were no match for their bare feet and vastly superior skills. Come sun-

NOWHERE NEAR GREENLAND

down, we repaired for drinks on the district commissioner's lawn, now furnished with tables and marquees. In those distant days, Africans were permitted to drink only beer and wine, but for this occasion Brian Hodgson made a special exception. And to take full advantage of what, who knows, might be a once in a lifetime opportunity, the chiefs and their cohorts rapidly downed copious cocktails of neat whisky, brandy and gin, and in no time all were spread in horizontal attitudes of total repose across the lawn. The D.C. sent for a lorry to cart them off and they entirely missed the spectacular fireworks display over the lake, by which Eddie Ratzburg made full amends for the earlier mishap.

The common alcoholic beverage of recreation in Tanganyika and in most parts of sub-Saharan Africa was beer, generally brewed from grains such as sorghum, millet or maize, but also from the root crop cassava and, where grown locally, bananas. Cassava beer, or 'pombe' was widely made in the lake province and had a characteristically strong yeasty smell which it imparted to those who drank it. However, this was sometimes distilled to make 'moshi' - which in Swahili means smoke - a dangerous form of methyl alcohol and there were many instances of multiple deaths from drinking it.

John Cooke was one of the two district officers in Musoma and was an experienced rock climber. I had a good head for heights, which perhaps matured early on the big dipper in Belgium, and he and I resolved to climb the topmost rock of the granite outcrop above the boma. This presented a near sheer face of perhaps forty feet on all sides, and our frequent close study of the problem had failed to resolve it. One weekend, while John was away 'on safari', (this being the accepted terminology in East Africa for a tour of work in the bush), I returned to reconnoitre the rock, and high up on one side I spied a small spur. If I could lasso this with a rope I could drag myself up and gain the summit. Back down I went for a long rope, and after a considerable number of casts managed to snag the protuberance. Now I had to leave evidence of my success, so back down again I went, inserted and stuck a label to the interior of an Imperial Pale Ale pint bottle, saying that this rock had been scaled by me on such and such a date, and filled it with sand. Armed with this memorial, I clambered up the kopje again, hauled myself to the top of the rock and placed it upon the summit. When John returned to Musoma, I suggested we have another go at the rock and fortuitously 'discovered' the possibility of lassoing the spur. After descending for the rope, I let John go up first, and it was hugely rewarding to hear his despairing cry that someone had been up before us! (Fifty years later I attempted the same lasso manoeuvre, but failed after many tries,

Into Africa

though I doubt that the beer bottle, exposed on the rock, could have survived half a century of storms and wind, or that there had been others nutty enough to make the climb).

During one of my lone reconnoitres of the outcrop one afternoon after work, I was bitten by a snake. Between the great rocks there is a dense mix of cactus, grass and bushes, and pushing my way through I believed I had been jabbed by the spike of a prickly pear behind my left knee. As I had already suffered a number of pricks and scratches, quite standard for this course, I paid no further notice. However, that night I experienced a throbbing ache in my leg and I developed a mild fever. Removing my pyjama trousers in the morning, they stuck to the back of my leg, and peering behind the knee I found there had been an exudation from two puffy, dark blue coloured punctures about half a centimetre apart. I went to see Pat Daly, the doctor at the hospital, and he confirmed my suspicion that I had been bitten by a snake; but as I was not yet dead the snake can have been only mildly venomous - possibly one known locally as a chicken snake - and he sent me off with a dressing on my leg and a couple of aspirins.

Possibly I have Achilles knees, because the next time I was to see Pat at the hospital was after the sharp terminal thorn of a sisal leaf had pierced my right knee and caused septicaemia. I had been on a joint safari with John Cooke in Majita 'A' in the south west of the district, a heavily populated and eroded area where sisal hedges had been planted to prevent cattle from grazing along the edge of gullies and washed-out areas. In our tent I awoke one night with pain and high fever, and daylight revealed a red line running from the knee to the gland in my groin which was very swollen. We set off in John's Land Rover for the fifty miles back to Musoma, and halfway there were flagged down by a bus. The driver passed John a note from the D.C. informing him his house had burnt down. The chimney of his kerosene-fuelled refrigerator had caught fire (one of two friends' houses that suffered this fate due to poor trimming of the wick), the flames reached the ceiling and spread to the rest of the house. I was in hospital for several days, and treating my infection Pat Daly diagnosed that I was also suffering from malaria, my very first attack, and subdued it with intravenous quinine. With a high fever, this was also the first time I experienced a hallucination, fancying that my bed was surrounded by a crowd of people roaring with laughter, though as far as John and I were concerned there was little cause for mirth. In that fire I lost my Garrard record player and the still embryonic collection of records I had lent to him.

NOWHERE NEAR GREENLAND

A subsequent encounter with Doc. Daly took place when I developed an abscessed wisdom tooth. I put up with the ache for a few days until I could no longer eat or sleep, and there was no dentist within a hundred and fifty miles, and those over very bad roads. Presenting myself at Musoma hospital, Pat said he could extract the tooth but regretted he had no anaesthetic for dentistry. I also regretted this with considerably more feeling as he wrestled the tooth with forceps, crunching it into several jagged pieces. During the seemingly endless time this took, I at intervals requested time out in order to lower my head to the level of my knees. However, the extraction was a total success in terms of pain relief, though a shard of root was left behind and voluntarily surrendered itself some months later.

The administration was encouraging people in Majita 'A' to move to Majita 'B', a sparsely populated and largely flat area of fertile land in the extreme south of the district, and I was to assist this by issuing the trans-located farmers with mosaic virus-resistant cassava cuttings for their new farms, which would in time provide their staple food. I was camping in that area, though this time occupying a small, thatched and isolated rondavel, and there I celebrated my 21st birthday, of which anniversary I had been too shy to inform my friends, spending the evening alone with a bottle of beer and a hyena that ambled past the door.

Musoma had no club as such, apart from the oval, fly-screened, mud-brick room on the airstrip, but Buhemba gold mine some twenty miles inland had an excellent club for its resident Canadian, South African and British miners, many with their families, and from time to time we would go there to drink and perchance to dance. The hospitality was generous, and there was always somewhere for bachelors such as myself to bunk down and sober up before facing a jolting drive home in the morning, for there were no paved roads in the district and their condition was typically lamentable, especially during the rainy season. The mine was situated in a bleak, hilly area of loose rock and thorny scrub and one often saw rhino there.

Musoma, and specifically the Bukwaya chiefdom, was the home area of Julius Nyerere, the first president of independent Tanganyika - soon to become Tanzania when it united with Zanzibar. At this time he was still a school teacher, for which he was given the title of 'mwalimu', and was in the process of forming the Tanganyika African National Union, or TANU. He came along with a driver in an old Land Rover to an agricultural 'field day' which we held in his area where we were demonstrating to farmers the benefits of ridging their land on the contour, and

Into Africa

other anti-erosion measures, and it was clear he already had a substantial following.

After six months I was transferred to Ukerewe District to replace an African agricultural officer named Ishingoma who was about to depart for Ibadan University in Nigeria to undertake a course in statistics. Ukerewe District comprised the largest island in Lake Victoria, measuring over thirty miles long and twelve miles at its widest point, as well as another dozen smaller islands including Ukara, almost round and about seven miles in diameter. Ukerewe was separated from the mainland by a channel some two hundred yards wide, across which a pontoon that could hold a couple of cars or one bus was pulled on a chain by half a dozen stalwart local men. The mainland side of the channel was the termination of the Kibara peninsula, which was also part of the Ukerewe district and to the east bounded by the Serengeti National Park. At Musoma I was loaded onto a bus together with my tin trunk, camping gear and suitcase, all of which were put on the roof, though, alas, without my record player and records. The journey took all day and I was met at Kabingo, the district administrative centre on the island, by the district commissioner Major Keith Battye, formerly of the Indian army and its civil service. I was shown to my 'house', which consisted of one room of the mud brick government rest house, with a concrete bath tub immediately next to the front door. This gave onto the main road, on the opposite side of which was my kitchen and long-drop lavatory. I also had the use of half a veranda which faced towards the tennis court.

For my transport, regional headquarters in Mwanza sent me a clapped-out 250cc BSA motorcycle which often refused to start, regularly shed supposedly integral components on the road, or would break down at the farthest point from home. I wrote a very bitter letter about this to the regional director, though its phrasing was larded with a certain mordant humour. So I was sent a new 30cwt Bedford lorry, complete with a driver called Changalawe, ('gravel' in Swahili - he told me the road was being repaired past the parental hut when he was born), which was just as well as I had not yet obtained a licence to drive. On my very first day at work I was walking the short distance to my office when the D.C. drove up behind me, stopped and said "Weightman, you look like a Greek trader, go and change your shirt for something more appropriate for a government officer." I was wearing a favourite plaid shirt of bright red, blue and green; a white shirt, or in a single pastel colour was what was deemed appropriate. A short while before this, the governor, Sir Edward Twining, had spotted a district officer in Musoma sporting a beard. His D.C. was forthwith instructed to tell him to shave it off or join the veterinary department.

NOWHERE NEAR GREENLAND

The great man came to Ukerewe while I was there. His portly, blimpish figure and jovial manner endeared him to the Africans, and when traditional dancers performed in his honour he jogged round in a circle with them, gaily waving his walking stick in time with the drumming. A few years later I was playing for Geita district in a cricket match at Mwanza against their team. Sir Edward was there, and when I came in to bat, appropriately low down in the batting order, I blocked away for several overs while a far better batsman at the other end made all the runs. Eventually I was caught, and as I came off the field, the governor said, "A fine, fighting duck, my boy!" When our team went in to field, I was placed at third man, and with a fast bowler hurling the balls down I stood at some distance from the wicket. One delivery was edged by the batsman and came flying at me fully eight feet from the ground, a certain boundary. I made a prodigious leap and somehow the ball stuck in my left hand, their best batsman was out, the game won, and subsequent compliments were somewhat less equivocal.

The population of Ukerewe island at that time was about fifty thousand, many of whom lived in homesteads comprising a close collection of thatched, mud-brick oblong huts on their own small farms, where millet, maize, cassava and cotton were most commonly grown. Cultivation was intensive and there were no fences or open fields, so cattle and goats were tether-fed at the end of a rope which was moved each day. Tall termite mounds rose up through the orange-red laterite soil, and in the millet fields small boys perched atop them manipulating a web of strings stretching to all corners of the ripening crop, at the end of which would be tied tin cans or gourds to scare off weaver birds which would otherwise descend in fast-moving clouds to strip the tall heads of grain. In the wetter west of the island, isolated stands of original rain forest still survived, and where these had been thinned they provided dappled shade for the growing of inter-planted arabica coffee and bananas. Streams, where they flowed out into the lake along the north coast, had formed small deltas which were planted with rice, and mature mango and orange trees were scattered in the fields throughout the island.

There was a good network of well maintained latterite roads running between rows of yellow flowering Cassia trees, and these were sufficiently wide for two vehicles to pass each other. Nansio, comprising two short streets of Indian dukas and a rice mill, was the main town and port of the island, served daily by the 'Tilapia' from Mwanza, four hours away to the south. This small passenger and general cargo boat was named after the most important food fish in the lake, where it was netted

Into Africa

and caught by line to contribute the major part of protein in the diet of the people. Later, R.I.Patel, a local shop owner, would build a cinema whose official opening I attended in the company of the district commissioner and the few other white residents on the island. We were seated in a kind of royal box set half way up the rear wall of the auditorium. The inaugural film was Sinbad the Sailor in Hindi and we sat through about seven reels before most apologetically escaping. Senior police inspector Joti, head of the illegal diamond smuggling squad, came to the island and showed us that there was more to the Nansio rice mill than met the eye. He took me down into a maze of tunnels dug beneath the mill where, he said, diamonds had been inserted into numbered bales of cotton destined for export, though I never quite fathomed why tunnels were necessary for this operation.

My very own pit latrine on the other side of the road from my one room in the resthouse was malodorous and upwind, and one day I decided that a good fire in the hole might render it less offensive, so I poured down a mix of petrol and kerosene. Simultaneously throwing down a lighted match and myself backwards, there was a very satisfying wooomf that lifted the shack's corrugated iron roof sheets. The smell, now heavily redolent of soot, kerosene and scorched organic matter proved even worse, so I poured down half a bottle of after-shave lotion. The resulting bouquet was quite indescribable and subsequently the cause of much unsolicited comment from passers by.

When I first arrived in Ukerewe district, the mainland Kibara peninsular was in the charge of another agricultural officer, a German called Kreig, but soon after I arrived he and his wife went back for long leave in Europe and he died there of cancer. I was then asked to look after his area as well as the islands. Kibara was generally sparsely populated, except by game since its Guta plain was contiguous with the Serengeti. In one year alone, over seven hundred cattle were reported killed by lion. Keith Battye shot a lion that had swum over to the island and he gave me its skull which had a complete set of most impressive teeth. I kept it for several years, mouth wide open in the wardrobe of my bedroom in the certain expectation that it would scare off burglars. As well as lion, porcupine were a major pest to the farmers in this area. Nocturnal animals, they ate their way at night through fields of cassava and sweet potato, and the department of agriculture employed a Seychellois fulltime to kill them in their burrows with arsenic-poisoned roots.

NOWHERE NEAR GREENLAND

Kibara was also considered the development area to accommodate an influx of people from Ukerewe island where there was limited land available for the growing population. Away from the lake there was no water for new settlements and their livestock, so one of my tasks during the dry season was to scout suitable sites for dams. Once identified, and with the local chief's assistance, labour from the community that would benefit from the dam would be enlisted to dig it. I would first have designed and pegged out the required structure - length, width, height and curve of the wall, spillway and freeboard, as well as the stepped tanks that would be excavated to add to water storage and provide material for the wall. Natural water courses, usually running down shallow ravines known as dongas, were the preferred sites, and while prospecting down one of these in the company of Stanislaus Andrea, an overweight agricultural field assistant, a mature female lion emerged from a bush just ahead of us. Stock-still in fright, we watched the lion saunter away and our unanimous decision was that this was no place for a dam! However, creating these small lakes was generally most satisfying and immensely useful to the people. Ideally, one required a site where the land rose only gradually behind the constructed barrage, and a colleague of mine working in Sukumaland south of Mwanza hit the jackpot. He was first alerted to his success by a formal enquiry from B.O.A.C. that requested the name of the new lake on their flight-path to South Africa, and which stretched back from the dam for several miles.

It was in Kibara, while looking at cotton fields that I came across a small group of Italian share-croppers living very simply in a pair of huts belonging to their Tanzanian landowner. There were just five of them, a young married couple with a small baby, the woman's unmarried sister and a single man. They spoke no English and very limited Swahili in which we attempted to converse, and I never learned how they came to be in that situation in such a remote spot. One day the woman came over to the island with her baby and sister. I gave them lunch, after which the mother crooned a lullaby as she breast fed her baby. Sometimes in my life I have been stricken in amazement by the beauty of a woman, and this was one of those occasions that, to the best of my recollection, so far number just four.

Keith Battye had a peaceable little black spaniel. Stan Dryden, the D.O. and Battye's assistant, had a large, and by him much beloved, white and very offensive bull terrier, pink around the eyes and pink showing through its much scarred and often suppurating skin as a result of the fights this dog almost daily instigated. In fact. Stan almost got the sack, or at least transferred, when his dog inevitably attacked

Into Africa

and almost killed the spaniel. Then, shortly before one Christmas, the D.C. asked me to move out of the rest-house to make room for friends of his, a judge and his family who were coming to stay. I thus moved down the road to the 'native authority' rest-house, with a smaller room but better and more conveniently sited lavatory. However, I protested to my superiors this somewhat high-handed treatment, hinting at resigning and returning to Kenya. As a result of this I was promised a real house, and within a matter of weeks the construction had commenced of a very pleasant two bedroom bungalow with a veranda and panoramic view of the lake, outside servants quarters, a garage and, oh dreamed of luxury, an indoor flushing lavatory. A few days after moving in, there was a thunderstorm with heavy rain which revealed that the back doorstep had been constructed sloping into the house, so that water poured into the kitchen. I found a jute sack, and while I was stuffing it under the door there was a lightning strike nearby and an electric shock threw me against the kitchen wall. Basic furniture had arrived from Mwanza, and in Nansio I had an Indian tailor named Karia, who incidentally had an amazingly beautiful wife, make me a set of cushion covers for a settee and four arm chairs. These were of corduroy, dark chocolate brown on one side and golden brown on the other. When I moved in, Stan's mud-brick house was being extensively repaired and rid of the termites that were rapidly consuming it, and he and dog came to stay with me. Said dog engaged in a fight, returned at night to repose on the sofa and bled and oozed all over my brand new cushion covers, and at a remove of fifty years I can well recall my acute displeasure. Bats soon invaded the roof-space of the new house, and a method developed by others to get rid of them was to observe where the bats went in and out, and then suspend an open-top, four gallon kerosene tin just below that point, because bats first have to dive before they take flight. But the design of the eaves of my house did not make this feasible, so as an alternative method I decided to gas them. I pushed a garden hose up the exhaust pipe of my Land Rover, led the other end under the roof and started up the car. This proved effective in the short term, but unfortunately I did not leave it long enough before I searched for gassed bats and nearly gassed myself.

At the centre of the island, some ten miles from Kabingo was a ginnery which processed all the cotton grown on the island. Its manager was Jack Leach, a Devonshire man who had flown Mosquitoes in the RAF during WW2 and had been involved in photo reconnaissance for the raids on the Ruhr dams. His engineer was Ian Somersett, a South African whose party piece was to stop a vehicle's motor by placing his hands on the spark plugs. The cotton was bought from the farmers by

NOWHERE NEAR GREENLAND

Indians who came down from Uganda every year for the harvesting season in Tanganyika, and they lived in the corrugated iron cotton stores scattered throughout the Ukerewe district and elsewhere in Lake Province where cotton was the principal cash crop. One of my tasks was to test the buyers' weighing scales against a set of test weights I carried around with me, and another was to check that the cotton had been correctly graded.. After the end of the buying season, I would supervise the fumigation of all the cotton stores where there was always a build-up of cotton pests that could be carried over to the next season.

One year, after the end of the buying season, I was issued with a projector and screen to show short films in the empty cotton stores. These promoted good agricultural practices, such as soil conservation, pasture management and the correct grading of cotton, and were interspersed with cartoons or films with a humorous theme. Among these was 'Muhemba's Unlucky Day' made in Dar Es Salaam, which told the story of a naive youth tricked into buying a 'money tree', which was merely a mango tree with paper money tied to its branches. This was always a free show, and because most in the audience had never witnessed cinema before, their vocal and physical participation greatly added to my own enjoyment.

Keith Battye looked every inch a military man and was a keen hunter of big game. I once went out with him in a boat to shoot crocodiles on the lake, for which he was armed with a large bore Holland & Holland rifle. We did not find a crocodile, but as we neared a small islet we made out a whitish green object sprawled over a rock at the edge of the water. I told Keith I thought it was a body, and so it proved, considerably decomposed and lacking head, feet and hands. A canoe with five people aboard had been lost some while previously, and these were evidently the stored remains of crocodile's meal.

Keith was eventually posted away to another district and not long after we received the news of his death. . In those days, the Colonial Service did not pay for their officers' children attending school in the UK to visit their parents in Africa for the holidays. Thus, every year Keith shot an elephant and with the money raised from the sale of the ivory he paid for his two daughters' return passage to Tanganyika. At Arusha he had obtained the £50 licence to shoot an elephant, and having shot one with good tusks he was waved down on the road by a game scout who informed him of a really magnificent bull elephant not far distant. Keith set off back to the boma at Arusha to obtain another licence. That done, he jumped back into the cab

Into Africa

of his International pick-up, and his gun lying across the front seat went off and killed him instantly. It was a mystery why an experienced hunter like Keith would be driving over rough roads with a loaded, large bore rifle with a hair trigger on the seat beside him. His bearer, with him in the truck, was exonerated of any blame.

Charles Parry (above L) and George Faurie (R)
Ukerewe Island, Tanganyika, 1955

The Public Works Foreman on Ukerewe was George Faurie, a grizzled and powerfully built South African of Huegenot ancestry. He lived alone next door and liked me to visit him after work to play gin rummy, as a change from his solitary games of patience, while he drank his customary Beehive brandy and water and chain-smoked Crown Bird cigarettes. He had a simple, formulaic and somewhat repetitive humour, and would regularly ask me "You saw that plank Barry?", to which I was expected to reply "What plank George?" "The plank the monkey f***** the cat on", and he would roar with laughter and slap his thigh. And as he held his hand of cards, he would sing in a pleasant but doleful voice "Hallelujah I'm a bum, hallelujah bum again, hallelujah give us a hand down to revive us again. I came to a house and I knocked on the door, and the lady said bum bum you've been here before, hallelujah I'm a bum……" etc.- and another: "and when I die, don't bury me at all, just pickle my bones in alcohol. With a bottle of rye at my head and feet, and then I know my bones will keep." Then in his seventies, George had fought in the Boer war, worked on the Union Minière copper mine in the Belgian Congo for many years and then panned gold on the Lupa river in southern Tanganyika for fourteen years between WW1 and WW2, about which he told many tales. Thou-

NOWHERE NEAR GREENLAND

sands participated in this gold rush, but as in California only a tiny few struck it rich, though there was apparently great camaraderie in the shared hardship. One day one of the older miners died. A wake was held in his house and much alcohol was consumed. Eventually the body was taken from the bed, placed in a coffin and carried to the cemetery. After a simple funeral, there was further drinking back at the house until the body was discovered still lying on the bed. So who among them had been buried? A general rush in panic to the graveyard ensued to exhume the coffin, only to find it empty. Eddie Ratzburg at Musoma, who was also on the Lupa, had told me the same story the previous year, so perhaps it actually happened. Another story which I have been told several times in different parts of Africa concerns a white overseer with a glass eye who would take it out to supervise the labour while he went off for a drink.

George shot a hippopotamus and cut a thick strip from its hide for me to make a 'sjambok', or 'kiboko' as a whip often made from hippo hide is called - kiboko being the Swahili for that animal, as well as slang for an old style tin opener. He hung it in a tree in the sun to dry, and when he gave it to me it was rock-hard and square in section, so I planed it down to a gentle taper with a wood plane and then soaked it in linseed oil to make it supple. But not supple enough, for I cracked it too soon and seven inches snapped off the end.

For one New Year, I drove all the way to Buhemba in Musoma district to attend a fancy dress party at the mine club. I decided to go as devil in disguise, presenting the black back of a waistcoat, topped by a white collared shirt worn back-to-front beneath my father's 1932 Hector Powe tailcoat. From between its tails curled my new 'kiboko', now blackened with boot polish and attached to a belt around my waist, and to whose extremity I had attached a triangle of black cardboard. Mr. Brown, the mine's chief engineer, was, as always, immaculate in his dinner jacket and brown shoes. I had to be back on the island in the morning to serve on a 'board of survey'. It was customary to hold such surveys on the first day of the year, which back then was not a public holiday, and usually included the local treasury, public works, and for me, this time, the post office. I had arrived back shortly before dawn rather the worse for wear, thrown down my devil's tail on the veranda, snatched an hour of sleep, and then gone to count postal orders, stamps and petty cash. This completed, I returned decidedly hung-over and photophobic to my house, and upon entering bent to pick up the 'kiboko' from the veranda floor. I failed to see a black snake lying right alongside it. It moved quickly to the corner of the veranda

Into Africa

and raised its head as though to strike. Instantly suspending my customary compassion for serpents, I snatched rocks from nearby in the garden and with them killed the snake, which I was later assured was a young mamba. The same day, I wrote off to Howse & McGeorge, chemists in Nairobi, to order a snakebite kit. This eventually arrived in a red tin box containing two vials of polyvalent snakebite serum from Port Elizabeth in South Africa, a small bottle of potassium permanganate, a syringe, a tourniquet and an illustrated booklet describing among other things the progressive development of symptoms leading to death, either from massive internal haemorrhage or nerve paralysis.

On another brief visit back to Musoma, I participated in a lively party at the 'club' on the airstrip. Pat Freeman, the gaunt Irishman who managed the bat-ridden Musoma hotel, was very much the life and soul, dancing every dance, whirling his partners around, drinking and standing drinks. At the end of the party, he went back to the hotel and shot himself through the mouth with a .22 rifle. He was apparently deeply in debt to local Indian shopkeepers.

When George Faurie went on long leave to South Africa he left me his two rifles, a .22 and a 9mm Manlicher Schönaur, and soon after I was called out one night to shoot a mamba coiled in the rafters of a hut. I let it be known locally that I now had snakebite serum, and once was taken to a hut where a man had been bitten. He refused to open the door and died. I also shot a puff-adder lying in the warm ashes of the fire in my houseboy's kitchen. These fat, relatively short, yellow-green snakes with a large head and massive, usually fatal bite, were a common sight basking on the roads. Pythons too were plentiful on the island, and men would call at the house or office carrying them in sacks to sell. I bought one for ten East African shillings and sent the skin for tanning to a taxidermist named Zimmermann in Nairobi. Not long after, while I was on home leave from Ukerewe, a Welshman named Charles White took over from me. One weekend he and a colleague were at my house when a man came round and sold them a python. They filled the bath with water and put in the snake still in its sack, weighed it down with rocks and left it to drown for several hours while they had a few more beers. Late in the afternoon they recovered the inert twelve foot python and photographed each other in the garden with the snake coiled around their necks. Then after a couple more beers in the house they went to retrieve the snake, but it had left, evidently not quite dead! One day I called on Ugo Fonari, the Italian doctor at the Catholic mission in the centre of the island. He said there was something rather interesting to show

NOWHERE NEAR GREENLAND

me in his garden. It was a python in the process of swallowing a dog, its non-hinged jaws fully agape, body pulsing, a really disgusting sight! And while I was still on Ukerewe, a lecturer name Mavis Skinner at the Bwiro teachers training college near Mwanza was attacked by a large python while walking up from the lake shore after a swim. It wrapped itself right around her and began to constrict, while Mavis strove to prevent its hooked tail from anchoring on her ankle and screamed fit to bust. Fortunately for her, an African cutting firewood nearby with a panga came to her rescue and killed and unwound the snake. It was said that the snake's mate had been killed near the same spot a few days earlier. Mavis almost immediately returned to Britain and did not return to Tanganyika. Of such things are nightmares made.

Other than for shooting snakes, I made little use of George's guns, though one weekend I accompanied Jack Leach and friends to the Guta plain on the mainland where I shot an impala. My bullet smashed its upper foreleg and it ran and ran with the leg dangling and flopping while we chased it through the bush. I never shot another buck, just guinea fowl roosting in the top of acacia trees which I shot for the pot, lying on my back with the .22 rifle during evenings in camp. Again on the Guta plain, which borders the Serengeti, I accompanied an Australian police officer attached to the Tanganyika police on a weekend's hunting. He shot first a topi, and then leaving the dead animal we drove on and he killed an impala. This, we soon discovered, was a heavily pregnant female, and after dismembering the animal for meat we left the still intact uterus and its foetus within convulsing in the sun. We drove back to look for the shot topi and circled and circled through the bush without success. We set up camp and from dusk and all through the night we could hear hyena feeding nearby at our kill. In the morning we found that every part of this large animal had been eaten or carried off, leaving only dung on a large, bloodied patch of grass.

George Faurie was eventually replaced by Tom Thomas, a diminutive and gentle Welshman married to Sylvia, an Australian girl from Melbourne. They adopted a serval cat as a pet and he taught me to say in Welsh "here's a health to all Welshmen and arseholes to all Englishmen", and being descended from Welsh on my mother's side I did not feel too badly about that. We were later joined by another Welshman named Charles Parry, small, genial, pipe-smoking, moustached, with a very red face that perhaps betrayed his fondness for spiritous beverages. He had come as foreman to the native authority public works which was engaged in various small-

Into Africa

scale building operations on the island. He had first arrived in East Africa as a soldier in WW1 and had never been on home leave since, reputedly because he had never successfully completed a tour of duty before being sacked. By his own account his career had commenced in the far north of Kenya, attached in some capacity to the administration. One day, Charles was in his bath, and presumably also in his cups, when an askari came to his tent with a cattle thief and asked Charles what to do with him. "Take him out and hang him", called Charles from his bath, and the askari did just that. Subsequently, Charles worked for the veterinary department, medical department, desert locust control, public works, agriculture, prison service, and several others besides. He was clearly not unemployable. Happily, but uncharacteristically, he completed his tour on Ukerewe island and went home on leave to Wales for the first time in forty years. Unfortunately I did not meet him again following his return to ask if he had noticed any changes, but the last I heard of him he was directing a gang of prisoners constructing a new crossing point for a ferry on the Mara river.

A young Scotsman named David Mowat was sent to Ukerewe to work with me for a few months. (We were all young then, and I took pride in the fact that at that time the official staff list showed me to be the youngest member of the Colonial Service in Tanganyika.) It gave great satisfaction to create one's own entertainment in the tiny communities of remote 'bush' stations. There was a flat expanse of sand stretching for many hundreds of yards inland at the extreme east of the island where the chain ferry then crossed from the mainland; though since the completion of the dam at Jinja and the consequent raising of the lake's level by several metres, this area is now under water. Remembering the holiday with my parents and sister at Westende in Belgium in 1938, and the sand yachts that swooped at speed along the firm, wide sands, I suggested to David we might build a sand yacht. Being keen on sailing, he readily agreed and we accumulated the required materials from dukas in Nansio. These included lengths of dexion - angled steel regularly pierced with slots and holes, much used for shelving - for the triangular frame, a pair of bicycle wheels, cotton cloth for the sail, and a discarded pram wheel which, placed at the apex of the triangle, would serve for steering. A length of bamboo for the mast, ropes and wire completed our requirements. So we spent several pleasant weekends building this craft - we even had a pennant at the mast head to indicate the direction of the wind - which when finished we transported to the launch site on the flattened-down top of a Land Rover. Unfortunately, the winds were too light and the sands too soft for us to achieve much more than a walking pace, sometimes

NOWHERE NEAR GREENLAND

aided by one of us disembarking to push! Perhaps we should have invested in another pair of bicycle wheels to spread the load on the sand, but David's time on the island was coming to an end, so we dismantled the craft and sold the components for what we could get. But we had had great fun building it and anticipating the great sport we would never have.

While David was still on the island, another young Scotsman was sent to work with me. He had just arrived directly from Glasgow where he had been active in the Salvation Army. Credulous with innocent wonder at everything around him, Fergus Brown was an ideal candidate for a practical joke. Thus, David and I meticulously searched a large scale map for the most remote spot we could find in northern Tanganyika and decided upon Yaida Swamp. This was some miles south of Lake Eyasi in an area apparently empty except for the iconic tufts of grass found in maps' keys to mark permanent swamps. On an official telegram form, ostensibly sent by the Director of Agriculture in Dar es Salaam, Fergus was instructed to make his own way forthwith to Yaida Swamp where he was to be in charge of a drainage scheme. This was placed in my official post box to which Fergus was sent the next day to see if there was any mail for us. He was naturally aghast and astounded by this peremptory order, and joined us to find where exactly was Yaida Swamp, for goodness sake. Naturally, we let him find it and we voiced our own astonishment and outrage. Then how on earth to get there? We proposed various implausible routes, such as looping up through Kenya or proceeding down to the coast and then striking inland for six hundred miles. And what did Fergus know about large scale drainage? Possibly a thousand square miles of inundated bog, and arguably the most extensive scheme since the Roman's unsuccessful attempt to drain the Pontine Marshes in 160 BC! And who, for example, would despatch or otherwise resettle the no doubt thousands of hippopotamous that for eons had peaceably dwelt therein. These were subjects for considerable calculation, discussion and helpful suggestions. I offered to lend Fergus my rucksack, and David volunteered his canvas bath, even though, in the circumstances, there was little hope of ever seeing them again, or him! We persuaded Fergus that he could quite reasonably delay his departure until after the weekend, and then posted him another telegram cancelling the first for unspecified "technical reasons". This was clearly beyond a joke, we said as we joined him in roundly denouncing the cavalier attitude and incompetence of officialdom. We never confessed our wheeze to Fergus.

One day, I was honoured by a visit from the deputy director of agriculture, one

Into Africa

Fuggles-Couchman, a large, blimpish man who had travelled all the way from Dar es Salaam, clearly not for the ostensible reason to look at the agriculture of Ukerewe, but for a glimpse of a very rare bird that was said to hang out in the Rubia forest at the far west of the island. A fanatical twitcher, he kept his binoculars glued to his eyes while he spooned cornflakes hoping to spot something extraordinary in my garden, and after breakfast we drove out west in search of this scarce bird. Crawling close behind Fuggles' voluminous Bombay bloomers through the dense and damp undergrowth of the rainforest, there issued little tweeting sounds as though from pursed lips at the front end of our tandem, and after an hour or so of this exercise he thankfully sighted what he most sought, though I did not since my view ahead was almost totally impeded.

Every year, I would be on a panel with the D.C. and his wife to judge the final of the primary school singing competition. This was to decide among the top ten of some sixty schools, and it made for a long and audibly challenging evening since the children sang at length with great enthusiasm . I had also to judge the primary school shamba competition from the start, so this took me all over the district, which was no bad thing from the point of view of becoming familiar with every part of it. The 'shamba' comprised plots to demonstrate water and soil conservation, the ideal spacing and weeding of plants, the benefits of animal manure, and so on, and there was an oral component to test the schoolchildren's knowledge. There was also a similar competition for secondary schools, and this included the management of livestock. One year, my colleague Charles White joined me in the judging and we set off across the Kibara peninsula in one of his two cars, both American of 1930s vintage. One was a massive, black Buick of which Al Capone would have been justifiably proud, and the other a Chevrolet drop-head coupe in which on this occasion we travelled. The canvas roof of this vehicle was rotten, and as we drove into a heavy rainstorm it split longitudinally between us, so that I was sitting out in the pouring rain and Charles was in the dry, hugely enjoying my predicament.

Charles was a keen hunter who claimed at least one elephant against his otherwise unblemished character, and when we were both serving in Geita district he burst through my bedroom door very early one Sunday morning while I was still lying abed, bearing the huge, hairy and still bleeding leg of a warthog he had just shot. He was also a keen auto mechanic, which he needed to be with the superannuated jalopies he owned, and would quite happily while away a whole weekend lying beneath one of them, beset by heat, intractable nuts, dripping oil and flies. Many

NOWHERE NEAR GREENLAND

years later, he would most appropriately own and operate a country garage in outback Australia.

One November 5th, we decided to have a fireworks party and most of our little community gathered at my house. A problem was that the only fireworks we could obtain locally were simple bangers, or firecrackers, but they would have to do. Come the dusk, we departed the house for the garden, and after aimlessly throwing firecrackers for a few minutes we divided into two teams and started to aim them at each other. In an inevitable evolution of this do-it-yourself entertainment, we learned to avoid their swift return by holding the lighted bangers for a second or two before throwing them. Equally inevitable perhaps was that when a banger landed at my feet I would overestimate the length of remaining fuse and attempt to chuck it back. Fortunately both doctors, Fonari and Daly, were in attendance and they took me to the bathroom to bandage my right hand which had been blown open by the banger. The burns were superficial, but I suggested they make the most of the occasion and put a bandage around my head as well. It had started to rain and everyone had come in from the garden and were sitting around in the living room expectantly awaiting our emergence from the bathroom. The head bandage entirely covered my eyes, so with arms outstretched my entrance more than fulfilled their requirement for further drama, and I felt my way out to kitchen to collect a hot coffee pot from the top of the wood-burning stove. Cups were distributed and Antoinette Daly was holding hers over her lap. Unfortunately, I could only see by staring straight down my nose and I missed the mug, pouring the hot black coffee directly into Antoinette's lap. She sent me a sweet, if brief, note the next day apologising for her precipitate departure.

Major Battye had been replaced as D.C. by Robert Paterson, a genial, ex-army officer with a record for gallantry, and with him Orpha his Welsh wife and their three young sons, thus considerably swelling to nine our tiny community of expatriates. One Easter weekend while I was having my hair cut on the veranda, Robert called round and told me a joke. There was this government officer having his hair cut. Happening by, his boss asked him, "Why are you having your hair cut during office hours?" "Well it grew during office hours, didn't it!" "Not all of it!" "Well I'm not having it all cut off!" At this point, a 'tarishe' came round to say that a swarm of locusts had landed outside a village on the north coast of the island. It was important to keep them moving, get them off the ground and to go somewhere else, so Robert and I collected our tennis rackets and rushed out in his Land Rover to the

Into Africa

invasion area. We located the swarm, and then accompanied by villagers yelling and banging on empty kerosene tins we rushed up and down over the locust covered ground, slashing with our rackets as they rose up in a cloud before us. Our weapons soon dripped and grew heavy with the clogged remains of these pests, but we successfully drove them off.

I had recently read in the pages of the Readers Digest an article about Harrods of Knightsbridge who claimed that they would 'send anything anywhere'. We had always had a piano at home, so why not here on an island in Lake Victoria? I wrote to Harrods, of course quoting the article, requesting the despatch of a second-hand German upright piano with a steel frame. They replied promptly saying that while they did not normally deal in second-hand pianos, Mr. Good of their music department would attend a sale on my behalf and purchase an appropriate instrument. They would also send me a tuning fork, the lever for adjusting the strings' tension, a felt wedge to place between multiple string notes, and a booklet on how to tune a piano. Crated and shipped by sea, this would cost me a total of £50. Thus the piano travelled on a freighter to Dar es Salaam, came up by rail to Mwanza and there was loaded aboard the 'Tilapia' for Ukerewe island.. Advised of its arrival, I was at the wharf to witness its unloading, only to see the crate immediately before mine swung off and unceremoniously dropped from a height of several feet by the dock's rusty little hand winch. Perhaps this proved fortuitous in concentrating the mind of the operator to take more care with the next one, which I later delivered unscathed to my house. The wooden crate was made to the shape of the piano and lined and padded with green felt wherever it might come into contact with the instrument's finely French-polished exterior.

I proposed that we should hold an agricultural show on the island, and preparations went ahead to inform the population on the several islands and mainland peninsula of the classes of exhibits, livestock, vegetables and handicrafts they could bring along. Prizes of tools, such as hoes, wheelbarrows, axes and so on were purchased, and on a school's football field we built a large number of stalls and created plots demonstrating the best practices for growing cotton, maize and other crops. Several VIPs flew up from Mwanza in a seaplane, and these included the provincial commissioner, 'Fanny' Walden, the regional director of agriculture Murray Lunan, and the deputy director of medical services who was Canadian. Our D.C. was now Alan Collings, an ex-Royal Navy man who met them at Nansio wharf and brought them to the show. All proceeded satisfactorily, the show was well at-

NOWHERE NEAR GREENLAND

tended, exhibits were judged, prizes awarded, speeches made, and our visitors were accompanied back to the wharf by a huge crowd of people who, like me, had never before seen a seaplane. This was at anchor in the bay a hundred metres or so from the shore and our august visitors clambered into a dinghy that would ferry them out. Standing in its bows was an African wielding a large paddle with which, obviously showing off to the appreciative and excited crowd, he made such enormous, theatrical scoops that the bow dipped below the surface and the boat sank some twenty yards from the shore. As it went down, in a perfectly horizontal fashion, the passengers in their suits and hats stood stiffly at attention as the water slowly rose up around them. At this, the crowd roared, howled, clutched each other and stamped with glee while Alan Collings tried with some desperation but to no avail to crank the engine of the district launch, which was tied up near the wharf and laid up for repairs. The VIPs bobbed about in the water and from beneath his trilby hat, still clutching a briefcase Fanny called out "don't anyone jump in, we're alright", though behind him the Canadian medic was near drowning - we heard later he had only one lung and thus was presumably less buoyant. Then two canoes put out from the shore and a rescue was quickly effected. Murray came back to my house, and the others to the D.C's for a change of clothes and a stiff drink, and I arranged my wet guest's wallet and its contents to dry on the top of my Dover stove. An hour or so later we all returned to the wharf and the VIPs were this time safely ferried out to the seaplane. We saw it taxi to the horizon and later learned it continued on the surface all the way back to Mwanza.

Our launch, the 'Mtemi' was out of service for some time, and both I and the D.C. needed to get to Ukara; in my case for some urgent soil conservation work. In the distant past, this craggy island had become considerably overpopulated, and under intensive cultivation its steep slopes became eroded and fissured by wide and deep gullies. All the stony hills bore traces of having been terraced, but most of the soil had gone leaving behind a grey underlay of granite boulders. The soil that had once clothed the island had washed into the lake where it formed deltas on which the people of Ukara now grew rice, and the interior was completely deserted. The culture and language of the people here was quite different from Ukerewe. They lived in round, tall-pointed, thatched huts, the thatch covering the whole structure to the ground so that they rather resembled inverted bouquets. And, perhaps unique in Africa, they organised bull fights. Each village had its bull ring, no more than a round stockade, and reared bulls to fight the bulls of other villages. Two bulls faced off in the ring and fought until one of them decided it had had enough,

Into Africa

when it would escape through the gap left in the stockade for that purpose. The fights were accompanied by much whistling and encouragement of the rival bulls, and, no doubt, there was some betting.

My soil conservation programme there involved creating 'check dams' at interval in the gullies by levering massive boulders into them and then lining the upper side with clay. With the rain, terraces of soil would form behind them on which crops could be grown, and we also repaired the old terraces on the hills, and along their outer edge planted a line of elephant grass. Such was the shortage of animal feed on the island, the men swam out into the lake to gather species of grass and reeds that grew in the shallows, and this entailed some risk. When I first arrived in the district, a doctor Smith was just completing a two year stay on Ukara where he had been studying the incidence of filariasis and its transmission. This disease results in elephantiasis which affected many people around Lake Victoria. He swam regularly from a large and rounded rock just offshore from the rest-house in the north of the island, and assured me he had never encountered a crocodile there. I therefore made it my custom to swim from this rock whenever I returned to camp after a long day's hiking around the coast and hills of the island . On this particular day, after I had been visiting Ukara for a year or more, I was particularly thirsty and called Tungaraza to bring a beer to the tent before I went for my swim. As he was doing so, he called out that there was a crocodile basking on the rock. It was young and probably only two metres long, but I never swam there again, thereafter contenting myself with a bucket shower.

With no launch at our disposal, Alan Collings, his wife Vivienne and I drove out to a jetty at Bugalora in the north of the island. There was moored an Arab dhow in which we intended to cross to Ukara. This dhow was a large, broad and clumsy looking craft with a crew of four, none of them Arabs, though Arabs still lived around the coasts and islands of Lake Victoria and had done so since the days of slaving. They generally operated small dukas and were involved in the trading of coffee and other local produce. In the light of early morning the waters of the lake were flat and white with the jagged silhouette of Ukara rearing blackly above the horizon just six miles to the north. We stowed our camping gear, clothes and food with the aid of the tarishe who was accompanying the D.C. The crew hoisted our single lateen sail, and in a very light breeze the dhow slowly drifted away from the jetty. We continued in this fashion so that by midday we had barely reached half way, and then what scrap of wind there was died completely and we were totally

NOWHERE NEAR GREENLAND

becalmed. It was now very hot. In a cardboard carton near my foot was a bottle of kummel liqueur, so to cheer us up and pass the time more pleasantly we swigged from it until it was empty.

In the late afternoon we noticed a wide, ominous, scimitar-shaped black cloud looming above the eastern horizon and clearly moving our way. Such sudden storms are preceded by high winds that can lash the shallow lake into a boiling fury. Still in a breathless calm, we sought measures to propel our craft towards Ukara now only a few hundred yards away. One of the crew took a long bamboo from the deck and probed the water for punting, but it was still far too deep. Upon the suggestion that we might waggle ourselves forward with the massive rudder, another of the crew took the long tiller and worked it from one side of the stern to the other, but after only a few ponderous waggles the rudder broke off at the stem and floated away in the gathering gloom, intermittently lit by the lightning flashes of the approaching storm. One of the crew gallantly dived overboard to retrieve it, and since there was the distinct risk of a lurking crocodile, Alan stood ready with his loaded .22 rifle, ready to ping a little bullet off its head and at least scare it away. The rudder was retrieved, and meanwhile Vivienne had been rummaging through the kitchen cartons and produced three frying pans and a saucepan with which, leaning perilously over the side, we attempted to paddle our clumsy craft and achieved some slight progress. A few puffs of wind ahead of the storm were now reaching us, but the nearby shore was a just a jumble of granite rocks. Two of the crew swam to these with a rope and once ashore began to tow us towards a short stretch of beach.

Once grounded, we hastily offloaded the tents and boxes. The rapid succession of the lightning flashes and peals of thunder warned us of the severity of the approaching storm, and Alan, Vivienne and the tarishe scrambled to erect their tent, first the inner tent and then the outer fly. I knew that, alone, I had the hope of raising only the outer fly before the storm struck. As I secured the ropes at the corners, the wall of wind howled in from the lake with the first large spatters of rain, and in the flashes I could discern Alan, wife and tarishe, at first hanging on to the bucking ropes of the fly, then being lifted off their feet, then letting go as the billowing canvas was snatched up and away into the darkness. Just as Alan and Vivienne crawled into the remainder of their tent it collapsed over them into a now sodden, lumpy heap. After a while, they burrowed their way out and ran over to join me in what was effectively a wind tunnel - or, rather, a rain and wind tunnel as it was

Into Africa

oriented east-west directly facing the storm. They plumped themselves next to me on my camp-bed, which promptly collapsed. Vivienne then pronounced herself very thirsty, and as all the supplies were beneath the ruin of their tent I heroically ran there with a torch, with difficulty located a bottle and ran back through the driving rain. Vivienne took a long swig. It was kerosene. Leaving her clutching at her throat and gagging, I went back a second time and returned with water. (In truth, I returned again with another bottle of kerosene, which was duly sampled, though it seems rather repetitious to mention it.) We spent a miserable night, with my guests eventually burrowing into their 'humpy', (as Australian aborigines call their huts). The next morning revealed the dhow over on its side on the beach, but it had nonetheless afforded its crew some shelter, and the airborne tent fly was discovered some distance inland. Local people arrived to provide porters, and in single file we made tracks for the rest house in the north of the island. Happily, when our work was done, we were able to make alternative arrangements for our return to Ukerewe island.

Alan & Vivienne Collings survey the ruins
of their tent
Ukara Island, Tanganyika, 1955

Chief Mataba of Ukara had been made chief in German times and forty years later remained autocratic and imposing in his old age, habitually wearing a red fez which conferred additional height and distinction. His deep and rasping voice suggested Louis Armstrong with tonsilitis. However, now in his seventies he was finding it increasingly difficult to walk to the farther villages of the island. The D.C. obtained permission to include a Land Rover for him in the local native authority budget, but the people of his island would have to make a road. As all the settle-

NOWHERE NEAR GREENLAND

ments were around the coast, a circum-insular road was planned and each village was apportioned a length to build. Very few people here had ever seen a motor-vehicle, and while it was understood that the road should be as level as circumstances allowed, and this was largely achieved on the individual stretches, there was frequently a step of one or two feet. where one village's work began and another ended. It was not understood that motor-vehicles did not do steps.

The Land Rover was towed over to Ukara on a pontoon and a considerable crowd awaited its arrival. I would have the honour of being the first to drive it. Once we had it on the road, and with the vehicle stationary, I put on an extempore show for the spectators, flashing and dipping the headlights, working the left and right indicators, and honking the horn which evoked shouts and applause. Then, when I opened the bonnet, panic seized the women and children in the crowd and they fled what they erroneously perceived to be the wide open maw of a monster, small children their twinkling legs not able to propel them fast enough fell flat on their face screaming, their running mothers yanking them up by one arm in their headlong flight. Then I put my head under the bonnet, revved the engine and waved to the crowd. "It's alright, don't worry, it's quite safe". Oh what fun it all was! Finally I slowly drove off with several men with hoes in the back to sort out the steps, with old Mataba standing regally upright at the front of the open vehicle holding on to the windscreen.

Unlike Mataba, Chief Lukumbuzia of Ukerewe was young and educated, speaking excellent English with what would today be described as a posh accent. He lived on the island in a large, white, echoing, bat-ridden palace constructed in a somewhat Moorish style and almost totally devoid of furniture. With him, I explored a little known part of the island which was under forest and included a swamp where there was a residual population of sitatunga, a rare species of buck whose habitat is in wetland areas such as the Okavango delta. Chief Lukumbuzia was later appointed Tanzania's ambassador to Sweden.

John Cooke and I were planning a climbing expedition to the Ruwenzori mountains in Uganda, also popularly known as the Mountains of the Moon, so named by Ptolomy the second century geographer who really had only a sketchy idea of where they were. We decided to get into some sort of training, and across the district's Kibara peninsula in a north-south direction ran a range of hills about nine miles long rising to more than a thousand feet above the plain. Its ridge was partly

Into Africa

covered in forest, and the rest in grass and savannah which supported a large herd of eland, the largest of all antelopes, but always nervous and difficult to approach. John arrived from Musoma with a young Irish nurse who was keen to join in the exercise, and we set off from my mainland house which had been the home of the late Krieg. This was some way from the southern end of the hill range, and my driver Changarawe drove us round to the northern end in the Bedford lorry and we started our hill walk. About half way along, the ridge dipped steeply and entered dense forest. I confidently led the way, having made this same walk alone a year or so earlier, and about an hour later we emerged at the very exact same spot we went in, which did little for my self-esteem. My truck was to meet us at the far end which we reached in the late afternoon. It was nowhere to be seen, so we trudged the extra few miles to my house. There a doleful scene awaited us. Tungaraza, my houseboy had invited Changarawe to teach him to drive and had driven right through the mud brick wall of the garage, partly demolishing it and the truck.(He was later officially charged with 'conversion not amounting to theft' and received a fine, which I paid and stopped out of his wages).

In order to make our climb in the Ruwenzori, we had applied to our superiors to take an extended local leave of three weeks instead of the two normally allowed, and this was readily granted, mountain climbing being regarded as a healthy and worthwhile pursuit. I had written off to the UK for an ice axe, crampons, climbing boots, sleeping bag and binoculars, and John, as an experienced climber already had the necessary equipment. We set off in his Land Rover, driving north to Kisumu in Kenya, circled round the top of the lake, along the top of the newly completed Jinja dam, and into Kampala where we stayed overnight at the Imperial hotel, and I received tremendous electric shocks from the bath taps. We drove on to Fort Portal in the far west of Uganda along a fiendishly twisting road, since straightened, which took us through the appropriately named town of Mubende. However, we had already been most impressed by Uganda, in comparing it with Tanganyika, for here there were bridges over the streams and rivers instead of drifts and chain ferries, and there had even been a long stretch of wide tarmac road between Jinja and Kampala. All the bomas were solid, imposing buildings and electrification was far more widespread - extending even to the hotel bath-taps! At Fort Portal we stayed comfortably at the Mountains of the Moon hotel and the next day reported to the boma where the district officer informed us we were making the climb at the wrong time of year. This was the rainy season, and what was rain down below was snow up above which would create unstable and dangerous conditions

NOWHERE NEAR GREENLAND

on the glaciers, and we would encounter problems crossing the rivers that guarded the approach to the high mountains. However, we had little choice over our timing; here we were, and he wished us good luck. (Nearly thirty years later, a conversation with Andrew Stuart, when he was the last Resident Commissioner in the New Hebrides before independence, revealed that he was that district officer.)

Some months earlier, we had read in the National Geographic Magazine an account of a climb made in the Ruwenzori. This expedition had recruited as head porter a man named Kule, and we determined to do the same. We drove out to Kule's village and arranged to hire eight porters, leaving for the mountains the following day. Back in Fort Portal we purchased the gear it was customary to issue each of them, namely a pair of tennis shoes and a blanket, and additional supplies of food to augment what we had brought with us from Musoma. Setting off from the village early the next morning, we noticed that none of the porters brought their personal issue with them. We had weighed out the loads for each man, which they carried in sacks on their backs with a strap around their foreheads, and these contained rice, sugar, dehydrated vegetables, buffalo biltong expertly made for us by Mrs. Ratzburg, maize flour, dried fish, kerosene, hurricane lamps and climbing equipment. It was to be a long climb up though the rainforest following the valleys of the Mobuku and Bojuku rivers towards the Portal Peaks. The rivers were narrow but in spate from the rains and ran steeply down over rock-strewn beds. These we needed to cross many times, Kule leading each time, secured by a rope and balancing from rock to rock, or wading in the rushing torrent, braced against its force. We followed one by one, now leaving the rivers behind and climbing up through the twilight of high forest where we encountered a solitary elephant. We came to caves in a cliff face where we were to spend the night. A storm was following us up the mountain and rain had just started to fall as we stood in a group ready to remove our loads. . There was a tremendous flash-bang, and the blast effect of an explosion as lightning struck right among us. Two of our porters lay injured, one of them unconscious, and some of the loads had burst open scattering rice, flour and sugar. We treated and bandaged the burns on the arms and legs of the injured porters, and seeing they were recovering well, suggested they lay up for a day and then descend back to their village.

The next morning, we stored provisions in a cave for our return journey in about ten days time, and continued up through the forest, reaching the bamboo line at about nine thousand feet. Then we climbed higher through thick mist into a forest

Into Africa

of giant heather and groundsel where the trunks and residue of their previous generations were heaped many yards deep on the ground. We broke from this cover to emerge at the edge of a vast bog, which stretched for a mile or two ahead to the base of another belt of steep forest, rising to the tree line at about twelve thousand feet. John and I were carrying more than we had planned to make up for the loss of the two porters, and progress through the swamp was effected by leaping from tuft to tuft of grass which flourished on the small hummocks that rose a foot or two above the mud. In doing this, I succeeded in quite badly spraining an ankle, on which I was obliged to climb for the next two weeks, and over the years it never returned to its original shape. Finally, all this slippery greenery was behind us and we were on rock with snow in plain sight. In the evening, we arrived at two huts constructed by the East African Mountain Club beside a pair of small lakes. This was as high as the porters would go, for above us now was the snow, ice and rock of serious climbing. This was to be our starting point for our attempt on Mount Speke, one of the four highest peaks of the Ruwenzori. Mindful and advised that here on the equator avalanches occur from about mid-day, we started out in the starlit dark of the early hours of morning. We trudged up steeply through deep powdery snow until we came to the summit ridge, with massive seracs on one flank that overhung a considerable precipice. Here and there rock broke through and our ice axes were ringing and crackling with electrostatic energy. On the summit was a small cairn of rocks, to which we added our own, and we stayed a while to enjoy the panorama of Uganda laid out thousands of feet beneath us; a rare view, since in these mountains it rains and snows for over three hundred and twenty day a year. We made a safe descent, though we saw the plumes and heard the rumbles of avalanches on the flanks of the mountain.

Very early the next day we crossed the valley and commenced our climb of Mount Stanley, at over sixteen thousand feet the highest in the range. The approach to the summit involves crossing an extensive glacier and we went prepared to bivouac overnight on the mountain. On the glacier we were enveloped in dense fog and heavy snowfall, so it was impossible to maintain our intended direction. There was also the considerable risk of crevasses, and roped up as we were, probing ahead with our ice axes, it would be difficult with only two on the rope to arrest a fall into a crevasse, let alone haul a person back to the surface, so we decided to abandon the attempt and returned to the huts by the lake. The next day we commenced a long trek to the foot of Mount Baker, the last on our schedule of summit climbs. This involved crossing the Scott-Eliot pass, which at fourteen thousand feet was

NOWHERE NEAR GREENLAND

mantled by deep snow through which our six porters walked barefoot, having chosen to leave our donated footwear behind. They possessed amazing hardiness, wearing only shorts and shirt, while we were swaddled in several pairs of socks, boots, vests, shirt, anorak and gloves. Nevertheless, we halted a couple of times to check their feet for incipient frostbite during the four hour crossing of the pass. We kept close to the face of a high precipice to our left, over which from time to time stones would come hurtling, though falling well clear of us.

After a hard day's trek we reached the huts, again beside two small lakes and dusted with snow. In what had now become our dinner routine, we made a stew, reconstituting the dried vegetables and throwing in rice and biltong. For the climbs we took with us just chocolate, water and the dry biltong to gnaw. Long before dawn the next morning we set off up a steep boulder-strewn ravine and were soon picking our way through snow. After some not very difficult climbing at the head of the ravine, we reached the summit ridge and a near- vertical pitch. I took the lead but quickly became stuck. The holds in the rock were covered in 'verglas', or sheet ice. My arms and legs began to shake with the strain and knowledge of the drop beneath me, and John talked me down the mini-steps I could no longer see. Then the weather closed right in, with dense mist rising up the gully and enveloping us, and heavy snow began to fall.

The author, near the summit of Mount Baker, Ruwenzori, Uganda, 1954

There was no choice but to retreat. Our gully of ascent had branched from time to time, and now in the conditions of almost nil visibility we took the wrong branch. Eventually at a lower altitude we broke out below the mist and snow and beheld

Into Africa

a magnificent, sunlit panorama of what we soon realised was the Belgian Congo. In the mist we had curved right round to the west and now faced a very long, pathless trek around the slope of the mountain to return to our camp. This we achieved by nightfall, arriving exhausted about eighteen hours after our departure.

We rested for a day, and then started back across the high pass, reacquainted ourselves with the blessed bog - though we were now travelling lighter and our leaps from tuft to tuft were easier - and made our way back to the head of the Mobuku-Bujuku river system. Kule wisely took us on a long diversion which led to a simple bridge across the Mobuku river, possibly now in greater spate than when we had crossed it a week before. Arriving back at the lightning strike caves in the forest, we found that leopard had scattered our stores and devoured the biltong. Early next morning, a Basanjo man appeared at the caves as we were preparing to leave. He offered us the magnificent pelt of a leopard, seemingly, if not actually a snow leopard, at least one from a high altitude since it had a great depth of fur. The owner was asking ten East African shillings for it, but as an honorary game ranger in Tanganyika, John refused it and, my appreciation shamed by his high minded example, so did I. Back at Kule's village, we paid off the porters, checked on the thunderstruck pair who had recovered well, and swam and washed in the broad and shallow, fast flowing river. For once, for someone who detests cold water, and this was really cold, it was delicious.

We commenced the drive back to Tanganyika, continuing to circle Lake Victoria in an anti-clockwise direction and stayed a night at a very pleasant lodge on its western shore. Crossing the equator we then drove on to Bukoba, the largest town and port on that side of the lake, near to where Clark Gable, Ava Gardner and Grace Kelly had recently filmed 'Mogambo'. Further south we came to Biharamulo, where John had been D.O. before being posted to Musoma, and then to Geita, a few miles inland from the southern end of the lake where there was a large and thriving goldmine. Supplies for the mine came in by lake to their jetty at Nungwe Bay, and it was to this bay that in the 1930s aviatrix Beryl Markham flew to evacuate a victim of appendicitis at the beginning of her classic book 'Flight to the West'. Entering Geita district we drove into an unmarked trench dug across the road by the public works department and broke a spring, and John was able to complain directly to Arthur Hammond, the local PWD boss with whom we were spending the night. (Later he was also to lose his house, set alight by his kerosene refrigerator.) And so we continued round through Mwanza and on to Ukerewe, where we completed

NOWHERE NEAR GREENLAND

the circuit of the lake, and John returned to Musoma.

There were two mission stations on Ukerewe, the African Inland Mission staffed by Americans and of an evangelical, protestant and somewhat dour orientation, and the White Fathers, Roman Catholics who operated a teacher training college, a clinic and were assisted by sisters. I attended just one Sunday service at the African Inland Mission, accompanied by the D.C. and his wife. The preacher man harangued the congregation, telling us that we were really no better than swine that rolled in the mud, got clean and then went right back and rolled in the mud all over again. Clearly a message there, but I believe the D.C, and his wife, upright in their pews, were somewhat offended and we did not return. The White Fathers, on the other hand, who on Ukerewe hailed from Holland, Belgium, Germany and Quebecois Canada, were most sociable. We played tennis with them and they came to our parties, though they did not dance. The sisters were similarly very friendly and relaxed and made an excellent liqueur from their oranges, and the fathers loved to have guests to entertain as this was the only time they were officially permitted to touch alcohol. Both came out for an initial tour of ten years, and the sisters had the right to only one leave in their home countries before they returned to Africa for life. The fathers were later allowed to take home-leave every seven years, when they were expected to raise funds for their mission and recruit newcomers to the calling. At that time the fathers received pay of just two East African shillings a day, but they and the sisters cultivated highly productive fruit and vegetable gardens, and one of their stations in the Belgian Congo manufactured 'white pops', strong cheroots which were distributed to all their missions in East Africa. They similarly distributed a 'snake stone' which also originated in the Congo and was said to suck out the poison from the site of a bite.

A curious phenomenon often seen above Lake Victoria, and the other great lakes of East Africa, is the eruption of 'lake flies' from the surface at certain times of the year. In their billions, these form a dense black column resembling a tornado rising several hundred feet into the air, at first vertically and then bending and dispersing in the wind. Sometimes there are several such columns at once which, seen from a distance, could suggest a great naval battle was raging beyond the horizon. When the flies come ashore they are attracted to lights, beneath which they can form drifts several inches deep. They are small enough to pass through mosquito screens, and would settle on the hot top of an Aladdin or Petromax pressure lamp where they would quickly cook and then char, giving off a strong smell of fish. It was com-

Into Africa

monly believed that if a canoe was immediately above the point where the flies erupted, all within it would be suffocated. The Bahaya people on the west of the lake roll them into rissoles, cook and eat them. Less frequently, water spouts occur over the lake, and one came ashore at Nansio while I was there, lifted up the entire roof of the covered market and plonked it down again trapping many people inside. It also showered down on the town a great quantity of small fish.

My first home leave was due in 1955 after I had been in Tanganyika for three years and Africa for five, but towards the end of my tour I was officially advised that I must first pass my oral and written Swahili exams or have my leave delayed until I had. This proved sufficient incentive, and as all my interactions on a daily basis with farmers and field staff were in Swahili it was not such a difficult task. I had arrived in Tanganyika from Kenya fluently speaking what was here derisively termed 'Ki-Settler', a simple and degraded Swahili frequently interspersed with English words, such as in 'Namna bloody gani!' which could loosely be translated as an irate 'what's going on here!' So it took me some time to tidy up my vocabulary and eschew old habits.

From Mwanza, I took a De Havilland Rapide bi-plane, made of canvas and wood and belonging to the 'Caspair Round The Lake Air Service', to Entebbe, then the only international airport in East Africa. We had called en route at Geita, where through its door I was handed a small wooden box to load onto the plane. I seriously underestimated its weight, since it was packed with gold ingots, and dropped it on the fragile floor of the plane, much to the annoyance of the pilot. Overnighting at Entebbe, I shared a room with an American pilot who offered to carry me for nothing in his cargo Loadstar, but I already had my B.O.A.C. ticket to London and I flew in their Argonaut, noisy and little more than a converted bomber. We put down at Khartoum, Cairo, Rome and finally Northolt, then London's international airport, whose terminal buildings consisted largely of spruced-up Nissen huts.

My parents and one sister were there to greet me, and if I remember correctly this was on the apron in front of the terminal huts, for things were much less crowded and formal in those days. They were not impressed that I now sported a neat van Dyke beard, then considered unconventional and an appendage of self-appointed artists, or possibly the natural prosthesis for a chinless wonder, which I was neither, and family hints almost amounting to nagging over the next few days finally persuaded me to shave it off.

NOWHERE NEAR GREENLAND

After a night in London, we drove down to Dorchester in Dorset where at nearby West Stafford my parents had a house that had been built by Thomas Hardy for his three sisters. Hardy had trained as an architect before he became a writer, and he also designed his own house 'Max Gate' just a mile down the road. In the garden on a somewhat bulbous pedestal was a brass sundial bearing the initials of Thomas and his sisters, and well spaced at the corners of the lawn there were no less than three summerhouses, one of which could be orientated on a turntable, and they were all keen bird watchers.

Talbothays, Dorset. Hardy sundial on plinth at centre, 1955

The upstairs lavatory, which faced towards Egdon Heath, we named the 'throne-room', since the seat was set and enclosed within a wide and magnificent mahogany bench. What great thoughts had Thomas Hardy, what muse while there seated, gazing at the bucolic scene beyond the window?

I bought a little Hilman Husky estate car, collected it from near Piccadilly Circus, which was scary since until then I had scarcely driven on more than African tracks devoid of traffic, and drove my mother to Paris. We stayed at the modest Hotel

Into Africa

Marie near Les Halles on the Rue de Rivoli, where a great fuss was made if you asked to take a bath. The manager was called and would personally bring you the bathroom key, and all this was inscribed as an extra on the bill. We visited the Louvre, the Folies Bergères, Les Naturistes, Versailles, Fontainebleau, had an amazingly expensive cup of tea at W.H. Smith & Sons on the Rue de Rivoli, which we could ill afford, since at that time the British were limited to taking only fifty pounds out of the country, and thus I had not the wherewithal to purchase the oil painting signed John Constable we saw in the flea market, priced at £90. I attended Louis Armstrong's farewell concert at l'Olympia, the famous Paris music hall. Backed by his All Stars, with vocalist Velma Middleton, he romped through the set programme, wowed the crowd with his gravelled sallies in French, and then kept singing and blowing his trumpet in encore after encore.

Sisters Sally and Jill with mother and me, Talbothays, Dorset, 1959

An advertisement in the personal column of 'The Times' announced that a lady was putting together a small party of young people to ski in Austria and there were one or two vacancies. It was high time I learned to ski, so I joined the party at Victoria station and was soon steaming towards the snow. The elderly lady, the organiser and grandmother of one of our party , was at the wrong end of the train when it divided near the Austrian frontier and she disappeared behind the Iron Curtain, to be reunited with us in Austria a whole week later. We were based in Solden and

NOWHERE NEAR GREENLAND

every day took the lift to the slopes of Hoch-Solden where there were a few chalets, a restaurant and Sir John Hunt of recent Everest fame, who was skiing there with friends. On the penultimate day of the holiday, by which time I had achieved, but never thereafter exceeded, a very modest proficiency on skis, my instructor asked me if I would like to attempt ski jumping. Just another of those things that seemed rather a good idea at the time. But when I became airborne from a high ramp of snow, I veered off-line so that the left ski landed on hard. compacted snow, and the right in soft, deep, powdery snow where it stuck, while the rest of me momentarily continued at speed, breaking my ankle and proving yet again that I have Achilles ankles as well as knees. I enjoyed a very comfortable rail journey back to England with two friends from our party, a bottle of cherry brandy, and my plastered ankle propped on the seat.

During this leave, I was invited to dinner by the son of friends of my parents at their neo-Georgian manor in Dorset. There were just five of us, my friend Michael, his mother, me and Vivien Leigh and her bearded companion, with whom she was associated in the current production of Tennessee Williams' 'Cat on a Hot Tin Roof' on Broadway, in which she starred. In fact, cats were the main topic of my conversation with her, for she deplored at length the quarantine laws that prevented her from being accompanied by her cat, to and fro across the Atlantic.

I had requested to be posted again to the lake province of Tanganyika, and this time the northern half of Geita district, which stretched along the southern shore of Lake Victoria, was where I was assigned. The small government station of some ten houses was situated in a scrubby patch of bush a couple of miles from the gold mine, whose well-appointed Lone Cone Club provided solace and entertainment to the local white population and their families. My house, unusually of red brick, was very small with just the one bedroom, but having a separate lounge large enough for my piano. I took over from a German called Decker whose personal vehicle was a curious Mercedes contraption called a Unimog. This stood high and square on oversized wheels and Decker and his wife sat bolt upright on a bench seat up front, and the steering column was also vertical, as on old tramcars. Tall, austere and very 'korrekt' we nicknamed him 'Double Decker', and in a house he had occupied I discovered a book in English critical of Hitler and his National Socialist Party. This book contained his evidently furious scrawls in red ink defending the Fuhrer and the Third Reich.

Into Africa

Geita district was largely covered by 'miombo' bush, which describes woodland with a mixture of tree species, many of them thorny and all of lowly stature. This bush was infested with tsetse flies, and the ground and vehicle tracks were littered with sharp stones. On a single trip to Mwanza, a mere sixty miles, I once suffered four punctures, with the tyres slashed and the inner-tubes pierced by the stones. I carried a vulcanising kit with many patches and a clamp to cope with such vicissitudes. Kneeling by the road, jacking up the car and repairing the tyres, invited the attention of the tsetse, no doubt seduced by one's copious sweat. They had the ability to touch down so softly on forehead, neck, arms and legs that one was quite unaware of their presence as they gorged, unless noticed by yourself, or someone who might shout, "Hey, you've a tsetse on your right ear!"; then 'splat!' and blood everywhere. A singular charm of the place was that where frequent streamlets meandered across the track, there were clouds of many coloured butterflies dancing just above the surface. I once came across two bicycles abandoned in the middle of this same road, belongings still strapped to their carriers and no-one in sight. While I pondered this enigma, my cab steadily filled with African bees and I had the answer.

Not long before I arrived in Geita, the mine manager's wife and driver were making their way to Mwanza with the week's output of gold ingots in order to deposit them at the bank. The car was ambushed halfway there by a recently- arrived central European employee who shot dead the woman and driver, drove their car off the road, hid the gold in the bush and returned in his car to the mine. The vehicle with its dead passengers was soon discovered and he was linked to the killing by witnesses who saw him driving on the road that morning. He subsequently confessed to the murders and theft, and back at the mine was handed a gun and he shot himself.

Fancy dress parties are very popular in small, isolated communities, perhaps because, in addition to the pleasure of play acting, they create a new cast of virtual characters and a change of faces. And so it was at the Lone Cone Club at Geita's gold mine, where I again trotted out my 'devil in disguise' costume, with which the people there were as yet unacquainted. Far into the evening, and somewhat the worse for wear, I was sitting drinking at a table with friends. The two short, red-tipped cardboard horns I had glued to my forehead to elaborate the original costume had already fallen off in the combination of heat, sweat and dancing, and my 'kiboko' tail was curled out of sight behind my chair. So when the young Cornish miner came over to our table, all he had in his view of me was my parson's collar

NOWHERE NEAR GREENLAND

above the reversed waistcoat and my black coat. He was maudlin in his cups and needed to confess his grief and guilt at putting down his old dog. Had he committed a sin? I should have declared myself straight away, but instead, egged on by my 'friends' who now with unctuous deference kept calling me 'Reverend', I cheerfully fell into the part they and the Cornishman had chosen for me and offered him heartfelt consolation; "It was an act of kindness, of love; the dear old dog is far, far better off" etc. I recall he asked me if I believed there was a heaven for dogs, and I certainly allowed for that possibility and the hope of a happy reunion, but I totally ignored my friends' suggestion I should make an immediate collection for a dog memorial. He then asked me if I would hear his confession. I replied that this would hardly be appropriate amid such ungodly surroundings and arranged to meet him out by the stone crushers, (huge and hideously noisy machines, but now at night blessedly silent), at three a.m. However, by that early hour my friends had forgotten all about this assignment, and so had I. At about 5 a.m. the Cornishman reappeared to tell me he had waited and waited for me by the stone-crushers. My dog-collar was now much askew, and he was somewhat peevish, so to admit my deceit would have invited a fight, or at least provoked invective such as "dirty rotten bastard!" so I was abjectly apologetic, and my friends were loudly critical of my uncaring negligence, and unworthiness for my chosen calling, which somewhat cheered him up.

My mother, stepfather and sister decided to come out and visit me, travelling by ship via the Cape of Good Hope and disembarking at Mombasa, and they would stay with me for five weeks. I wrote to my superiors asking if it might be possible to allocate me a larger house, but as nothing was available in Geita they proposed to transfer me to the Ukiriguru agricultural research station about eighteen miles south of Mwanza, from which base I would carry out extension work among farmers in the south of that district. The research station was set among stony hills, barren but for scrubby bush and a number of resident leopard and hyena. My house, a mirror image of that in Nansio, was at the foot of one of those hills, and leopard and hyena regularly roamed the station at night, and in Mwanza town they competed in scavenging from rubbish bins.

Meanwhile, I had been planning to climb Kilimanjaro with Noel Carter, the chief surveyor at Geita mine, and I would meet my family in Nairobi immediately after the climb. Noel and I intended what we grandly called 'an east-west traverse of the massif', our starting point being the Rongai forest station. We progressed to great

Into Africa

detail in our arrangements - exact timetable, equipment, rations, porters, hut bookings, etcetera. I moved into my new house at Ukiriguru and Noel and I were about to leave for Moshi on the southern side of the mountain when I received a telegram to say that my parents' ship had broken down at Beira and would not now arrive at Mombasa until a week later than scheduled. This completely threw out my plans and I had to abandon the climb. At least Noel carried my ice axe to the summit, together with my old school woollen scarf which his wife had fashioned with additional windproof material into a hood.

I drove up to Kenya to meet my parents and sister in Nairobi and we stayed at the Brackenhurst hotel at Limuru outside the city. Its rooms were in separate chalets, dotted around magnificent gardens surrounded by a tea estate, and each chalet had a heavy, carved, antique door imported from Zanzibar. From the hotel, the summits of both Mount Kenya and Kilimanjaro could sometimes be seen, far to the north and south respectively. After a few days there, while they regained their land legs, I took them by car to Kisumu and my parents boarded the lake steamer for Mwanza. I then drove with my sister back to Tanganyika through Kisii, and once we had crossed the border and the streams and rivers reverted to flowing over the roads rather than under them, I asked her to wade through the water ahead to ascertain the depth, assuring her that crocodiles never strayed this far upstream. For years after, she averred that I could not have been absolutely sure of this. With my parents and sister staying at Ukiriguru, I camped in the garden, and on many nights a leopard would 'saw' - the guttural sound they make when hunting - outside my splendid and presumed cat-proof tent.

We were invited to dine by the provincial commissioner, Fanny Walden. He lived in the former German provincial governor's house situated on the top of a granite outcrop in the middle of Mwanza. The only approach to it was by a long flight of steps, and the ground-floor of this large house was paved with blue and white Dresden tiles. Fanny had an African mistress who acted as his housekeeper, and kept modestly in the background at times of official entertainment. However, his other house staff of long standing tended to the imperious when dealing with guests. At a small dinner, one of the diners took one more potato than the number of guests yet to be served allowed. "Rudisha moja, Bwana!" - or 'Put one back, sir!', he was commanded. Princess Margaret stayed here when she came to Tanganyika on a royal visit not long after the end of her romance with group captain Peter Townsend. Her royal entertainment included a magnificent display of traditional

NOWHERE NEAR GREENLAND

dancing given on the airfield by a number of the local tribes. This included one by the fifty wives of Chief Mwajabere of Zanaki in Musoma district. I had seen them dance at the coronation celebrations five years previously, but while for that occasion they had swayed, stamped and chanted bare-breasted, now all mammary movement had been stilled and encased in fifty pairs of identical pink brassieres. A regatta at dusk, of hundreds of lamp-lit canoes along the Mwanza shore, glided by unseen by royal eyes as the princess was that evening indisposed.

The Tanganyika African Union founded by Julius Nyerere now wielded considerable political power, and as a means to hasten the day of independence he had ordered a campaign of civil disobedience. Farmers were told to ignore our advice concerning soil conservation, and to return or throw away any free fertilizer they had been issued. There had also been some minor riots in Mwanza and other parts of the country. Tanganyika was administered by the British as a United Nations Trust Territory, and preparing Tanganyikans for the government of an independent state had long been official policy; but the promised emancipation was not coming soon enough for Nyerere and his colleagues, who like all politicians seek power in their time. To assist the administration in rural areas that were thought to be 'disaffected', I was formally gazetted as a supernumerary district officer, and went from village to village holding 'barazas', or official meetings, specifically to explain to the people the role of the administration in preparing them for government, and the part they should play. I also discounted rumours, common at the time, that in the future there would be no more laws or taxes, the banks would print and distribute as much money as the people wanted, and Europeans would have to reduce the number of cars they owned - just as herders in overgrazed and eroded areas had been required to sell off a number of their cattle.

A small detachment of the Kings African Rifles arrived in lake province to demonstrate their firepower, as a warning of likely response to violence. I was asked to help organise one of these exercises, and the result was somewhat farcical. Having made sure that the large field which was to act as a range for firing mortars was clear of local people, I stood with a large group of them in front of a cluster of huts. I waved the all clear to the soldiers who with their mortars were about a kilometre away. They fired the first bomb which (I trust), was intended to fall well short of us. Instead it fluttered over our heads and fell with a tremendous bang on the far side of the settlement. Great shouts and cheers from all around me who apparently did not appreciate that this was not intended (or was it?), and I must confess to

Into Africa

some disquiet during the rather long pause that followed, which I hoped indicated that the range was being more carefully calculated before the next mortar bomb was launched in our direction. This fell into the field well short of us, as did all the others that followed, and thus were a great disappointment to everyone in the crowd, except me.

My great friend Revell de Valda, the same who had trodden the thespian boards with me in that definitive amateur production of Shakespeare's Tempest, and whose father had written books of his explorations in South America, went out to Malaya to plant rubber the year before I left for Africa. He came to visit me while I was in Geita and arrived just as I was recovering from an attack of rheumatic fever, the first since I had left Kenya, and again undiagnosed. The symptoms were the same: fever, pain migrating from joint to joint and a very erratic heart beat. He deplored the rough conditions in which I lived - the lack of proper roads, electricity and convivial female company, my miserable little house and the tsetse flies. Why not come to Malaya? I had the opportunity to stay on in Tanganyika at least until Independence, which had already been scheduled for 1961, when I would receive my 'lumpers', or a gratuity, for the years I had served there. This sum would not be inconsiderable, relative to my meagre resources. However I decided that this money would not compensate for another two years of self-inflicted hardship, from which, I had by now convincingly been persuaded, I apparently suffered. So, before finally leaving Tanganyika in February 1959 I tendered my resignation from the Colonial Service and applied for interviews in London with the two major rubber plantation management companies in Malaya. At Dar es Salaam, I boarded the British India ship 'Uganda' for Venice, and from there took a train to Oslo, and then onwards north to Mjolfiel to ski.

While in Mwanza the previous year, I had been treated for bilharzia, otherwise known as schistosomiasis, which I had almost certainly contracted from swimming in Lake Victoria. This is an occupational disease of rice growers throughout Africa, and is passed to man by a small freshwater snail which acts as an alternate host. I had returned from Norway after two weeks of mainly cross-country skiing feeling extremely fit, but after a month of mooching around at home in Dorset, I experienced some undue fatigue and reported to the tropical diseases hospital in London for a check-up. It was established that I still had bilharzia and I was to spend another six weeks as an in-patient undergoing treatment, this time with intravenous injections of antimony. These are highly toxic, and may only be administered by a

NOWHERE NEAR GREENLAND

doctor slowly depressing the plunger of a syringe over a period of twenty minutes while he checks on your vital life signs. About midway through the first injection I passed out and my heart stopped. Upon resuscitation, there was a considerable team around my bed, and a young Welsh nursing sister lilted "We thought you'd gone!". The doctor asked how I felt and I said "marvellous", as indeed I did, having just had an extraordinary near-death experience. This was of becoming, not diminishing; and then returning to only two dimensional space, quite flat in black and white. The temporary shortage of blood to my brain did not adequately explain to me these profound impressions which transcended common reality, and certainly in that instance death had no sting. (And if one day, and I hope not too soon, at the very end of my life - or not the very end of my life - I shall know I have passed this way before).

Many years later, after leaving Africa, I read a book written by a female East German economist who had worked in Tanzania in the 1980s. She made much of the former oppression of the native people by the British colonialists, how the natives had been forced to grow cash crops to feed the greed of Britain's industries and consumers, and of the 'struggle' for independence. This conformed very much to the communist style of rewriting history to justify their own ideology, of newly emergent nations need to glorify their road to independence, and that of their first generation of politicians to conjure up exaggerated notions of victimhood. An old man on Ukerewe had once deplored to me the departure of the country's former German masters, when people obeyed and respected authority and did not, as today's children do, he said "poke sticks into the spokes of my bicycle wheels when I ride by". The British administration worked almost entirely through the traditional chiefs or tribal structures to administer law fairly and prevent them acting as despots, and always attempted to reconcile tribes that had a long history of mutual hostility, rather than acting to divide and rule which would have created chaos rather than the general tranquillity that reigned. I spent most of my time reinforcing the food security of the people through the promotion and improvement of food crops and the protection of their land, and little was required to encourage the growing of cash crops since the people's own need for money to purchase basic consumer items provided them with sufficient motivation. Taxation was limited to just a few shillings a year for able bodied men only, and primary schooling and medical care were free.

The current and largely accepted argument that all colonial enterprise in Africa

Into Africa

has been irredeemably bad, disregards the fact that in less than fifty years it brought many societies from the equivalent of the early iron age, with no writing, wheels or permanent structures, to the technologies and enlightenment of the 20th century, put a complete stop to inter-tribal fighting, and to a large extent left their native languages and traditional cultures intact. Fortunately, for the majority of these countries, colonisation was limited to administration, with little or no settlement by European farmers. South Africa, Namibia, Zimbabwe and Kenya are among the exceptions, and in Kenya I experienced the inevitable antagonistic attitude of the settlers towards the colonial administration which saw it as overly protecting the rights of the African people. In the early 1950s, governor Mitchell was for that reason refused membership of the Rift Valley Club.

All countries recast their history into the form with which they are comfortable. And such are the current negative connotations of 'colonialism', that in an act of wilful amnesia and political expedience the United States of America, for example, denies it was ever a colonial power, when it was, and is, the most successful of them all. In a fit of exculpatory togetherness in victimhood, a US Ambassador, addressing an audience in west Africa, complained that his country too had once been colonised! In the footsteps of the British, the USA colonised half of the north American continent, (and hence was too preoccupied with that to join in Europe's 19th century grab for Africa), which settlement was made secure and permanent by the near-genocide of its native people - unlike, say, colonialism in India and Africa. It went on to neo-colonise Russian Alaska, former Spanish and French possessions in north and central America, colonised many Pacific islands, had a colonial adventure in the Philippines and settled Liberia with its former slaves. America, Canada, Australia and New Zealand are today's leading colonial powers; to a smaller degree China with its settlement of Tibet and Taiwan, and to a limited but tenacious extent France, for the sake of francophonie. The current neo-colonisation of western New Guinea (Irian Jaya) by Indonesia appears of concern only to fellow Melanesians in the region.

Colonisation has been part of man's story since Homo sapiens first came out of Africa and replaced the Neanderthals wherever they found them. Two thousand years ago the Bantu people commenced their aggressive expansion south from their heartland in today's Nigeria, progressively invading the whole of Africa south of the Sahara and reaching the Cape of Good Hope shortly before the arrival of the first Dutch settlers. On the way they replaced the hunter-gatherer Bushmen, or San

NOWHERE NEAR GREENLAND

people, of whom in countries like Tanzania, only small pockets of linguistic evidence remain. Successful colonisation demands the maintenance of demographic superiority, (Israel's current dilemma), which was achieved in the Americas.
None of the indigenous Guanche people of the Canary Islands survived their colonisation by Spain; the Caribs of the Caribbean and the aborigines of Tasmania disappeared altogether.

The former colonised countries, particularly in Africa, which to a large extent have managed to retain their own languages and native culture, may be said to have been 'technologised' rather than 'civilised' by this process (though the French still speak of their ongoing 'mission civilizatrice'), for most often the countries with the most highly developed technologies are in a literal sense the least civil. Is the bombing and blowing up of tens of thousands of men, women and children more civilised than eating just a few?

Almost exactly fifty years after I had left it, I went back to Ukerewe Island where in my time the population had been fifty thousand. Now it was three hundred thousand, and where a network of two-lane roads had run between avenues of trees there were now only narrow sandy tracks barely wide enough for a vehicle, no trees, and fields of cassava extended to their very edge. Cassava, because it will produce a harvest in soils too exhausted to grow successfully any other food crop. So great now was the pressure on the land and the need for food, I saw no sign of cotton or coffee, and the ginnery at the centre of the island lay derelict, the manager's and engineer's substantial houses in ruins, gardens gone, and now used as shelters and yards for livestock. My own house at the government centre had fared well structurally, though it had not seen a lick of paint inside or out in half a century. The current occupier, the district magistrate who hailed from Arusha, very kindly showed me around and deplored the total lack of money for maintenance. His internal walls were black and his furniture was made from packing cases. The garden too was gone, as again the need for food had pushed cultivation to the very walls of the house, and subsequent erosion had removed more than a foot of soil from around their base leaving now redundant lavatory, bathroom and kitchen pipes high in the air. Where once we had a tennis court, there now remained just one rusting upright pipe that once had supported one end of the net. I would make the analogy of the Romans leaving Britain after nearly half a millennium of occupation, when their great network of roads deteriorated for lack of need and maintenance, great villas crumbled together with their under-floor central heating systems and

Into Africa

disappeared, for they were incompatible with the resurgent indigenous culture and its values, and tribalism returned. Over this very long period of colonisation, hundreds of thousands of Britons were enslaved and many transported to Rome in chains. Is it now too late for Britain to seek compensation for this from Italy, or at least from Rome?

The massive, exponential increase in the human population of African countries that have been largely dependent on home-grown food, and the water to sustain it, presents their governments and development agencies, not only with the need to find a solution to the increasing impoverishment of the land and people, and a chronic and increasing dependence on food aid, but with a considerable dilemma. In the minds of most politicians, the size of population is sacrosanct as an expression of national power and importance, and all rightly believe in the preservation of human life through the prevention and cure of illness and the maintenance of civil order. But given the finite nature of natural resources, these tenets are currently proving incompatible. Sixty percent of Malawi's rural population, for example, is now perennially dependent on food aid. For how long can we predict with any confidence that this will endure without interruption; five, ten, fifty, one hundred years? Any interruption, even for just one year, due, say, to international strife, plant disease or a reduction in grain surpluses in the developed world, will result in mass starvation. (Currently, a new strain of black rust is spreading to devastate wheat crops in a widening area of the world, and increasing amounts of grain in the USA are being grown for ethanol production.) Can the bountiful results of a second 'green revolution', possibly based on plant genetic modification and affordable to small farmers, be realised before this grim possibility comes to pass? Or will this be prevented by a prior population collapse due to HIV? Meanwhile, working away to further increase population growth, the pharmaceutical industry and epidemiologists are now confidently predicting that a malaria vaccine will soon be at hand, which in Africa will save the lives of five million children a year. The effects of climate change through global warming, for which the predictions based on current models may not be reliable, are another factor that will have a bearing in this complex formulation for the future of the continent.

PENINSULAR MALAYA

NOWHERE NEAR GREENLAND

UNDER RUBBER

In August 1959 I flew from London to Kuala Lumpur on the inaugural flight of the Comet IV airliner. It had already touched down in Singapore where there had been a large crowd to greet and photograph this jet-powered wonder, just as there had been at the previous stop of Colombo. The sleek-lined Comet, with its four engines neatly enclosed within the wing surfaces, flew much higher, faster, and for its passengers much quieter than the piston driven planes that had previously served this route. There were few passengers on the plane, but a young scion of the Wedgwood pottery family occupied the seat next to me. Looking down from very high over the Mediterranean, I observed that surely some of those small islands beneath us would be entirely covered at high tide. He then witheringly reminded me of a fact I had known since prep school, "there are no tides in the Mediterranean" he said, no doubt mistaking my subsequent silence for humble subservience, rather than rueful reflection that it was not inevitably rewarding to test my humour on complete strangers. As we approached Kuala Lumpur, descending through grey scattered cloud which would soon gather to give the city its regular afternoon shower, I made out the giant dredgers at work on the tin mining pools whose colour resembled strong milk tea, as did that of the rivers that converge here and give the city its name, meaning muddy confluence. The roofs of red and orange tiles, grey corrugated iron and the flat white tops of a few modern buildings created a mosaic among the green of suburban gardens and the sur-

Under Rubber

rounding steep forest-covered hills, while in the distance serried ranks of rubber trees extended to the horizon. Tin and rubber were then the mainstays of Malaya's economy.

I was met by Majid, the Malay driver of the manager of Sengkang Estate to which I had been appointed as an assistant manager. A sturdy brown man, he was wearing a well-pressed white shirt, dark trousers and the round, black, traditional Malay hat called a 'songkok'. Driving out through the city I was assailed by the unfamiliar odours of the east, many pungent and pleasant, some with the hint of vegetable and animal decay, whose unique and subtle combination contributes as much to the character of a place as its appearance, indelible in the memory and instantly recallable. We drove out past the high white walls and corner guard towers of Pudu prison, where communist terrorists of the 'emergency' were still being hanged, then on down a fine tarmac road of a quality I had never seen in Africa, through sixty miles of continuous rubber estates, broken only when we passed through minor settlements of two-storied Chinese shop-houses and the modern town of Seremban, state capital of Negri Sembilan.

My bungalow-to-be was eighteen miles south of Port Dickson on the road to Malacca. In Malaya, the tradition is to designate an address by its nearest milestone. Thus, I was to live at 'eighteenth mile', while my manager lived at 'fourteenth mile', and another assistant manager at 'twenty-second mile'. And, somewhat whimsically the Tamil Indians, who comprised a quarter of the country's population, still termed every public road as 'company road', in collective remembrance of the East India Company. However, I had arrived in Malaya several weeks earlier than expected, and my bungalow was still being redecorated, so I was initially lodged in a small Chinese hotel of half a dozen rooms on the sea front just outside what is locally called P.D. though Port Dickson is a minimal port and more of a small seaside town. One could say in that respect it was the Margate of Malaya, being less than two hours drive down a good 'company' road from the capital. The hotel was clean and airy with high ceilings, and comfortable with simple but excellent Chinese food. There were few other guests there during the week, but at weekends it filled up with cheerful Chinese businessmen from K.L. entertaining their girlfriends. They were always highly sociable and I was generally invited to join them for pandemonic meals and boisterous ball games on the beach. However, these weekends were hardly relaxing, for my experience has been that the Chinese are the noisiest people on earth. Without apparent discomfort they tolerate and snore

NOWHERE NEAR GREENLAND

through colossal noise levels, and I have often seen their children undisturbed at their homework surrounded by complete bedlam – presumably a survival mechanism for living in close contact with large numbers of people whose language demands much shouting for normal conversation. Whoever named the game of Chinese Whispers was quite probably deaf. (When a few years later I was on Jeram Padang estate, I was regularly kept awake at night by the incessant barking of a dog which was chained on the veranda of the Chinese shop about a hundred yards from my bungalow. Exasperated, and armed with my hippopotamus hide whip to physically remonstrate with the animal, I purposefully strode down through the moonlight to the shop where the owner and his family slept soundly behind shutters, within arms length of the source of my irritation. As I raised my 'kiboko', the dog lunged and promptly bit me on the leg. The moonlit rubber trees alone bore witness to my rueful laughter as I limped back to my bed).

My bungalow at 18th mile Sengkang, with my mother and dog Pontianak, 1961

Because for the time being I was about seventeen miles from my place of work, the manager's Land Rover would collect me at the ungodly late hour of 7 a.m. and take me straight to the field where I would immerse myself in the multitudinous activities pertaining to rubber production that required my supervision. Starting with the tapping, I would mark with a broad yellow crayon any wounds on the tapping panel or excessive bark consumption, this colour uniquely employed by me as other overseers used red. I would also check the latex cups on the trees for cleanliness,

Under Rubber

and see that the tapping paths along the tree lines were free of weeds. I might then check on the bulldozing of jungle for new planting (unlike in Africa where forest is always termed bush, here in Malaya it is jungle), the digging of drains through swamps, the surveying and construction of terraces on steep land, the grafting of rubber seedlings in nurseries, the planting and fertilizing of trees, the spraying or hoeing of weeds and the inspection and treatment of trees for root disease. This would usually involve several miles of walking, giving one a good appetite for breakfast when returning to the bungalow at around 11 a.m.

I would set out again before noon, when the tappers had collected their latex from some five hundred cups and were carrying it to the weighing stations in heavy, brimming pails, often balanced on a wooden yoke across one shoulder or pushed on a bicycle. Here, after recording the amount against the tapper's name and the field of origin, the latex was poured into a large holding tank and prevented from coagulating by the injection of ammonia gas. Transported to the estate factory by tanker lorry, it would then be manufactured into one or more products for eventual export. By 2 p.m., when all field activities had ceased for the day, I would make a final check of the work so that an appropriate plan could be made for the morrow. I was then free for the rest of the day, except at the end of the month, when there would be the 'check rolls', or detailed wages ledgers to complete, as well as production statistics and other returns to submit to management.

However, once I moved into my bungalow on the estate, the daily work routine would require me to attend 'muster' in the pre-dawn dark at 5.30 in the morning, when, at a point near the labour lines, all the weeders and tappers would attend rollcall and then disperse to their allocated places of work in far flung parts of the estate. But for these few halcyon weeks following my arrival, I had a late breakfast every day with manager Charlie Ross, his wife Nancy and their children. He had started his career in Malaya before the Second World War, during which he was captured by the Japanese and put to work on the notorious death railway in Burma where he lost many friends and colleagues. He was a compact, feisty Scot who believed in hard work from himself and his assistants. He had a most equable temper and a ready sense of humour, and I never heard him swear or tell an off-colour joke - quite exceptional among the rubber planting fraternity. He liked to recount tales of the fierce managers under whom he had worked as an assistant, particularly one Harry Piper who on his morning round of the estate discovered an assistant still in the bungalow celebrating his birthday with a friend. Cordially invited

NOWHERE NEAR GREENLAND

in, with a toast he wished the assistant a very happy birthday and promptly sacked him. He was also a man who Charlie claimed could spot a single blade of 'lalang' (Imperata cylindrica), from half a mile away. This tall, voracious and invasive grass spreads both underground and by feathery, wind-born seeds, and it thrives in impoverished soils. If not controlled, it will swiftly overwhelm a plantation and severely depress the yields of rubber. "Lalang", said Charlie, "has been responsible for more planters being sent packing back to Britain than for any other reason", and this was no doubt recounted as a cautionary tale which I would do well to heed. Indeed, every day tens of thousands of labourers throughout Malaya were employed in lalang control, either by wiping each and every blade with oil, and then following up and digging out every last root, or by spraying with herbicide - using sodium arsenite until it was banned because of frequent accidents and suicides. Lalang, for which the different methods of control were the subject of endless debate among planters, scientists and economists, is totally inedible to livestock and a fire hazard, though Charlie said his malnourished fellow-prisoners on the death railway resorted to eating its boiled leaves and rhizomes. Originating in South America, it is a most successful species and now a curse throughout the tropics.

While still at the Chinese hotel I had a local teacher come in for an hour each evening to teach me the Malay language, and every day for several months I went to work with a list of ten new words that were likely to be of practical use and made an effort to use each one. After six weeks, I passed my Incorporated Society of Planters written and oral Malay exams with distinction, much to the chagrin of some young planters who had made little progress in this regard over a vastly longer period. The same system, with which I was familiar from Africa, also obtained here, namely that unless and until you pass your local language examinations you will receive no promotion or increase in your salary; ever. Until a few years previously, planters had been required to learn Tamil, whose people then made up the majority of plantation labour. But with increasing numbers of Malays and Chinese employed in the industry, and since independence from Britain two years previously, when there had been a major political campaign to encourage the Chinese, Indian and other ethnic minorities to speak the Malay national language, or bahasa kebangsa-an, the policy had changed. In gaining fluency in the language I was considerably helped by the fact that many Arabic words that had been assimilated into Swahili were also to be found in Malay, less the vowel that terminates every Swahili word. Thus, karatasi, karani, fikiri, kalamu, fahamu, respectively

Under Rubber

meaning paper, clerk, think, pencil, understand, become kertas, karan, pikir, kalam, paham in Malay.

On Sengkang estate the majority of rubber tappers were Chinese, most of them Cantonese from south-east China, plus a few Tamils and even fewer Malays. However, it was the Tamils who provided the majority of workers for other essential plantation tasks such as weeding, pest and disease control, drainage and fertilizer application, as well as the clerks and overseers. Generally, the tappers were women and would have two regular 'tasks', each comprising some five hundred trees to tap on alternate days, seven days a week. Replacement tappers were borrowed from the field gang, to which they may previously have been demoted for substandard tapping, whenever a regular tapper took a day off or was sick. Most tappers wore head scarves, trousers and long-sleeved shirts, stiff and impregnated with black, coagulated latex that washing could never remove. Such clothing provided some protection from the myriad mosquitoes that swarmed in the shade of the trees. Tapping consists of making a shallow diagonal cut across half the circumference of the trunk to remove a thin sliver of bark to open up the latex vessels. Commencing at the first light of dawn, this requires considerable skill, since removing too much bark, or wounding the tree by tapping into the cambium layer from which new bark is generated, reduces the tree's economic life and yield, and might result in the tapper being relegated to the weeding gang.

Women make the best tappers. They have a light touch and are generally sober, alcohol being the downfall of any who attempt this skilled work when drunk or hungover. On Sengkang, as on all estates, many of the women tappers and weeders were young, and some still becoming even in their drab and latex- stained working clothes. As a yet young bachelor coming from six largely celibate years in the African bush, they were balm for deprived eyes, but ever mindful of the planters' crude maxim 'never shit on your own doorstep' I limited myself to quiet, satyric appreciation. Nearly half a century later I can still conjure the image of those who were the object of my restrained admiration, Chinese, Indian and Malay. Two of them, on different estates, evidently aware of my admiration, came and sat for hours in the drive of my bungalow awaiting a summons that never came, while I paced restively within or buried my head in a cushion. Another, a sublimely beautiful Tamil girl, one Sunday morning in a vast field in a very remote part of the estate, came marching towards me down the very same line of young rubber seedlings. Quelle coincidence! Nearby, the grassy bank of a river, shaded by tall

NOWHERE NEAR GREENLAND

trees, beckoned. I hastened my pace and passed her at speed, bestowing a taut smile and a quick greeting, thinking "Oh God, don't look back or you are gone, just keep going".

With a work force comprising Malays, Tamils and Chinese, one quickly became aware of distinct ethnic characteristics in their work situation. Experience has generally shown that indigenous people do not make satisfactory or dependable labour on foreign-owned plantations. Thus it was in the Americas, Australia, Malaya, Fiji and the New Hebrides where workers were provided by African slaves, kidnapped Melanesians, indentured Indians, Chinese and Vietnamese. To be dependable, this labour has to be entirely dependent on the plantation and completely detached from external ties and obligations. In Malawi, African politicians with large estates recruit their workers from villages as far away as possible within the country to minimise any contact with their families, and the demands they may make upon them. Thus in Malaya, Malays were rarely employed as tappers since this work requires absolute regularity of attendance, and seasonal work in their own rice paddies, and social occasions such as weddings and funerals made for frequent absence from work. So Malays were generally employed for miscellaneous tasks such as weeding and short term contract work, and could afford to adopt a take it or leave it attitude to employment since they always had their own productive land at hand to return to.

Tamils were brought to Malaya from India specifically to work on the rubber plantations, and for many years until after the Second World War made up the great majority of the labour force. They were particularly dependent on management support and intervention since they frequently suffered family problems, indebtedness, quarrels and the men from demon drink - usually palm toddy which had been allowed to ferment beyond the legal limit. On Sengkang, there was an area reserved for the traditional cremation of their dead. However general inebriation or a rain shower would sometime interrupt the proceedings, and driving past I would observe that recent mortal remains required further combustion, and would instruct the Tamil headman accordingly. They also made good bush lawyers with a strong penchant for litigation, and the plantation workers' trade union was founded and dominated by Tamils. The Chinese, on the other hand, were inscrutably self-sufficient, sober, dependable and very hard working, and I recall only once in five years when my intervention was called for.

Under Rubber

Shortly after my arrival at Sengkang I let it be known that I was always available at my bungalow to respond to any emergencies that might arise during the night. So when the call came one midnight, it was from the Chinese headman who told me that one of their number, a young man, was seriously ill and required the attention of a Cantonese doctor who lived at the nearby village of Pasir Panjang. So we set off, but all there were fast asleep and the headman shouted and threw stones against the first floor shutters of a shop-house. Eventually a shutter was flung open and a conversation ensued with the man upstairs. However, the dialogue soon evolved into shouting and sharp exchanges, and terminated when the shutter was slammed shut. The headman seemed very downcast, but beyond telling me that this doctor refused to attend the patient, and that it would be quite useless to take him to Port Dickson hospital, he would not tell me the nature of the illness beyond that it was something special, "luar biasa", out of the ordinary.

Back on the estate, I said I would like to see the sick person and was led to a house in the labour lines. Clearly there was considerable concern as there was a crowd gathered, both around the door and within the house. I went through into the bedroom, and made my way to the bedside. There lying on his back on the sheets, eyes closed, was a naked young man with two slivers of bamboo lashed to either side of his penis. I sought an explanation and was told that the splints were to prevent his penis from disappearing inside him, from whence it would never again emerge. I explained as best I could that this was an anatomical impossibility, and firmly promising this I eventually persuaded an old lady by the bed, who I believe was his grandmother, to untie the cord. During the unbinding process, the crowd outside pressed at the open window, and those inside stared intently at the vulnerable member. With the young man now goggling down the length of his body, there was complete silence and possibly a cessation of breathing as the cord and splints were removed, and the somewhat blue member, now with a flush of fresh blood, re-assumed a rosy hue but remained an external organ. The word of this passed outside and all around there was excited chatter and some laughter. Happily vindicated, relieved that the lad's mind had not overcome matter, and thinking but not saying I told you so, I went back to my bungalow. This had indeed been "luar biasa". (Many years later I related this episode to a doctor friend and he found this condition, presumably hysterical, described and named in his medical dictionary.)

Near the Chinese hotel where I had been lodged, was the most lively establishment in Port Dickson, the Sirusa Inn. Harry, the son of the Indian manager, was an ac-

NOWHERE NEAR GREENLAND

complished water skier and a super show-off, who daily demonstrated his masterly manoeuvres, skiing backwards on a table top, on his bare heels, swivelling, swerving and leaping entirely for the benefit of the fair sex, from whom he trusted this athletic investment might bear early dividends. He also most altruistically introduced me to a number of young lady telephone operators at the Seremban exchange who, Malay, Chinese and Indian, provided me with a sequence of compatible friends. These included Siti, a gentle Malay girl whom I took out most often. Then, when I had not seen her for some months I encountered her, heavily pregnant, in a Seremban street. We agreed we should meet later for lunch after I had

I exhibited my genuine snake juice at Parties Malaya, 1961

completed my morning business, during which interim I had decided I was the father, would take full responsibility and would marry the girl. However, when we met and I had launched into my speech of liability, she gently interrupted to say that the father was an Italian who for the time being had done a bunk, but whom she hoped would return to her. When a couple of months later I called at her house she had suffered an induced miscarriage, and the two women relatives caring for her were ready to beat me with broomsticks, when Siti called out that I was not the culprit - who, incidentally, had never returned. I saw her a few times after that; she was a really sweet girl and I was grateful for her honesty.

Under Rubber

In those days there was little socialising between the Malay, Indian and Chinese communities, except perhaps among the higher educated echelons of society, and certainly any boyfriend-girlfriend relationship was practically unheard of. However, there was ready association between all ethnicities and Europeans, whose higher earning power offered prospects of a good time and possibly a good marriage, which made for an expatriate bachelor's corporeal paradise. Some of my planter colleagues had long-term live-in girlfriends known locally as 'keeps', and some entered into marriage. However, by the law of the land, if a European married a Malay woman he had to take a Malay name, be circumcised and embrace Islam. These planters were cynically termed 'gangplank Muslims' who would abandon all pretence to that faith once they boarded ship to return to Europe, though presumably there was little they could do to redress any minor surgery.

Not long after I arrived, a Tamil tapper reported to one of the overseers that Chinese tappers in tasks adjoining his were stealing latex from the estate. This they were doing by pouring a proportion of their latex into holes in the ground, removing it at night, by which time it had coagulated into solid lumps, and selling it to rubber dealers in a nearby village. When rubber trees reached the end of their economic life, after about thirty years when all the high-yielding bark had been tapped away, they were poisoned by painting an arsenic paste on a frill cut around their base. The trees died, the trunk and branches rotted and fell, and the stumps decayed, leaving a line of sizeable holes in the ground. By this time, a new generation of rubber trees would have matured in the interlines parallel to the poisoned trees. (These days the old trees are felled and the light wood is used for furniture, palettes, etc.) It was into such holes that the stolen latex was being poured. The overseer, one Lopez, and I recovered many large lumps of rubber from these holes, but putting my left hand down one hole too many I was bitten by a snake on the ring finger. I flipped out the snake with the end of a stick and killed it. Lopez then tied a hanky around my wrist, and with another made a tourniquet around my upper arm. Putting the snake in the boot of my Austin A40 car we drove five miles to the estate clinic at Pasir Panjang. The dresser had used the last of his anti-snake bite serum to treat a tapper bitten by a king cobra, so he applied potassium permanganate to the wound in order to neutralise any venom still remaining at the site. But this did nothing for the venom that had already entered the blood-stream, so he recommended we drive the further fourteen miles to the hospital in Port Dickson to obtain an injection of serum. (My own South African polyvalent anti-snake bite kit was still in my sea baggage en route from Tanganyika.)

NOWHERE NEAR GREENLAND

Arriving at the hospital, there was a long queue of Malays, Chinese and Tamils waiting to see the doctor. Although, as a true Brit I abominate queue jumpers, I thought that just this once I might have fair excuse to be delinquent, so I advanced to the head of the line and informed the Indian doctor of my predicament. Where, he asked, is the snake? Followed by the whole queue and others who came running across the hospital compound having picked up the word snake in any one of three languages, I produced the dead serpent from the boot of my car. "Not poisonous", declared the Tamils and Chinese. "Poisonous", said the Malays, "you bit by that you dead in ten minutes, lah!" "Not poisonous", repeated the dissenting faction. "Poisonous", reiterated the Malays, and so it went, with me, Lopez and the doctor looking from side to side as though following a rally at Wimbledon. "So," said the doctor, "I am not telling if snake is poisonous or not poisonous, you understand, but side effect of serum can indeed be utterly damaging, so take this serum immediately to game department in Seremban, and if snake is truly poisonous go to general hospital and get the jab". So off I set for the state capital of Seremban, another twenty miles away, headlights on and overtaking fast-moving traffic, Lopez sitting beside me ready to take over the driving if I conked out. My hand was by then swollen and painful and Lopez eased the tourniquets from time to time. We arrived outside the game department only to find it had just closed for lunch. "Try the veterinary department", said Lopez, and we just caught the last person on his way out. "Poisonous", said the Malay veterinary officer, so off we went to the state hospital. There a motherly Scots nursing sister gave me a pilot dose from my vial of serum, scolding the Port Dickson doctor for not having done the same, and when after ten minutes there was no sign of anaphylactic shock, I was administered the full dose and despatched to a hospital ward where I spent the rest of the day rapidly recovering. I returned to the estate in the evening, and next day preserved the snake in an alcohol filled demijohn. For a while thereafter, I exhibited my genuine snake juice at parties, though since then I have been a tad more circumspect in putting my hand into holes in the ground.

Shortly afterwards, we received another tip-off regarding theft. This time a heap of rubber had been discovered in tall grass beside the 'company' road. With an overseer and a Ghurka night-watchman, I lay in wait for half the night, being bitten to bits by mosquitoes. After seemingly endless hours, by which time I decided I was in need of a blood transfusion, three men approached and started stuffing the lumps of rubber into sacks. We jumped up, shone our torches and the men ran off into the darkness. The overseer recognised the men as our own tappers and they were duly convicted. Previously asked by the magistrate if I recognised them or would know them again, I said no, which no doubt earned me points in the Chinese community, but I could hardly explain that after such a short time in the country all Chinese looked the same to me!

My mother and stepfather visited me while I was still at Sengkang. During my morning field work, he would take a stroll around the plantation and return towards midmorning when we would all take breakfast together. So that he could greet those he met along the way I instructed him to say 'upper harbour' which very closely approximates 'apa khaba' for how are you, and in reply 'harbour bike', for 'khaba baik', I am fine. This worked very well but often initiated a long, one-sided conversation in which my stepfather remained largely speechless. They stayed for about two months, during which time we visited Fraser's Hill, a hill station some five thousand feet above sea level to the north of Kuala Lumpur, where we stayed for a couple of days and played a round of golf. Then we drove up the east coast of Malaya, through Kuantan and Kuala Trengganu to Kota Bharu and its famous 'Pantai Chinta Barahi', or beach of passionate love, though we witnessed no supporting evidence for its name. In the early 1960s there were no bridges across the several big rivers that flow into the South China Sea, and crossing them by ferry was picturesque but took a considerable time.

This part of Malaysia was and still is entirely Malay, very traditional and conservatively Muslim. The sunlit stillness of the rural scene, with its scattered kampongs of high-pitched, atap-thatched roofs, surrounded by coconut palms, mango and durian trees, and the brilliant yellow-green patchwork of young rice paddies, was gently broken only by the shimmering air and the slow plodding water buffalo ploughing dark soil. Palm-girt rivers and white sand beaches, the translucent light, the gentle pace of life and calls to prayer, were for me in no small measure enhanced by the total absence of rubber trees.

While my parents were still with me, we were invited to dinner with Freddy Cunningham, a retired planter who had been in Malaya since long before the Second World War. He had known Somerset Maugham and, like other planters of his era heartily disliked him for too thinly disguising the identity of friends and acquaintances in his stories about Malaya. Freddy was a bachelor and servants had prepared and then served a fine and formal meal which was followed by the ritual with a decanter of port. He lived in a spacious bungalow on the seafront just north

NOWHERE NEAR GREENLAND

of Port Dickson, and when not long after he bought a house next to the golf course at St. Andrews in Scotland and left Malaya, he gave his bungalow to his Chinese cook.

After we returned to Port Dickson my parents took a ship to Georgetown on Penang Island, where they stayed for a week at the Eastern & Orient Hotel, with its 18th century cannon arraigned on the fine-cut lawn along the sea front. In the spacious, circular, entrance lobby one could partake of light refreshment, but should also be aware that it is a 'whispering gallery' like the one in St. Pauls cathedral, where even hushed words are carried round its walls to the tables of complete strangers, and perhaps the very subject of one's unflattering comments. While they were still there, I drove back late on a Saturday night from Kuala Lumpur, and on the 'company' road to Malacca, within sight of the lights of my bungalow, I fell asleep at the wheel approaching an abrupt right-hand bend. The stout, white, concrete post that marked it - one of the common genre known as 'planter's friends' - knocked the left front wheel clean off, the car somersaulted and then skidded down the road on its roof. I was stunned, but luckily not knocked out when the roof caved in almost to the steering wheel. The engine was roaring, the lights were still on and I could smell petrol spilling onto the road. Disorientated and upside-down, I found it difficult to locate the key and turn off the engine, but this I did and then kicked out the window of the jammed driver's door and slid out through the small space, thereby cutting my back and arm on broken glass. I left on the side lights of the car since it was inverted immediately after a bend, and then walked the remaining half mile to my bungalow. I phoned Charlie Ross, and he came to take me to his house, where his wife Nancy, a former nurse, bandaged my light injuries while I chattered away feeling as bright as the proverbial button. However, by the next day shock had set in and I was a trembling wreck. Nevertheless, concerned that my car might cause a further accident, I set out very early with a lorry and a team of workers to recover it, only to find a small crowd and several parked cars already gathered at the spot. There were my blood stains on the driver's door and a few spots on the road beneath it, and I overheard the bystanders speculating as to how many people had been killed. Three, I believe was the common consensus. The extent of the damage to the car made me appreciate how lucky I had been,

My bungalow at 18th mile was built in very traditional style, all wood with a shingle roof, a wide veranda along two of its sides, and set on brick piles a metre from the ground. The high ceilings were tongue-and-groove boards, and the bathroom

Under Rubber

was equipped with two huge water-filled earthenware 'Siam' jars, from which, armed with a dipper, one could ladle a perfectly adequate shower, or within which one could enjoy a deep bath. A raised and covered board walkway led from the back door to the kitchen, and under the bed in the main bedroom was a trapdoor, through which in the event of an attack by communist terrorists, one might escape to the cover of the rubber trees which surrounded the garden. However, though by 1959 the 'emergency' was still dragging on in the states of Pahang and Johore, where communist gangs were still battling security forces and making sporadic attacks on rubber plantations, all had been quiet for a few years in the state of Negri Sembilan, now said to be the rebels' chosen area for rest and recreation.

Lesley and Perky
Bukit Tersunyum
Malaya, 1971

Ronald. B. Perkins lived at Bukit Tersunyum, which translated means 'smiling hill', on his small rubber estate between Sengkang and Port Dickson. This overlooked Cap Rachado at the narrowest point in the Straits of Malacca, one of the world's busiest shipping lanes which divides peninsular Malaysia from Indonesia. From his house high on the cliff, and the capacious wooden deck cantilevered out from it, ideally situated to salute the downing of the sun with a whisky stengah in hand, you could discern Pulau Rupat, a small island abutting the east coast of Sumatra

NOWHERE NEAR GREENLAND

some twenty miles away. From the deck, Perky would call out to Ah Soh, an ancient amah who had served him for many years, to replenish the drinks. Perky, as he was generally known, was a small, bustling, bespectacled bachelor with the complexion of one who had spent his life in the east, but who had retained the lilting Welsh accent of his youth. He was celebrated for his book on estate surveying, essential reading for young planters, and had known Charlie Ross from their years in captivity by the Japanese, and their survival on the death railway in Burma.

Tamil firewalking
Sengkang Malaya, 1960.

Trough with coconut water
in foreground.

An excellent host, Perky had here entertained General Auchinleck of World War Two, north Africa fame, and Brigadier Thompson who created the concept of 'new villages' during the Malayan emergency; these effectively severed the communist terrorists in the jungle from their essential supplies of food from the local population. His advice to the Americans to adopt a similar strategy during the early days of the Vietnam war went unheeded. Perky was the president of the Port Dickson Club, a venerable institution to which the clubhouse bore inelegant and perilous witness. As the tennis member on the committee, I attended meetings on the upper floor of the club, which largely consisted of rotting boards, so we met in the safest part of the room near the top of the stairs, where drinks could be delivered to us at minimum risk to the steward. Needless to say, the tradition of stamping on the floor to summon the next round of drinks from the staff below had long been proscribed.

It was therefore timely that a new clubhouse should be built, and Perky as president would officially open it. Some time before he had been delivered a massive beige

Under Rubber

and brown Bentley from the U.K, but its leather upholstery had been extensively scrawled upon in a graffiti of indelible ink, probably in the London docks as an expression of the envy so endemic in the British character, so the car was sent all the way back and another was sent out. The day for the formal opening dawned, but on account of some personal and prolonged preparation for the event, Perky opened the club by driving the Bentley clean through the wall of the billiard room.

I had another accident with my car when driving south from the Cameron Highlands where I had spent a few days over Christmas. In a rain shower, I encountered on a wooden plank bridge a car being driven by an Indian on the wrong side of the road. Braking, I went into a long skid and we collided. No injuries, only minor damage but loud remonstrations from the other driver. A Malay policeman came along and agreed that I was entirely in the right, but would we drive back to the nearest police station where photographs would be taken of our vehicles. While the photos were being taken, a heavy lorry came from the north and a Volkswagen from the south. Both drivers' attention was taken by the police cameraman, and they crashed head on. A pregnant woman and a small child in the car were both seriously injured, these still being days before the use of seat belts.

There were Hindu temples on each of the three divisions of Sengkang estate, and every year on a particular date the Tamils would hold a temple ceremony. On my division there was to be fire-walking. First a long shallow pit was dug about ten metres long and two wide, and an estate lorry assisted in transporting loads of dry rubber wood collected from around the plantation. Nadison, my gardener, informed me he intended to participate in the fire walking, and requested three days leave to prepare for the event. This involved prolonged praying and the offering of fruit to his deities; so to my own I offered up prayers for Nadison, and made sure he mowed the lawn before his initiation began. As with barbecue cooking, the walking would not commence until the flames had died down, and the fire was reduced to glowing coals. I was ready near the side of the pit with my camera, but not close because the heat was tremendous, and prepared to record the walk of some dozen men, among whom Nadison was about the fourth to go. Most walked, some strolled, and two or three ran, but none was harmed. The only concession to prevent burning, was a wooden trough filled with coconut water at the far end of the pit to douse any hot cinders stuck to the soles of feet. My photographs, with more than customary blur, testified to the shimmering heat by the distortion of their images.

NOWHERE NEAR GREENLAND

A very great friend of mine, who for years had a Malay keep, and a son by her who became the captain of a jumbo jet, went back to England on leave, met a beautiful Anglo-Irish girl and they became engaged. He returned to Malaya and she was to follow a few months later. Meanwhile he asked me to be his best man at their wedding in St. Andrews cathedral in Kuala Lumpur, so I went out and ordered a new grey suit for the occasion from a Chinese tailor in the Batu Road whose name was Soon Fat - which possibly inclined his clients to order an extra inch at the waist. My friend was then managing a plantation whose northern section was cut off from the rest by a deep ravine, across which there was a wooden-planked suspension bridge, mainly used by tappers carrying latex. He was cycling across it on a round of inspection, when the front wheel of his bike suddenly jammed between the planks and he was thrown over the side of the bridge into the ravine, landing on his back.

Aware that his back might be broken, he called out to the tappers above him to bring a door onto which he might be rolled. This was done, and he was carried on this in a truck to a hospital in K.L. There it was confirmed that his spine was fractured, and he was put in a plaster cast from which only his head, arms and legs protruded. However it became progressively less amusing for him to be so closely encapsulated in the heat and humidity of Malaya, without the benefit of air conditioning, and I bought him a long knitting needle to scratch persistent itching. He was due to be hatched from this carapace just a week before the wedding, and I was despatched to order a plank bed at the top hotel in K.L. where they would spend the night before their honeymoon on Pulau Langkawi.

My company 'adopted' the cruiser HMS Belfast while she was at the Changi naval base in Singapore for six months undergoing a refit. We had a series of about twenty ratings and two officers come to Sengkang for two or three days at a time. The ratings stayed in former army barracks near Perky's estate, and the officers at our Eden bungalow, a luxurious facility on a beach nearby, where our managerial staff could spend weekends and holidays. I took these parties around
the estate in a lorry to show them rubber trees, the tapping process and the factory where the latex was coagulated into sheets and smoke-dried.

Following the visit of the last party, I was invited to accompany the Belfast for a week on its proving trials in the South China Sea. I was allocated the spacious 'admiral's' cabin in the stern, and the ship undertook a series of daily exercises in-

Under Rubber

cluding simulated gas, submarine and nuclear attacks, but her main armament of eight inch guns was never fired, since according to the captain this would cost twenty thousand pounds a round, and the navy couldn't afford that. Communicating bulkhead doors would automatically roll shut moments after the general alarm had sounded for a mock attack, and I was frequently left isolated in the luxury of the admiral's cabin.

I was shown over every part of the ship, drank 'pussers rum' in the stokers' mess where the Bugis Street sign they had collected was proudly displayed - a Singapore street of considerable notoriety. And one morning with one of the officers on the

Abandoned by ms Jutlandia in Genoa, July 1963

gun observation platform above the bridge, I noticed wisps of smoke being emitted from the forward eight-inch gun turret. I brought this to the attention of the officer who immediately informed the captain, as the smoke was being vented directly from the magazine. Alarms went off and men in protective gear entered the turret to descend to the magazine. There was a certain tension while the cause was investigated; was the Belfast about to blown to smithereens? But it was merely a battery which had overheated and created the fumes.

Singapore was a popular destination for planters in search of recreation, (though

NOWHERE NEAR GREENLAND

certainly not rest), and the Great World Cabaret, a vast dance hall, provided this in the form of 'taxi dancing'. A singer, generally Chinese, would warble love songs to the accompaniment of a live band, while perhaps sixty young ladies, Malay, Chinese and Indian, sat along one side of the hall awaiting invitations to dance, and their aspiring partners sat at tables and partook of refreshments on the opposite side of the dance floor. The form was, that on entering the hall you bought, generally from an elderly Chinese woman or 'nonya', a book of ten tickets which entitled you to ten dances with any girl or girls of your choice. Between dances you would walk over and choose a partner, or possibly run if there was likely to be competition for the same girl. If you really fancied the girl, and wanted to take her to a meal or a hotel, you could 'book her out'. The earlier in the evening you did this, the more you had to compensate the management. Or, you could wait until the end of the evening's dancing and take her off without having to pay.

Lopsided in Lotus position but probably not meditating
Malaya, 1964

That was usually after midnight, and the risk in that was that the girls you found most attractive might already have been whisked away. You could even book out the singer, but she cost significantly more. The band would also play music for 'rongeng', a traditional Malay form of dancing where you move in small to-and-fro steps with elbows akimbo, in front of, but never touching, your partner. In peninsular Malaya there were similar establishments employing the same formula, though on a much smaller scale and they were naturally a popular haven for single men.

Under Rubber

When at Sengkang, I occasionally attended concerts of Cantonese opera in Port Dickson. These were highly colourful, stylised and traditional with elaborate masks and costumes, but for ears schooled in western music, the sounds created were decidedly outlandish. The clash of gongs and cymbals, the thumping of drums, the keening of pipes and strings, accompanied the often harsh caterwauling and whining of the protagonists - necessitated perhaps by the half dozen or so formal tones of the Cantonese tongue. I also went to a number of performances of classical Indian dance, graceful, flowing and seductive, with a tender, lilting voice accompanying the quick changing, rhythmic rattle and pops of the tabla, a sweet singing sitar and the cheerful, unbroken melody of a hand-pumped harmonium. I was struck by the incuriosity of my fellow Europeans for Chinese and Indian music, invariably being their only representative at these concerts.

Once or twice a month there would be shows of either Indian or Chinese films in the labour lines of my division, the former always filled with singing and romance and the hilariously overemphasised gestures and movements that typify the national style of acting; the latter, generally originating in Hong Kong, were usually more sober dramas, with elements of martial arts, lascivious landlords, implacable war lords and betrayed young maidens.

After three years in Malaya, I was due overseas leave and boarded a Danish ship - the Jutlandia at Port Swettenham, bound for London and due to call at Aden, Port Said and Genoa en route. This elegant small liner with four raked masts was built to carry just over sixty passengers; however we had only half that number aboard and tranquillity reigned as we puttered across the Indian Ocean. I often lay on the upper deck at night watching the masts swing in a slow arc across the stars, and there was no unseemly rivalry for deckchairs, no queues for meals, and lunch was a long, leisurely affair of Danish cold table, with rollmops and many other kinds of seafood, deliciously prepared and elegantly presented. We arrived at Genoa to find that the port was on strike. The first officer believed we could be held up there for several days and suggested to me and a fellow passenger, a Scots tin miner, that we might like to go ashore and spend a day or two at Santa Margarita, a small seaside town a few miles down the coast. So, armed with towels and swimming shorts, we set off by bus, checked into a hotel there and spent the rest of the day on the beach. Next morning we had misgivings about being away from the ship, the beach had been overcrowded and you had to pay to walk on it, so we decided to return to Genoa.

NOWHERE NEAR GREENLAND

As we entered the port area, we looked out for fellow passengers who might be taking coffee at one of the many sidewalk cafes, but none was to be seen. We made our way down to the wharf where the Jutlandia had been tied up, and where she had been, there was now an ominous empty space between two other docked ships. My Scots friend rushed to the warehouse opposite the vacancy, "Jutlandia? Jutlandia?" he shouted to an obese docker. "Partito! Partito!," the Italian yelled in reply, expressively waving his burly arms. Our ship had indeed departed, quite possibly with our passports. We made our way to the shipping line's agents in the town. Here we were regretfully informed that the ship had given the striking dockers a large quantity of cigarettes and spiritous beverages in exchange for being promptly unloaded and loaded, and as it cost the company a large sum of money to keep the ship alongside, she sailed as soon as this operation was complete. The purser had handed our passports to the agents, for which receipt we were profoundly thankful, though apart from damp towels, swimming trunks and two toothbrushes we would be travelling exceptionally light for the rest of our journey to Britain. I had with me only a small sum of Italian lira, but fortunately my friend had with him a few travellers cheques. We walked to Genoa's magnificent railway station and booked two second class tickets through to Calais on a train leaving that evening. Later, we attempted to enter a museum and then an art gallery, but were refused entry because we were wearing shorts, and thereafter spent the rest of the day lingering over sidewalk cups of coffee. We were ill-dressed for the chilly crossing of the channel, and on arrival at Dover a customs officer, informed that we had come from Malaya, asked to see our luggage. He fished around disbelievingly among our few steaming garments and purposefully wrote down our names.

Arriving at Victoria station late on a Friday afternoon we proceeded directly to a gent's outfitters. I had told my friend that I had previously stayed with my parents at the Norfolk hotel in Surrey street, just off the Strand, and that they would know me there, but we would need to buy long trousers, a shirt and tie and, being barefoot in trainers, a pair of socks and shoes. To gain entrance to the dining-room, a cardigan instead of a jacket might just pass muster and would be a lot cheaper. So we ordered two of each of these items from a bemused shop assistant, blowing the full balance of the travellers cheques, and walked to the hotel with our heterogeneous collection of brown paper parcels, and booked in.

Of course they had absolutely no recollection of me, unshaven in my khaki shorts, trainers and now decidedly grubby aertex shirt, but after a certain amount of eye-

Under Rubber

brow twitching at reception we were admitted. However, shortly after I arrived in my room, the management telephoned to ask when our luggage would be arriving. I had to go down and explain, for to miss a train is understandable and commonplace, but to miss a ship in mid-voyage somehow smacks of irresponsibility. Not for another week, when our ship comes in, I told them, and no we couldn't give them a deposit until we had been to the bank on the morrow. They were very conciliatory and accepted my Zeiss Contessa camera as surety. My bank was in Dorset, but my friend's was with the Bank of Scotland in the City, so on the Saturday morning, after a leisurely breakfast of porridge and kippers, we decided to stroll over to tap his resources. We proceeded with some confidence towards our destination but, shades of Genoa, where the bank should have been was now an empty building site, with a bulldozer completing the final scraping-up of rubble. My friend ran to get an explanation from a conveniently placed policeman, who told him the bank had "relocated down the street, right at the traffic lights, down to the next intersection, turn left and it's the second building on the other side, but the bank closes at eleven on Saturday mornings, so you will be lucky…" But determined to be lucky, we had already started running. Catching one of the very last of the staff to leave the bank my friend thankfully parleyed a withdrawal.

We now had a week to kill in London while the Jutlandia made its stately way through the Mediterranean, past Gibraltar, across the Bay of Biscay and finally up the channel to the port of London. The trial of Dr. John Ward was in progress at the Old Bailey, and we stood in an unmoving queue for hours hoping to see Christine Keeler and Mandy Rice-Davis in the flesh, but eventually gave up and went to the cinema. Over the next several days we went to the zoo, sat in the Strangers' Gallery in the House of Commons, took in concerts, plays and art galleries, and finally presented ourselves at the London docks to collect our luggage, just as the Jutlandia came alongside. We were given a cheery though somewhat ironic and ribald greeting by our erstwhile fellow passengers, who had strung graphically illustrated streamers over the gangway intimating that we had fallen victim to sirens or had otherwise been delayed by some form of carnal entrapment.

My parents now lived at Wyke, just outside the small town of Gillingham in Dorset, and my new car, which I had ordered from Malaya, was awaiting collection from the local garage. This was an MGB sports model in British Racing Green, with leather seats and wire wheels. In this I drove my stepfather to Bournemouth to watch the British hard-court tennis championship, got lost with my younger sister

NOWHERE NEAR GREENLAND

in a maze of lanes around Bransgore in the New Forest, and then went with my elder sister to Scotland for a week's holiday on Skye. She was navigating and somewhere we inadvertently turned left and drove the length of Wales, finally emerging somewhere near Chester. (I will recount my near arrest in Edinburgh as the 'Weasel' of the Great Train Robbery, in the chapter on the New Hebrides.)

At the end of my leave I flew back to Malaya, but this time was to be based on an upcountry plantation, Jeram Padang, still in Negri Sembilan and near the small town of Kuala Pilah. This was managed by a tall, heavily built, lugubrious Irishman who appropriately answered to the name of Paddy and had the reputation of being a notorious sacker of assistant managers. Fortunately, I had a colleague there who was extremely bolshy with a huge chip on his shoulder - possibly because his father could afford to send only one of his sons to public school, who had subsequently become a name at Lloyds - and happily he conducted most of Paddy's lightning. Standing in the back of an open Land Rover and wearing a solar topee, Paddy would be driven slowly around the estate early every Sunday morning, passing very close to my bungalow with the implied inference of why are you slacking while I am hard at work on the Sabbath? My colleague Jerry duly fulfilled the company's ulterior motive for sending him to work under Paddy, and before long he was dismissed.

Jerry returned to England, obtained a grant to be trained in Bristol as a plumber, made a fortune in that trade and bought a manor house in Yorkshire. I had visited him once at his cottage in Hampshire, and was with him when he banged hard into the bumper of another car in a car park. The driver leaped out to remonstrate, but my friend got in first, "What do you think bloody bumpers are for if not to bump, you idiot!"; so the aggrieved and now dumbfounded party got straight back in his car and drove off in silence. Not long afterwards, Paddy built a splendid swimming pool in the garden of his bungalow, and charged the not inconsiderable cost in the estate accounts to 'emergency water supply'. So the next time the visiting agent came down from K.L. he was sacked. He eventually returned to Britain where he opened a hairdressing saloon in Bristol.

Lionel, another assistant manager on the estate, was a huge man of Dutch and Chinese parentage. He lacked almost all his upper front teeth but had an extremely pretty Indian wife, a schoolteacher who used to visit my bungalow to discuss literature and the cinema. Born in Indonesia, his father was the manager of a rubber

Under Rubber

plantation in Java, and by Lionel's account was a harsh man hated by his employees. One day, on an inspection round of the estate, the Javanese overseer accompanying the manager pulled a ripe papaya from a tree, sliced it in two with his parang and gave half to Lionel's father, who died in agony shortly afterwards. The overseer had smeared strong poison on one side of the parang's blade.

I loved travelling in my open car in Malaya, particularly at night when the heavy scents of tropical flowers, durian fruit and spices were magnified in the warm air wafting around me, though I held my breath when passing Chinese vegetable gardens which were regularly manured with 'night soil', possibly for those who promote recycling the very essence of organic and energy conservation farming.

A couple of years later, time for overseas leave came round again, but I had not been back in Dorset for long, and was busy building a low wall along the drive of my parent's house, when I was summoned to London by the chairman of the plantation company, Sir John Hay. He wished me to return to Malaya almost immediately to take up a position of visiting agent, based in their head office in Kuala Lumpur. It had been customary for candidates for this post to be drawn from outside the planting fraternity, but the chairman thought otherwise, and from the vibes in the office when I arrived, it was immediately obvious to me I was most unwelcome. So, ostensibly for me to learn about a new method of manufacturing 'crumb rubber', I was sent after a few days to the company's latex factory near Malacca. I learned later that Sir John Hay had terminal cancer, and this was a means to get me out of head office until he had passed away when, presumably, I could then safely be transferred back to the field.

The manager of the rubber factory was a Northern Irish protestant, a bluff and cheerful man who seemed really happy to be among the myriad pipes and tanks, the clanging and mephitic pong of the production process, in which lumps of discoloured, coagulated rubber floating in the stagnant water of large concrete tanks, and stinking like a lavatory, were processed together with the latex; but never was I so out of my element. The manager was primarily preoccupied with bookwork, so the maintenance of hygiene and the general supervision of the manufacturing process were my responsibility. This included clambering down ladders into the many huge, stainless steel tanks every morning to check that they had been scrupulously cleaned. I was busy about this work one morning, when I heard my name being called. It was the manager. He rubbed his hands together and said "You know

NOWHERE NEAR GREENLAND

what? You know what? They've shot the bastard!" Who? I replied. "Kennedy, they've shot the bastard!" I was due to go back to my bungalow for breakfast, so there I switched on the radio and heard the breaking news.

Shortly after Sir John Hay died, the company offered me the management of Glendale estate, but as I was rather fed up with being 'messed about', and after more than five years was also somewhat bored with rubber trees, I decided to resign and gave three months notice, which period I spent on Middleton estate. The manager there was a large, irascible and diabetic Yorkshireman who shortly after I left sped his car at night into the back of an unlit timber lorry and was killed.

Coming back for breakfast there one morning, I found my gardener poking around with a broom beneath my MG in the carport. He had discovered a cobra in the act of swallowing a frog, and it had glided under my car and disappeared somewhere in the general direction of the propeller shaft. I got into the car, started the engine, revved it loudly and ran the car forwards and backwards for a few yards. No snake. Then with the engine off I could hear it hissing every time I shifted the gearstick. I then belatedly thought to close the air vent that led into the cab beneath the dashboard. Eventually we gingerly opened the bonnet and there was the snake low down in the engine, whence it was dislodged with a rake and killed.

But there is no living in most tropical countries without having close encounters with snakes. Nancy Ross, wife of Charlie Ross and then on Tanah Merah estate, went to take pullovers from the bottom drawer of a chest of drawers, prior to returning to Scotland for home leave. Coiled asleep in the drawer was a king cobra. Slamming the drawer shut, she called for assistance, but the snake evaded attempts to kill it, crawling up behind the other drawers until this piece of furniture had been entirely demolished. And once while I was watching a bulldozer clear jungle for planting rubber, it uprooted a huge tree, exposing a nest of dozens of writhing cobras. The driver quickly backed off and with the next pass buried the snakes beneath tons of earth.

I decided I would go to New Zealand and perhaps read Chinese at Auckland University, since while in Malaya I had studied Cantonese for two years and Mandarin for one. My last few days I spent in K.L., largely because a Chinese garage at Pataling Jayah needed to prepare my M.G. to travel for five weeks as deck cargo on a New Zealand steamship travelling from Port Swettenham to Auckland. When I

Under Rubber

left my car at the garage, I specifically asked for it to be driven carefully down the new motorway to the port. No problem, said the Chinese garage owner, my son will do that himself. The very day before I was due to sail, the garage rang me at the Federal hotel to say my car had been involved in minor accident, and that there had been some damage to a door. I was not at all pleased that harm had befallen my iconic vehicle, and told them to inform my insurance agent, then repair it and drive it down to Singapore and load it onto the ship there in a week's time.

An hour or two later, I received a call from the insurance agent who worked in a subsidiary of my company. He said, I really think you should go and take look at your car; and there in the centre of the garage floor was just a heap of junk, a mess of twisted metal, no sign of a door, let alone a slightly damaged one. The garage owner was weeping. His son and a friend had been catapulted out through the top when the car came off the motorway at high speed in a rainstorm, and they were now in a critical condition in hospital. The insurance man said he could give me a cheque immediately for the write-off value of the car. I went back to the hotel, and there saw advertised in the Straits Times an M.G.B. sports model, low mileage, for sale in Singapore.

The next day I took the train to Singapore, vetted the car, tomato red with boring wheels but in excellent condition, and I bought it. A day or two later the New Zealand Steamship Company's 'Wairimu', a small and ageing cargo ship which carried a maximum of eight passengers, crept in from Port Swettenham, and I went down to the port to witness the loading of my car. First to be loaded was a large and magnificent mauve and black Renault dating from about 1910, which was on its way to a motor show in Christchurch. It was pushed onto a palette, and four cables were attached, one to each corner, and hooked to the main cable above. Lifting commenced, the four cables tautened and the sides of the Renault were crumpled and crushed inwards. The newly-created wreck was nonchalantly pushed off the palette and my car, being much narrower, was loaded without further incident.

My fellow passengers were a motley lot, and had all come out overland from the UK and joined the ship at Calcutta. First was a New Zealand family of three, mother, daughter and son, renowned for pushing a pram for charity from the southernmost tip of New Zealand's South Island to the northernmost tip of the North Island. They were now returning from pushing the same old pram from Lands End to John O'Groats in the U.K. to publicise tourism in New Zealand. They

NOWHERE NEAR GREENLAND

had driven out in a Land Rover across Turkey where, inadvertently entering an army camp, they were briefly arrested for spying; then on through Afghanistan and into India. I was to share a cabin with the young son. There was a New Zealand boat builder, who with friends had driven an old ambulance as far as Kathmandu and had sold it there, and a young, newly married Northern Irish couple who rode their motorbike to Nepal for their honeymoon, and also disposed of it there, since selling vehicles in that country was then unrestricted by red tape and taxes. The crew of the 'Wairimu' and the junior officers were all Maoris and South Pacific islanders, and the captain an elderly Kiwi. My cabin mate had bought a variety of exotic musical instruments in India, including a sitar and tabla, but was given to playing a mouth organ when lying in his bunk. I made him an offer for this instrument that he could not refuse and carelessly mislaid it over the side.

As it transpired, we were due to depart Singapore on New Year's Eve, then steam non-stop for five weeks to Auckland. While in Singapore I had bought an Akai open reel music system with two large speakers and a number of tapes, mainly classical but including one of Louis Armstrong. There were no entertainment facilities for passengers on this ship, and our modest dining-room on the upper deck was also our wardroom. We were naturally inclined to celebrate the New Year, so I set up my music system, bought some beer from the steward, and the seven of us enjoyed some very loud Sachmo. Hardly loud enough though to drown the din on deck, where the crew was enjoying the mother of all wing-dings. The pram-pushing lad stuck his head out of the porthole for a look-see, and was immediately bludgeoned with a bottle. He slumped back among us and we carried him groaning to the sick bay where someone, perhaps the ship's carpenter, sewed up his scalp. The next morning the captain declared the ship dry, and it would remain so until the culprit was apprehended and punished. As we slowly plodded south through the Sea of Arafura, a mutinous mood descended upon the ship, but someone in the crew saved the day, and possibly us, by proposing a charade to which we were all invited. A life-sized dummy in sailor's rig was dragged to the boat deck, a brief funeral service was held, and this substitute culprit, shrouded in a New Zealand flag, was consigned to the deep and slid overboard from a stretcher. The captain, thus mollified and roaring with laughter, declared the ship wet again, whereupon the crew, as though to make up for lost time, went on a collective blinder, and the ship all but ran ashore that night on a small island.

We had to call upon our own initiative for amusement and recreation on this long

Under Rubber

voyage, and the ship's carpenter generously provided us with the wherewithal to make kites. Some days of preparation were followed by flying them over the stern. Then one got entangled in the wireless aerial strung between the masts. This was recovered only with some difficulty, and the captain was not at all pleased. The next day one flew down the funnel and all further kite flying was forbidden.

Entangling a kite off Waimiru's stern, 1965

We were then passing among the myriad Indonesian islands that sprinkle this passage, and for several days we sailed through many thousands of banded sea snakes, always in pairs, which presumably gathered in this part of the ocean for breeding.

With no kites, at least there were always islands to see on this voyage, to gaze at through binoculars and somewhat wistfully speculate about the lives of people that lived on them. From Thursday Island we sailed on down the length of the Great Barrier Reef, and the captain proudly showed me a number of large, hand-beaten iron nails, which years before he had collected at the site where Captain Cook careened his ship the 'Resolution' at Cooktown.

The s.s. Wairumu eventually hove into Auckland and was immediately surrounded

NOWHERE NEAR GREENLAND

by police and customs officers who had received a tip-off that the ship was carrying drugs.

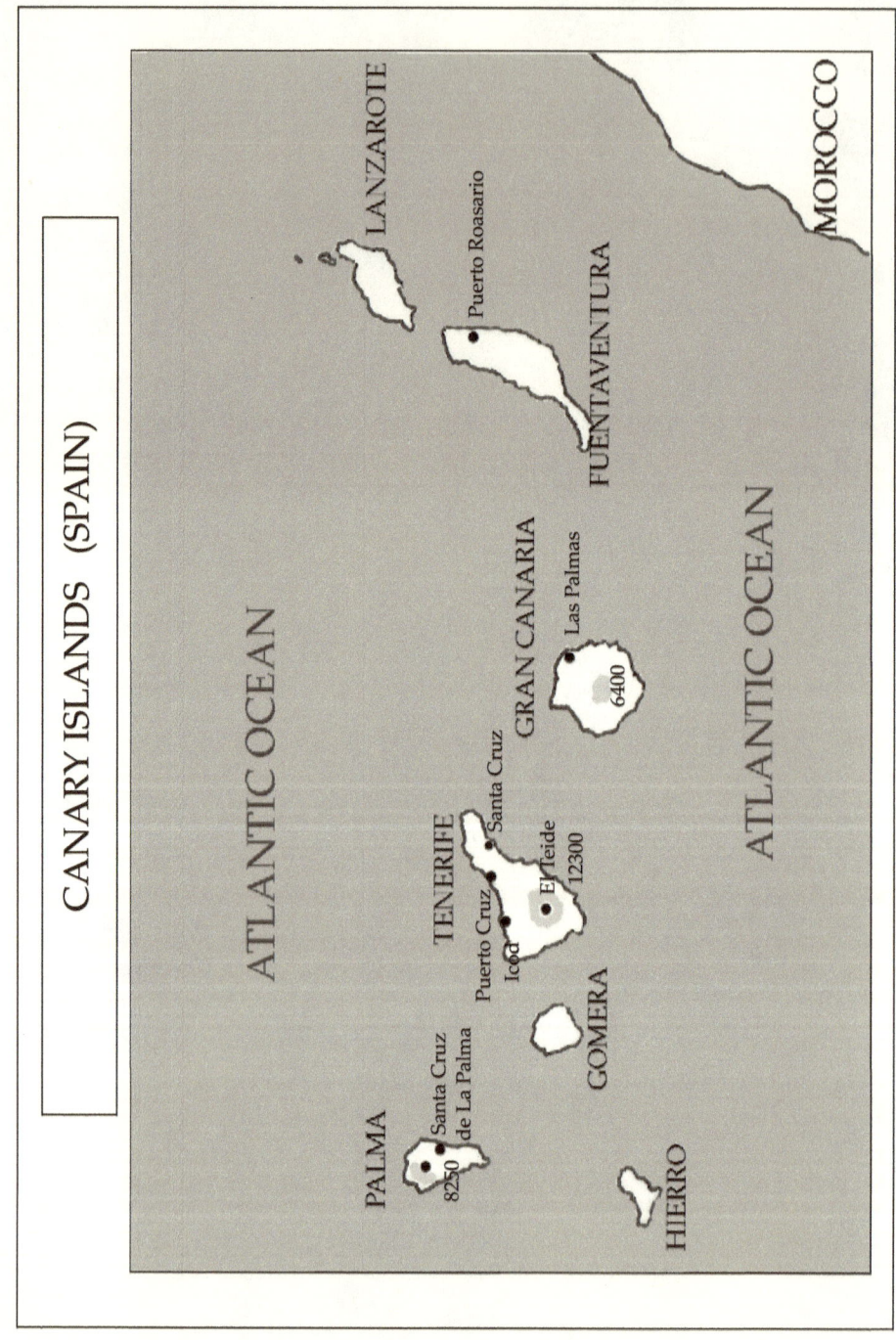

NOWHERE NEAR GREENLAND

KIWIS AND CANARIES

In the customs shed at the ship's dock in Auckland, I declared my cabin baggage, my household possessions which were in the hold and my car which was on the deck. Some items such as my African drums, buffalo hide Masai shield and wood carvings would have to be taken away for fumigation, but for the time being my crates would remain in the bonded warehouse until I had an address to send them to. I produced the papers for my car, and to my horror was told that because I had not owned it for a full year I would have to pay 86% duty, almost as much as buying the car again, and money that I just did not have. I explained the circumstances under which I had had to buy this particular MGB just before boarding the Wairimu, and the customs officer conceded that if I could produce documentary evidence from my insurance agent concerning the crash of my former car, which I had owned for more than a year, customs would reconsider this matter of duty; but meanwhile the car would remain in the bonded warehouse.

I checked in at the Great Northern Hotel on Queen Street just a few hundred yards from the dock. It was a hot, late Sunday afternoon and I decided to go for a stroll in the city. The streets were almost deserted and I crossed Queen Street, only to hear the short blast of a police whistle. Why had I not crossed the road at the authorised crossing point? Because there was no traffic in sight, I replied. This was no excuse, I was informed and told to remember that in future. On my walk I no-

Kiwis and Canaries

ticed a white line painted down the centre of the pavements on either side of the road, and later I discovered that unless turning to go into a shop, or to cross the street - at an authorised crossing point of course - one should keep to the left of the line. This kind of petty regulation, I found, was typical of Auckland in 1965. Dinner at the hotel, or tea as it is called throughout New Zealand, was at six p.m. Sharp. If you arrived at five past six and soup had already been carried round to all the other guests, you missed out. And presumably if the hogget, potato and peas had been dished out when you even more belatedly rolled up, you would have to make do with just the treacle tart and custard. My room was very hot and small, and overlooking the busiest street in New Zealand, it was also very noisy; that is to say until around 8 p.m. when Auckland closed down for the night, excepting on Sundays when it was closed all day.

After two nights there, I decided to look for alternative and cheaper accommodation. I took up the phone book and almost at random chose an hotel in an area near the harbour bridge. This was a quiet, private hotel owned by an Irish New Zealand family that was very much into horse racing, discussing form and dashing down to the betting shop in the afternoon to place their bets. There were one or two elderly resident guests, including a retired, quietly spoken accountant who had survived the great earthquake in Napier in the 1930s and never tired of retelling this most dramatic event in his life. On the black and white TV screen in the lounge room, I watched the bulletins of Winston Churchill's final illness and then his funeral. I had a pleasant room, but after my first night there I awoke covered in red, itching bites. I flung back the bedclothes, and there against the white sheet was the evidence. Fleas! The room was infested with fleas! I was too embarrassed to mention this to the management, and during the day purchased a large can of aerosol insecticide. Before I got into bed that evening, I sprayed the whole room, stripped off the blanket and top sheet and sat on the bed zapping anything that moved, and there were still many surviving 'jumpers', as fleas are somewhat congenially called in New Zealand. I then sprayed all my clothes, emptied the can on myself, and went to sleep wondering if in large doses a pyrethrum-based insecticide could prove fatal to humans. Apparently not, and I awoke next morning free of any new bites and walked over to the registrar's office of Auckland University to investigate what courses I might take there. It was agreed that I might gain immediate admittance as a mature student. However, there was no Chinese language course, so I chose Russian instead, and for my BA decided to add the subjects of psychology and philosophy. These would at least make a change from tropical agriculture and

NOWHERE NEAR GREENLAND

I was, anyway, keen on Russian literature and had read a few books on the other two subjects which had interested me.

Meanwhile, I had been recruited by Pat, the son of the hotel owner, to join him in being a waiter at the Colonial Room for a couple of nights a week. This was then the most upmarket restaurant in Auckland, situated on the other side of town, and I had a dinner jacket in good condition which I would be required to wear. The cook was a large, cheerful Dutchman called Bill Fenimar, who combined the best of French and British cuisine, and one of the rewards of my job, in addition to a wage and tips, was to choose any dish from the menu for my dinner. A New Zealander who came in one evening, unaware of the fare offered, told me he thought the food was far too fancy, and what was the matter with good, plain, honest New Zealand food like hogget, potatoes and lambs fry. On arrival at the airport, new to the country and the design of its bathroom furniture, Bill had mistaken the small, low mounted hand-basins for urinals and used one as such, much to the disgust and horror of others in the facility, and his own huge embarrassment.

The papers concerning the accident to my car arrived from Malaya and I presented them to customs. All right, they said, you can bring in your car duty free, but if you sell it within two years you will have to pay the full duty. I was delighted. This was probably the first MGB sports model to be brought into New Zealand and proved to be the object of some attention. At that time there were strict monetary exchange controls in force, and any New Zealander wanting to buy a new car had to have access to overseas funds. Few did and the roads still abounded with WW2 models, and even some of earlier vintage. Coming back into Auckland one day on the motorway from Hamilton, I branched off onto a byroad at rather excessive speed and was almost immediately flagged down by a couple of police motorcyclists. Here's trouble I thought, but they only wanted to take a look at my car.

Pat was a 'chippie', or carpenter, and drove around in an old dun-coloured Ford Prefect whose rear springs had long since collapsed under the weight of the building materials he habitually carried around on its roof. Thus, with its nose in the air, and high wings consisting of 8ft x 4ft ceiling boards, it looked as though it might attempt to take off, if only it could get up the speed. The car, with its broken seats piled with the tools of his trade, and sundry boxes of screws and nails, off-cuts of mouldings and architraves, was also infested with fleas, and I did my very best to avoid travelling in it. Pat was engaged in the general upkeep of his father's properties around the city, but was also in the lucrative business of converting houses into flats for rent. In Auckland there were many traditional, large, kauri timber-framed and clad houses set on concrete piles coming onto the market. Their four or more bedrooms exceeded the needs of their often now ageing owners, as they did the needs and budgets of the many young people coming to work in this fast growing city. Their conversion was a relatively simple matter of banging in wood framed partitions, blocking or putting in extra doors, and engaging plumbers and electricians to put in pipes and wiring for the new bathrooms and kitchenettes. Pat was a skilled carpenter, and made a nice job of mahogany-veneered island units, cupboards, doors and suchlike. He seemed never to encounter any problem or delay in obtaining the required planning permission, and probably had his father's influence in the right quarters to thank for that. One day, he asked me if I would like to assist him in this work at the weekends. He was then working on a house in Remuera, one of the better suburbs of Auckland, and if I assisted him he would rent me one of the three new flats at a reduced rate. Since making my first bookshelf at the age of five, I had always been prepared to turn my hand to carpentry, so I agreed. An incentive for him was that I would occasionally let him borrow my car, particularly when he needed to impress the fairer sex, though this need arose far more frequently than I was prepared to lend him the car.

I was enjoying my lectures at the university. I was quickly able to write in legible Cyrillic, but was struggling with the Russian grammar which I found more difficult than German, of depressing memory from my schooldays. The psychology was quite fun, though I did not really enjoy handling white rats, and I thought the philosophy course was overly preoccupied with semantics.

Once I had moved into my completed flat, Pat announced that we were then going to redecorate the exterior of a large rooming house on Norana Avenue. However, he had a tenant living in the basement flat and was due to deliver to her a carpet. I went along to assist, and thus met my future wife, Lesley. Then aged twenty-one she had been married to an English sheep farmer who had recently settled on a farm near Nelson on the South Island. Just a few months after their marriage, he overturned the tractor when crossing a stream and was crushed to death. She then moved back to Auckland, where she had attended art school, to be with her sister and was considering becoming a dress designer, for which as a skilled artist she had considerable talent. She had been born in Harare, Zimbabwe, when it was still Salisbury, Rhodesia, and her father was a civil engineer. He went up to Nyasaland

NOWHERE NEAR GREENLAND

in the 1950s to survey the site for a hotel on Lake Nyasa, and contracted cerebral malaria from which he died. Her mother then married her deceased father's younger brother who was a carpenter, and the family, including Lesley's three sisters, moved to New Zealand and settled in Whangarei in the north of the North Island.

We started work on painting the very extensive roof of the house, sloshing grey paint from the roof ridge and working it down with brooms towards the gutters. We had previously removed decayed metallic mosquito gauze from the windows of the ground and first floor, so that we would have access to paint the window frames. The ground and upper floor of the house each had a corridor running their whole length, with the rented rooms and bathrooms on either side, a communal kitchen at one end and a lounge room at the other. The tenants were mainly young working people, but there were also retired couples and elderly single men who in New Zealand were designated senior citizens. Pat was experienced in dealing with the needs and complaints of these tenants, be it an electric fire, a spare blanket or a defunct light bulb. Shortly after we had started work on the roof, an elderly Irish couple complained about a single man in the room adjoining theirs. Late into the evenings, there would be a persistent tapping sound emanating from his room, as well as a strong chemical smell. Mr. McKay was uncommunicative and also very furtive, looking up and down the corridor before emerging from his room and scuttling off to do his daily shopping. Clearly he was a suspicious character. Pat was familiar with the eccentricities of his tenants and probably would have taken no action in this case.

However, one morning when we were moving the ladder, by which we gained access to the roof, we noticed some metal filings on the ground floor windowsill immediately below Mr. McKay's room. Back sloshing paint on the roof, we discussed the significance of this find and came to the astounding, but to us irresistible, conclusion that in all probability Mr. McKay was a counterfeiter! The furtive behaviour, no obvious source of income, the tapping, the smell of chemicals, and now the metal filings on the windowsill, all added up, and clearly pointed towards Mr. McKay being engaged in engraving and etching metal plates. His Irish neighbours had also reported that he regularly made a phone call at a certain time of day, so Pat decided to hover around the central corridor and do a spot of eavesdropping. What he overheard did little to diminish our suspicions. Mr MacKay had said things like, "it's getting a bit hot over here, what's it like over there Frank", and, "I

Kiwis and Canaries

am sure they are watching me". So, when he emerged next morning at his regular time to go shopping, we decided I should shin up the ladder, climb through the window into his room and have a quick squiz. Pat, meanwhile, would keep watch from the roof for Mr. MacKay's return. I duly entered the room, and there against the wall was a large, iron-bound wooden chest, festooned with chains and padlocks. There was nothing else in the room which could fuel suspicion so I descended and reported to Pat. He then decided, or quite possibly we jointly decided, that there was now sufficient evidence that Mr. MacKay was up to no good and it was timely for us to request the police to investigate.

Later that morning, we had a meeting at Auckland's police headquarters with detective sergeant Knight of special branch, and on hearing us out he became visibly excited; overly so we thought, because he said he would immediately request authority for a search warrant and come round to the house with two constables after lunch. Pat protested that this was not exactly what we had in mind. Perhaps at this stage, some discreet preliminary investigation of Mr. MacKay's background would be more in order. But sergeant Knight had the bit between his teeth. Possibly there had never been a case of counterfeiting in New Zealand before and here was the chance for him to go for fool's gold, so to speak. With pen poised over his notebook he asked, "Now what shall we say on the search warrant we are looking for?" Somewhat flattered by our sudden recruitment, we readily assisted him: Inks?, yes; Engraving tools?, yes; Acid?, yes; Banknote paper?, yes; Metal plates?, yes; and so on. We returned to the rooming house with a sinking feeling that things had really gone a bit too far, too fast. Then, as we made our way along the side of the house, on the way back to our ladder and the roof, we noticed, crumpled in the flowerbed, the disintegrating, metallic, mosquito gauze we had torn from the window frame beneath Mr. MacKay's room. Here, all too clearly, in an instantaneous and stunning revelation to us both, was the source of the metal filings we had discovered on the window sill. Aghast, we realised that the most crucial piece of evidence pointing to counterfeiting had gone a'glimmering. Back on the roof ridge, our now drastically revised and intelligent analysis of the situation indicated that Mr. Mackay was actually suffering from some form of paranoia and was now in need of our protection from the heavy handed police.

We drew lots to decide who would go down to tell sergeant Knight when he arrived with his cohorts, that it had all been a terrible mistake. Show him the mosquito wire and get him to back off. The lot fell on Pat, and when we saw the police car

NOWHERE NEAR GREENLAND

approaching he clambered down to meet them at the front gate. Safe on the roof, I remarked a certain amount of arm and gauze waving, and then the police disappeared into the house. Pat rejoined me, and said there was really no stopping them. He sensed they thought he had been intimidated into delaying their investigation. Five minutes passed, then ten, fifteen, twenty. This was a good sign, we thought. They must have found something after all. Then finally the police emerged onto the drive below, and Pat went down again to talk to them. Mr. MacKay, the detective sergeant commenced sternly, is a senior citizen, a pensioner, and the pension is the source of his income. They had ordered him to open the wooden chest, which, with the removal of the sundry chains and padlocks, was duly accomplished. Inside the chest they discovered cheese, bacon, sausages, bread, butter, jam and other groceries which Mr. MacKay kept secured in fear of them being stolen. As for the tapping sounds, these were associated with Mr. MacKay's regular evening exercises, and the chemical smell was that of Sloanes Liniment with which he rubbed down his body afterwards. There was certainly no evidence whatsoever that this senior citizen was engaged in any kind of illegal activity, and they departed back to headquarters in a sort of disappointed huff.

Pat was worried for Mr. Mackay after this experience. Sometime before he had asked Pat for an extra pillow and a room heater, so that evening, filled with remorse, Pat went round with the requested items and tapped on Mr. MacKay's door. At first it was opened just a crack on the chain. Then much relieved to see Pat there he said "Come in, come in, you will never believe what happened to me today! A squad of policemen came round and said they wanted to search my room for inks, paper, engraving tools, metal plates.......it was amazing! They thought I was a counterfeiter!" Pat expressed himself similarly astounded, and only a week or so later Mr. Mackay took rooms elsewhere.

We still had another week's work to complete sloshing paint over this huge roof, which happened to overlook the next-door garden. While we were up there, we noticed that a woman from the next-door house would every day carry a plate of food to a shed at the end of the garden. We had also heard very human-like groans coming from this shed. Was someone, we wondered, being held hostage there? Or possibly a relative against his or her will - from the groans alone it was hard to ascertain the victim's gender - until, perhaps, that person signed over their wealth to the heartless woman? However, due to the very recent and unfortunate episode with Mr. MacKay, we were understandably loath to return with a new tale for de-

Kiwis and Canaries

tective sergeant Knight. Nevertheless, we imagined a possibly scornful and humiliating reception, along the lines of "What is it this time, gentlemen, Martians?" And we saying "No, you must believe us this time, officer, this is really serious. Coming from the shed in that garden we have heard......" Of course it is entirely possible that through this wretched coincidence of events, an incarcerated person was not saved from a terrible fate, and a wicked criminal was never brought to book. (On the other hand, if we were merely introducing Auckland's ace sleuths to a decrepit dog in a shed, we risked arrest for wasting police time.)

We read that there was to be a total eclipse of the sun, the centre of whose path would pass over Cape Kari Kari in the far north of North Island, so Lesley and I decided to drive up there to witness the event. On the way we stopped at Whangarei to meet Lesley's parents, where he was a carpenter and they both taught ballroom dancing. At Kari Kari a few dozen people had gathered in a field high above the sea, many with smoked glass or dark negative film. An elderly gentleman showed me his antique, brass-rimmed binoculars, inherited from an uncle who had fought in the Zulu wars, which he had brought along to observe the activity around a giant rocket the Americans proposed to launch some hundreds of yards away. This, in its flight, would analyse the unique properties of the solar corona during the brief period of full eclipse

The mid-morning light progressively darkened as the moon's shadow moved across the sun and the air grew chill. One by one the stars appeared, and then with a roar and a bright streak of flame the rocket rose into the night-like sky, its trail of vapour and fire dissipating and then disappearing into the zenith. Then, after five minutes the bright necklace of the corona was broken by a growing crescent of bright sun, and the birds began their second dawn chorus of the day.

Seven years later, on leave from the New Hebrides, we came back to Whangarei and organised a fancy dress party to which Lesley's parents and friends were invited. This was given a biblical theme and held in the local dance hall. A white tented table dispensed Beersheba, and another Gadarene's Wine; however, my mother-in-law had ordered, or at least been delivered, several cases of sherry instead of white wine, which mightily smote disciples, Pharisees and Romans alike.

(Thirty years on, I would again come to this area, this time with my great friends Revell and Deirdre de Valda, visiting the kauri museum near Dargaville. Nearby,

NOWHERE NEAR GREENLAND

many giant and ancient Kauri trees have been excavated whole from a swamp. Here I purchased a small wooden bowl, authentically dated to forty five thousand years before the present.)

Lesley and I decided to get married. She was soon to return to England to stay with her late husband's parents in Kent. I decided that after the second semester I would drop out of university, follow Lesley back to England, and probably return thereafter to some country or other to resume my career in tropical agriculture. Meanwhile, we took at trip around New Zealand in my open car. We went to ski on Mount Ruapehu, inhaled the sulphurous fumes of Rotarua, visited Nelson, Christchurch, and Lesley's sister in Timaru. We then clambered around on the Franz Joseph glacier below Mount Cook, drove over to Greymouth on the very wet, west coast of South Island, and then returned to Auckland via Plymouth and the west coast of north Island. I saw Lesley off on the Shaw Saville ship 'Gothic', which until recently had served as Her Majesty the Queen's royal yacht, only to have her return a few days later because the ship had broken down with serious engine trouble shortly after leaving Wellington. The ship managed to get away a week or so later, and en route to England via the Panama Canal had called at Pitcairn. Here Lesley saw elderly islanders, who had been living in New Zealand, lowered in harness into boats riding alongside in a heavy swell. This required very skilled timing on the part of the man on the winch, to avoid the person on the way down being met by a rapidly rising boat.

A month or so later, I followed on the Greek liner 'Ellenis'. The shipping company offered a special deal to encourage tourism in Greece, whereby one could continue on to Piraeus free of charge for a whole extra week after calling in at Southampton. So I decided to do this, with Lesley and my mother joining me at Southampton. We would have a holiday in Greece and also get married there. The ship was carrying mainly young people from New Zealand and Australia, going to work for a while in Britain or holiday in Europe. The popular film 'Zorba The Greek' was still of recent memory, and there were well-attended Greek dancing lessons every day. There were also Greek language lessons, and having recently learned the Russian alphabet, which differs by only a few letters from the Greek, I made better progress than with the dancing. The voyage called first at Sydney and then Tahiti. In Papeete, I hired a scooter for the day and drove right around the island, visiting the newly opened Gauguin Museum, which sadly did not possess a single original work by the artist, and in the evening watched a spectacular display of 'tamurai'

Kiwis and Canaries

dancing by a bevy of swirling and undulating vahines. Tourism here was still very low key, and it was several years before the French military came to the island for their two decades long series of atomic bomb testing at Mururoa atoll.

The Ellenis passed through Panama and then called at Curaçao in the Dutch Antilles, where we were delayed for an extra day because a pregnant passenger was crushed against a wall by a drunken taxi driver and killed. The island had a desolate appearance, and there were large areas of prickly pear, formerly plantations where cochineal insects were scraped off the cactus to produce colouring for the confectionery industry. With a New Zealand film director and his wife I went to the only nightclub in town. This proved to be quite a dull affair, though we hung on until midnight. When we came out to walk the mile or so back to the ship, the streets were alive with scuttling cockroaches, so we invented a game whereby one could not proceed without landing squarely on a cockroach, and we still made good progress. It was rather like hopscotch, and after deliberating whether to call it hoproach or cockscotch we chose the former. Half-way back to the ship, we were caught in a thunderstorm and sheltered in the front room of a house that opened straight onto the street. There, a few mulattos were dancing in a desultory manner to a wind-up gramophone. When we came out again there was not a live cockroach in sight.

The Ellenis was three days in Southampton, since this was also the start for its return voyage to Australia and New Zealand, and it was boarded by a decidedly miserable-looking horde of British emigrants bound for those countries, their appearance accentuated by drab, dark-coloured, winter clothes and winter-white complexions. There was, however, still plenty of space left for the Greek emigrants who would join the ship at Piraeus, possibly to occupy the spacious but basic dormitories I had caught sight of on the lower decks. I now rejoined the ship with Lesley and my mother, but, as I tried to convince them, its former cheerful, youthful atmosphere had been totally usurped by crowds, queues, apprehension and gloom. This was only made worse by a very rough passage through the Bay of Biscay, when the rails were lined with heaving passengers, and the stairs and companionways were slick with vomit. However at least Lesley, my mother and I, all hardy sailors, no longer had to queue at the doors of the dining room.

We stayed a few days in Athens, which was familiar to my mother who had worked there in the 1950s, and Lesley and I went to see an Anglican priest to ask if he would

NOWHERE NEAR GREENLAND

marry us. Not so simple he said. First of all, Lesley had not been baptised, and then, he intoned, there were various other rules and regulations concerned with residence, birth certificates, permits and so on. We had naively thought it would be easy, so there was to be no wedding in Greece. We then all took a ferry to the island of Samos, birthplace of Pythagoras, and hard by the Turkish coast within sight of Ephesus. My mother was to be with us for only a few days since while in Athens she had arranged to sail back to England on the 'Canberra', and she left Samos aboard a Dakota. Lesley and I were very taken with Samos which, unlike many smaller Greek islands whose landscape had been reduced to a skeletal appearance by millennia of occupation, was still lush with extensive forests and vineyards. Our roaming around was given some purpose when we decided that we would like to buy a piece of land there. Though we walked for miles in the mountainous interior, including visiting a remote monastery where a monk gave Lesley a donkey ride up a steep hill, we really wanted something by the sea. Near Pythagorean there was a delightful little, grass-covered promontory, complete with a small stone ruin, facing across the straits towards Ephesus and the mountains of Turkey. Lesley and I had swotted Greek from Southampton to Piraeus, and armed with our phrase books we now endeavoured to find out to whom this piece of land belonged. Unfortunately, not long before our arrival in Samos, a native of that island who had made a fortune as a restaurateur in Montreal, had returned to the place of his birth and paid a huge sum for a very small piece of land. He was soon followed by an English lord who, not to be outdone, had paid more for even less, and now everyone, it seemed, wanted to show us a piece of land they had for sale at, no doubt, a highly inflated price. News travels quickly on a small island, and the fact that we arrived with my mother who had a title, had certainly not helped matters. So we were whisked around in ancient vehicles to look at a plot almost on the airfield ("Very convenient, yes?"), a steep hillside with a view of a quarry where dynamiting was a daily event, another piece behind a butcher's shop, and so on. We had so fallen in love with that little promontory, which became more and more beautiful by comparison with everything else we were being shown, it became that or nothing. But unable to make any headway in that direction, we regretfully returned to Athens aboard the twice weekly DC3.

Regrouping and eating pistachio nuts at a pavement cafe on Santagmatos Square, we read in an English newspaper an advertisement for the sale of a small restaurant in Tenerife. At least that gave us the idea to go to the Canary Islands, so off we went. But instead of the quaint palm-thatched cafe on the beach that we had imag-

Kiwis and Canaries

ined, the restaurant turned out to be a neon-lit establishment on the ground floor of a skyscraper in downtown Puerto Cruz. Recoiling from that, we took a bus along the north coast to the little town of Icod de los Vinos, and after a night in the hotel there, we rented a fourth floor apartment with an uninterrupted view of the sea at the Playa San Marcos, a small cove with a black sand beach a mile or two below the town. Half a dozen brightly coloured fishing boats were drawn up on the steep sloping sand during the day, the largest of which was named Ma Jesus, and some of whose catch went to the four or five wooden kiosks along the top of the beach, which served fish meals to their customers sitting at tables under canvas awnings. On our first morning at the beach where, having put away our Greek phrase books, we were already studying hard to master simple Spanish, a lame middle-aged, local inhabitant worked his way along the tourists selling seashells on which he had painted a picture of the Teide, the snow-tipped volcano in the centre of the island which rose over twelve thousand feet. Having made the sale of a nicely painted seashell to us, he asked if we would be interested in buying a piece of land. Although we already had such an idea in mind, the question so soon after our arrival was perhaps premature, and he did not appear to be the kind of person with whom one would enter into serious real estate negotiations. So we said no thank you, and went back to our Spanish.

We had called in at Grand Canaria on our way to Tenerife, and had spent Christmas with Lesley's late husband's sister and her German botanist husband who was writing a book on ferns. We were driven around to see something of the island, but found it rather stark, dusty and unattractive. By contrast, the north side of Tenerife was lush with banana terraces along the high cliffs of the coastline, and rose steeply through neat vineyards and fig trees to fields of tomatoes and potatoes, and on up to the dark green belt of pine forest skirting the high moonlike, lava-strewn plateau that surrounded the Teide volcano. The hillsides were lightly sprinkled with the white walls and red-tiled roofs of small farms and villages, and everywhere a network of stone channels carried irrigation water from galleries hacked deep into the upper slopes to serve the cultivated fields all the way down to the coast. We bought a large scale map of all the Canary Islands and made a plan to visit some of them in search of our ideal domain.

First we took a plane to La Palma, in the north-west of the islands and way off the tourist track. This is essentially a huge, sleeping volcano which rises twenty one thousand feet from the ocean floor, and its summit, over eight thousand feet above

NOWHERE NEAR GREENLAND

the sea, attracts copious rain to the steeply tilted fields that cover its eastern slopes. This island has gained recent fame from the giant telescopes that now scan the heavens from its summit, and also some notoriety from a dire prediction that the whole, unstable, western slope of the volcano, several cubic miles of earth and rock, will one day shear off and tumble into the Atlantic below, causing a massive tidal wave that could devastate the eastern seaboard of the United States and destroy New York.

We passed our first day there at Santa Cruz de la Palma, its major town on the south east coast, and walked to a small restaurant adjoining the evaporation ponds of a former salt works. We were the only clients and the proprietor, noting our approach, put on a record of German marching music. Lesley physically restrained me from breaking into a goose step and stiffly raising my right arm, and our host apologised when he realised his error, though he had no alternative tune at hand to match our ethnicity. As Germans make up the great majority of tourists in the Canary Islands during the European winter months, his was an understandable mistake. The large proportion of elderly or middle- aged German males, in the company of very much younger women, persuaded us that perhaps many of the former were ostensibly attending business conferences. One day at the Playa San Marcos, when there were unusually large waves breaking on the shore, one of them knocked over a massively rotund German and rolled him several times up and down the steep beach like a barrel, while his friends, shouting and floundering in the foam, desperately tried to grab his spinning arms and legs as he passed them at speed, first one way and then the other.

We took the bus from the town to explore La Palma. Its roof was piled high with bundles, crates, furniture and small livestock, and our fellow passengers comprised only peasant farmers, wrinkled and coloured like walnuts, the women in black, the men in dark leather jackets and blue serge, with heavy working boots. There was no coastal road, so the old bus with its cracked, brown vinyl seats, swayed and ground higher and higher, rounding hairpins as the road zigzagged upwards, with precipitous drops first on one side, then the other. We sat right at the back, and being the only tourists aboard we aroused some curiosity among the other passengers. Whenever our driver successfully negotiated a particularly horrendous bend, they genuflected and then all turned with smiles and encouraging nods, as though to say, "Don't worry, Miguel (or God, perhaps?) knows what he is doing". In the morning haze, the blue sea far below joined seamlessly with the sky, so we that we

Kiwis and Canaries

seemed to be crawling over the rugged surface of a small, separate green planet. At what was presumably the end of the road, we endeavoured to sleep that night on a narrow iron cot, in what we took to be a workman's hostel. However, as there was an unceasing clatter of boots on bare boards, either these men were engaged in some kind of shift work or they had another reason to come and go so frequently. The next day we repeated this journey in reverse, though now instead of being tilted right back in our seats, we were pitched forward and hanging on to the back of the seat in front of us. In terms of looking for a pretty plot of land, this had not been a fruitful trip, but it had not lacked interest.

We next decided to visit Fuertaventura, low-lying, and hence a near-desert island attracting no rain, and not far distant from the dry coast. of Africa. We flew there on a day trip, and though we were impressed by the beaches, we did not take to the sparse and struggling vegetation that lay behind them. My abiding memory of that visit was of having mistaken the loo signs at the tiny air terminal, and being followed in, and then chased out by a large lady with a broom before I had time to adjust my zip.

So, we came back to the Playa San Marcos, and shortly thereafter, along came the man with the painted shells again. We did not buy another shell, but this time agreed to go and see his piece of land. We arranged to meet him and his wife, and with them walked eastwards a couple of miles along the coast to the hectare or so they had to sell. It was bordered on three sides by banana terraces, but the whole of the north side ran along the top of a two hundred foot high cliff, falling straight into the sea. To the south was a clear view of the snow capped Teide, soaring high above the pine forest and green fields below. There was also a fine outlook, stretching along the rugged coastline to the east and west. The land itself had served largely as a dumping ground for stones cleared from the neighbouring banana fields, but there were a few fig trees and struggling vines, and here and there patches of grass between the stones. However, the real clincher for us was the cave. In the middle of the property, the ground rose into a hump of smooth black rock, on top of which was a wooden cross, and beneath it the four feet high, semicircular entrance to a cave. We wanted to explore it immediately, but our landowner called out that it was "muy peligroso" so we curbed our impatience for another day . He and his wife, he said, had never been inside it.

The cave had been formed by an ancient lava flow, which had covered ground

NOWHERE NEAR GREENLAND

whose soil was later eroded or flushed away, leaving an eight to ten foot high space between the cavern floor and the roof. It had almost certainly been lived in by the now extinct Guanche people, whom the Spaniards had discovered living here when they invaded the islands in the sixteenth century. They had lived in caves, using inaccessible ones high on the cliffs to store their embalmed dead, as well as in settlements on the Tenerife plateau. The Spaniards claimed that when they arrived, the Guanches had no knowledge of boat building, but would occasionally float between islands on inflated goat's bladders. There were affinities between the Guanche language, now largely lost, and that of Berber people living on the African mainland, and the native population was from time to time supplemented by castaways and the shipwrecked.

Lesley and I went to visit the last stronghold of the Guanche, a deserted, ruined and now protected village called Masca, in a remote, high and stony area of the Tenerife plateau. Here are the remains of a few stone buildings, some still rising almost to roof level. I have always had weak ankles, which literally let me down when I was learning to skate, and which I have subsequently seriously damaged when climbing and skiing. When walking, I would not infrequently turn my ankle over and go into a rapid, unchoreographed dance routine in order to regain my balance and avoid keeling over. Unfortunately, this occurred in Masca, and at a stumbling run I crashed against the corner of one of its precious buildings, and it fell down. Fortunately the rumble and cloud of dust went unnoticed by the guide and other tourists who were intently peering at something some way away. "Another place on which you have left your mark" said Lesley, as we hastily rejoined them.

We told the landowner we were definitely interested in his piece of land, and the next day, armed with a torch, matches and candles, we returned to explore the cave. After a short, vaulted entrance, this branched out left and right, forming quite a large room. At its extremity on the right it sloped down into rubble, and perhaps here was scope for some excavation and extension. Near the back wall of the main space, there were a few large stones arranged as though once used for cooking. Otherwise there was no sign the cave had been visited, no tin cans, no plastic and no graffiti. We immediately started making plans, deciding where we would make an entrance drive to the property, and where we would build a simple house with magnificent views of sea and mountain.

Kiwis and Canaries

We also rekindled plans to get married and went to see Mr. Fox, the British Consul in Santa Cruz de Tenerife, the administrative capital of the Canary Islands. The consulate was situated in a beautiful, seventeenth century town house, whose finely-carved black balustrade on the first floor, surrounded on three sides the paved courtyard below. We climbed the wide wooden staircase and met with Mr. Fox in a spacious, dark-panelled room with a high, beamed ceiling. We produced the few documents he asked for, answered a very few questions to his entire satisfaction, and he agreed to marry us the following week. It was a very simple early afternoon ceremony, with just Mr. Fox and the bespectacled Spanish clerk he called in to be a witness, and who also kindly photographed us somewhat out of focus with the consul at his desk, Lesley in a dark blue suit, and me in dark blue blazer and grey trousers.

We stayed on at the Playa San Marcos for another two months or so, engaging a lawyer in Icod de los Vinos to assist us in the purchase of our piece of Tenerife. This, with the complications inherent in foreigners purchasing land under the then military government of the islands, was to drag on for another ten years. We were also attempting to purchase more than the maximum number of square metres allowed to a foreigner on one title, so we would have to divide the property into three separate titles, one each for Lesley and me, and one in the name of my sister Jill. And the fact that the land belonged to an extended family, many of whom had an interest in it, and some of whom were living in Venezuela, did not make for rapid completion.

Lesley was now pregnant; we had done all we could for the time being to advance our side of the purchase, and we decided to return to England. There I took a job as a labourer on a farm near Sturminster Marshall in Dorset, while looking for another posting in agriculture overseas. Lesley and I lived in a small farm cottage near a railway line. Farming had become far more mechanised in the fifteen years since I had laboured on a farm in the New Forest, and it no longer seemed the healthy, physical job of manual skills it once had been. Now, I found, the whole process of harvesting wheat required just two people, steering and manipulating wheels and levers; one driving the combine harvester which cut and threshed the grain in one operation, and the other bringing a high-sided trailer alongside to be filled automatically through a tube from the combine's giant hopper. Then back with the grain to the silo at the farm where handling was again all automated. To someone like me, for whom machinery holds less than a superficial interest, and

NOWHERE NEAR GREENLAND

loathing its noise and the pace of work it imposes, this was neither fun nor healthy living in this beautiful countryside.

Meanwhile, I had two offers of work in Cameroon; one with the Cameroons Development Corporation, which was managed by the Commonwealth Development Corporation, and the other with the Department of Agriculture there. However, papers for the latter posting, which I preferred, were stalled endlessly somewhere on a government desk in Yaounde, so I accepted the former. Our son Matthew Paul was born at Poole Hospital in the November, and a few weeks later I left by air for Douala. Lesley and our son were to follow some six weeks later.

CAMEROON - WEST AFRICA

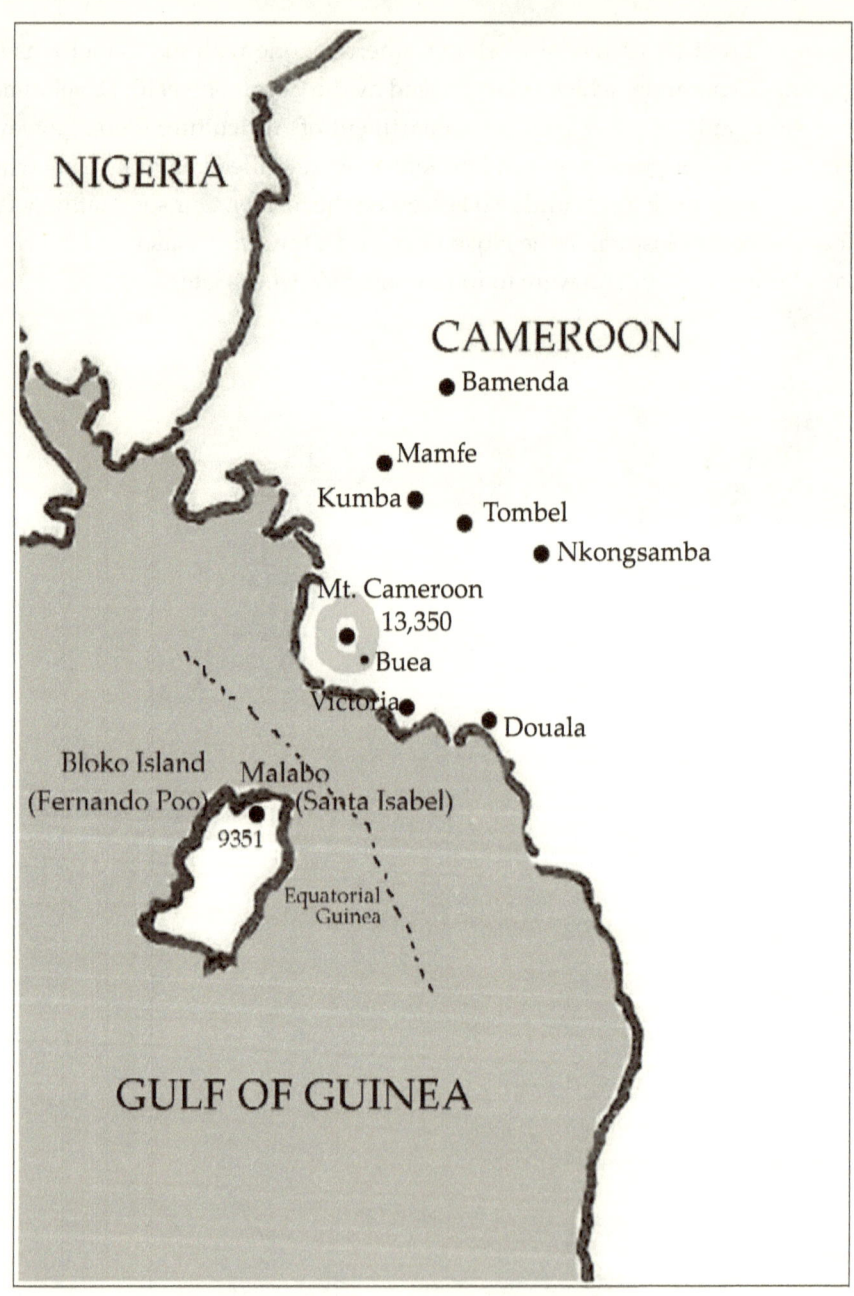

NOWHERE NEAR GREENLAND

A SAD CHAPTER

I arrived at Douala, Cameroon's major seaport and largest city, early in the morning aboard a UTA flight from Paris, transported in just a few hours from English November chill to the heat and humidity of the West African coast. At the airport to meet me was Dennis Jackson, a tall, early middle-aged and somewhat pear-shaped Welshman with a florid complexion. He was my fellow assistant manager on Mukonje estate, some one hundred miles away by road in what had been British administered West Cameroon. This, four years previously, had voted in a referendum to be amalgamated into former French administered Cameroon, an area ten times larger and now an independent republic, rather than become part of Nigeria, from which the British had governed it. This choice was certainly influenced by a local dislike of the Ibo people, the principal tribe in neighbouring Nigeria and the dominant traders in this part of Cameroon.

Before leaving the airport, Dennis downed a couple of large bottles of cold beer, product of Brasseries de Cameroun, and then we set off for Mukonje, an African driver at the wheel of a Land Rover. The tarmac road climbed gently inland through small fields of bananas, cassava and sweet potatoes, past roadside clusters of corrugated iron-roofed shops and bars, and, more strikingly, every few hundred yards the recent or rusting wreck of a crashed car or lorry. Traffic was

A Sad Chapter

generally light, though we frequently met or were even passed by the huge, thundering, articulated green lorries of Brasseries de Cameroun. In fact, beer was the dominant theme of this trip, since Dennis insisted on stopping every few miles for another bottle of beer at one of the many diminutive roadside bars.

Thus we eventually arrived at the area manager's house on Mukonje, considerably later than the hour for which I had been invited to lunch. Duncan, the area manager who was responsible for the three or four Cameroons Development Corporation rubber and cocoa estates in this corner of Cameroon, was a slightly built, middle-aged Scotsman with piercing blue eyes and a serious drink problem. We arrived at his house, just as he and the minister for posts and telecommunications were finishing an extended lunch. After making markedly slurred introductions Dennis, completely sozzled, was driven away to his apartment over the estate shop at the plantation centre, and the honourable minister took his leave soon after. Duncan had kindly invited me to stay with him for a few days while some repairs were made to my bungalow, and until I had equipped it with the essentials for living there with my wife and baby son. I therefore put my luggage in one of the bedrooms, and Duncan offered to take me over to look at my assigned bungalow, so that I could make some notes on what I thought needed to be done before the arrival of my family in a few weeks time.

Mukonje estate was gargantuan, and it was seventeen miles from Duncan's house to mine, most of the way under a gloomy arcade of mature rubber trees, with an occasional sunlit space where rows of young rubber trees had been planted amid a green, leguminous, creeping cover crop. In smaller open spaces, were labour lines consisting of a dozen rows of long, single-storied whitewashed buildings, where tappers and weeders occupied one or two rooms, depending on family size. At intervals between the rows were the shower and lavatory blocks and there was a crèche, a corrugated iron roof surrounded on all sides by a half wall, for the labourers' infants. We were driven to my bungalow in a black Austin saloon car by Duncan's driver. The bungalow had been built some fifty years before by the Germans, when Cameroon was one of their colonies, and they had carved out the estate from the rain-forest. It was wooden, clapboard-clad, white with a red corrugated iron roof set on high concrete piles, and overlooking a ravine several hundred feet deep, at whose base was a hydroelectric power station, also built by the Germans. A massive, steeply-angled black steel pipe carried water to it from a small dam at the top of the ravine. The ravine itself was thickly wooded, as was its far side for a distance

NOWHERE NEAR GREENLAND

of several miles, through which ran the former border between West and East Cameroon.

Duncan sat on a settee in the living-room while I made my inspection of our future home, which comprised two bedrooms, a living-room and bathroom. That done, I informed him I was going to make a tour around the exterior of the house, look at the long-overgrown garden, the outside kitchen and the servant's two-roomed flat beneath the bungalow. When I returned to the living-room, Duncan was still sitting, or now rather sprawling, on the settee. I mentioned the few things I had noted down, for instance the fly screening was torn or disintegrating in many places and needed to be replaced - and perhaps a cot for the baby could be obtained from CDC central stores? Duncan stared fixedly at me with his pale blue eyes, his head tipped slightly back, his jaw jutting out, his face very pink. I did not immediately realise what had happened, for mentally he had passed out and no longer knew who I was.

Duncan, Lesley, Irene (Peace Corps!) and Dennis
Bekili, Cameroon, 1967

He said nothing, and then suddenly got to his feet, amid a clatter of falling empty miniature liquor bottles such as one is served with on aeroplanes, bid me goodbye, and with rapid and rather jerky arm and leg movements, made for the door and the flight of wooden steps leading down to the yard where his driver was waiting with the car. It was quite clear I was going to be left behind, seventeen miles from anywhere with no transport, no food or means of cooking it, no light which was

A Sad Chapter

still to be connected, no water because the tank had been emptied for cleaning, no bed clothes, no luggage, and already a degree of jet lag. I was indeed in a strange country. He got into the back seat of the car, shut the door and told his driver to take him home. Fortunately the rear window was open so that I could speak to him, and the driver, seemingly understanding and possibly accustomed to a situation of this genre, sat rigidly gazing at the windscreen and made no move to drive off. I reminded Duncan that he had invited me to stay at his house for a few days, that it was really not possible for me to stay at the bungalow, but was brusquely told to push-off. I stayed crouching by the window, the driver with his hands resting on the steering wheel and Duncan glaring back at me.

We seemed to have reached something of an impasse. Since he had no idea of who I was, I then adopted the role of a hitchhiker and asked if he wouldn't mind just giving me a lift down the road. This led on his part to a lot of hostile questioning, where had I come from, where was my own car, where was I going etc., which I answered somewhat evasively, and eventually but with considerable ill grace he opened the door and allowed me to sit beside him. He then lit a Gauloise cigarette, his driver started the car and off we set down the long road beneath the rubber trees. Meanwhile, Duncan had firmly decided that I was a member of the Peace Corps, and resumed his harangue with repeated remarks such as "Bloody Peace Corps people, you've only been in the country for a year and you think you know everything, and now you come begging me for a lift", and so on, all the time staring at me with his blue eyes and accidentally singeing holes in my shirt as he waved his Gauloise around. Then, as we reached the estate airstrip, whose runway crossed the road at right angles, he ordered the driver to stop the car.

I had already learned that day from Dennis that this area of Cameroon was under a dusk to dawn curfew due to terrorist activity on the part of the Bamilike tribe, many of whom became disaffected from the government following independence, believing they had not been given sufficient representation in parliament. They had launched sporadic attacks on army posts, had ambushed cars and murdered their occupants - one recent victim, a Greek trader, had been decapitated - and also killed a number of the neighbouring Bakossi tribe. The latter were cattle people of the savannah, whereas the Bamilike were agriculturists from the forest, and they had a long history of mutual antipathy. Because of the security situation, the estate's wages were currently being delivered each month by plane to the estate airstrip. So Duncan now announced that we were going to wait for the plane - a yellow

NOWHERE NEAR GREENLAND

aeroplane he informed me - carrying the wages. We sat there in the car on the edge of the airstrip in the gathering darkness, with Duncan mumbling on and I mostly silent, though from time to time slapping at my smouldering shirt, which at least was keeping the mosquitoes away. I was by now exhausted and becoming increasingly angry and impatient, so eventually I leaned forward and very quietly asked the driver to drive on. A roar came from an instantly reactivated Duncan, "How dare you tell my driver what to do, who do you think you are, bloody Peace Corps", and so on and so forth. So we sat there some more, a lot more, until eventually headlights lit up the car from behind us. The liquid latex tanker lorry was returning empty to the estate after delivering its load to a central factory. It lightly beeped its horn, so our driver started the car as though only to move aside, allowed it to pass, and then thank God kept going, sans observations from Duncan.

We arrived, by then at about ten o'clock at night, at the centre of the estate where there was a factory and junior staff housing, offices, the factory, garages, storage sheds and Dennis' flat above the estate shop. We were then only a couple of hundred yards from Duncan's house, which was up a short but steep drive, and to the west by day enjoyed a distant but spectacular view of Mount Cameroon, an active 13,350 foot volcano and by far the highest mountain in West Africa. However, Duncan now commanded the car to stop at the estate shop where he got out, sprawled over the bonnet and yelled for Dennis to come on down from his flat and socialise. Whereupon, eschewing this opportunity for partying I left the car unnoticed, climbed the short way in the dark to Duncan's bungalow, locked myself in my bedroom and wondered what sort or madhouse I had come to. I determined that next day I would go down to CDC headquarters at the coast and request an alternative posting. Then I went to sleep.

The next morning, with some trepidation, I presented myself at breakfast. Duncan was already at the table, but now I was seeing his Dr. Jekyl, a charming, welcoming Scotsman, somewhat the worse for wear but with a disarming and somewhat lopsided, apologetic smile. He said his driver had told him something of the previous night's happenings of which he had absolutely no memory, but was infinitely sorry for whatever had occurred. He did hope I would excuse him and that I would be happy here working on Mukonje. I replied that I thought the bungalow was rather too isolated, to which to bring a few weeks old baby, and that, at least to start with, we might be better off on one of the CDC rubber plantations down at the coast. These were clustered around the small port of Victoria, and

A Sad Chapter

near Buea, the diminutive administrative capital of West Cameroon. It would be rather too lonely here for Lesley with absolutely no neighbours, and then there was the curfew factor, which with the bungalow right on the edge of the forest, introduced an element of menace and would, anyway, greatly limit our social life. Despite these arguments, somehow Duncan's charm, which was not without an element of pathos, persuaded me to stay, or at least to give it a try, and thus I made the worst decision, not only of my life but for that of my wife and son.

This was the time of the harmattan; from November to March a hot, dust-laden dry wind blows west and south west from the Saharan interior to torment the coastal regions of West Africa. A beige, and even brown haze banishes blue from the sky and fogs the stars. This is the season for heightened irritability and heat rash, with the tiny, biting 'black flies' guided to their feasts by the sweat of their victims. Heavy, oppressive and unrelenting, the dust dulled the green shine of the rubber leaves, permeated the houses and built up sleeps in the corners of eyes. April would bring the start of the rainy season which would last until October, and some areas on the coast, to the west of cloud-breaking Mount Cameroon, experienced over three hundred days of rainfall a year, with the CDC Edenau oil-palm estate claiming a localised 800 inches (66 feet!) annually, the highest precipitation in the world. Rain would bring myriads of mosquitoes beneath the dark shade of the rubber trees, where they bred in discarded latex cups, contracted malaria from the tappers and passed it on to their next blood donor. Mud brought chiggers that bubbled up in eggs beneath the toenails. It was not the most enviable of climates.

In line with the localisation policy of CDC, a very charming Cameroonian, Clitus Tita, was the substantive manager of Mukonje estate, and though he was entirely competent as an administrator, he knew absolutely nothing of rubber and the management of labour. Having been a planter in Malaya for six years, where the standards of rubber cultivation and tapping were the highest in the world, and the labour hard working and skilled, I was quite dismayed by what I found on Mukonje. The tapping panels were a mass of knife wounds and the bark consumption was voraciously high. A major part of the problem was that this work was entirely done by men who lacked a woman's light touch, and their control of the tapping knife and visual acuity was far too often impaired by strong drink and its after-effects. However, unlike in south-east Asia, it was not traditional for women to do this work, so I could do no more than instruct the overseers to be more active in marking the wounds with their thick red crayons and recommend

NOWHERE NEAR GREENLAND

the worst tappers for transfer to the weeding gang, provided competent replacements could be found.

Moreover, the field workers who did the weeding, pest and disease control, pruning, etcetera were back home before nine in the morning, having completed a task which was less than a third of the norm for Malaya. I had a meeting with the field workers, and told them I did not consider two hours work was a fair exchange for the pay they received, and I doubled the task for the number of trees to be weeded or inspected for root disease, the length of tapping path to be sprayed, and so on. Predictably, the labour immediately went on strike, so I proposed that we would do away with task work altogether and they could all work the full official hours, from seven in the morning until three in the afternoon, with a half hour break for lunch, more or less the hours put in by the tappers. This work schedule, enforceable under the labour code, was not at all welcome, so eventually we came to a compromise whereby I slightly reduced my proposed new task size, and issued all the weeders with new hoes. At least, they were all still able to complete their work by eleven in the morning.

One morning I went to inspect a field on the far side of the tarred main highway from West to East Cameroon, which ran right through my division of the estate. Here young trees were to be brought into tapping, and the outline of the new tapping panels had already been scored on the bark, supposedly at five feet from the ground, but in fact all over the place. With my mind on how to rectify this, I drove back to the main road and continued along it towards another entrance into the estate. As I came round a corner, I saw a Peugeot taxi hurtling straight for me on my side of the road. Idiot!, I thought, and then almost immediately realised that I was the idiot driving on the wrong side of the road. Driving in West Cameroon had only a short time before been changed to the right, bringing it into conformity with former French Cameroon. I immediately swerved into the ditch. Meanwhile, the taxi skidded broadside on, the back door flew open and a large number of loaves of bread followed by a lady of very ample proportions tumbled out onto the road. I got out to apologise to the taxi driver and help the uninjured woman to her feet, but it seemed the driver, already accustomed to this kind of mishap following the recent lane changeover, was quite unperturbed and the large lady was shaking with giggles. I had started to collect the loaves from the road, when another taxi rattled round the corner from the direction of East Cameroon, and finding a car broadside across the road it screeched to a stop. The driver, clearly the worse for drink, leaped

A Sad Chapter

out and wanted to fight the other driver whom he accused of stupidly parking his car in such a reckless and irresponsible fashion. Protesting that it was entirely my fault I managed to separate them, peace was restored and the large lady and all her loaves were loaded back into the taxi.

At the time the changeover to the right was proposed, West Cameroon still had its own prime minister and parliament, and one of the elected members suggested that for reasons of safety this new rule of the road should be phased in gradually, with at first only buses, lorries and other heavy traffic driving on the right, to be followed a week or two later by cars, motorbikes and bicycles. Fortunately his proposal was not adopted. (One is reminded of the story, that had the channel tunnel been designed for road traffic, French drivers approaching England were to accustom themselves to the British rule of the road by driving on the left of the tunnel, and British drivers heading in the opposite direction should practise driving on the right.)

Mukonje estate was just a few miles from Kumba, the largest town in West Cameroon, along whose main street at least half its mud-brick, ramshackle, tin roofed buildings were bars, many with rooms at the back where the bar girls could offer their customers a form of horizontal relaxation. This general dereliction was greatly leavened by the cheerful, brightly coloured shop signs proclaiming 'Her Majesty Queen Elizabeth II Bicycle Spares', 'Kumba World Wide Furniture Emporium' and 'All At Sea Hairstyles'. The diesel, smoke-pumping, box-bodied buses were also emblazoned with confidence-building logos, and we followed one with 'Heaven Help Us' writ large on its rear, its entreaty somehow made more earnest by the lack of an exclamation mark. We also gained regular amusement from the headlines and items in the West Cameroon newspaper. One front page trumpeted 'WOMAN LOSES LIP IN FIGHT OVER BUCKET', and another 'CHICKEN KILLED BY BEING STRUCK ON THE HEAD ON SEVERAL OCCASIONS'. Perhaps the best story concerned a woman working in the field, who took a nap in the branches of a tree. When she awoke, still in the tree, she found herself out at sea, about a mile from land. Apparently there had been some kind of flash flood.

Kumba's large central market comprised small, single storey brick-built shops, surrounding and facing into a quadrangle filled with open stalls selling freshly killed meat, not so fresh fish brought up from the coast, veritable cornucopias of fruit and vegetables, and every kind of ware from plastic buckets, clocks and curry

NOWHERE NEAR GREENLAND

powders to clothing. It was invariably windless, swelteringly hot and crowded, with the intermingled smells of decay, urine, sweat, strongly perfumed soap and spices, but always lively and colourful and it served all our shopping needs, there being no general stores or supermarkets in the town. A regular sight near the entrance to the market was a naked lunatic festooned in chains, the loose ends of which he would swing around his head as he charged at people, especially children who baited him, though these were mock charges and he never harmed anyone. He was known as 'Chain Worker'.

Because of the local security situation, there were checkpoints on all the roads into town. These were manned by French-trained gendarmes from East Cameroon, who wore paratroop-style camouflage uniform, wrap around shades and carried automatic weapons. They sauntered up to the cars with a casual arrogance, were often drunk and one did not refuse them when they asked for a lift.

While still in England I had bought a Land Rover in Dorset and had it shipped to Douala. It duly arrived with many of our personal possessions packed inside, including a carry cot which we had bought from the man who sold us the car. Shortly before Christmas I drove it down to Douala to collect Lesley and Matthew, and without a single stop for beer we returned to Mukonje. The tiny black flies, the vector of filaria which causes elephantiasis, were very common in this part of Cameroon. They cause an itching bite and are small enough to pass through mosquito screening. The nuisance could be reduced by not sitting too close to the windows where they could sense their prey. A regular cot had still not been provided by CDC and we put an extra layer of gauze over the carry cot, though this made it rather hot and airless for Matthew.

Dennis had by now been transferred to the Tombel estate on the border with East Cameroon, where good use was to be made of his previous experience with tea in India, as he was now to oversee the establishment of a tea nursery and subsequent plantings, the rest of the estate being under mature cocoa and rubber. This was an isolated posting, where the security situation was worse than our own, with an entirely Bamilike labour force surrounded by Bakossi villages. Not only was Dennis an alcoholic but also homosexual, the former addiction perhaps by reason of the latter disposition, for he was a most unhappy person requiring constant support and cheering up, which Lesley and I provided to the best of our ability. He was lonely, and frequently drove the thirty miles to our house for company, and so it

A Sad Chapter

became routine that I would put on our Louis Armstrong tape, whereupon Dennis would take down a pair of maracas from where they hung on the wall, shake them high above his head, and slowly pirouette to the music with tears streaming down his woebegone face. Duncan, also living alone and lonely, would sometimes be with us at the same time, always largely sober on arrival, but progressively and routinely becoming more inebriated to the point when his blue eyes adopted their bellicose stare and his jaw was thrust out. During this metamorphosis, he maintained the charade that he did not drink at all, and would accept only offerings of fruit juice. However, his trouser pockets bulged with miniature bottles of spirit, and these would clink with his every move. After downing a glass of orange juice, he would excuse himself and clink his way to the bathroom. Then preceding the sound of the flushing lavatory, there would be yet another clink as an empty miniature bottle struck the gravel below the bathroom window, which sequence of events followed at regular intervals during his visits. As far as I know, both Duncan and Dennis paid the wages of their drivers, which enabled them to combine social mobility with their drinking habits.

Lesley and I agreed that Duncan sober was one of the nicest men we had ever met. He was polite with an old worldly charm, generous, gentle and humorous, nothing was ever too much trouble for him. He was really a lovable character and needed our help. He had a wife in England who was a teacher, a beautiful teenage daughter and two young sons, one of whom was to prove fatally diabetic. They came to visit just once while we were at Mukonje, and it was great to see them together as a family, but covering for Duncan was gaining progressive importance in my work, writing his reports, completing the regular returns that head office expected from him, and apologising for his no shows at CDC headquarters' meetings on the coast.

There was considerably more social contact between Africans and Europeans at management and professional levels in Cameroon than I had experienced in East Africa. We were invited into their houses and vice versa. We enjoyed the opportunity to enjoy Cameroonian home cooking, especially the many variations on the theme of groundnuts and the abundant use of chillies. The chewing and sharing of kola nut, which gives one a mild high, was both a solitary habit and social ritual, though it was too bitter for my taste and I did not persevere to acquire it. There were red and white varieties of kola, and the latter, said to have aphrodisiac properties, was nicknamed 'kick starter'. A great friend of ours was Pius Fusi, the OCPD, or officer in command of the police district, based in Kumba. He had been

NOWHERE NEAR GREENLAND

trained at England's Hendon police college, and was the epitome of smartness without swagger, with a natural air of command and a good sense of humour. Surviving from colonial times was the gloomy Kumba Club of high ceilings, whizzing ceiling fans and red cardinal polished cement floors. It was frequented by expatriates, many of whom had known better days, and the higher echelons of local Kumba society who were now enjoying theirs. The club provided high bar stools along a well-stocked, dark hardwood bar, light snacks and a crumbling tennis court where an intimate knowledge of its topography was the key to winning.

A more lively club just out of town occupied a large, unprepossessing, prefabricated hut that had been the road camp of McAlpine civil engineers when they were constructing a road there some years previously. Here were held regular dances, well attended by Cameroonians and which featured the catchy, syncopated West African 'highlife' music. Pius was a great dancer, though like so many compatriots and expatriates alike, he was on most days 'of the drink taken' any time after noon, and at these hops he would become progressively paralytic. For some reason he would then despise his own kind, sink deeper and deeper into his chair, slowly shaking his head and repeating "dirty people, dirty people".

One weekend morning, Dennis drove over from Tombel for a coffee at our place, and then Duncan arrived and both went through their usual routine accompanied by Louis Armstrong. Around noon they left, or were perhaps politely shooed out as both had the air of people with nowhere to go anytime soon. There had been a shower or rain and it was very hot and humid. I placed Matthew in his carrycot close to the window, suspending its straps over the window fastener to raise it higher to catch any breeze there was. The cot was now higher than the table beneath it, so I piled books on it to support the cot at either end. We decided to go for a short walk to the dam which fed the hydroelectric station. Our housegirl had her own small baby, and she was outside the flat below our house. We asked her to keep an ear out in case Matthew cried. We walked to the dam and returned after about fifteen minutes. We then went to the bedroom. The carrycot had tipped up, back towards Matthew's head where the supporting books had slipped away. Matthew had choked on regurgitated milk and was dead. We both frantically tried mouth to mouth resuscitation, but it was seemingly too late. We drove him to the nurse at the estate clinic, still desperately trying to revive him, but she confirmed he was dead. The house girl had heard nothing. Perhaps her own baby was crying. I reported the death to George Kissob, the district commissioner, and he ordered a

A Sad Chapter

post-mortem which found that death had occurred as described. The overseers on my division came and held a wake in our living-room, deeply grieving for us as was their custom, and we were deeply touched by their gesture, and the estate carpenter worked all night to make a tiny coffin for Matthew. A Swiss minister officiated at his funeral. They say you never recover from the death of your child, and writing this forty years later I weep at the memory of it. Our marriage too was forever shadowed by his loss and was never the same again.

Devastated is today a worn-out word, used even to describe a merely disagreeable surprise, but in the old sense of the word that was what we were, and also suffering from no small degree of shock. Duncan ordered that we take a few days holiday, so we drove through part of East Cameroon, and returned down from the highland town of Bamenda, through Bafusam and Upper and Lower Mamfe. The long road from the latter towns to Kumba was so steep and narrow, that up and down traffic were on alternate days. As it was, our progress was very slow and dusty, since we encountered many hundreds of long-horned cattle being driven down this road to the market in Kumba. The only other memory I have of that trip is of a hotel bedroom in Foumban. Its lavatory was in the room completely unscreened, and the washbasin emptied directly onto the tiled floor.

Dr. Brian Duke was a filaria specialist who had been researching this disease for some years in Kumba. Though not Scots, he was a keen Scottish country dancer, and his suggestion that he might hold a weekly highland fling at his house, and teach the traditional steps to the uninitiated, was heartily taken up by the younger expatriates. These mainly comprised volunteers from America (Duncan's damned Peace Corps), Ireland, Germany, Holland, France and the UK. Apart from Lesley and me, the only other representative of the planter community was David Wimblett, who worked at the Cadbury Fry cocoa plantation at Ikiliwindi, and who was later to go to the Gilbert Islands (now Kiribati) in the South Pacific, and there marry a local girl. Our Scottish dancing to Jimmy Shand records was nothing if not enthusiastic, and our good doctor seemed unfazed by the scant heed we paid to the finer points of prancing on toes and heels, and with the brawny young Dutch girls vigorously swinging their partners, giving literal meaning to a highland fling, some of us were bouncing off Dr Duke's wooden walls like stones from slingshots.

Brian Duke also introduced us to Barombi lake. This was a deep volcanic lake, nearly a mile wide and set in a thickly wooded crater not far from Kumba. A steep

NOWHERE NEAR GREENLAND

track, slanting down the interior face of the crater, led to a small bathing hut at the edge of the water where Brian kept a rowing dinghy. At the Kumba Club, I had encountered an American civil engineer named Ed Gunderson who worked for the Public Works Department. On several occasions I had found him at the bar, slowly shaking his head and gazing into the depths of his beer, repeating "It's godda have a bottom, it's godda have a bottom", his voice and eyes expressing the dread, the horror, that there could actually be a bottomless lake and it was right here in Kumba. For someone had once assured him that Barombi Lake had this possibly unique quality, and the image of its dark, infinitely deep waters really spooked him.

The Barombi Lake Depth Probe ready for launch, Cameroon, 1967

So, to put his poor mind at rest, and satisfy our own curiosity, Lesley and I decided to measure its depth. We obtained a yard long piece of six-inch galvanized steel pipe, painted its exterior gloss white, and decorated it with the crossed flags of Britain and France, and the letters BLDP - for Barombi Lake Depth Probe. We bought a roll of sisal twine, and Lesley spent a whole day tying markers on it at intervals of ten feet, and a larger coloured marker every one hundred feet. On the interior of the pipe, I secured a maximum-minimum thermometer, and protruding from its bottom end, an aluminium tube that once had held an expensive cigar, to bring up a core sample from the bottom of the lake. "That is if it has a bottom", commented Ed when we showed him our sophisticated, heavy piece of equipment, with an albeit finite, thousand feet of string attached.

A Sad Chapter

Yes, it was all seriously scientific, and even Dr. Duke was impressed. He rowed us out to what we all agreed was approximately the centre of the lake, and we began slowly to lower our probe into its black depths. Down and down it silently went. Then at about one hundred feet the string broke and our heavy probe must have hit the bottom at tremendous speed. Dr. Duke was not impressed. In fact he could hardly believe it. As we mutely held our now limp end of the broken string, the atmosphere in the rowing-boat must have been similar to that at NASA Control following a failed shot at Mars. However, not to be entirely defeated in our mission, and not least for Ed's sake, we tied a stone to the remainder of the string and lowered that overboard instead. It duly found bottom at about four hundred feet. Although he didn't say so, we think Ed was really disappointed. The lake with no bottom had been his very own American dream. (Some years later a very similar crater lake, Lake Nyos, not many miles distant, emitted a tremendous belch of toxic gas from its depths, and suffocated in its vicinity two thousand people and their livestock.)

Dennis' place on Mukonje had been taken by a Scotsman called Jock who now lived in Dennis' former flat above the estate shop. Not only was he an alcoholic living alone, but he also was homosexual, and soon after his arrival had taken to soliciting young boys on the estate. Pius Fusi got to hear about it, and one day phoned me to say that if Jock did not desist he would arrange for the police to set a trap, and he would be duly charged and almost certainly deported. I asked the manager, Clitus Tita, to relay the warning, which he did. Whereupon Jock went on such a bender, he ended up in hospital and was later flown back to Britain under medical escort. He left behind a black spaniel whom Lesley and I temporarily adopted, but very soon after were alarmed to find it foaming at the mouth. As rabies was endemic in the area, we drove it with some trepidation to the vet in Kumba, leaning forward as far as possible to put some distance between us and the dog in the back of the Land Rover. However, we learned after tests that the dog was suffering from 'hair ball', as a result of persistently nibbling its long and hot coat, and the vet, taking a liking to the dog, adopted it.

Down at the bottom of the gorge below our house, and living in a couple of rooms tacked-on to the building housing the hydroelectric turbine, was old, white-haired Alphonse who had faithfully tended this whirring and humming contrivance for about forty years. One day, the plantation was visited by an elderly German who had worked on Mukonje before the second world war, and I took him down the

NOWHERE NEAR GREENLAND

steep track to meet Alphonse. There was mutual recognition; they hugged, patting one another's backs, a few tears were shed and photos were taken. Alphonse had told me stories of life on the estate under German management. One concerned a particularly fierce manager who was woken from his post-prandial siesta by a young assistant. Throwing open the shutters, he shot the horse from under the young man and banged the shutters shut again. On another occasion, it was nearing Christmas and the manager was desirous of obtaining a turkey. He described in some detail to his houseboy exactly what he wanted, and some days later the servant returned with an ostrich.

It was some years since I had climbed a mountain, and the 13,350 foot summit of Mount Cameroon beckoned from a distance of only fifty miles. Good friends of ours in Kumba were Steve and Sue Gartlan. He was a primatologist from Bristol University, and would spend many days in the forest recording and observing the behaviour of chimpanzees and monkeys. They were keen to join us on the climb, as were David Wimblett and Pius Fusi. This volcano had quite recently undergone a major eruption, and a massive lava flow had cut the main road between Kumba and Victoria on the coast, but for the time being it was quiet and probably safe to climb. From a technical point of view there was no serious climbing involved, it was just a long hard slog of over two vertical miles. We planned to stay a night at a mountain hut about three quarters of the way up, and then set off for the summit early the next day. We also expected to descend all the way down on that second day. After a night at Buea, the little capital at its foot, we drove up at dawn to the prison farm on the lower slopes of the volcano where the track began and we left our vehicles. We slogged up through the rainforest all morning, and in the afternoon emerged onto steep open moorland. Some years before, Lord Douglas Hamilton piloting a plane from America, had crashed with his son somewhere on these slopes, and the wreck had still not been found. Apparently it was important from the point of view of inheritance to establish which of them had died first, and everyone on the mountain kept an eye open for the wreck. (It was discovered by a local hunter sometime during the 1970s)

Near sunset, we reached the hut at about ten thousand feet. It was already very cold with a bitter wind blowing, and we were dismayed to find that much of the hut's wooden cladding had been scavenged for firewood, so that there was little protection from the icy blast. We had collected firewood along the trail, and also had a primus stove, so we were able to make a hot meal, and we clustered close to

A Sad Chapter

the fire for as long as the wood lasted. After dark, we were joined by two young French meteorologists. They were also doubling as vulcanologists, and scampered up the mountain every week to take readings of temperature and seismic movements at the summit. We spent a miserably cold night, but before we had stirred the French contingent had already departed for the top. We set off, but Pius was now finding the going extremely difficult, and his shining black skin had turned dull grey. He sat down and said he would go back down to the hut to wait for our return. We continued on up, but Lesley was soon having such problems with her hip joints, or perhaps it was the upper thigh muscles, that she was using her hands to lift up her legs at every step. At about 12,000 feet she finally seized up, and David, Sue and Steve all declared headaches from the altitude and did not feel sufficiently motivated to continue, and they would stay with Lesley until I came down. I clambered on up, now somewhat slowed by the height, until I reached the highest point on the crater rim, and looked down the almost sheer inner face to the thinly fuming depths at the centre. I was carrying a stick and thrust it deep into the ash of the rim, and when I withdrew it the end of stick was smoking. After a few minutes, I started on down, running and leaping on the bare, steep scree to join the others. At the hut we found that Pius had already started down, and we did not catch up with him until we reached the bottom of the mountain in the early evening. By then, with the protracted use of seldom used muscles, we had all lost sensible control of our legs, and imitating the ministry of silly walks were wandering all over the place. As we were about to pass the prison farm compound, we all made a concentrated and seemingly superhuman effort to walk straight, and so made it back to our cars without arousing the audible mirth of the incarcerated.

Up a long, steep and winding mountainous track through the forest high above Tombel was a quinine plantation named Essusong, from which the bark of the quinine trees was sporadically harvested. Though it notionally came under Dennis' management, he had never yet been up there, because this forest was home to Bamilike 'maquisard' terrorists. One day, Lesley, a Peace Corps friend and I drove up with Dennis to Essusong. We were in the middle of a convoy of three vehicles, in front and behind us heavily-armed military. Somewhat incredibly, the Germans some seventy year earlier had built a castle up there for their estate management, though it probably had also served as a hill station retreat from the heat of the plains below. The castle, massively built complete with crenulations, had stood empty and bat-ridden for more than a generation, its walls already festooned with the roots of strangler figs and epiphytic ferns, and under slow siege from the en-

NOWHERE NEAR GREENLAND

circling and advancing forest. Clouds drew a chill and grey skein over this lonely scene, and after a picnic on the castle's roof, we descended again to Tombel, cheered all the way by the singing of half a dozen children of the estate workers we had taken aboard our truck, "Oh white man, oh white man, no go for see white man, no go for see white man, Oh white man…….." the piping sweetness of their voices keeping well at bay whatever intended harm might be lurking around us.

Despite the lighter and brighter interludes of our existence there, Lesley was generally depressed and the house held profoundly sad memories for us. I was on the lookout for employment elsewhere overseas, and we had subscribed to the airmail Daily Telegraph. One day we saw that the Crown Agents were advertising the post of Agricultural Extension Officer in the New Hebrides, so I decided to apply. Consulting my set of Encyclopaedia Britannica, we learned that these islands were located in the South West Pacific, that their Melanesian people were insanitary, living largely in the ways of their forefathers, and that fevers abounded. However, that particular article had not been revised since it was written in 1923 and we rather hoped that things had somewhat improved in the interim. We had also learned that the New Hebrides was a 'condominium' jointly administered by the French and British following a convention agreed between them in 1906. This ambivalence was curiously reflected in West Cameroon, with its British trained police and anglophone parliament within the much larger territory of francophone 'Cameroun', as well as the recent confusion concerning the correct side of the road on which to drive, and our Barombi Lake Depth Probe painted with the crossed flags of Britain and France (as displayed on the driving licence I would obtain on arrival in the New Hebrides).

On the morning of New Year's Day 1967, a holiday for labour but not for management, Duncan, Dennis, Clitus Tita and I were having a meeting in Duncan's office. A phone call came through from Tombel estate telling us there had been some kind of attack on the labour lines; they had been set on fire and it was believed there could be many dead. For the moment, there were no other details. Duncan rang the police in Kumba, and they said that the police post at Tombel had reported a serious incident, and that army and police reinforcements were at that moment on their way to the scene. We rang through to the Tombel estate office, and asked that someone stay there and let us know what was going on as soon as they had anything to report. They said there were three of them sheltering in the office, and that there was no way they would be leaving it. We waited in suspense. Most of the

A Sad Chapter

labour force at Tombel comprised members of the Bamilike tribe, so who would attack them?

An hour later a policeman came on the line from Tombel office. The army was asking us to send over two or three lorries to carry dead bodies to Kumba. No other details, except that the army had taken charge of the situation. We arranged for two five-ton lorries from Mukonje and another from our Mvu estate to be despatched there immediately. Dennis and I also set off for Tombel in our respective Land Rovers. There we found a large army presence. They were all francophone, and as we found out later, mainly Bamilike. They seemed excited and fired up by what had happened, and were shouting and pushing people around. I found an officer and told him the lorries were on their way. We were not allowed anywhere near the labour lines from which smoke was still rising, but we could see that some of the houses were blackened by fire and smoke, their corrugated iron roofs buckled or fallen in. Then a Tombel lorry filled with dead passed us, grey arms dangling over the side, here and there a limb protruding from the stiffening heap inside.

We spied a police Land Rover among the many army vehicles, and then Pius Fusi who came over to talk to us. He confirmed that the army had taken complete control of the situation, specifically to calm the people down and keep the Bamilike and Bakossi apart. He indicated two large groups of men, women and children sitting down, some fifty yards between them and surrounded by soldiers. Our other lorries arrived and were directed through to the area of the burned houses. But additional bodies were now being carried or dragged in from the bush and neighbouring areas of the estate, where they had fled the attack but had been cut down. One lorry was detailed to carry the wounded to Kumba hospital, many with bloody rags covering deep cutlass wounds to head, arms and body. We learned from Pius that the assault on the labour lines was a revenge attack on the Bamilike by the Bakossi, but did not get the full story until the next day.

It transpired that early on the morning of the attack, a Land Rover driven by a popular Bakossi schoolteacher had been ambushed on the main road by Bamilike terrorists, and he, his wife and two children had been murdered. The incensed local Bakossi people then carried out their reprisal three hours later. Sixty-eight men, women and children, all Bamilike, were dead, cut down or burned alive in their houses. These victims had nothing to do with the killing of the teacher and his family, which was carried out by Bamilike 'maquisards' operating in gangs from the

NOWHERE NEAR GREENLAND

forest, but they happened to be of the same tribe. Hundreds of Bakossi men were later brought into the prison compound in Kumba where, under the army's largely Bamilike supervision, they were starved and tortured, and many of them died. Months later, following a trial, some of the survivors were formally executed by guillotine in East Cameroon.

Meanwhile, Duncan's condition was becoming dire and he needed more and more support. One weekend he and Dennis came over to the house, and soon Dennis was dancing, crying and shaking the maracas, and Duncan had become aggressive, shouting and drilling us with his blue eyes. Lesley and I exchanged looks; we had had enough. We must now adopt a defensive mode to survive this torment. I switched off the music and asked them to leave the house immediately, now! I bundled them out. Dennis went, quietly sobbing, but Duncan was highly offended. I couldn't talk to him like that, who did I think I was; I would be dismissed, and so on, and still muttering imprecations he was driven off home. We felt bad about, it but we had to get through this terrible time.

Shortly after that, Dennis suffered a bizarre and eventually fatal accident. At Tombel, he and an overseer went to inspect a field of cocoa that bordered the highway from east to west Cameroon. They had parked their car on the verge of the road at the bottom of a long hill, and were about to climb through a wire fence. Then over the brow in the east, came a lorry laden with 44 gallon oil drums. Halfway down the hill, the driver lost control, the lorry slewed sideways and overturned releasing several dozen full barrels of oil rolling at high speed towards Dennis and the overseer. The latter nimbly dived over the fence and got out of the way. Dennis, not being built, or in condition for any kind of speed, was not so lucky and was run over by one of the drums. It fractured one of his legs in two places and he was evacuated to a hospital in Douala. Not long afterwards, because of poor circulation exacerbated by drinking, he had to have that leg amputated. Some months later Lesley went to see him in hospital in Wales where, she said, he wept. Soon afterwards we heard he had died. Poor man.

One morning I went over to Duncan's house. I was to go down to the coast to represent him at a meeting, and needed to collect some papers. He met me at the top of steps leading to his front door. "There are people in my bathroom", he whispered. "Who are they?", I asked. "I don't know but I can hear them talking" said Duncan, "and they won't come out. They have been there all night". I went to listen

A Sad Chapter

at his bathroom door. Silence. I tapped on it; no response. I then cautiously opened the door. The bathroom was empty. Duncan had a strange vacant air and looked exhausted. I believed he was now suffering from delirium tremens. I told him that Lesley was nervous to be left alone while I was down at the coast and might I bring her over for him to look after her. He readily agreed, with his old world gallantry, and I drove back the seventeen miles to collect her. I told Lesley that when I got to the coast I would explain the situation to T.S.Jones, the general manager of CDC, and suggest that Duncan be packed straight off to hospital.

By now very late for the meeting, I left Lesley at Duncan's gate. He met Lesley at the top of the bungalow steps, appeared to have a fit and tumbled down into the garden unconscious. Lesley retrieved his denture from where it had fallen into the grass, bent over Duncan and tried to revive him. He came round, but almost immediately became very amorous, and Lesley had to push him away. She eventually helped him back into the house and onto a sofa, and then phoned his doctor in Kumba. Meanwhile, I was driving down to the coast. The road was not only appalling with huge pot holes the whole way, but was also extremely dusty. Attempting to overtake a vehicle was really dangerous because of the dense and long trailing plume of dust, and because of the dust I failed to see the general manager of CDC driving in the opposite direction, and we probably passed when I was about halfway to the coast. He knew I was coming down to represent Duncan again and had sensed from the lack of direct communication that something was seriously wrong. So when I reached the coast and was told the GM had left for Mukonje, I immediately turned around and drove all the way back again. Meanwhile, the doctor had sedated Duncan and put him to bed, and Lesley had given the GM a stark account of how Duncan had been that morning and over the previous few months. The next day, Duncan was taken off to hospital down at the coast. Lesley and I went to see him there, where he cheerfully complained of the absolute nonsense of even being considered a sick person. He was soon flown back to Britain, where he was diagnosed as having advanced terminal cancer, and died not long after.

We had by now heard from the Crown Agents in London that I was being considered for the post in the New Hebrides, all strangely prescient, and was asked to report to the British Consul in Buea for an interview. His office was at his residence, a fine two storied house with a distant view of the sea, and set in an extensive English garden of gently sloping lawns, rose beds and herbaceous borders. The only

NOWHERE NEAR GREENLAND

other time I had been there was to attend a midday reception to celebrate the Queen's birthday. The expatriates and African dignitaries were gathered on the lawn in their lightweight suits, clutching their drinks and canapés. The police band struck up the strains of God Save the Queen, and we all hushed and stood to attention. I was standing next to the secretary for education, a tall and portly Englishman, and halfway through the anthem there was a heavy thud. Rigidly at attention, he had keeled over backwards, felled by his drink, and many previous ones no doubt. The anthem over, he was picked up, brushed down and carried to his car. Could it be that had there not been the tradition of senior Africans and expatriates employing drivers for their personal transportation, there might have been less excessive drinking? - or just more car accidents, with an accelerated rate of attrition? As it was, I had never been, and was never again, in a country where drunkenness and alcoholism was the way of life, and too often the way to death for so many. Only a year after leaving West Cameroon we heard that our good friend Pius Fusi had died of cirrhosis of the liver.

The interview with the consul went well enough and he recommended me for the post. We were soon informed by the Crown Agents, that a passage on the Italian liner 'Marconi' had been booked for us to travel from Genoa in early January, bound for Sydney via Las Palmas, Perth, Melbourne and Adelaide. We would then embark on the 'Polynesie', which would carry us via New Caledonia to the New Hebrides. We started to make arrangements to leave Africa and to sell the Land Rover. A few months previously we had bought an African Grey parrot. It was very young, and on being assured by the African who had caught the bird that it was female, we named her Boudicca. She lacked the red hair of her royal namesake, but at least had bright red tail feathers. We had been inspired to buy a parrot by the hilarious antics of another, owned by the manager of Barclays Bank in Kumba. Somehow, he had trained this droll bird to roll over on its back and croak "Death of Nelson, death of Nelson". It could also accurately imitate the sound of curtains being closed, bolts being shot, and then say "Good night all", the nightly sequence of events as our friend closed up his house before going to bed. Boudicca was a quick learner, could soon repeat her name, and went on to develop a considerable vocabulary, sound effects and a limited repertoire of classical and martial music.

We needed to find a ship travelling to England via Las Palmas so that we could leave our personal effects with shipping agents there, and Boudicca with Lesley's in-laws who still lived on Grand Canaria, and then pick them up when we passed

A Sad Chapter

through on the Marconi. We discovered that at about the right time, there was a Spanish banana boat bound for London via Monrovia and Las Palmas, and due to leave Fernando Poo (now renamed Bioko) the small Spanish island possession off the coast of Cameroon, and only a short distance from Victoria. We hired a barge from the local port authority, and with our personal effects, Boudicca and many of our friends who were keen to make a day trip to Fernando Poo, we set off on the three hours crossing. The island, an ancient volcano with highly fertile soils, rose steeply up through cocoa plantations to a rainforest-covered summit at nearly 10,000 feet . A large proportion of its population was Ibo, who had been brought across from Nigeria to labour on the very extensive and productive cocoa estates, though they were later to be repatriated, if not previously killed in the reign of terror that ensued when the island became independent as part of Equatorial Guinea the following year.

The small, hot and humid port town of Santa Isabel (since renamed Malabo) founded by the British in the 1820s as a base from which to suppress the slave trade, was neatly laid out with Spanish colonial style buildings and flowering roadside trees, though it was clear the expatriates were already pulling out and a number of shops were boarded up and cafes closed. Lesley and our friends enjoyed a good meal at the Spanish Club, while I busied myself with the port authority and recruited labour on the spot to unload our crates of personal effects from the barge, and then load them onto the Spanish ship which was already alongside. Fortunately I had brought with me sufficient US dollars to satisfy both officials and labour who, all African, were cheerfully and cheekily offhand with an air of "We don't have to be polite to them anymore". We went aboard the banana boat with a number of local residents and their children, who were leaving for good and making tearful farewells to their African servants and Spanish friends. We said goodbye to our own friends, who had still a few more hours to spend on the island before returning on the barge to Cameroon, a beautiful country where we had made many good friends, but for us had also been a catastrophe.

REPUBLIC OF VANUATU
Formerly the New Hebrides

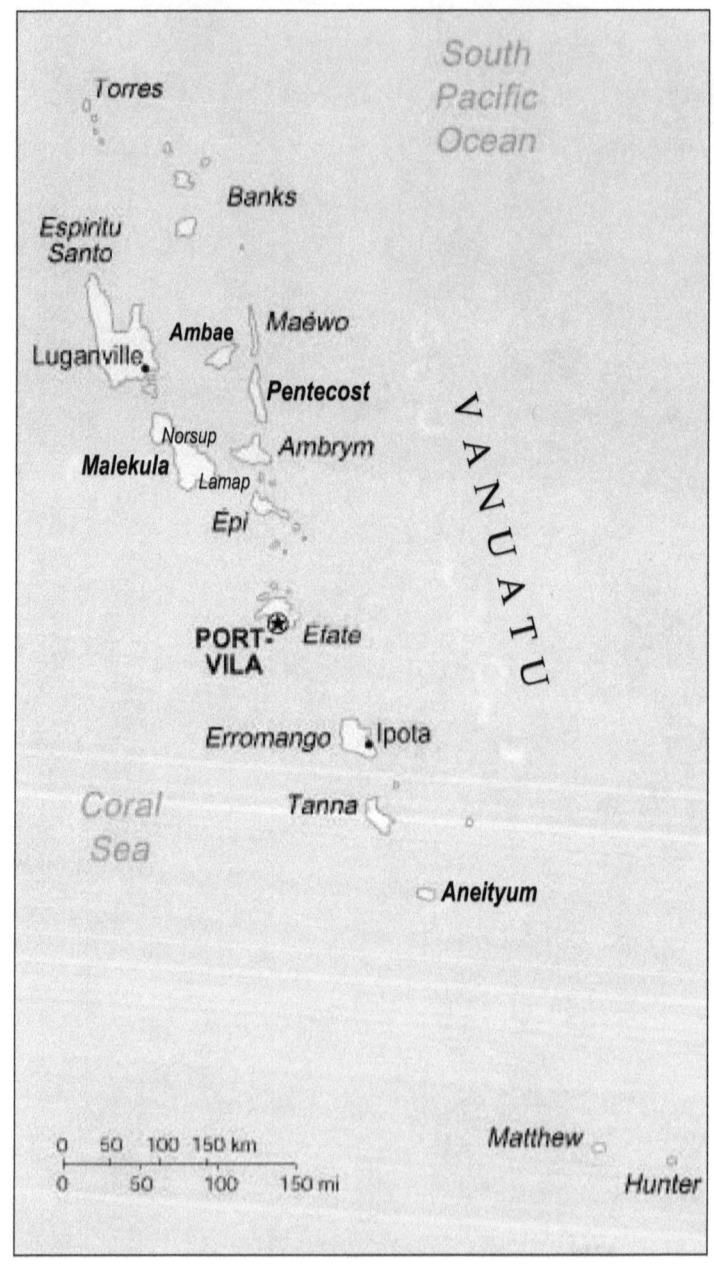

NOWHERE NEAR GREENLAND

TO CORAL STRANDS

Lesley and I arrived in the New Hebrides (now the Republic of Vanuatu) in February 1968. Our outward journey had commenced in London where we entrained for Paris, and onward from there to Genoa where we were to embark on the Lloyd Tristino passenger liner 'Marconi' bound for Sydney. Our trip thus far had been uneventful, except that when having dinner in the dining car, somewhere between Paris and Genoa, we were joined at our table by Marcello Mastroianni and a companion, possibly his agent. The smallness of the table did not even afford us the excuse to ask the Italian mega-star to pass the salt, and our crippling native reticence prevented us from gushing about how much we had enjoyed his performances in Fellini's 8 ½ and Divorce Italian Style. However, a large middle-aged Italian lady progressing down the carriage recognised her idol and, simpering and rolling her eyes, went so wobbly at the knees that she passed our table at a low crouch. Most generously the government of the New Hebrides Condominium had booked us first class passages, so our berths aboard the Marconi were quite luxurious, as was that of our parrot Boudicca, which was housed for the month-long voyage in a large hutch, one of a line on the top deck near the funnels for the comfort and safety of pets accompanying their owners.

The Marconi's first port of call had been Las Palmas in the Canary Islands where

To Coral Strands

the previous month, en route to England from the Cameroons, we had left Boudicca and our household effects in the care of Lesley's relations from her first marriage. At one point, while transferring the parrot to the ship, I left her in charge of Lesley while I went to find a taxi. Boudicca was covered in her cage on the pavement in the centre of Las Palmas, and as a very dignified Spanish businessman passed by, Boudicca let out a piercing and prolonged wolf whistle. This stopped the gentleman in his tracks, and I was sorry not to have personally witnessed the look of utter astonishment he gave my wife. Dinners aboard the Marconi were quite a formal affair, and the chefs excelled every night with the presentation of magnificent ice sculptures that accompanied the ceremonial entry of equally stupendous desserts.

An Elizabethan dress from menu cards for Lesley; Robinson Crusoe for Boudicca and me.

Meanwhile, Lesley excelled at the fancy dress parties, using her considerable artistic talents to make an Elizabethan dress entirely from menu cards for herself, and a Robinson Crusoe outfit for me, to which Boudicca added an exotic touch, perching and squawking on my pseudo-banana leaf sunshade. We carried off the first prizes, as we did for the best hats at a subsequent do, Lesley having placed me beneath her accurate replica of the ship's funnel. The film "Who's Afraid of Virginia Woolf" was showing in the ship's cinema, and we watched it three or four times, enjoying the fine performances of Richard Burton and Elizabeth Taylor, which in her case we thought surpassed anything she had done before.

NOWHERE NEAR GREENLAND

When we docked at Sydney, we had to declare the arrival of Boudicca to the quarantine authorities. Since it was, and still is, strictly prohibited to import birds of that species into Australia, our parrot was to be placed in quarantine ashore until we took our connecting flight to the New Hebrides. (In fact, we had been due to continue our voyage on the 'Polynésie', a Messageries Maritimes vessel that made regular voyages there, but our ship had been delayed and missed that connection by a couple of days.) We were told by the quarantine officials that we would have to buy a new parrot cage, in which Boudicca would be taken ashore, and that the old one would have to be destroyed. We duly bought a new cage at a department store in downtown Sydney, and no less than three quarantine officers came aboard to transfer Boudicca into her new cage and escort her ashore. Up on the top deck, two of these officers spread wide their raincoats, while the third, a safe pair of hands, crouched in the slips to defend Sydney against a parrot attack. I removed Boudicca from her hutch, and once she was firmly secure behind bars, one of the officials took the old cage, which was also in the hutch, and unceremoniously dropped it overboard into Sydney Harbour. I have since fantasised that one day ships will run aground there on a reef of old parrot cages.

We took the UTA flight from Sydney via Noumea to the New Hebrides. We were assured that Boudicca had already been loaded into the hold, though if she was squawking to confirm this, we were unable to hear her as this was a very noisy, black smoke belching old DC4. The islands of the Condominium of the New Hebrides eventually rose above the eastern horizon. We landed at Luganville on Espiritu Santo, at the old World War Two airfield on the plateau to the west of the town and entirely surrounded by creeper-festooned tropical rain forest. At the time, this was one of just two international airports for the New Hebrides, and our passports were stamped in the stifling heat and humidity of the small corrugated iron shed that served for arrivals, departures and any other activity that deserved protection from the weather including, in a tacked-on lean-to, those catered for by a long drop, pit latrine.

Espiritu Santo, locally called Santo, is the largest of the eighty-three islands of Vanuatu which extend from north to south in a Y-shaped volcanic chain, rather like the separated metatarsals of a two-toed sloth. A chain of mountains, rising to over six thousand feet, runs the length of the west coast, its outline softened by the green blanket of forest that covers it, much of it beneath an over-blanket of Meremia peltata, a vigorous vine that swarms over one hundred foot trees as though they

To Coral Strands

were daisies. The steep and broken terrain on this and many of the other islands has thus far protected the forest hardwoods from large scale logging and, due to the cyclones that regularly rage through them, many of their stands are sparse and not commercially attractive. Here and there are massive banyans whose aerial roots develop into a labyrinth of crutches supporting massive branches, all festooned with epiphytic orchids and ferns, and roosting, inverted fruit bats.

Santo's only town, Luganville, on the island's south east corner, is on the site where a vast US military camp was built in the early 1940s to support the campaign against the Japanese in the Pacific. On this remote island, where a whole year's development might once have celebrated the building of a wooden church or the planting of a hedge, the speed and size of its creation must have been truly astounding to the local inhabitants. Miles of hardtop roads were constructed from living coral bulldozed from nearby reefs, and then spread, rolled and watered so that the coral grew into a solid surface, which over some stretches has endured for sixty years. Coconut plantations were flattened to create three airfields, land was reclaimed from the sea, and docks, cranes, hospitals, workshops, barracks, fuel depots and more than forty cinemas appeared as if by magic. The great scale and speed of this build-up was not without cost. The liner s.s. President Coolidge, then serving as a troopship, and a destroyer sank after striking their own mines in the Segond Channel opposite the town. The former is now a national monument and a major tourist attraction, bringing scuba divers from all over the world to dive the world's largest, easily accessible wreck. Mike Ratard took me to see the remains of a US single engine fighter plane in the forest reserve above his father's plantation on the small island of Aore just across the Segond Channel. The pilot's seat was deeply embedded several feet up in the trunk of a large tree. Similar wrecks litter the forests of Santo and some are still being discovered. A line of three planes in the sea off the west coast of Pentecost island bears witness to where they simultaneously ran out of fuel having got lost in thick cloud while returning from Guadalcanal in the Solomon Islands.

For some considerable distance from Luganville, there still survive dozens of rusting, now only partly earth-covered steel sheds built to contain munitions. In the town itself, Quonset huts, the US Equivalent of the British Nissen hut from the same era and resembling excavated half-sections of underground tunnel, once created a uniformity of architectural style that arguably reflected the vision of Baron von Haussman. Until 1972, an extensive cluster of the genre, originally a US offi-

NOWHERE NEAR GREENLAND

cers' mess, provided Santo with its only hotel, while just opposite another had survived as a cinema. The Hotel Corsica burned to the ground on a windy night, scattering through the town the multitude of cats, rats and cockroaches that had long called it home. No longer would guests be kept awake by the yowling and thunderous scampering of cats across its hot tin roofs, of which there was a huge area over the cavernous lounge, dining room and bedrooms of this corrugated complex, clicking and banging night and day as it expanded and contracted, and loudly drumming under the rain. Also ended was that establishment's only live entertainment, when late of an evening the well-oiled and genial manager, Alan Brown, onetime student for the priesthood, took pot-shots at the cats with his pistol from his place at the bar. He was never known to have hit one, but certainly added to the holes in the roof.

Resembling those once built in South Africa to permit the u-turning of sixteen inspanned oxen, Luganville's main street is most likely the widest in the South Pacific, though once its WW2 coral surface had worn away it became a quagmire of sticky brown mud every rainy season until it was sealed before independence in 1980. This permitted Carmen of Carmen's Bar, veteran comforter of US servicemen and customarily dressed in black and red, to ride her bicycle slowly and gracefully up and down the street. Mao's Bar on the waterfront held lively dances on Saturday nights for which they would sometimes engage a live band. One that I heard was from Fiji, and its lead singer, who just happened to be an albino in heavy shades, gave a heartfelt rendition of 'A Whiter Shade of Pale'. Today's low profile of the varied and nondescript buildings that line the main street, interspersed with still vacant lots, make it seem even wider than it is, and crossing it one feels wary of being run over by vehicles just appearing in the distance. The wide street also gives the place a certain lack of intimacy; there is little shade from trees, and the town bakes in a humid, high noon glare, suitable only for mad dogs and smiting the incautious tourist. Residents walk fast only to escape the sun, and the customary laid-back pace of their daytime activities may reflect the lingering effects of kava, or one or two many beers the night before, or possibly it is just that they have nowhere to go in particular.

Luganville has always lacked the capital Port Vila's pretensions to sophistication, its Chinese shop windows displaying to little advantage a look-alike jumble of kerosene lamps, children's clothing, plastic wares and other odds and ends; its cafes are found in tacked-on wooden verandas, and the Chinese restaurant is a large,

To Coral Strands

bare, undecorated room with absolutely no view because it has no windows. Only the Hotel Santo, which succeeded the Corsica on the same site, can claim to have style, with its buttresses forming the pillars of an arcade, and it offers a degree of modern comfort not found elsewhere in the town. The immediate waterfront, entirely on reclaimed land, is a litter of bricks and bits of ancient concrete, accessible only through yards and mostly ill-kept gardens, though on the west side of the town near the covered market, there is a pleasant public garden where in 1980 the French opponents of an Anglophone-led independence dug up the tree planted there by Queen Elizabeth in 1974. A new concrete bridge across the Sarakata River now replaces the old single lane steel lattice bridge which had been thrown out of line by an earthquake in 1971, and around the mouth of the river there are half-derelict boat yards and the decaying hulks of small inter-island vessels stranded on the inter-tidal mud.

Luganville was the centre of Vanuatu's coconut industry, and until the coming of the finance centre and tourism to Port Vila in the early 1970s, was the self-claimed commercial capital of the country. Coconut plantations, almost all French owned, extended northwards up the east coast of Santo for fifty miles, and their cattle were kept primarily to mow the grass beneath the palms. These supplied the abattoir in town, as well as exports of choice beef to Japan through the now long- abandoned and derelict Japanese fish freezing and packing plant at Palakula to the east of the town. Most of these plantations today, with an ageing and diminishing population of coconut palms, have progressively become cattle ranches, while their sparse survivors of cocoa and coffee have languished untended since the several thousand Tonkinese, who had long been the mainstay of plantation labour, were repatriated to North Vietnam in the early 1960s.

Many half-castes, (a term still politically acceptable in Vanuatu), whose provenance in most cases stems from liaisons between French colons and indigenous women, still live in and around the town, though in 1980 many left for the neighbouring French overseas territory of New Caledonia which, at the time, offered a haven for disaffected francophones. Most of those who left had supported the francophone separatist movement, which, had it succeeded in its rebellion, would in all probability have swiftly relinquished its authority to France. Those who remained continue as before to fill management positions on the plantations, and serving as artisans and clerks with government and commercial enterprises, and are far better integrated into local society than the Chinese shopkeepers. Few ni-Vanuatu (the

NOWHERE NEAR GREENLAND

term used since independence to define indigenous Melanesians) and none of their villages are found in the vicinity of Luganville, since all their land for many miles around was alienated to foreign ownership more than a hundred years ago. Though this was returned to the customary land owners when the country became independent in 1980, nearly all the land is now leased to expatriate agricultural interests, and the indigenous people remain in the villages where their forebears resettled several generations ago.

To set Espiritu Santo in the geographical context of the other islands in the archipelago, I will give a brief description of them, for the present as far south as Efate. To the north of Santo lie the Banks Islands, rearing high out of the ocean, some to more than two thousand feet, most of them displaying their fiery origins with active or quiescent cones. Among the actively volcanic ones are Gaua and Vanualava, and Uruparapara comprises the lofty horseshoe rim of an eroded volcano, whose crater is now submerged beneath its deep bay. Further north are the low-lying Reef and Torres-Islands, the latter almost within sight of the southernmost Solomon islands. To the east is the high sugarloaf shape of Ambai, distinguished by three name changes in thirty years, Aoba - Omba - Ambai, and the supposed inspiration for James Michener's Bali Hai. Here, three thousand feet up at its centre, are two crater lakes, one blue and one green, beneath one of which a dormant volcano awoke in 2006, and the island's population was evacuated to its relatively safe shores until the eruption subsided a few months later. Farther to the east, one above the other, are the long, narrow and very wet islands of Maewo and Pentecost, the former distinguished for ancient irrigated taro systems, the latter famous for the Pentecost Jump, the mother of all bungees. Then back to the west, across an inland sea within the Y of the islands, is Malekula, the second largest island of Vanuatu, whose steep forested hills were home to the Big and Small Nambas, though nearly all have recently moved down to the coast and exchanged their penis wrappers for Y-fronts. An almost certainly apocryphal story ascribes the origin of the name Malekula to a Portuguese discoverer, who after relieving himself in the bush inadvertently cleansed his behind with nangalat leaves. Contact with the leaves of this tree on the skin produces a stinging itch which can persist for more than a week. 'Male kula' is approximate Portuguese for sore buttocks.

Appropriately at the epicentre of the north-south axis of Vanuatu is the island of Epi. Eighteenth century maps show this island as named Api, which is the Malay word for fire, and perhaps reflects the early eruptive nature of the island. (A num-

To Coral Strands

ber of Malay words are common to the many local Vanuatu languages (lima: five; mati:dead; tlinga:ear; mayat:corpse, mata:eye, etc) To the north of Epi is Ambrym, island of sorcerers and two massive active volcanoes, perpetually crowned by their high plumes of smoke and ash which are frequently carried by the south-east trade winds to dust the forests and crops of Malekula with inorganic fertilizer. Between Ambrym and the mile high, recently re-awakened and now uninhabited volcanic island of Lopevi, lies Paama, whose 19th century resident missionary wrote a book entitled 'Between Volcanic Fires'. Perhaps the most densely populated island of Vanuatu, its forests have been entirely replaced by food gardens, and under demographic pressure the traditional means of maintaining the soil's structure and fertility by fallowing have been abandoned. This has resulted in land degradation and falling crop yields, though the volcanoes on either side from time to time contribute a bountiful, though acidic, dusting. A unique feature of Paama is the evidence of a wide and deep ditch, dug in the distant past to encircle the island a short distance inland from the sea, its purpose being to confine pigs to the village areas and deny them access to food gardens, for whose crops of taro and yams they have a voracious appetite.

Immediately south of Epi are the Shepherd Islands, a half dozen remnants of the island of Kuwae which according to oral history blew to pieces in 1452 and now encircle an active underwater volcano. Another thirty miles to the south is the island of Efate, home to Port Vila, the capital, whose vine-festooned forests are progressively being encroached upon by timber extraction and the extensive cattle properties sprawling inland from the coast. On the north west of Efate is the deep Havana Harbour, where the American 6th Fleet dropped anchors in World War Two, and lost them all as the chains rattled out in a vain attempt to find the bottom. Here in the mid 19th century, the establishment of one of the first Christian missions was greeted with great communal feasting, but when the boat that had carried the missionaries to this shore sailed away, they all became the fare of a follow-up feast. Along the south of this harbour are white sands, coconut plantations and the circum-insular road, which for much of its length is no better than a potholed coral surfaced track.

South-westwards it climbs up steeply through almost savannah-like vegetation of grass and mimosa, in the rain shadow of a range of wooded hills topped by Mount Macdonald; then it snakes down and drops steeply over the escarpment into the valley of the Mele River which flows out over black basaltic sands and makes the

NOWHERE NEAR GREENLAND

shallow sea of Mele bay dark and forbidding. This bay lies between the long arms of the Devils Point and Pango Point peninsulas, around the broad base of which extends the town of Port Vila, its harbour sheltered from the west by two small islands which provide a safe anchorage for boats, even in most cyclones. The narrow main street, flanked by flat-topped buildings of mainly three or four stories, alternately shabby and passing smart, comprises the central business district, and a web of lesser, potholed roads runs inland through upmarket residential areas to outlying suburbs of crowded, borderline slums. Despite the developers' chainsaws and recurrent cyclones, the capital still retains many of its trees, among them mango, cassia, poinciana, casuarina and rain-tree. Over the years since 1968 the town has changed little, though it is now larger and more congested, and the sea front, once an indented confusion of sand, stone and lumps of concrete, has been straightened and tidied by the construction of a sea-wall. The greatest change in the countryside around the capital has been the progressive disappearance, through senility, of coconut palms, and the replacement of their former plantations by cattle ranches.

Having officially entered the New Hebrides, with our passports stamped in the hut by a policeman in a British-style uniform, while at another small table his French counterpart was similarly preoccupied with Gallic passports, the DC4 took off again and banged and belched its way south to Port Vila. With noses pressed against the scratched and shivering windows, we gazed down at the many islands passing beneath us, bays, white sand beaches, reefs and mangrove shores, with rainforest clothing the hills almost down to the coast, along which cultivated clearings, coconut plantations and thatched villages were tenuously linked by the thread of coral tracks.

Landing about an hour later at Port Vila, we and our parrot were greeted by Monsieur Beaugendre, the Director of Agriculture, Livestock and Forestry. We later learned that under the Condominium, whereby the New Hebrides was jointly administered by Britain and France, each Condominium department - as distinct from the separate national departments of the two colonial powers - was headed either by a British or French civil servant. Thus, for example, treasury, posts & telegraphs, meteorology and geological survey by Britons; and agriculture, public works and mines by French. We checked in at the Hotel Rossi on the sea front in town, and our very first meal there was shaken - but not stirred, since our fellow diners barely raised their faces from their plates - by a not inconsiderable earth tremor, a feature of not infrequent occurrence in these islands. Hélène Rossi, charming daughter-

To Coral Strands

in-law of the elderly hotel owners, took an immediate shine to Boudicca, and she was delighted when we told her a couple of days later that while we were being posted forthwith to the island of Malekula, the parrot must stay at the Rossi to await judgement as to her ultimate fate from Dr. Valin, the Chief Veterinary Officer, temporarily away on a trip overseas. What had transpired was that someone in the Department of Agriculture had meanwhile unearthed a regulation utterly prohibiting the importation into the New Hebrides of any bird of the parrot or pigeon family. Hence M. Beaugendre's ruling.

We flew up to Malekula, the only passengers that day in a small high-winged Dornier aircraft piloted by an irascible Frenchman who, when we landed on the grass strip at Lamap in the south of the island, howled at a local man who wanted to load a car battery, and shouted at the agitated catholic priest who served there as agent for Hebridair and Air Melanesia (known to local wags as Air Melanausia). Sans battery, we continued to Norsup in the north east of Malekula where we were met by M. Yves Tanguy, manager of Plantations Réunies des Nouvelles Hébrides, the largest coconut plantation in the archipelago, who drove us to his house and greeted us with champagne. Well and truly welcomed, he then drove us to our house which was less than a hundred yards from his own.

Whereas his house had been constructed of clapboard and corrugated iron in the 1920s, to a traditional design of surrounding, mosquito-screened verandas and wooden louvres, our own was an altogether more modern, single-storey structure of concrete blocks with no veranda at all. (Although almost all houses in the islands are of a single storey, the term bungalow is never used, unlike, say, in Britain, India and elsewhere.) With a garden sloping steeply down to the French primary school some fifty feet below, it commanded a magnificent view over Norsup bay and its small offshore island, and in the very far distance on a clear day, the thin, dark line of Pentecost could be perceived on the eastern horizon. The interior of the house had been newly redecorated, and three men, Thadee Malovane, Rosario and England, all - including the latter! - from francophone villages to the north, were busy up ladders painting the exterior walls white and the gutters and window frames bright blue. The day after our arrival, a Land Rover drove up behind the house. Darvall Wilkins, the British District Agent, a red-haired Australian in his mid-forties, had come to inspect the work he had organised and was surprised to find us already installed.

NOWHERE NEAR GREENLAND

Norsup was built around the centre of the PRNH plantation, and prior to our arrival was, as far as expatriates were concerned, a predominantly French community. The exceptions were the Italian mechanic Joseph Migotti, the part Fijian field manager Peter Wright, and an elderly Tonkinese carpenter named Twat. The French included the assistant plantation manager Patrick Gallay and schoolmaster Fiol and their families, and they were soon to be joined by two more married teachers and a doctor for whom houses and a hospital were already under construction.

Dawn view from Norsup house. Malekula, 1968

The rest of the community comprised the plantation workers - some one hundred Gilbertese and Wallis Island copra cutters, and New Hebridean and Fijian mechanics, drivers and stockmen. Women were hired from nearby villages to harvest the cocoa pods from the fifty hectares of that crop, and Big Nambas from the northwest plateau of the island came down to cut copra from time to time, donning shorts over their penis sheaths, and squatting in small tin huts at Aop bay a couple of miles from the plantation centre. At this centre were the management office, workshops, a former cotton ginnery, a bakery, copra and cocoa drying beds, a rudimentary abattoir, and the plantation general store where we soon discovered that the employees who bought on credit against their wages paid more than we did, despite the fact we also bought on credit. As in the old song, they owed their souls to the company store. A long line of humble, workers' quarters skirted the south

To Coral Strands

shore of Norsup bay, and raised walkways led to an equally long line of privies overhanging the water.

Norsup was also the centre of French administration in north Malekula and the assistant French district agent, Maxime Carlot, was stationed there. His boss, Monsieur Guy Boileau, was established in the agency at Lamap, near Port Sandwich in the far south east of the island, where Captain Cook anchored for a few days in 1789. About four miles down the coast from Norsup was Lakatoro, which Darvall Wilkins, commencing in 1963, had created as the British district agency. Originally sited on a small, French-owned coconut plantation, Darvall transformed it over the years into the likeness of a botanic garden. Sparing many fine trees, the upper part of the station was cleared from the forest, into which it imperceptibly blended where the land rose steeply over a series of coral cliffs and terraces, long uplifted from the sea to a height of nearly two thousand feet. The staff houses, thatched courthouse and church were on the higher ground with a view of the sea and offshore Uripiv Island, and the lower land had been made into a sports field with an adjoining, immense, sago palm-thatched social club; and towards the sea was the agricultural station of which I was now assuming command.

We had quite naturally moved into the largest of our three bedrooms, which had an en-suite bathroom. But we were to discover when Dr. Valin came to stay with us a few weeks later, that this part of the house was considered to be a chambre de passage, for visiting officers of the department such as himself. But we did not agree that an integral part of our house and the best bedroom should serve as a rest house, so we stayed put and accommodated him in one of the smaller bedrooms. However, Dr. Valin, presumably as a matter of principle, continued his occupancy as though he was in a rest house, and though my wife, an excellent cook, prepared every meal for him during his stay, he partook of none of them, taking his meals in the houses of our French neighbours. An awkward situation, though we respected his expectation to be independent of our hospitality. (There was, anyway, already a perfectly adequate Condominium rest house only a few hundred yards away.) We converted one of the bedrooms into my office, and early during his stay we raised with Dr. Valin the question of Boudicca's continued residence at the Hotel Rossi. However, he was adamant that she stay where she was. In bringing the prohibited parrot to the New Hebrides, we had presented him on his return with a fait accompli; but thus far and no further, Boudicca must remain in Vila. Nevertheless, some months later, following our further pleading, he finally relented

NOWHERE NEAR GREENLAND

and we collected our parrot, by which time she was whistling the first few bars of the Marseillaise.

However, my relationship with the outwardly jovial doctor was never to be on a happy footing. Shortly before my arrival in Malekula he had shipped at considerable expense a fine bull to the village of Pinalum, where it was to serve the cows of local farmers and thus upgrade their stock. Some time later I was speaking to him on the radio telephone, and he asked me for news of the bull. I went to Pinalum to enquire, only to find, oh horrors, that it had been shot and eaten. Evidently the bull had proved bad tempered, had broken fences and chased people, so it was shot. Reporting back, it was then a case of the messenger being shot! Dr. Valin was most displeased, and, moreover, this was an anglophone village, so what more could one expect!

By the late 1960s, New Hebrideans were just starting to invest in foundation herds of two or three heifers and a bull, just enough to graze the grass under their coconuts, though except for a few professional stockmen they had no previous experience with cattle and were afraid of them. However, the Condominium Agricultural and Industrial Loan Scheme had just been inaugurated, so New Hebridean farmers could now obtain through this scheme their livestock, barbed wire and posts for fencing. Fencing also demarcated their land, which was perceived as a means of strengthening, or at least demonstrating, customary ownership. In fact, a very large proportion of the loans granted under this scheme was for fencing materials. I had quite a fine but small herd of Illawara cattle, (an Australian variant of the British shorthorn breed), at the Lakatoro agricultural station, whose progeny were for sale to New Hebridean farmers at a highly subsidised price. One farmer who came along, looked at them and said "No, mifela wantem sotleg". The short legged cattle referred to, he had seen on a plantation in the north east of Malekula where they were very decidedly inbred, but at least they were less intimidating and quite incapable of jumping fences!

We shipped breeding cattle to other islands in the district, but on Malekula we took them as far as we could by tractor and trailer along the coastal tracks, and then drove them on foot overland to their destination. The latter operation had to be done very carefully in this hot and exceptionally humid climate, and some inexperienced farmers, who chose to drive the cattle themselves, ended up by chasing them until, within hours, the animals died from exhaustion and dehydration.

To Coral Strands

Charles Rogers was one of two young volunteers who came out from the UK in 1968 to work with the newly-founded British cooperatives movement. Strangely, they were initiated into their work by being sent to cut copra for Ham Harris, a planter in North Efate; and then the Chief Cooperative Officer, apparently still not quite knowing what to do with them, sent them up to me in Malekula. They stayed with us for a week or two, (incidentally eating us out of house and home!), and it was decided that Charles should stay and work with me. I had just then received a new, shiny blue Ford tractor and trailer, and needed to transport two young breeding cattle up to Vao. Charles, coming from a farm back home, was no slouch at driving tractors, so I gave him the job; but said wait for me at Orap, because the river there is tidal and it can be tricky unless forded in exactly the right place at the right time. An hour or two after his departure I set off to follow him in my Land Rover. At Orap, there was Charles with my precious tractor, trailer and cattle way out in the sea with waves breaking over the whole ensemble. First we untied and swam the cattle ashore; then to free the tractor from the trailer, stuck fast in the sand, I had to dive down, a lump of coral in hand, and bang out the pin that linked them together - not so easy with the waves and churned up sand, but it was accomplished. We then drove the tractor onto dry land, and later gave it a good wash down with unsalted river water, and likewise the trailer, though I have no memory of how or when we got that out. Since then, in all the years Charles Rogers has been in Vanuatu, I believe he has never totally immersed another tractor!

In my work as an agricultural extension officer in Tanganyika, I had become accustomed over a period of six years to spend long periods in the field, or 'on safari' as it was termed there. In fact, like other Colonial Service officers in the districts, we were enjoined to spend at least twelve days a month on safari. Thus it was quite natural for me to find that Darvall Wilkins, formerly a district officer in Tanganyika, was spending an similar proportion of his time 'on tour' as it was called here, and to follow suit. Anyway, I loved field work and was therefore naturally inclined to give this priority over paper-pushing in the office or pottering endlessly around an agricultural station, as was clearly favoured by some of my colleagues and superiors. By its nature, successful agricultural extension, which basically means the dissemination of help and ideas to farmers, as with district administration demands close and frequent contact with the people in order to engender trust and continuity. Its aim is basically to enable them to farm their land in a sustainable and more profitable way, and so raise their standard of living, and with it the general status of their health. And I speak here of contact with 'the people', since the vast majority

NOWHERE NEAR GREENLAND

of them here in the islands were directly involved in agriculture.

To visit individual farmers on their holdings, discuss its suitability for one or another crop or livestock, examine constraints posed by land, labour, communications and markets, etc., was to look for some way, if at all possible, to assist them in a practical manner. This I would always do in the company of the local agricultural assistant, whose job this also was, in the hope that my example would be followed. Such visits would generally follow a meeting in the village nakamal, quite often in the evenings since farmers like to get out to their fields very early in the morning, and complete the hard physical work before the sun is hot and high in the sky. These meetings were always well attended, often by the whole community, since there were no competing attractions such as television, and very few radios, though church times had to be avoided. At these meetings, I would expound themes topical for the time of year, impart specific information I wanted to get across, such as disease control or agricultural loan opportunities, deplore the generally horrible quality of copra which depressed the price farmers received, and then encourage a general discussion touching on their perceived needs and problems.

I soon learned that New Hebridean farmers were highly individualistic, and that while group demonstrations of some technique or other were useful, they did not share information readily, somewhat holding to the principle that 'knowledge is power', so why dissipate it through sharing and lose the advantage over one's neighbour? Traditionally there were times when a group would get together, as in Africa, to effect some particularly arduous task such as land clearing, or the digging of irrigation channels for the intensive cultivation of taro, and the ones who benefited from this work would reward their neighbours in kind, here with food, in Africa with beer. Otherwise, farmers were quite secretive about what they did on their land and what they planned to do with it, so after my meetings there were always a reticent few waiting for me in the dark outside, to take me aside and sotto voce invite me to visit their farm, or place an order for a Berkshire pig, a Rhode Island Red rooster or a hundred cocoa seedlings. Some of these orders might be delivered on copra trading ships, but more often I took them with me on my next boat trip to the area. Fortunately, the captains of the government touring vessels were most accommodating to me in this respect, though doubtless the redoubtable and recently departed curmudgeonly Captain Kirkwood would have thrown a navy blue fit had I asked him to load a pig aboard! For him you had, at the very least, to remove your shoes to walk his holystoned decks.

To Coral Strands

From the need for evening meetings, it followed that I would often sleep in the villages, though if I was near our boat's anchorage I would sleep aboard. The hospitality of the villagers was touching, since if there was no house specifically reserved for visitors, one of them would vacate a room their own for me. I always carried with me the very basics of simple meals, such as rice, tinned meat, bread and jam. The former would be cooked for me, to which my hosts would invariably add island food such as taro, manioc, kumala, plantain, cabbage and even the awesome laplap, and we would all partake.

Opening of the new Catholic Church at Norsup, 1968

Though often delicious, the latter, a type of pudding made from a variety of root crops or breadfruit, with added coconut cream, has a very high specific gravity, seemingly about that of lead on the periodic table, after swallowing a quantity of which it would perhaps be imprudent to attempt swimming. And one would always be shown the ples blong swim, or washing place, usually a small stream just outside the village, often where it met the sea.

Every village was punctilious about its ablutions, made in the late evening and at dawn, for which there were separate sites for men, and women with their children. As a visitor, one was accorded complete privacy, and at night after a hot and humid day in the field, it would be near idyllic to lie in the flow of a cool stream, lazily lathering oneself and gazing up through palm fronds at the stars. Whether there was ever an impatient queue silently lurking behind bushes nearby, just wishing

NOWHERE NEAR GREENLAND

to hell I would hurry up, I never discovered!

The next day, I might walk on down the coast, possibly after visiting inland villages, and that evening or the next meet up again with the touring vessel. I would also stay at the agricultural assistants' houses, simple abodes of two bedrooms and a living room, walled and partitioned with woven bamboo, with an outside kitchen, pit latrine, a place to shower and a water tank. We built some twenty of these in the islands of my responsibility, shipping to the nearest beaches the materials in kits comprising corrugated iron, cement, dressed timber, ceiling board, gutters, water tank, etc., with the bamboo locally provided. Once, ferrying such a load on a large outrigger canoe, from a point south of Lamap to the Maskelyne Islands, we sank. Fortunately, the cement was destined for the next trip, and pushing and swimming alongside the waterlogged vessel for a mile or two we reached our destination, though the ceiling of the resulting house remained conspicuously warped. In later years, when there were more airstrips in the islands, I was able to make more inter-island flights when no touring vessel was available.

Once, due to poor communications or inadequate preparation, I arrived in the Maskelynes when every single able-bodied man and most of the women had departed elsewhere for a church assembly. My plan had been to take a canoe along the south coast of Malekula to the offshore island of Akhamb, and then on to Milip village and walk round to South West Bay. But there was only one very old man left at Pescarus village, and when I explained my predicament he shook his head, which was, anyway, already shaking with age. Bislama has a very descriptive term for the extremely aged, 'bon bon', meaning bone bone, when all the flesh has shrunk to outline the frame beneath, and this would have well described him. However, he was also shaking his head because he believed his little outrigger was perhaps too humble for me. We went to the place on the beach where it was hauled up high among the beach morning-glory, and it looked fine to me, though judging by the flowering vines swarming all over it, it was clearly quite a while since it had been taken to sea. My own doubt was that maybe he was too frail for the task, but a light south-easterly breeze was blowing to help us along and I accepted his offer to take me. The Maskelynes are the only place in the islands where sails are the rule rather than an exception to propel their outriggers. My captain duly staggered from behind his house, carrying a short mast with an old sail furled around it. Unfurled, it was really beautiful, with a pair of trousers sewn right into its centre.

To Coral Strands

Off we set, just him and me and my rucksack, and the little sail filled. He sat in the stern, steering with a paddle, and I sat on a small wooden bar across the thwarts facing him. We sailed a mile or so off the coast, where dark rain-forest tumbles right down to the shore from a jumble of hills behind, and the villages and beaches are few and far between. It is, in fact, rather a sinister coast, and became more so to me as the old man recounted its history. On that small offshore island, Lanour, uninhabited now and covered in bush, once stood a fine house where a whiteman lived with his island wife and children. From his boat he bought copra along the coast and ran a small trade store. One night, the bush people swam across to the island, murdered them all, stole the trade goods and threw their bodies down a well, where they are to this day. And over there, in the bay where a small creek runs into the sea, mister so-and-so and his partner were at anchor for the night. He went below to light a lamp, the whole boat blew up and they died on the spot. And further on, over there near Faroun, there used to be a village whose people had come down from the interior to live on the coast. They were notorious poisoners and murdered many people, even people on Akhamb island about a mile across the sea from their village. So one day, the people of Akhamb got fed up and went across and killed them all. There used to be many villages along this coast, but the people were all poisoned or died of fever, and now there is just dark bush. With this thin, ancient man, his gnarled hands, weather-worn face and quavering voice, in his little old canoe with the patched sail, one could not help but be reminded of 'The Old Man And The Sea'. It was a great privilege to sail with him the whole of that day, and hear the stories from his childhood and youth at the beginning of the twentieth century. I will not say near-forgotten stories, because the tradition of oral history is still strong in the islands, and I am sure that in the Maskelynes and on Akhamb I could be corrected on details and supplied with names I have forgotten.

While I loved being out in the field and could never have exchanged this life for one of regular office hours, I do admit to having felt occasional flashes of resentment or jealousy when struggling up some wet and god-forsaken hillside on a Saturday or Sunday afternoon, imagining the camaraderie and cool beers at that very moment being enjoyed by the office wallahs in their comfortable homes and clubs in Vila. There was an occasion when I had agreed to help the British district education officer in delivering wages to teachers on Ambrym and Pentecost. On a Friday morning, I radioed the financial controller at the British residency in Vila to ask if the required money could be sent up on the milk run, as the early plane to Malekula was called, on the Saturday morning. "The answer is no. The answer is

NOWHERE NEAR GREENLAND

no", came the very abrupt reply, with no explanation as to why not before he hung up. I was convinced he just couldn't be bothered to go out to the airfield on a Saturday morning. As a result, those teachers probably had to wait until the following month to get paid. The officer in question was renowned for having worked in Vila for several years, without ever setting foot beyond Efate, and would have had no inkling of the practical difficulties we often faced in carrying out our work. When years later I became the Director of Agriculture, I did my best to get myself and my officers out into the field as frequently as possible, for there lay the realities of any situation, often misrepresented or misunderstood from reports. Ensconced in an office, demanding reports and returns to justify a daylong sedentary habit, only limited the time for creative activities by those in the field.

Towards the end of 1968, the Condominium proposed that I should accompany Dr. Valin on a two weeks tour to study tropical pastures and beef production in Queensland. Flying via Noumea we were joined there by some fifteen Caldosh (New Caledonian colons), all cattle ranchers and their veterinarian. Starting in Brisbane, I found myself sharing a room with Dr. Valin. However, this soon led to disagreement, for when we retired for the night Dr. Valin wanted all the widows tight shut and I wanted them wide open; after all it was a hot night and there were no malarial mosquitoes to worry about. But then appreciating that all French like to sleep with the windows closed, seemingly clinging to the ancient belief that night air is evil, I let him have his way. However, I spent a very restless night and, besides, Dr. Valin was a large man seriously inclined to flatulence. So, for the rest of the tour at the various places we visited, Cairns, Makay, Bundaburg, Townsville, the Atherton Tableland, etc., I took a single room at some additional expense to myself; but Dr. Valin was aggrieved.

That we were star-crossed colleagues was confirmed, when a year or so later I was visiting the island of Paama, and discovered at a cooperative that almost all their tins of beef, canned in Vila, were blown. I sent one of these cans back to the assistant director of agriculture, David Allen, with the request that there should be some investigation as to the pathogens responsible and questioned whether there were any problems with the canning process. I was amazed to receive from Dr. Valin, a few days later, a copy of a several pages letter he had despatched to the two resident commissioners, my director and both district agents for CD2. This accused me of a destructive, nationalistic attitude and sabotage against French businesses and enterprise, and he wanted nothing more to do with me! I was astonished. Some year

To Coral Strands

or two later, I visited the same cannery and saw the workers, cigarettes in mouths, pushing boef en gelée into the cans, with ash falling from time to time into the meat. And at least I was considerably cheered by a sense of schadenfreude when I subsequently read of the good doctor's visit to Tahiti to promote New Hebrides canned meat products. The first tin he personally opened within a close circle of interested spectators turned out to be blown, and presumably all then stepped back smartly from the squirting pong!

I had early on met the Bostonian Catholic priest Father Bertrand Soucy at the Walo Rano Mission, a few miles up the coast from Norsup. An advantage of working for the Condominium agricultural service was that it trained and employed equal numbers of francophone and anglophone 'agricultural monitors', who were its grass-roots extension agents in the islands, and this gave me access and acceptability in both francophone and anglophone communities and the opportunity to visit them. This 'entrée' was not shared to the same extent by officers of the British and French national services, who tended to be greeted coolly by those missions that did not share their language. Father Soucy very kindly found us an attractive, very black, blond-haired young lady from Wala Island who would assist my wife in the house, and he duly brought her to the house with the request that we concern ourselves with the protection of her morals. A gene for blondness is often expressed in Melanesians, though arriving from Africa, where this feature is not found among the people, we had first believed it to be the result of bleach from a bottle. This combination of blond hair and black skin is both startling and attractive, and so it was found by the young New Hebridean overseer at the French primary school nearby. He was responsible for starting up the school generator, which also supplied power to our house from 6 p.m. every evening, and he turned it off at 10 p.m. unless someone was having a party. We had housed the young lady in pleasant servant's quarters next to the garage, but after switching off the electricity he adopted the habit of scrambling up through our steep garden to dally a while with her. Such dalliance, as we discovered too late, led to pregnancy, and after admonishing us for our lack of vigilance Father Soucy drove off with her back to the mission. Sadly, this young man died two years later from a heart attack.

While she was still with us, a mature coconut palm was struck by lightning right by the house. The path of the lightning was quite clear on its trunk, and with a trowel she dug where the strike had passed into the ground. She then produced a 'tut blong tunda', or thunder tooth which she said had been created by the light-

NOWHERE NEAR GREENLAND

ning. This was the size of a large molar, of the colour, feel and weight of ivory and was lightly striated. We later collected a couple more from the Wala-Rano area, but eventually lost all of them. People to whom we showed them, hazarded that they were the product of superheated, compressed sap, or possibly they were simply the beaks of parrot fish. They were, and remain to me a complete mystery.

On Friday 13th December 1968 the barometer started to fall, the skies were black and the wind was blowing fitfully from the east. This indicated that the eye of the depression, or cyclone into which it developed, was to the north of us. At lunchtime we strained to hear the weather forecast from Radio Vila, and as the wind began blowing in great gusts we were usefully informed that we should expect showers with bright intervals. Such was pre-satellite meteorology. Father Soucy had brought in his Ford pickup truck for repair by Mr. Migotti, but by late in the afternoon it was still not ready and he was anxious to get back to the mission. I offered to drive him the six miles or so up the coast, along the narrow, twisting, muddy track between the coconut palms. Arriving at Wala, the father gave orders for battening down the mission, and then very kindly offered me Bourbon whisky in his study, where on his desk was the altimeter from a WW2 aeroplane. As the air pressure dropped, so, according to the altimeter, we virtually climbed higher and higher. I believe we were at about 3,000ft, though not quite as high on the Bourbon, when I announced I really ought to head back home. Thus, sufficiently fortified, I drove back through the horizontal blizzard of rain, falling fronds and coconuts in time to help Lesley fortify our own house before the full force of the cyclone struck an hour later.

Dawn revealed that apart from two now prostrate Panama cherry trees - one our parrot's favourite perch - we had not fared too badly. We were faced with a major mopping up operation in the house (glass louvres admit a lot of water when it strikes them horizontally at high pressure), and half the garage roof was missing. The major damage, we soon heard, had been in the south of the island about forty miles away. Tom Layng, seconded from the British Service as chief Cooperatives Officer, was due to tour that area in the 'Mangaru'. He was asked to report on damage to buildings, infrastructure, casualties and morale, and I joined him to assess damage to crops, and what food and planting material assistance might be required. We found that three villages in the Maskelynes had been flattened, including the house I was building at Pescarus for the agricultural monitor - the same one for which I had recently sunk with building materials. Fortunately there were no injuries there or at other centres along the coast, and though morale was low, with many people just sitting around in a daze and not doing much to help themselves, their houses of woven bamboo walls, bush poles and corrugated iron - some of which materials could be collected up and re-used - could soon be rebuilt. I had some disagreement with Tom since I considered that his report, to be sent back by ship's radio to Vila, rather over-dramatised the situation in a grandstanding sort of way. However, there had been serious damage to crops and, as is typical with cylones, sea spray had been blown a mile inland and salt was killing whatever plants the wind had spared.

Lesley introduces Jones to Boudicca. Malekula, 1969

Food aid would be needed for a time, and sweet potato cuttings, which produce a crop relatively quickly, would have to be brought in from unaffected areas.

Not long afterwards, a Catholic priest called at our house one afternoon, asking us to show him on his map the track across to Brenwei on the other, western side of the island, where he intended to celebrate with the magnum of champagne he had with him the birthday of a nun working in the dispensary there. We advised him that not only was it rather late in the day to start across, but that the footpath would frequently be obscured or blocked by fallen trees, as the result of the recent cyclone. Nevertheless, he set out, evidently trusting more in God than our advice. Around lunchtime the following day, he arrived back at our house, much scratched,

NOWHERE NEAR GREENLAND

limping and his clothes torn. He had lost his way and spent the night under a tree, though apparently not too bad a night after downing the magnum and perhaps then singing himself to sleep. But he had lost his camera and suitcase and had had a frightening experience, as anyone who has been bushed will appreciate. But on the morrow, he walked due east towards the rising sun until he reached the boundary of the plantation. Now, how was he to find his camera and suitcase again? Fortunately, there were Big Nambas returning home that day. He accompanied them, and with their expert tracking skills soon found the missing items. A few years later, we heard that the sister, who was reputed to be a German countess, had married a priest, and following summary excommunication had opened a bookshop in New Caledonia. However, whether it was the same priest who had failed on that occasion to celebrate her birthday in a congenial manner, I know not.

One weekend, a party of about ten of us decided to climb to the top of the highest hill behind Lakatoro, whose summit is some sixteen hundred feet above sea-level. We planned to camp at the top and carried the necessary light camping gear and food. The hilltop had been manned by American coast-watchers during World War Two, on the lookout for movements of Japanese ships and planes. Their hut had presumably long disintegrated, and we could find no trace that they had been there, not even an old Spam tin. However, there was still a small grass clearing, which presumably they had made, and an old inhabitant of Litzlitz village told us that the Americans had grown vegetables up there. It was the hot season, but relatively cool at the top, and John Naupa and a couple of others obligingly descended into a nearby valley to fetch water, as we had drunk all of our supplies on the way up. But as dusk fell, we were besieged by clouds of the most enormous and voracious mosquitoes. We had not brought clothing or nets to defend ourselves against this plague, unforeseen so high and far from the coast, nor did we have insect repellent; so we retired early into the part protection of our sleeping bags, arms over faces and spent a rotten night.

The next morning at dawn, towards which we faced, the mosquitoes had all gone and in the eastern sky there was a magnificent comet with a long bright tail. We enjoyed this wholly unexpected spectacle with a very early breakfast, which was as well since once the sun rose, we were newly besieged, this time by a plague of flies. This was again extraordinary as there were no cattle for miles around, just rain-forest, in which roamed a few wild pigs and a number of wild dogs. Anyway, the comet had by then disappeared in the brightening sky, and we were already

To Coral Strands

wearied of brushing the flies from our eyes and mouths, so we hurried back down to sea-level to spend the rest of the weekend in relative comfort. Was there something malign about that summit?

A few years later, when the memory of the flies and mosquitoes had faded, Darvall and I discussed the possibility of establishing a little hill station up there. A sort of mini-Simla perhaps? At least, the all round views were magnificent and it was significantly cooler up there than down by the sea. So one afternoon we set off, and I was to guide Darvall to the top. Mistake number one: like the priest we set off too late. Mistake number two: like the priest we lost the path. Mistake number three: we persevered for too long trying to get to the summit, though it was already clear that we could not get all the way down again before dark. That was enough to put us in serious trouble. Added to that, it was a totally moonless night, the bush was thick and there were sheer drops where the upraised coral reefs met the original limestone mantle of the island. Before long it was absolutely pitch black, like being in a cellar strewn with unidentifiable obstacles, and many times we worked our way into the centre of thickets only to have to back out again. Then we remembered the wild dogs. Hadn't Jack Barley, captain of the m.v. Navaka, recently been treed by them at Lambubu? Was that a distant bark? Or not so far away, perhaps? This was what it was like to be both bushed and blind. Should we stay put until dawn? No, our wives will be worrying. Indeed, Lesley always became extremely anxious whenever I returned later than expected, which stemmed from the death of her first husband, and in fact at this moment she was bravely riding our little Honda 50 motorcycle up a very steep track we had recently cut into the forest, calling out our names, but we heard nothing.

At long last, lower down, we saw the lights of Lakatoro far below, but we could see them only because the hill fell away almost sheer at that point. No way down there. Later, much later, around midnight, we eventually came out of the bush and blundered onto a road which we didn't recognise until we had walked along it for quite a way. At last we stumbled through the back door into Darvall's well-lit kitchen, to find his wife Ida and Lesley waiting for us. We were covered all over in scratches, bruises, torn clothes and twigs. They were furious, of course, but mightily relieved, and somehow the subject of the hill station never arose again.

Another cyclone sprang upon us without warning when I was proceeding up the west coast of Pentecost in George Mitchell's copra boat 'Marum', the regular gov-

NOWHERE NEAR GREENLAND

ernment touring vessels either being out of action or otherwise unavailable. With me was the acting district agent, George Filor, and we had collected a woman suffering from pneumonia at Bwatnapne and were taking her to a dispensary in the north of the island. The winds were already gusting strongly from the north, were moving round to the west, and the seas had rapidly become very rough. We were clearly on the edge of a hurricane, and George Mitchell radioed Oscar Newman to ask him where we could find shelter. Fortunately, after a while we were able to raise him. "There is only one place on that coast", yelled Oscar, "back the way you came, at Loltong. Get behind the reef at Loltong". The seas by then were huge and the wind shrieking, and turning round against the cross-seas was a most hazardous manoeuvre, setting our boat almost on its beam ends. But we made it back, anchoring behind the reef, and the contrasting calm seemed almost miraculous. I then did an Eagle Scout thing, and ran up the coast some miles to Abwatuntora dispensary to fetch antibiotics for our pneumonia patient. It was an exciting trip, mainly through small coconut plantations, with heavy fronds flung at me and nuts thumping down. The medical assistant had closed the dispensary against the storm, but obligingly opened it for me and gave me the needed tablets. (In Britain, I would have been asked, "But where is your prescription?") And then back to Loltong, but with the north-west gale now strong behind me, I practically flew back. George Filor and I were found separate tiny huts near the beach, where we laid up for three days until the seas eased and we could put back out again.

On Malekula, the east coast track from Norsup went south as far as the Pangkumu river, the largest on the island. This had formed a small delta, and divided into several shifting streams before it met the sea, and so was hard to bridge. There are beautiful multicoloured, river-tumbled stones at its mouth, and Lesley and I twice went there to collect them. In mid-1968 she drove me as far as the river, and wading across I walked on down the coast through Tisman and Aulua to Lamap. At Tisman lived the formidable Oscar Newman, where he managed a coconut plantation for a French company, and based his copra trading business for which he had two or three boats plying round the islands. He also bought and then sold boats to the British and French governments. One of those was the district Condominium launch 'Pangkumu', used in alternate two-week periods by the district agents. It had been a Brisbane river boat, apparently for drinking parties, since wherever you were onboard a glass holder awaited within easy reach, and I believe I counted eighteen of them. The captain was a still-inclined-to-be-pugilistic, former boxer named Puyu Festa, and I also occasionally used this boat for touring. Once I was

To Coral Strands

at Tenmaru, waiting with Virhambat, chief of the Big Nambas, and one of his cohorts whom I was going to carry with me to Norsup. The Pangkumu arrived from Santo two days late, and once aboard I had a stand-up row with the captain. This was the first time in his life that Virhambat had ever set foot on a boat, and already nervous and made more so by our altercation, he said that if we carried on like that he wanted to be put back ashore immediately, so rather shamefaced we shut up.

Anyway, on the occasion of my walking down to Lamap, I stayed the night with Oscar, always a genial host who regaled me at dinner with his scurrilous tales of buggery in the church, adultery in high places and wholesale murder, rape and arson among the local populace. Lurid deeds were ascribed to Oscar, and perhaps this was his way of attempting to level the playing field. He also recounted how he kept ahead of the game in the keen competition of copra trading. He radioed false positions of his ships, and transmitted messages of there being huge amounts of copra to pick up where there were none, and none where there was plenty, and had his competitors steaming in all directions. Once married to a white Australian lady, he now had a number of New Hebridean wives, each ensconced in her own solidly built and well-equipped little bungalow on the property. Allegedly for forcing himself on one of his younger wives too soon after she had born him a child, she decided to poison him, and according to the doctor in Vila who treated Oscar when he became very unwell and all his hair fell out, she had given him sufficient thallium rat poison to kill several horses. However, once out of hospital alive, and throughout her prison sentence, which she served as the cleaner at the rest house at Lakatoro, he brought her gifts of food and home comforts.

John of Blacksands, the latter being a small village just north of the Pangkumu River, was an enterprising New Hebridean, a small businessman who had long had bad relations with Oscar, almost certainly over women as they did not live far from one another. The last time I saw him at his house, he was lying in bed with a grossly swollen testicle upon which someone unnamed, he said, had invoked nakaimas - black magic. One day in the 1970s, John was in Luganville looking for a lift back home the day Oscar was setting off in the m.v.'Tisman' and he took John aboard. Somewhere off Malo, they fell into an argument and a while later John went overboard. A witness told me how he had heard a shout and a splash, and saw the lighted torch John was holding wavering down and down in the dark water. A few weeks later, Pierre Theuil and Charles Savoie, whose enmity with Oscar went way back, claimed they had heard John had swum ashore on Malo.

NOWHERE NEAR GREENLAND

Whether they started the rumour or not, which persisted for some weeks, there was nothing to it, though Oscar was said to have been greatly discomforted. Not long afterwards, Oscar suffered his own tragedy on the same boat. Sleeping on the hatches with his family, on a hot night and calm seas while travelling south from Santo, the 'Tisman' hit a freak wave. Far too late they discovered a toddler had rolled overboard and a prolonged search failed to find the child. Shortly before Independence in 1980, Oscar was under siege on his plantation from those who claimed customary ownership to the land. Eventually an angry mob gathered, Oscar was prevented from firing upon it by Jerry Marston, the then British district agent at Lakatoro, and was forcibly evacuated under armed guard. Transported to Vila, Oscar died there about two years later.

This time, on my walking tour, when I reached Lamap I paid a courtesy call on Monsieur Boileau, the French district agent, in whose chambre de passage I was to spend the night. However, I found the FDA and his wife at home, ears glued to the radio, listening to news of the riots and demonstrations in Paris that brought down the de Gaulle presidency and government in that August of 1968. In the evening, however, they broke their vigil and we played tennis on a floodlit court. Returning to Norsup, I immediately went down with an attack of rheumatic fever, my first since leaving Africa, and was out of action for several days.

Unlike some of his people who came down to Norsup to cut copra, Chief Virhambat proudly wore his nambas (penis sheath) and nothing else wherever he went. I had invited Virhambat to always stay with us when he came to Norsup, and he greatly preferred that to staying in one of the little tin huts at Aop. Since her Panama Cherry tree had been blown down in the cyclone, and Boudicca had greatly alarmed everyone by flying out onto the reef, then to the top of a giant banyan tree, and subsequently from branch to branch from which she was eventually grabbed, loudly squawking, by one of a mob of totally inebriated Gilbertese, we had taken to keeping her on our newly built, screened veranda. Virhambat greatly admired our parrot and coveted her red tail feathers, so he was delighted to sleep on the veranda with her and his customary bodyguard.

In 1969, my mother, then seventy-three, came to stay with us at Norsup. One morning, Virhambat who had stayed overnight joined us at breakfast. Sitting in his nambas, a picture of dignity next to my mother, he perfectly disposed of his cornflakes, bacon and eggs, wielding the cutlery as to the manner born, but was clearly sus-

To Coral Strands

picious of the sausage. It would have been a good photo opportunity, but might have spoilt the moment, as I knew the chief did not regard sympathetically those tourists who climbed up to his home village of Amok to focus lenses on their nambas and bare-breasted women.

While my mother was staying with us, we attended an evening dance at a small thatched hall in neighbouring Tautu village. The name given to the then popular style of shuffling your feet absolutely flat on the floor, while pumping your partner's arm up and down as though signalling in semaphore, was 'Texas dancing'. This, to the romantic crooning of Gentleman Jim Reeves, or the slow and lugubrious lyrics of country and western singers, was accompanied by incessant loud clicks and pops from the girls, almost all of whom would be chewing bubble gum; so one's memory is of the shhh-shhing of the feet and their percussive accompaniment. Many such dances were given in the Lakatoro Metemet club and none was ever considered a success unless it 'kasim daelaet' (kept going until daylight) around five a.m.

In the course of my work I did not have much cause to visit the custom villages on the islands of Pentecost, Ambrym and Malekula, since their people were completely self-sufficient in their need for food, both from crops and livestock. They supplemented the growing of yams and taro, and the rearing of domesticated pigs and fowls, by maintaining traditional hunter-gatherer activities. They hunted and trapped pigeons, flying fox, wild pigs and even rats, and gathered many species of fruit, nuts and other edible plants growing wild in the forest, as well as wild honey and a species of termite scooped from the hollowed out, dead branches of trees (which I tentatively tried; very acid!). Freshwater prawns were three prong speared in mountain streams, and people living near the coast hunted fish - on Pentecost with bow and arrow. This was the way all the people of the islands had once lived. Those that still did so, for the main part living in the hills and away from malarial mosquitoes, generally enjoyed better health than the people down on the coast. These had been rapidly converted to religion, and diets based on rice, sugar, sweet biscuits, and tinned meat and fish, which they paid for with their labour and the growing of cash crops; they also paid with fever and diabetes. However, for limited periods custom people would also cut copra on the plantations in order to buy basic consumer items, such as kerosene for lamps, matches, salt and stick tobacco.

NOWHERE NEAR GREENLAND

The most remote of the custom people are the Small Nambas living in the high, rugged, forested terrain in the centre of south Malekula. In the 1960s their numbers could still be counted in hundreds, but by the 1990s were down to a mere dozen or two, the rest having moved down to the coast, now at least sartorially missionised and wearing skirts and shorts. Lesley visited them in 1970, together with the anthropologist Jean-Michel Charpentier and Claudia Huffman, travelling up the Pangkumu river from the east as far as Yabogatas village.

The previous year, the Small Nambas had been visited by Kal Muller who was taking photographs for an article in the National Geographic magazine. He had climbed up from South West Bay where, he wrote mysteriously, he heard rumours of people living in the interior!

Claudia Huffman among the Small Nambas. Malekula, 1970

This route is by far the toughest, crossing a whole series of steep lateral valleys, switchbacking up a thousand feet, down a thousand feet for hour after hour. I followed that track in 1972 when I went up with Earl Dorney, the Tasmanian doctor at Lakatoro. The two agricultural field assistants who accompanied us, carried two roosters and a young female pig to widen the gene pool of the Small Nambas' isolated livestock, as well as packets of various vegetable seeds such as Chinese cabbage, pumpkin, beans and tomato. The Small Nambas guide who escorted us from

To Coral Strands

the coast had two fingers missing from his right hand. Two years previously he had been carrying a small pig along this same track in the interior, when he was ambushed and shot at close range by a man with whose wife he had been dallying. He lost his fingers and the pig in his arms was killed. That he was able to make his escape was probably because the assailant's gun was typically an old muzzle loader. Now, nearing the first Small Nambas village, our guide exchanged cheerful greetings with a man on the path, the first we had met since leaving the coast. Afterwards, he told us that this was the same man who had shot him. Evidently, honour had been satisfied. In Yabogatas village and in a hamlet nearby, Earl carried out a health check and distributed pills, while I presented the pig, rooster and seeds to the chief and carried out an informal nutrition survey.

Twelve years later the prime minister, Father Walter Lini, making his first visit to the area, invited me to join his party which included three of his ministers and several other members of parliament. I advised that we should follow the much easier river valley route up the Pangkumu from the east. However he was adamant that we should start from South West Bay and return the same way. Some twelve of us duly set off through the forest and slogged up and down the helter skelter steep track, whose surface for the most part was slippery red clay. In the late afternoon, by which time I had been liberally dishing out glucose tablets to our flagging delegation, we could hear rhythmic drumming coming from way ahead and far above us. Then, while we were taking a rest, which we were doing at increasingly frequent intervals, an emissary from Lundumbwe, the capital of the Small Nambas for which were heading, came down to impart the good news that all was ready for our ceremonial entry into the village; the bad news, was that upon arrival we were all expected to participate in a custom dance of welcome.

Muddy and tired, we clambered up the last few hundred feet to the settlement, where the chief, in full regalia of feathers and pigs' tusks, gave each of us a decorative necklace. As he did so, we peeled off left to join the circular dance around an ensemble of slit gongs, whose drummers accompanied our rhythmic shuffling and stamping with their own dirge-like chanting. Round and round and round we went in the gathering gloom, and we were grateful indeed when a great ground oven was opened up, and steaming, fragrant laplap leaves were unwrapped to reveal our meal of pork, taro, yams and plantain. Quite absent from the pork here was the blubbery excess of fat, which almost totally excludes lean meat on pigs fed on coconuts at the coast. Later, we all retired replete to a leaf hut built specially for

NOWHERE NEAR GREENLAND

our visit, where a thick layer of leaves had been laid to soften the hard ground. However, we were immediately joined there by at least fifteen village dogs, who evidently also appreciated the comfort, but had us scratching away all night at their vagrant fleas. We came down the following day, for much of which largely gravity-assisted exercise I was in the sole company of Sethy Regenvanu and Father Walter Lini, and once we were at a lower altitude and encountered coconut palms along the track, the prime minister demonstrated his expertise in opening green coconuts for us to drink.

The Big Nambas lived on a high plateau in the north west of Malekula, and their main settlement, Amok, was cunningly defended by a maze of paths lined on either side by thick hedges of impenetrable cane. A guide was essential to find the centre of the village. I first went up there in 1968, and was treated to new culinary experiences, such as navisu, the flowering head of a tall grass cooked in a bamboo cylinder. Less delicious was the acrid, bright pink flesh of fruit bat, or flying fox, thrown whole onto the fire in the communal nakamal and cooked fur, guts and all. And perhaps even more daunting was the kava, chewed and spat into bowls by youths, the strainings of which were then ceremoniously handed to one to drink. Giving one at least temporary pause, was the knowledge that tuberculosis was quite common in these traditional communities. I also spent a memorable night in the tiny hut deemed a rest house, but proving rest-less since the surface of the sleeping platform consisted of un-split giant bamboo stems, laid lengthwise. Reclining upon a sheet of corrugated iron, lacking the raised nodes of the bamboo, would arguably have been more comfortable.

('Nambas' is the name for the penis sheath. There is no physiological difference between the big and small nambas people, only that the sheath of the former is more elaborate, with a bunch of deep purple fibre tucked under a wide leaf belt.)

The drink of kava, traditional in many South Pacific islands, is obtained from the many-branching roots of the shrub Piper methysticum. Though once commonly chewed for its preparation, this practice is now strictly limited to a few custom villages in Vanuatu, and elsewhere the fresh or dried roots are ground, usually in hand-cranked machines or in the villages with a chunk of abrasive coral. Water is then mixed with the mash, squeezed and strained through coconut fibre and the liquid is ready to drink. It then has the colour of grey mud, but is of a somewhat thinner consistency with an earthy, bitter taste, which explains all the hawking and spitting that inevitably follows swallowing it. One attempts to down all it in one go without breathing, as with, say, a less than fresh oyster, quinine or castor oil. Physiologically it is non-addictive, and while no-one enjoys the taste, it is easy to adopt the social habit for the quiet and restrained camaraderie of the nakamal, and the combined effects of the analgesic, soporific and anaesthetic properties, to mention just a few, which induce a very pleasant, tranquil state. Over-indulgence goes to the legs rather than the head, and while perambulation might be impaired, there is no way anyone in that state will resort to argument or violence.

Round and around we went in the gathering gloom. Lundumbwe, 1984

The Presbyterian missionaries and some other denominations were quick to condemn its use as heathen, but the Catholic and Anglican prelates were as quick to take up the habit of drinking it themselves, some of them several shells a day (kava is traditionally drunk from the half shell of a coconut) for fifty years with no negative side effects save a minor flakiness of the skin.

NOWHERE NEAR GREENLAND

Lesley also went up to Amok in the same year to do some sketching. This coincided with the visit of a red-haired American anthropologist who, with the somewhat naive idea of better blending into the background, wore only nambas and ended up with a burned backside that would have been the envy of any troop of self-respecting baboons. In the late 1970s, the French built a road to Amok, by then almost the only remaining Big Nambas village still living in custom. But this served only to accelerate the migration of its people down to the coast, leaving Chief Virhambat and his family almost the sole occupants. He died a few years later and now the plateau and its villages are deserted.

Two of Lesley's pictures from her trip to the Big Nambas. Amok 1970

Lesley, who had been at art school in New Zealand, took up painting again, mainly in oils and pastel. Her strength in figure painting was an excellent grasp of anatomy and musculature, and she took up the challenge of depicting the local people, skilfully interpreting the modified play of light on black skin. Her only 'landscape' showed coconut palms bowed and their fronds streaming in a cyclone. That painting is now in Scotland, as is one of two superb drawings of old Chief Teinmal of Ambrym and his son, Tofor, for which she made sketches when we attended Tofor's grade taking ceremony in Fanla in 1969. Lesley held two or three very successful exhibitions in Vila and sold every one of her works, many of which went to France.

To Coral Strands

An exception was an oil painting of a Big Nambas man which she presented to the Cultural Centre in Port Vila and which mysteriously disappeared some years ago.

The largest custom village in the district was Bunlap, above the south-east coast of Pentecost. Then presided over by the charismatic and humorous Chief Bong, it occupies a commanding position above Bay Barrier, where the rugged, heavily forested land tumbles steeply down to an arc of white sand beach. This is the weather coast, or 'big sea' side, where waves from the whole width of the Pacific crash against the reefs, roar through blow holes, and throw ashore all manner of flotsam. Like Maewo, the similarly high, long and narrow island immediately to the north, it enjoys deluging rainfall and abounds in waterfalls and cascades.

Humorous Chief Bong of Bunlap carrying water in bamboo.

South East Pentecost, 1969

Bunlap adjoins the Bay Barrier Catholic mission, where visiting boats need to negotiate a narrow channel between the reef and a sand bar at the very top of the tide to gain safe anchorage. By long-established agreement with the mission, the men cover their nambas with a pair of shorts and women cover their breasts, when they cross over the mission land that straddles the path to their village. As Bong

NOWHERE NEAR GREENLAND

remarked, this was a one-sided agreement, and to be fair, the priest and his flock should remove their trousers and dresses when crossing over his land. He was not above discussing fate and philosophy with the priest of the day, whose parishioners, he pointed out, suffered just as much from stomach ache and being struck by lightning as his own people. An outstanding feature of the village was the central midden, where one clambered onto a high lattice of hardwood poles to do one's business above a squirming morass, in which pigs happily rooted and grunted. It could be that women had their own separate amenity, but somehow on that detail I could not bring myself to enquire of Margaret Jolly, the charming Australian anthropologist working there at the time.

From Bunlap, I once walked the length of the east coast of Pentecost to the north, perhaps a distance of twenty miles, in the company of two of my agricultural field assistants. For long stretches of the way there are no tracks, and where the reef or beach do not provide a path, or high headlands plunge sheer into the sea, detours up steep hillsides through bush and rainforest have to be made. We arrived in the late afternoon at one of the few and far separated villages on this coast and were warmly welcomed. It was a beautiful setting, with a clear stream tumbling over cascades from the hills behind, and running out over golden sand into a shallow lagoon behind the reef. In the evening we were entertained with kava in the sago-palm thatched nakamal. Near the entrance was a wood fire, whose flickering light threw moving patterns on the leaf roof above us, and fitfully lit the celebrants sitting quietly on low benches where it met the ground. One by one, stooping with respect as we approached the kava-maker and his bowl, we accepted our half coconut shell of the bitter grey liquid, and having drunk it returned to our places on the bench and thought quiet thoughts in the gloom.

Later, leaving the nakamal after two shells of kava, I noticed a tall, rusty gas cylinder standing next to the fire. Attached to it by a piece of wire was a short length of pipe. So, as I had seen in other villages, this served as the village bell, to be clanged whenever the occasion demanded. Passing close to it, I idly shook the cylinder and the liquid gas sloshed about inside. It was full. The village headman had followed me outside and he explained that the bottle had been washed ashore some years before. As the wheel valve at its top had almost corroded away, and its heavily rusted side was warm from the fire, I explained that their bell was a potential bomb that could explode at any time, and suggested that I might attempt to empty it next day.

To Coral Strands

Thus, early the next morning, we very carefully carried the heavy cylinder to the shore and slowly rolled it down the beach and into the quiet water of the lagoon. Watched by all the people of the village gathered along the beach, and armed with a hammer and a short length of leaf spring to act as a cold chisel, I waded out into the lagoon pushing this unexploded bomb before me. As the prevailing wind was from the sea, I had already ordered that there should be no fires or lighting of pipes in the village until I gave the all clear. I then began gently tapping the valve, trusting that as it lay half in the water and the chisel was wet, I would strike no sparks.

The village gas gong. North east Pentecost, 1970

Suddenly the whole corroded top of the valve snapped off, and the bomb became a torpedo. It shot off at high speed, jet propelled by the high pressure gas roaring out behind it. Then, deflected by small waves in the outer part of the lagoon, it changed direction, then changed again and charged back towards shore. The crowd which had been gleefully clapping, whooping and jumping up and down, now began a rapid and disorderly retreat to higher ground, while I warily watched the unguided missile, knowing that in the water I couldn't outrun it but might just dodge it. However, before it reached me or the shore, and possibly because accumulating ice in the valve deflected the jet, it took to zooming in circles, then, finally

NOWHERE NEAR GREENLAND

as the gas ran out, swizzling round and round like a catherine wheel before it lay quiet and still on the water. As the gas slowly drifted ashore I followed after it, pushing the now exhausted cylinder before me. Many hands came to help return the village bell to its former pride of place in the nakamal, which was effected once we had ensured no traces of gas remained inside it. The wire and pipe were reattached and the villagers then took turns at clanging the cylinder which, they averred, now had a higher and sweeter note than before.

The hazards of gas had three times marked my earlier life. As a toddler, I had stood on the head of my bed, and reached up to turn on the gas tap that had once fuelled light to the bedroom at our house in Abbots Langley. Fortunately it was summer, the windows were open and my father came upstairs to see if my sister and I were properly tucked in, and turned off the hissing gas before we came to any harm. Then in Malaya, I moved into a newly completed house, the first I had occupied that was not a bungalow. A new gas refrigerator was delivered and fitted. That night there was a clamorous thunderstorm, one bang seeming right overhead. Then I heard my Chinese cook, who slept next to the kitchen shouting "Ayor! Ayor!", and as smoke billowed up towards me I ran down the stairs to find him dashing around the kitchen, extinguishing with a flailing apron burning curtains, dishcloths and smouldering cupboard doors. The copper pipe carrying gas from the bottle outside had been cracked during installation. The kitchen had filled with gas, which was then ignited by the kerosene refrigerator's pilot light. I ordered an electric replacement the very next day.

More recently in Norsup, the gas cylinder ran out while Lesley was cooking dinner. I rolled a new one from the garage and stood it upright outside the kitchen door, but I could not unscrew the steel protective cap over the wheel valve. This cap had a hole running right through it, into which I then passed a large screwdriver to turn it, but as I did so it somehow also opened the valve. As the gas rushed out, it quickly formed a block of ice over the cover, and there was then no way I could remove it to turn off the tap. While I quickly extinguished the light on the nearby kerosene refrigerator, Lesley sped to the bathroom to turn off the water heater there. Then we separately ran to our neighbours to warn them to take similar precautions. It was a large cylinder and it took about half an hour to empty itself. There was little wind and we stood at a distance waiting for the gas cloud to disperse. Afterwards we had a cold supper.

To Coral Strands

More tragically, not long after I had been transferred to Vila, a great friend of ours was involved in a fatal accident with gas. Chris Weaver was a brilliant young administrative officer in the British service, still in his twenties, lively with a sharp mind, a great wit and a devout Catholic. At Tagabe, with Kirk Huffman working the camera, we had started shooting 'double over backwards' films. In other words, you carried out the actions backwards and then projected the film in reverse. Thus in one simple take, I walked backwards around the lawn dragging the lawnmower. Reversing the action for projection, this showed me mowing the lawn forwards, but leaning back, stiff armed at a ridiculous angle, legs moving strangely and turning corners in a very weird manner. Then, to practise the opening of a more elaborate scene we were developing, we filled our mouths with pieces of apple, started the camera and then fished out the pieces one by one with a spoon and placed them on an empty plate. This was also most amusing when played backwards. However, the full scene we were devising was to show us repeating this at a picnic on the beach, and then running backwards fully clothed into the sea and disappearing beneath the surface. Back the other way, we would emerge miraculously dry from the water, run up the beach with a most peculiar gait and then strangely manipulate food, including fish, into our mouths. In a previous take we would have cast the fish from one of the plates into the sea. We also practised drinking backwards, that is squirting water from our mouths into a glass and then running it backwards. This also we found hilarious. Then during this totally original, creative and artistic endeavour, Chris was summarily despatched to Santo to prepare and supervise an election and for his stay he rented an apartment from a local expatriate. But there was a slow leak of gas from a cylinder within the house and when he returned one evening from drinking kava, undressed and proceeded to light a mosquito coil. the whole house blew up. Chris died from his burns about ten days later in a Sydney hospital.

At the time of his death, Chris was betrothed to Vicky Haywood who had come out to the New Hebrides to be with him and undertook a number of short term assignments for the British administration in Vila. During my next leave in the UK, I was invited to spend the weekend with her parents, General and Mrs Haywood who lived at Chartwell Lodge in Kent. Memories of that stay include a private visit to Winston Churchill's former home, and late one evening hearing the sweet sound of a piano drifting across the garden from the house next door, where lived the great and by then retired Australian pianist Eileen Joyce. I had attended a concert she gave at the Bournemouth Winter Gardens in about 1949, when dressed all in

NOWHERE NEAR GREENLAND

white she played Grieg's piano concerto, and then Beethoven's Emperor concerto for which she wore deep red. During a crescendo towards the end of the first movement of the latter piece, a piano string broke and jangled with adjacent strings. During a brief pause for the piano, Eileen Joyce attempted to pull it clear before the music demanded her re-entry. She succeeded, clearly using some force, which was both dramatic and disquieting for the orchestra and audience who greatly feared she might injure her hands. I was with my mother and sisters in the front row, and a red rose from the bouquet, with which she was presented at the end of the concert, fell near my feet. This I retrieved, and treasured until it was eventually claimed by natural disolution.

During an early leave from the New Hebrides, in the early 1970s, which Lesley and I spent mostly between London and Salisbury, we were due to spend the weekend at the house of a friend of her brother-in-law, a fellow psychiatrist who lived in Stratford-upon-Avon. We had been told that there would be tennis, so on that Friday afternoon, still holding Harrods in high esteem from my good experience with their piano in the 1950s, I entered their establishment to purchase a racket. Having made my selection, I proposed to pay by cheque on my bank in Dorset. I was then asked for my banker's card. I explained that I lived on an island in the South Pacific and had never owned or heard of such a thing. So the assistant said, "Let's see if we can help you, sir. Let me take you to meet our chief accountant". Climbing somewhere up into, or possibly among, the gods of Harrods, we met this elderly, kindly, almost Dickensian figure in a black coat and high winged collar, the chief accountant no less. Of course they would like to assist me. Was there perhaps someone he could ring to vouch for my identity? I suggested my mother, but explained that she no longer bore the same name as myself. He telephoned the number I gave him and the brief conversation I overheard went something like this: "Lady Venning? Good afternoon, this is the Chief Accountant of Harrods...... yes..... yes, thank you my lady, I have your son here, Barry Weightman......yes..... yes of course I will......... yes indeed, and thank you kindly, Lady Venning, goodbye." And then to me: "That was indeed your mother. She asked me to tell you that you have left behind a pair of old grey socks and she is sending them on." Mothers!

We had started this leave travelling by ship from Sydney to Singapore, and then visited old rubber planting friends of mine in Malaysia. From there we flew to Bangkok where we were lucky not to be in a neighbouring hotel that was consumed by fire one night, killing many foreign tourists. We went on to Bombay, and

To Coral Strands

were intrigued to note that the miles of giant sewer pipes lying on the surface, awaiting interment across low-lying and evil-smelling land between the airport and the city, had families living in them at either end, and we wondered if there were perhaps more families living further inside the pipes. Coming into the city at night and new to India, we were aghast to see how many thousands slept in the street, on car roofs, under cars and on charpoys in shop doorways. And when we were taken to a high point near the main hospital to admire the lights of the city, the small park into which we attempted to step was so completely carpeted with sleeping people, we retired immediately to our waiting Ambassador taxi.

From there we went on to Rome, where I arrived with acute conjunctivitis. Our Australian travel agent in Sydney, a charming Mr. Reid, who was more than ninety years old, had booked us into a top hotel in the Via Venitto. Almost blind, I was led by Lesley into its splendour, where we were told the staff were all on strike. We could stay there, but would have to make our own beds. and the restaurant was closed. However, as a great concession, we could order sandwiches. This we did, though due to language difficulties our order created some puzzlement, discussion and shrugging of shoulders between the two loyal staff, scabs or whatever they were. We had imagined one sandwich to be a small triangle of bread, such as eaten with a slice of cucumber at a game of croquet. Instead, a tottering tower of huge rounds of bread was delivered to our door, the bearer of which departed laughing and shaking his head. These kept us going for the next two days, though when we left, we put the surplus of at least half of them in the wardrobe. For the first of these days I lay in the dark with antibiotic and a cool bandage on my eyes. On the second day I was able to see well enough to visit the Vatican museum. After many galleries, we had reached a small modern one and were studying delicate Egyptian artefacts in their brightly lit glass cases, when two archetypal American tourists arrived at its entrance. They looked around and then consulted their guide-book to the museum. "Say," the man addressed the gallery's guard, "is this the Sistine Chapel?"

On Ambrym, the island of alleged sorcerers with their dread art of 'nakaimas', or black magic, feared throughout the islands of the New Hebrides, only one custom village had survived into the 1960s. This was Fanla, on the lower slopes of the volcano overlooking the north coast. Here, Teinmal, a small, bent and wiry old man with a large nose, was chief, and Tofor his tearaway son, with a reputation for witchcraft, murder and a penchant for wearing heavy wrap-around shades, was

NOWHERE NEAR GREENLAND

his heir. In 1969, when Teinmal possibly believed he was not long for this world, he decided to raise his son to the grade of Mal, the highest level in the customary grade system, and preparations were put underway for the ceremonial killing of a large number of pigs. A lofty, pulpit-like dais was raised above the 'nasara', or dancing-ground, in the centre of the village, beside which stood a collection of slit gongs. Hollowed out from logs through a long narrow slit, each was crowned by the huge-nosed head and wide, red-circled eyes that characterise Ambrym slit gongs, though here also bearing the carved crossed hands unique to gongs made for the chief. These instruments ranged from the tallest on the island, perhaps over ten feet high, which when struck with a heavy stick would emit a deep, echoing boom, to smaller ones, only a yard high which gave out a sharp clack. On the day of the ceremony the dance ground, dais and slit gongs were bedecked with red hibiscus flowers. Tofor's head was shaved, and into his scalp had been hammered hundreds of small, sharpened wedges fashioned from the basal part of giant fern fronds. Foreign guests had been invited, and Lesley and I had travelled overnight from Sarmette on Malekula to Ambrym with a dozen friends on the 'Baleine Noire' an elegant black yacht belonging to an American named John Houston Sussex. It was a sultry black night of rain and constantly changing light winds, so sails were soon lowered and we motored the rest of the way. However, the cabin and cockpit of the yacht quickly filled with the grey fog of diesel fumes, and everyone aboard, including Captain Sussex, was copiously sick.

Once ashore, the steep walk up to Fanla somewhat cleared our heads, and we joined the small crowd clustered around the nasara. Tofor, resplendent in garlands of flowers beneath his strange and cruel skullcap of spikes, mounted the dais and loudly harangued the assembly at length in the local language. Then, with the killing of his first pig (the rest would follow later) with an ornate pig hammer, the drumming, singing and dancing commenced. Often dancing solo, old Teinmal was the star. Rejuvenated, he leapt and stamped and whirled like a dervish, arms spread wide, the heavy circles of pigs tusks around both arms, and the great triton shells in his hands increasing his speed and momentum as he circled the nasara to the thunder and clacks of the drums. He truly danced with all his might. That over, he withdrew to one side and quietly smoked his long-stemmed clay pipe while younger dancers took his place. Lesley made a very beautiful drawing of Teinmal in that repose, and also one of Tofor with his hammered scalp. Just two months later Teinmal passed away.

To Coral Strands

Encircled by Protestant, Catholic and Seventh Day Adventist villages, Tofor increasingly felt that Fanla, and the age-old traditions of the island it represented, were under siege. With the creation of local councils in the 1970s, he felt further excluded from power and influence beyond the confines of his own village.

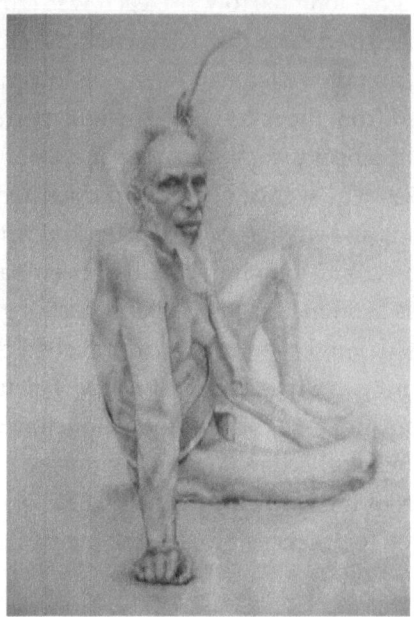

Chief Teinmal of Fanla
relaxes after dancing.
Drawing by Lesley Weightman
Ambrym Island, 1969

With the growing political awareness and ambitions among the majority of New Hebrideans, the French administration was inclined to woo that small fraction of the population that held fast to custom, since with little or no formal education and scant knowledge of the outside world, they would surely be the very last to demand independence. Thus, despite his reputation, they strongly supported Tofor to be the sole representative of the country's chiefs in the recently created Representative Assembly, the great majority of whom had long been converted with their people to one sect or another of Christianity. However, he failed to be elected, and increasingly frustrated, considerably increased his consumption of red wine. Then one day in 1975, he decided to take affirmative action to demonstrate his power and authority over the people of Ambrym.

With Jerry Marston, assistant British district agent at Lakatoro, we were aboard the 'Rocinante' and had just completed a visit to West Ambrym. Rounding Dip Point,

NOWHERE NEAR GREENLAND

where in 1913 the volcano had completely destroyed the Presbyterian hospital and village, consigning them both to deep water, we were headed for a visit to North Ambrym. Soon after rounding the point, we encountered crowded canoes being paddled strongly in our direction, and then on past us to the west. Then more and more canoes as we proceeded, men and women straining over flashing paddles, their children's' tousled heads just visible above the thwarts. Probably a bigfala lafet in West Ambrym, we thought, maybe an important marriage, but they must be late because they are all paddling like hell! Then, as we spied our landfall at Fonah, there gathered on the narrow beach and on into the coconuts beyond was a huge crowd. Chief Willie Bongmatur of Magam Presbyterian village, recently Tofor's rival and victor in the election to the Representative Assembly, was at the forefront of the crowd at the water's edge. We dropped anchor. Jerry was in his bunk going down with flu and I went ashore in the dinghy. Certainly the crowd didn't seem hostile. Excited, perhaps, but apparently quite eager to see me.

As I stepped onto the sand, Chief Willie immediately explained the situation to me. For several days, Tofor had being going round to each and every village in North Ambrym, swearing on his manhood, unnaturally sustained in a near-perpendicular posture by his nambas, to cause fire and brimstone to rain from the volcano upon the heads of all the people. The volcano would in fact detonate and destroy them all, their villages, their crops and their livestock. There would be complete and utter devastation. Even now he was in communion with the spirits of the volcano, and very soon this would all come to pass. His accredited powers of sorcery lent considerable weight to his words and explicit body language, and hence all the canoes fleeing the area. Chief Willie said stoutly he didn't believe a word of it himself, but would the government please straight away send a police patrol to arrest Tofor and remove him, before the people were stirred to even greater panic and the volcano exploded - quite possibly by sheer coincidence. I said I would go back to the boat and immediately radio David Browning, the acting British district agent at Lakatoro, to relay his and the people's disquiet and urgent request. I duly raised David, and on hearing my account he roared and roared with laughter. He didn't believe a word of it, because by rotten luck, Sod's and Murphy's law combined, it was April 1st! I then managed to get Jerry to the radio to croak his corroboration of my report, and to tell David we were setting off immediately back to Lakatoro, as our boat might be needed to transport an arresting patrol to Ambrym. Back on the beach I assured Willie that help would soon be at hand and we departed.

To Coral Strands

Constables were quickly collected from Lakatoro and Lamap for a joint British and French police exercise, and they climbed up to Fanla to arrest Tofor the following day. He was nowhere to be seen; but he saw them, from the top of a tree and stayed up there until they had all sailed off again. A few days later the joint force tried again, approaching the coast out of sight of Fanla. This time they were able to arrest Tofor in his village. So they set off with him down the steep path to the coast and the waiting boat. He was in the middle of the single file of police, and halfway down, according to the constable immediately behind him, Tofor spun round, gave a terrifying yell and disappeared - we presume into the thick bush at the side of the path, though the constable and his colleagues believed this was quite patently an example of the paranormal. A week or so later, third time lucky, Tofor was arrested in a night raid and transported to Vila where he spent some time in prison, presumably for spreading alarm and despondency on a truly ambitious scale. He died in Fanla in the mid-eighties, probably from cirrhosis of the liver.

It was on the Condominium vessel 'Rocinante' that I did most of my touring in the islands. Captain Guenet was just ending his time when I arrived, and I believe I had only one enjoyable trip with him before Majie Bochenski took over from him and captained this ship until I left in 1986. Majie was a small, wiry Pole with a shock of short white hair, a boyish grin and heavily accented English. He was born in Vladivostock and had only recently enlisted in the Polish navy when war broke out in 1939. He and his ship evaded the Germans and he served with great distinction in the free Polish navy throughout the war. He was awarded their highest distinction for bravery, following an action in which a group of torpedo boats under his command sank or damaged, without loss to themselves, a number of German E boats. After a long period of piloting in the Middle East after the war, partnership on a trading vessel brought him to the New Hebrides in 1960. Majie was a fine seaman and navigator, and he was also very cautious, a quality that must have kept him off many a reef. His faithful and long serving crew would lightly make fun of him when he ordered soundings to commence when the Rocinante was still far offshore, and I remember how distressed he was when the bows very lightly touched a shoaling sandbar off Sakau in the Maskelynes.

I often shared the four-berth cabin with other touring officers, though as a regular customer I always had the same bunk, the top one on the starboard side where there was a small sliding window, from which I could peer out at the sea and passing islands. Meals were taken at a table on the deck of the wide stern, and while

NOWHERE NEAR GREENLAND

eating one could always give a hopeful tug at one of the lines being trawled astern. The cook, and perhaps Majie himself, had some bizarre or perhaps merely avant-garde ideas of what victuals to combine on the plate. Thus boiled carrots and sauerkraut with a fried egg in the middle was always something of a surprise breakfast, and fresh tuna with tinned spaghetti seemed original, but there was always ample food, hot and on time, or ready whenever one returned from a long hike, wet, tired and hungry well after any scheduled mealtime. A French colleague once asked me to join him in an official letter of complaint about the food, but I had absolutely no complaints to make. As a navigator, the stars were Majie's trusted friends, and he shared his knowledge of them with me while we sailed at night through calm seas, or when the Rocinante lay gently rocking at anchor. The planets were his delight, and I remember him waking me in the early hours of one morning to see a conjunction of four of them in the western night sky. In all the years I sailed with him, his ship and passengers were never at risk, or if they were he never let on. Majie died in 1990 soon after his retirement.

It was during my mother's visit to Norsup that the plantation's Gilbertese labour decided to go on strike, though she was by no means the cause. They had recently arrived from Ocean Island to find their assigned living quarters in a deplorable state of repair. Meanwhile the assistant manager, his boss being on leave, had somewhat insensitively put them to building a tennis court. Once a week, there was a free cinema show on the extensive upstairs floor above the old cotton ginnery. That week it was to be the Hollywood biblical extravaganza 'The Story Of Ruth' and we took my mother along. When the lights went up for Mr. Migotti to change the reel, it was revealed that many of the Gilbertese there were extremely drunk and apparently involved in a fiercely whispered argument. Then, at the end of the second reel, the lights came on again and it was clear that the swaying man clutching a knife and advancing on Solomon, a much detested Wallis Island overseer, had drawn the short straw and badly misjudged the moment to make his assassination attempt. Peter Wright pluckily disarmed him; he was removed from the hall and the police were sent for. At this point, many of his fellow Gilbertese got up and left the show. Down went the lights again for the third reel of Ruth, but soon afterward a lurid red glow suffused the hall. The strikers had set the copra dock alight. Dried copra being more than sixty percent oil, burns fiercely, and it did, all one hundred tons of it. The Story of Ruth was abandoned for the rival attraction, and we would now have had to read the bible to find out how it all ended, at least in the original version. Certainly, my mother enjoyed her evening enormously.

To Coral Strands

There was a small group of sadly neglected plantations just south of Lakatoro. One was run by Bill Gidley, a former sailor in the Royal Navy and originally from Cornwall. He was taken off his ship, sick, shortly after WW2 and nursed back to health by Madelaine Corlette, whose father, owner of the plantation, had married a woman from Ambai. Bill married Madelaine and they returned to the plantation at Bushmans Bay. By the time I saw it, bush had encroached on all but the last few acres of ageing coconuts around the house, which was a WW2 Quonset hut, much of which was taken up by the plantation shop. This was fairly typical of New Hebrides plantations, by now managed by the second or third generation after the original colons, who with their labour had done all the hard work of clearing the bush and planting coconuts. With a productive life of sixty to seventy years, each palm with only minimum care would with great regularity - barring cyclones - provide an even cash flow by delivering to the ground a lovely bunch of coconuts every month of the year. No dangerous harvesting from the tops of the palms as, say, in Sri Lanka; just let the ripe ones drop - unless, that is, they are specifically harvested to drink green.

Cattle were kept to mow the grass so that nuts on the ground remained visible, and were thus more easily collected. The flesh of the coconuts was then shelled out, spread on a platform, and made into low grade copra over a smoky fire, and this was generally exported to Marseilles for making equally low grade soap. A few plantations employed hot air driers to make a better product for a higher price. Little or no agricultural knowledge or skilled management was required for these operations, with the exception of preventing the grass from becoming overgrazed, especially during the dry season, by selling off an appropriate number of livestock. Unfortunately, most planters fell at this low hurdle, and in the worst cases, as represented by this little group of plantations near Lakatoro, grass was replaced by every kind of noxious weed, some up to two or more metres high, so that not only was there little feed for the cattle, but it became a challenge to find a fallen coconut. Left on the ground for some weeks, these nuts germinated and sprouted, their leaves providing at least a small amount of forage for the meagre cattle. Under such a regime, planters found that their time could more profitably be spent in their store selling trade goods to the local people.

Pierre Theuil owned the property almost next door to the Gidleys. He was the second generation of the family on this piece of land and already into late middle age, the last of three brothers on adjoining plantations. With unintentional irony, his

NOWHERE NEAR GREENLAND

property was named 'Plantation Idéale'. Well, yes, that is if you wanted to take a bunch of botanists to see perhaps the most comprehensive and concentrated collection of noxious weeds in the South Pacific. Among them there was coral berry that horribly tainted the milk of any cow that browsed it; herbe balai, which was good only for making brooms; the vicious thorn-covered piko or wild aubergine that grew higher than a horse; castor oil, lantana and herbe gendarme, all highly toxic to livestock; Bidans pilosa, whose sharp seeds hooked into your socks and took ages to extricate; Elophantopus, false tobacco and blue rats tail, all totally inedible; guava, highly invasive with worm-infested fruit and wood like iron; and so on. In sunlit glades where a number of palms had fallen through age or lightning strike, and flying birds and fruit bats excreted the seed of lime trees, pawpaw and wild tomatoes, as well as tree seeds from the forest which rapidly grew into saplings, one was witnessing the intermediate stage of a deranged garden of Eden returning to the rainforest, from which it had originally been cleared and was now reclaiming it.

Pierre was a smallish, round man, with thick spectacles, small retroussé nose and a red face. He had a very loud voice with a distinctive Australian twang and spoke what might be termed Froz. He was proud of and claimed direct Irish ancestry through the name Lynch. In fact, he looked Irish, and his general demeanour was one of cheerful belligerence, though occasionally he would give vent to despondency, waving his arms and shouting "Pas un sou, pas un clou, pas du tout, c'est la misère Monsieur" (Pierre was also fond of repeating the pun, "Monsieur, je ne suis pas un vrai Theuil, mais un fauteuil.") His two overwhelming passions in life were that activity commonly associated with the procreation of children, and forever wrestling and tinkering with worn-out machinery and scrap metal. For the first he had a delightful woman named Anna, with whom he took up when she already had seven children by another Frenchman, and with whom he had many more. A few years into the relationship they came into Norsup to be formally married. We presented him with a wide-brimmed Mexican hat for the occasion, and he later stopped by our house for a celebration. At home, the children lived in permanent hunter-gatherer mode, and hence were fit and well fed; though this was to be interrupted for a few hours each day, once the French had built a school for them at nearby Rensarie, which initially catered almost exclusively for the numerous offspring of the Theuil and Savoie families. We always invited the Theuils to our Christmas party. The children, ranging from toddlers to teens, with always a preponderance of girls, would be immaculately groomed and well behaved, some

To Coral Strands

standing on chairs in the kitchen to reach the sink and help with the washing-up. (The huge excitement engendered by our hot water taps reminded one of the children in Steinbeck's 'The Grapes of Wrath'). As our parties continued into the night, the children would crash out on all the beds in the house. We never saw any of the colons and their families at occasions hosted by the French, official or otherwise. They were just not invited, even to the 14th July celebrations, possibly because they were not perceived as a credit to French culture, not reflecting the rayonnement, or la gloire, perhaps, but they were nevertheless engaging and genuinely delightful people, largely independent of our culture's materialism and status symbols, and rich in living.

The centre of Plantation Idéale was where Pierre indulged his second passion. This comprised a large Quonset hut entirely crammed with ancient and rusting machinery, including the chassis and wheels of WW2 trucks and the remains of a bulldozer whose blade had been powered by cables rather than hydraulics. Out in the open air - there was no room inside - and surrounded by old pumps, massive cylinder blocks and other unidentifiable objects, long since cannibalised, was a workbench where Pierre in T-shirt, oily shorts, pink plastic sandals and clouds of flies would happily manipulate, bang and clang away at stubborn lumps of metal. Of any final, useful application I remain ignorant, though it is entirely possible that some were incorporated into his very ancient Land Rover. This had no silencer, and its thunderous approach could be heard from a considerable distance. Lacking even a windscreen, the vehicle was entirely flat topped, excepting, perhaps, a heaving heap of children, and the odd bag of dried cocoa beans or copra to barter at the Norsup shop. He drove like some Rommel in the rainforest. There were rarely brakes, and wanting to stop for a chat, Pierre would sail past while changing down into low gear and then turning off the engine, so that he would come to a jolting halt some hundred yards down the road, steam escaping from the battered radiator, which he would now take the opportunity to top up.

One morning in Migotti's yard, I had stopped to change a punctured rear wheel on my Minimoke and leave it for repair. While I was attaching the spare wheel, Pierre roared up and we were soon joined by Bill Gidley in his old International pickup. Both started a conversation with me, but Bill whispered where Pierre shouted, so that I was alternately drawing near and recoiling in this interchange. Having been somewhat distracted from the task in hand, I eventually set off to drive to Lakatoro, and halfway there was amazed to be overtaken by a wheel. As my vehicle eventu-

NOWHERE NEAR GREENLAND

ally slumped down on its rear axle, the wheel continued at high speed between the coconuts and disappeared into the bush. It took me a quite while to find it, though the hub had been ruined with the bolt holes worn into large ovals.

At the time of independence in 1980, the Papua New Guinea Defence force was brought in, primarily to put down the Vemerana rebellion on Espiritu Santo. A detachment was sent to Malekula to check for dissidents there. At Plantation Idéale, a two-way radio was discovered - almost all planters had them, though this one probably didn't work - and Pierre was badly beaten up, this treatment only ceasing, I was told, when he revealed he had a large and long-established inguinal hernia. He left for New Caledonia soon afterwards, and sadly, died there. Presumably his beautiful mixed-race children, now grown up, are still living there or in France, and happily some of the family Theuil are still in Vanuatu.

An elderly near-neighbour of his was Charles Savoie, married to the sister of Chief Wilfred of Fonah in north Ambrym. Near the beach he had a fine, round, thatched fare in which was displayed the framed photograph of a French admiral in full dress uniform, whom he claimed as a close relative. Charles, soft spoken and somewhat sibilant, would receive me there with a show of old world manners and pour me a drink of unchilled lime juice or Ricard pastis. His shy wife never joined us. He lived with her in a shed nearby, within walls and roof of corrugated iron which must have been incredibly hot. Right against the front of the shed were deep wallows of black mud, where his enormous Large White and Berkshire pigs, almost motionless on their sides but venting an occasional happy grunt, drowsed away their days in porcine bliss.

The French agricultural officer whom I replaced at Norsup, though he was gone before I arrived and I never met him, was married to a Tahitian lady, and had worked solely with the plantation sector, though there was little to show for his efforts. By all accounts his wife was very attractive, and a French neighbour in Norsup admitted to me that he had once spent some hours in dalliance with her. He recounted the following story: suspicious of her activities, the husband followed her to Santo. He discovered the house where she was, and parked immediately outside was a man's bicycle. Putting two and two together he immediately went to a nearby shop, purchased a hacksaw, sawed through the crossbar and soon had entirely bisected the bicycle. No sooner had he completed this and stood back to admire his handiwork, when he was accosted by the furious owner, who had noth-

To Coral Strands

ing whatever to do with that house or his wife.

Radio communications in the islands could be a physically strenuous affair. In the Abwatuntora local council office in north Pentecost, one furiously pedalled a wheel-less bicycle to generate the signal, handlebars in one hand, microphone in the other. As a distant voice annoyingly replied "You are very faint", you reflected as you pedalled even more furiously "How right you are!" and delivered your breathless message. Leaving north Pentecost on the 'Lopevi' launch one day, the radio was loaded aboard to take to Vila for repair. It was tied to a stanchion above the upholstered bench on which I was reclining. In heavy seas it broke free and the wretched contraption fell on me. Being temporarily stunned, alas, I missed the chance to toss it overboard.

While the great majority of my time and effort was directed towards improving New Hebridean smallholder agriculture, I did what I could for the plantation sector, in terms of crops, livestock and especially pest control. Never mentioned in South Pacific tourist brochures is that, for the most part, its islands are overrun with rats. The indigenous species is the small, rural Rattus exulans; but introduced from the time of Captain Cook onwards - and possibly earlier in the New Hebrides by de Quiros in 1606 - are the black or roof rat, Rattus rattus, a major pest of agriculture, and the large, short-tailed Rattus norvegicus, which frequents urban habitats such as sewers and warehouses, and was once notorious for disseminating the plague with its fleas. It was immediately evident to me on arrival that the roof rat was not only causing enormous economic damage to the principal crop, coconuts, but also to cocoa. Everywhere there were prematurely fallen, green coconuts lying on the ground, with rat-gnawed holes right through the husk and shell. Similarly, cocoa trees carried on their trunks and branches thousands of rat-destroyed pods, sometimes as much as 90% of the crop. Funded by my budget, I obtained foot-wide, rolls of sheet aluminium from Japan to band the trunks of coconut palms, about ten feet from the ground, above the point where they could be bashed with bushknives, a habit of locals whenever they pass close to a tree. This would prevent the rats from climbing them, and those already nesting in the crown would need to come down as they can not thrive on coconuts alone. But this would work only in regularly-planted, wide-spaced palms whose fronds did not meet to touch one-another, and not in the dense, self-planted traditional groves where palms were of all ages, waiting for their chance to reach the light and bear nuts, and where access up just one would provide access to all. However, the former represented the great majority of the national resource, and demonstrations were established on a few palms at various points throughout the islands in my charge.

Showing pepper-cuttings to Ida Wilkins and Miss Emery of the FCO. Lakatoro, Malekula, 1970.

The large plantation at Norsup banded many thousands of palms in this manner, and more than thirty years later most of the bands are still in place (palms are monocotyledons and the girth of their trunk does not increase with age). However, few plantations followed suit, and very few New Hebrideans did so on their smallholdings, for unfortunately the rumour had spread that the aluminium bands attracted lightning, which was not the case though difficult to demonstrate to the contrary, but it was entirely sufficient to short-circuit this initiative. There was better success with cocoa, and we made many thousands of blocks of bait, about the size of a small bar of soap, which incorporated warfarin, coconut and meat meal impregnated in paraffin wax. The blocks were nailed to the trunks of the cocoa trees, above the height where they could be reached by dogs or pigs, and were shipped to all the islands where cocoa was grown, and were widely used. However, poison being traditionally the principal means of despatching enemies, it was important to demonstrate that these blocks could not practically be used for that purpose, or accidentally dissolve in water supplies; so farmers were somewhat

To Coral Strands

reassured, when at meetings I would drink Coca Cola from a glass in which I had immersed a block of this insoluble rat bait. Over the years there were no accidents, and chickens that frequently scavenged crumbs of bait at the sites where we made it, were apparently unaffected.

In 1969, I arranged for a three-day workshop on cocoa production and rat control to be held at Lakatoro. This would be attended by agricultural field assistants from the three districts of the New Hebrides where cocoa was grown, as well as by a number of local farmers. We had invited two cocoa experts from Papua New Guinea, and the rat control officer from the South Pacific Commission based in Noumea, to give talks and make field demonstrations in their respective subjects. Fred Klekham OBE had long experience of working with smallholder cocoa growers in PNG, and he was accompanied by a man named Wilson who specialised in other pests and diseases of that crop. Our rat expert from Noumea was also named Wilson (and we still had a volunteer at Lakatoro named Wilson), so to distinguish the former he became 'Rat Man Wilson'. It was he who provided the memorable highlight of the workshop. Having the day before set out a line of baited cage traps between the coconut palms on the agricultural station, presumably, if I remember correctly, to confirm the species of rat responsible for the damage, we all traipsed down the following morning to witness the results. I had of course earlier given Rat Man Wilson a huge build-up, telling the farmers that this was the "namba wan man long Pasifik long killem rat" which, of course, was why he was here, "from hem i gat big fella savvy long killem everi rat i ded". (the best man in the Pacific for killing rats, because he has great knowledge in killing dead every rat).Success! All the half dozen traps had caught a rat. Expert at handling these wild creatures, he gently removed them from the cages without once being bitten. Then, with a pair of nail scissors he deftly removed the middle toe on the front left foot of each rat. That done, and murmuring terms of endearment, such as "Off you go then, you little cheeky chappie you", he set each one free. There was complete astonishment among the craning spectators. Clearly, the apparently painless and near-bloodless snipping of one toe was not going to kill the rats, by then happily scampering home or shinning back up the coconut palms. Or could it? Was this some kind of 'nakaimas', or black magic? Were the scissors poisoned, perhaps? Afterwards, the questions piled in. Unfortunately I did not know the pidgin word for "boffin", and the term "nerd" had not yet been invented.

Once when touring south east Ambrym, I found myself sharing the simple thatch

NOWHERE NEAR GREENLAND

and bamboo rest house at Toak with Darvall Wilkins. Retiring for bed, I waited until Darvall had tucked in his mosquito net, and then doused the hurricane lamp. A few moments later all hell broke loose, shouting, squealing, swearing and the sounds of smashing mosquito poles, of ripping net and finally of a camp bed overturning. In the pitch black, I imagined some frightful attack by a madman, but Darvall had merely tucked himself in with a rat.

On another occasion, when staying at the house of agricultural monitor Willie Rau, high up on the Pentecost plateau, we had retired to bed in separate rooms, and lamps were extinguished. Again a terrible commotion soon broke out, and then the sound of running from the house. From the front door by the light of the full moon, I could see Willie chasing someone through the village, particularly the flashing white soles of their bare feet. Eventually he came back and explained that he had been woken in the dark by the feel of someone's hands around his throat. With a yell he pushed the person off, and took up the chase when the latter fled the house. It was a young woman who had become deranged as a child after witnessing the death of her parents in a fire. Willie then shut and locked the front door, but the girl returned and sat on the doorstep weeping, and repeating "Willie, Willie, Willie" well into the night. It was the saddest sound.

It was again with Willie that I had the following experience, which should, perhaps, be entitled "taking the biscuit". We had walked down the wild east coast of Pentecost where there are no roads, not even tracks for long stretches, and the hills rise steeply to two or three thousand feet from the sea. It was already quite late in the day and we were to climb up to the village of Wijamwel high on the plateau, but were uncertain of the way. Reaching a small coastal hamlet, which was deserted but for one young man, we asked if he would guide us and help me by carrying my rucksack. No sooner had we asked, when he grabbed the bag and set off at a run up a precipitous path through the forest, all the while laughing and singing. We quickly realised we had chosen unwisely. Calling out slowed him not one jot, but by good fortune I had retained a packet of biscuits, and we discovered that by shouting "Biscuit!" he would stop until we caught up with him. However, no sooner had he taken his reward, he would set off again at the same mad pace as before. Happily, in repeating this stratagem, the biscuits just lasted until, in the near dark, we reached our destination. I paid off our friend, and asked someone in the village to open up the store so that we could buy something for the evening meal. However, our guide followed us in, and whatever I ordered he ordered: a packet

To Coral Strands

of soup...... a packet of soup; a tin of beans......a tin of beans, and so on. The poor chap was going to spend all his earnings, and perhaps more than he had, so we gave up and just took the packet of soup.

Another of my clients for cocoa seedlings, rat bait and Berkshire piglets was Albert Joseph of Pinalum, known to the local people as "Black Negro". Born in Port au Prince in Haiti, he had served a spell in the French Marine, carrying coal from Cardiff to his home country, before sailing around Cape Horn to the South Pacific in 1901. He settled on Ambai in 1903 and operated his own copra trading vessel between the islands. He also participated in the evacuation of the population from Dip Point, north Ambrym in 1913, when a volcano erupted beneath the settlement and destroyed the Presbyterian Hospital, then the largest in the New Hebrides. He moved to Pinalum just north of Norsup in the 1920s, bought a piece of land and opened a shop. He was a keen farmer but did not enjoy a good relationship with the authorities, probably because he had once illegally traded in liquor. Though already in his nineties when I first met him, he was still a fine figure of a man, slim but powerfully built, well over six feet tall and graceful in his manner and movement. We always spoke in French, and at his store he would show me the latest Grand National Irish Sweepstake ticket he had bought, as he had all his life without success. He died, probably 106 years old, in 1984. I very much regret that I did not record, and do not now remember in any detail, the tales he told me. After I had left Malekula in 1975, I did try to persuade Kirk Huffman of the Cultural Centre in Port Vila and Paul Gardissat of Radio Vila to interview him, as his memories of the old days stretched more than a generation further back than perhaps anyone else alive, but, alas, without success. I last called on him during a brief visit to Malekula, the year before he died. By then he was much shrunken and blind, and clearly living in considerable poverty. I wrote to the French ambassador describing his situation, and suggesting they might afford some assistance to Albert who was most probably their oldest citizen in the whole of the South Pacific, though I do not know if anything resulted from this. (In the early 1970s, the Burns Philp ship 'Manutai' went into dry dock at Palekuka, Santo for her hull to be surveyed. I happened to be staying in Luganville at the Hotel Corsica, and there met the man sent over from Australia to do the job. Amazingly, he was in his nineties and like Albert had participated in the evacuation from Dip Point, and remembered him well.)

When I first arrived in early 1968, there were still many small stores dotted around the coasts of the islands. These bought copra locally and sold a variety of fairly

NOWHERE NEAR GREENLAND

basic consumer items to nearby villages, continuing a tradition of such small-scale trading that had obtained for nearly a century. One I called upon in north Ambrym operated out of a small corrugated iron shed near the beach, and displayed a string of brassieres slung above the counter. The trader was a small, elderly Frenchman, and when he stood up an extra-large cup settled neatly on his bald head. Stores such as these purchased their stock from the bigger trading vessels, like the Henri Bonnaud operated by Ballande, the largest French trading company in the New Hebrides, which sold forty-four gallon drums of Algerian red wine. This was at the time the British administered cooperatives were being established throughout the islands. They soon numbered more than a hundred, and the French soon followed suit in their areas of influence, particularly where the Roman Catholic church and their francophone schools predominated. These cooperatives all bought copra and sold consumer goods, and in a very short space of time, all the small traders, unable to compete on price and scale, and with the New Hebridians' national pride in their first foray into commerce, disappeared. I once accompanied Darvall Wilkins to the small catholic island of Vao, where he had arranged to hold a meeting. But no-one showed up, all the men having been rendered horizontal by just such a drum of Algerian wine, now standing empty on the beach.

One former small trader was George Florence, a Mauritian, who lived in a small hut just south of Aulua, on the island of Malekula. Many years before, he had killed his trading partner in a drunken fight, and served a long sentence for manslaughter in Vila, where he tended the grounds of the British paddock. When I met him, living alone except for his dog, he was fashioning light shades from nautilus shells, bisecting them lengthwise to expose the beautifully sculpted air chambers they contain. He also maintained the lawnmower for the nearby Presbyterian mission and did other odd jobs around the place. Now old, a small, quiet and seemingly gentle man, he soon after died, and his body was not found for some days afterwards when passers by were alerted by his barking dog.

In the mid-1970s, a new pest arrived in the islands, the Giant African Snail, Achatina achatina. No-one knows whether it was introduced as a pet in the pocket of a schoolboy, on the bottom of a crate from South East Asia where this pest was already common, or by a Frenchman in mind for a snack. Where there are no natural predators, this snail will wildly multiply and devastate food gardens, ornamental plants and tree seedlings. It was a serious pest in Malaysia, where we had to protect every rubber tree seedling with a ring of methaldehyde poison bait. The snail first

To Coral Strands

appeared in the New Hebrides, as one might expect, in the area of Star Wharf in Vila. Unfortunately, it was not recognised for what it was until the first snail, or snails, had laid eggs, and each one can lay thousands. These are deposited underground or under stones and are both hard to find and impossible to spray, though a scorched earth approach might be effective, but not always appropriate for the site affected. Anyway, these snails soon broke out from their original beachhead, and before long the roads in Vila and the outside walls of the houses throughout the town were plastered with them - the walls because the snails were in search of lime to grow their shells. Soon, the front line of the snail army could be encountered crawling north up Klems Hill, and creeping south east towards Teouma, and a snail's pace no longer seemed so slow. The smell of the crushed and rotting snails on the hot and sunny roads was most memorable. Worst of all, there was devastation in the food and market gardens around the town, though collecting the snails by hand twice a day would somewhat reduce the damage. Collected snails could be killed by crushing them, liberally sprinkling with salt or detergent, or by throwing them in the sea, though the agricultural department advised that if first boiled, and their shells then cracked, they were relished by pigs as a high protein feed. Ultimately growing to almost a hand's length with very hard shells, they were far too large to be tackled by any of the local birds, so some other form of biological control would have to be found. Meanwhile, measures were taken through publicity and freight inspection to prevent the snails from being carried to other islands. However, before long they were found around Simonsen's Wharf in Luganville, and again they broke out into the town and surrounding countryside before they could be contained.

Eventually, it was decided to introduce other species of snail from Africa that cannibalise this pest, which is why in its own country it remains only a minor nuisance. Those introduced were first multiplied at the Tagabe agricultural station and then secretly released at selected sites. Secretly, because everyone wanted some for their own garden, and the size of individual colonies could have been reduced by desperate collectors to the point of being unviable for multiplying, at which they were by no means as prolific as Achatina. Meanwhile, French-owned snail canning factories had sprung up, first in Vila, then in Santo, perhaps on the principle of 'where there's muck there's brass', and the product was shipped to France, both in tins and frozen in large blocks of ice. I had the occasion to inspect the cannery in Santo. Sacks and sacks of snails were being brought in by truck, pickup and bicycle for sale by the local people, and in buckets by small children who made quite good pocket money thereby. The snails were boiled in large vats, and then women at long tables winkled the flesh from the shells with metal picks. But live snails, escapees, crawled everywhere, including across the manager's desk and the ceiling of his office; quite an amusing sight, and I had rather hoped to see one peering from his shirt pocket. Needless to say, although cheap and in plentiful supply, they were hardly one's first choice from the menu of local restaurants.

Lesley surveys the weighing of snails
Port Vila, Efate Island, 1978

The local Kiwanis service club then introduced a 'Snail Collection Day', and this was held annually for several years. Each time, more than thirty tons of snails were collected by hand, both in Vila and Luganville. In bulging, oozing and extremely heavy sacks, these were brought in to weighing points, and the name of the collector and weight of snails were recorded. Spot checks were made to ensure that deceased snails were not being brought in, though the smell would have been a dead give-away. Prizes were awarded to individuals, and to collectives such as villages, women's clubs, schools and cooperatives, for the heaviest weight of snails collected, and there was a special prize for the largest snail found. The latter usually attracted photographers, and his or her (I understand they included hermaphrodites), picture was published in the local press. The many tons of snails were then taken by lorry to the town dump and bulldozed into the ground. I believe it was about four years before the cannibal snails, particularly the relatively elegant, slim, pink Eug-

To Coral Strands

landina, began to have a genocidal effect on their African diet, and by a year later the pest's population had collapsed and the canning factories closed down. Fortunately, they did not succeed in spreading to any of the other islands, though a small beachhead on Malekula was exterminated in time. Before the introduction of the cannibal species, naturalist snail specialists in the UK and elsewhere in the world complained that these would go on to attack and cause the extinction of indigenous snails unique to the islands. However, this might take a very long time to eventuate, if at all, on Efate, Santo and Malekula, and one may hope may never occur on the other eighty islands.

We very much enjoyed living in the French community at Norsup. Fortunately, Lesley was an excellent cook, so our little dinner parties were generally a success, and French was invariably the language of conversation. She introduced them to many 'Anglo Saxon' dishes, which evinced many questions and comparisons, including, I remember, mint sauce for which she was pressed for the recipe. We also often dined at their houses, as there were no restaurants at which to entertain, and we were struck by how openly critical the French guests could be of their compatriot hostess's cooking, such as "What is this supposed to be for goodness sake?", holding up an offending morsel, or merely peering closely at their plates and sadly shaking their heads. This would inevitably give rise to lengthy culinary discussions, though these merely changed the drift and not the subject of what was, anyway, always the principle topic of conversation at table. During such talk I would always be the polite and somewhat detached listener, since my own knowledge, if not interest in the subject, would have been limited to superficial observations on, say, baked beans or boiled eggs. Lesley would sometimes modestly preface the presentation of her main dish with an apology, if it was not up to her own exacting standards. I advised her not to do this, since with the French this simply engendered suspicion and subsequent peering and prodding at the food. Rather, serve it with aplomb, as though the somewhat over or underdone whatever was exactly as intended. Certainly, though, I never remember them to have been openly critical of Lesley's cooking, as they were with each other's.

However, in Norsup it was not always easy to find the makings of a good meal. Beef supplied by the plantation was from cattle grazed on their tough pastures and comprehensive collection of weeds beneath the coconuts. Furthermore, these animals were run and gunned down from the back of a truck, often after a lengthy chase, so the meat was invariably tough, requiring much pounding with wooden

NOWHERE NEAR GREENLAND

hammers, wrapping in pawpaw leaves or prolonged marination, and failing these measures, prolonged chewing. Seafood was also not plentiful, unless you went out and caught a fish yourself, and cases of fish poisoning (Sigiatura) were not infrequent, so there was some nervousness about eating reef fish. There were no local fishermen venturing out to catch deep water, pelagic fish such as tuna, so those of us who frequently used government touring vessels were privileged, since these always trawled a couple of lines, and we would often return home with good sized slabs of fish for the deep freeze. Every three weeks or so, either the Konanda or Manutai, Burns Philp trading vessels, would drop anchor in Norsup Bay and Lesley and I would go aboard with our fellow expatriates and local people to shop at their shipboard stores. We always had the impression that whatever could not be sold in Vila would be put aboard these ships to sell in the islands, since many of the tins had been bashed, lacked labels or were time-expired, and quite possibly qualified on all three counts. Sometimes we just took the supercargo's word for what he thought was inside, and opening them combined hope with apprehension. The flour and rice were generally full of weevils, and I can remember Lesley sifting and sifting again to get them all out, though their smell and acrid taste would linger. Once and once only, Lesley bought two trays of twenty-four eggs. All forty-eight proved to be rotten. Complaining six weeks later, when the same ship came around again, was somehow rather lame. These ships bought copra, cocoa and other produce during their passage around the islands, and were overrun with cockroaches. Nevertheless, they were a welcome sight and diversion when they arrived.

Getting provisions sent up by plane from Vila, or down from Luganville, was not so easy and was expensive. Unless you had a regular, preset order, you would have to be at the plantation or district agent's office to pass your requirements by radio. The Norsup plantation had its own store with a rather limited range, tinned fish taking up most of the shelves, but it always had good French champagne, and excellent French bread was available there every day in the form of baguettes. There was no market, though roadside sales made some fruit available throughout the year. Like others, we had our own vegetable garden, but it was difficult to maintain any production during the hot and rainy cyclone season from October to March. However, small cherry tomatoes grew wild in the bush and fields, wherever cattle could not get to them, and were an excellent standby throughout the year. We rarely drank fresh milk since this was inevitably contaminated by coral berry, which grew prolifically in the local pastures and imparted a horrible taste; so tinned powdered milk was the norm in those days before the packaged, long-life product

To Coral Strands

appeared on the scene. Occasionally an ocean-going yacht would drop anchor in the bay, decanting their hardy crews ashore. They were always delighted to come up for a good hot shower, soak in the bath or enjoy other long-missed, creature comforts, but did not always appreciate how difficult it could be there to get provisions. Thus a rare rasher of bacon or treasured egg did not always get the degree of appreciation they deserved, and we expected.

Being at Norsup, we acted as something of a bridge between the French and our fellow anglophones at Lakatoro. However, when we first arrived in 1968, the only other person at Lakatoro with English as his first language, besides Darvall's family, was the young volunteer named Wilson. With prison labour, he had started making a vehicle track behind the station, with the intention of taking it right across the island to Lambumbu, where there is a deep inlet and safe anchorage, providing a good starting point for touring the west coast of Malekula and South West Bay. Always keen to be involved in this kind of creative, pioneering work, I offered the services of the ancient Fordson Major tractor we had at the agricultural station. Progress on the road had reached the top of a very steep slope. In fact, it was really too steep except for four wheel drive vehicles in low ratio, in dry weather. Anatole Lingtamat, our agricultural monitor and tractor driver, had succeeded in getting the old tractor to the top, where it did good work pulling felled trees away from the road trace. Unfortunately, at the end of work it had stalled facing downhill at the top of the steep slope, and we failed to start it on a very tired battery. Recklessly, I decided we could push start it, and taking the place of the driver I would engage the clutch once it got up some speed on the steep slope. Well, I made a complete hash of it, and ended up hurtling down the hill with the engine still refusing to start, unable to engage a lower gear and the brakes failing. The new made surface was by no means level, as some tree stumps had not been cut entirely level with the ground, and struggling to keep the tractor pointed straight down the slope, the only part of me remaining in physical contact with it was frequently my hands on the wheel. While this was going on, I was very mindful of the fact that my wife's first husband, a young Englishman who went to the South Island of New Zealand to farm sheep, had died beneath an overturned tractor only months after they were married. Just maybe this made me strive harder to master the situation. Eventually, near the very bottom of the hill, the old tractor started and slowed, and a ragged cheer drifted down to me from the work gang up above.

We were also being helped in this work by the people of Tautu village, whose cus-

NOWHERE NEAR GREENLAND

tomary land this has been before it was alienated, and still remained up ahead, beyond the Norsup plantation reserve. They had for some time opposed the further expansion of the plantation into the forest, and had even pulled up some of its fence posts. When at independence in 1980, twelve years later, the French pulled out somewhat precipitately, they left behind a stack of confidential correspondence in their residency's yard, with strict instructions to minions that it should be burnt. But it wasn't, and one of the letters, appropriately retrieved by an anthropologist, was from the French district agent to his resident commissioner claiming that my involvement in this road making, which eventually traversed the plantation's forest reserve, was an overtly provocative and political act. Which it wasn't. Another incredible letter was from the French resident commissioner, in reply to one from the French district agent, by then based at Norsup, who had informed him that I had held a party at my house to celebrate the death of President Pompidou. This was attended by a number of our French friends and their names were now requested so that they could be disciplined. As they were not, I can only assume their authorities eventually gleaned the vital information that the date of my birthday fell three days following the death of their president. Yet another letter concerned a colleague who was witnessed by an informant to place his hand on the buttocks of a New Hebridean on Akhamb Island! And it was either the Chancelier or the Directeur du cabinet at the French residency in the early 1970s, who at Vila airport introduced me to his two daughters who were about to share the same flight with me to Pentecost, and curiously added the aside, as though to imply he knew all about me, "Un homme très dangereux". As he seemed so serious, I should have asked, "In what sense, monsieur?". As it happened, both girls were very sick on the flight, though this was apparently due to the very rough conditions rather than any fear of their fellow passenger who was kept busy passing them paper bags.

In 1970, Fiji achieved independence from Britain, and the small Fijian community in Luganville threw a party to celebrate the occasion, to which the British and French district agents were invited, as were practically the entire expatriate community and many local persons of mixed race. I was at the time looking after Northern District for my colleague, Mike Ratard, who was on leave, so I was also included. All went well until Chris Turner, the British district agent, made his speech of thanks to the hosts. He congratulated Fiji on its emancipation, wished it every success in the future, and remarked that this was an event that might one day be celebrated by other territories in the Pacific. At this, the French district agent and the manager of the Banque de L'Indochine et Suez who were sitting next to

To Coral Strands

Turner, abruptly stood up and left the party. The next day, the Sarakata bridge and a number of walls in town were found scrawled with graffiti in French, English and Bislama, expressing such sentiments as 'à bas les pokens', 'f*** off English', (somehow the term Britanniques has never caught on), and others were directed at Chris Turner himself. A senior technician at public works, who was of Japanese and local extraction and appropriately known as Tokyo, was said to be the ringleader behind this and certainly he had access to all the paint. It was such francophones of mixed race who were most fearful of independence, especially of one under an anglophone government, when their hopes of the New Hebrides becoming a French overseas territory, then still very much alive, would be dashed. Tokyo's boss, M. Pommadere, was a cheerful and charming man, who occasionally came to Malekula to inspect works in progress. He was distinguished by the shiniest, baldest head imaginable, and as he never wore a hat, it was a complete mystery to me why, in those days before sun-block, he was never felled by sunstroke.

There was indeed a palpable paranoia afflicting some of the French at this time, which perceptibly increased during the political developments engendered by anglophone New Hebrideans during the mid-1970s, and the phrase 'la menace d'Australie' was frequently heard or read in local French newspapers. Admittedly, some of us blithe and mischievous spirits were inclined to encourage this syndrome. The flat, very shiny aluminium sheeting I had imported to band the coconut palms, gave Jerry Marston and me an idea. In the bush immediately above Lakatoro, we would build a great rocket, using a single stack of 44 gallon oil drums as the core, around which we would wrap the sheeting, and eventually top it with a nose cone painted with a Union Jack and the logo for radioactivity. Towering high above the bush this would clearly be seen from the road, and. Lakatoro residents would be briefed to parry any questions with "What rocket? I see no rocket".

Thus thrown upon our own resources for entertainment in this remote community, where we shared the dying embers of two empires, from which would erupt the occasional sputter, pop or puff of smoke, we expanded our practical jokes into a form of theatre, as well as directing our energies to devising some elaborate fancy dress parties. So we decided, possibly because the vast, thatched Metemet club building at Lakatoro remotely resembled a Saxon baronial hall, to hold a mediaeval costume party. Lesley worked for weeks, helping to design and make the elaborate outfits, including a prominent codpiece for the French district agent, M. Lecuyer (who had once worked in Lamberene and known Albert Schweizer), and some-

NOWHERE NEAR GREENLAND

thing filmy for his 'soit-disant' cousin. As a knight, I had a coat of chain mail made entirely from the aluminium pull tags of beer cans, and Lesley made a magnificent bishop's costume, complete with a tall mitre of embossed, golden cloth, for the district education officer, George Hart. Peter Wright wore a monk's long brown habit, complete with cowl and impressive crucifix. Darvall Wilkins was resplendent in tight hose, red knickers and tunic, and his wife Ida in a fine gown, bodice and a veiled, tall conical hat. All French, British and New Hebrideans at Norsup and Lakatoro entered into the spirit, and the spirit duly entered them as the party progressed.

Ida and Darvall Wilkins
at mediaeval party
Lakatoro, Malekula, 1971

A whole pig and young steer were roasted on spits, there was much courtly dancing, wassailing and merriment, and a volunteer, Richard Brittaine, played the minstrel and sang a couple of ballads.

Lesley kept the bishop's outfit, and much later when George Hart was about to board the plane at Norsup to depart on long leave, he was required to remove his travelling clothes, which were put with his suitcase in the aircraft's freight compartment, and don the bishop's robes and mitre. Tall and gaunt with a pointed red

To Coral Strands

beard, this firm adherent of the Church of Scotland looked imposing indeed. Thus he travelled non-stop to Vila where we had alerted the Catholic Mission to the arrival from the north of a high prelate of their church.

'Bishop' George Hart departs Malekula by plane
for Port Vila, 1973

On another occasion at the airfield, we contrived a demonstration to lament the departure of the French count who was also our doctor. On his arrival with wife and four children at the departure point, he was met by bed-sheet banners reading in French and English "Don't go doctor, we need you", amid a crowd of walking and bedridden wounded. We had wheeled a couple of beds to the edge of the airstrip. One held a sufferer whose head and arms were totally bandaged, and whose severely injured leg was raised up on a pulley. At the other bed, a white-gowned aide vigorously pumped a red liquid through a transparent tube, which disappeared under the bedclothes and re-emerged lower down to return the same liquid into the bucket. I was lying in a wheelbarrow, my legs folded under me with bloody

NOWHERE NEAR GREENLAND

bandages wound around the stumps of my knees. Lesley had a large raw steak held with a bandage to her cheek (sorry about the flies!), and there were other examples of sickness - faces peppered with bright red spots, and mutilations. The doctor enjoyed it hugely, and then the plane arrived. Two elderly nuns en route to Vila, who were sisters at the French hospital in Santo, stepped down, and seeing what clearly was the result of some terrible catastrophe rushed towards us, arms aloft and uttering little cries of comfort and pity. The scene was complete.

Interval at the Gala opening of the Lakatoro opera season.
Darvall & Ida Wilkins, Simon Westwood, Margaret Ponninghouse,
George Hart, and Lesley & Barry Weightman, 1972

One variation on the theme of fancy dress was to stage the opening of the Lakatoro Opera Season with a performance of the Beggars' Opera. For this, about eight of us at Lakatoro donned dinner jackets (yes, they were still part of one's portable wardrobe in those days) or long evening dresses, and sat along the veranda of George Hart's house listening to the opera being played through big speakers in the moonlight of his garden below. This 'gala opening' was duly reported on the news next day by Radio Vila, including the fact that we had enjoyed a champagne interval.

To Coral Strands

On one of my departures on leave for Europe, when timing the connection with onward flights was vital, the agent, Peter Wright, regretfully informed me that the one vacant seat on the plane from Santo was, after all, taken, but he would speak with the passenger concerned. With him I approached the open door of the Islander plane, next to which was sitting a completely bald man in sunglasses. When addressed by Peter, he shook his head vigorously, sat tight, and spluttered angrily away in some Germanic-sounding language quite unknown to me. This continued for a while, and we appeared to have reached a mutually incomprehensible impasse. I had reached the point of giving up, when the Lakatoro volunteer Alan Hardiman removed his sunglasses and identified himself. Entirely for the sake of this little joke, he had completely shaved his head and shaved off his long-established and luxuriant moustache.

On this occasion, Lesley was already in Vila, and was to travel south to spend time with her parents in the North Island of New Zealand, and I was to travel north to England via Kashmir, where I had booked a holiday aboard a houseboat on Dal Lake. My houseboat, most un-ethnically named 'Mona Lisa', was moored next to a footpath-wide, stone pier built out into the lake, and comprised two bedrooms, a dining room, bathroom and sitting-room, all richly appointed with locally-crafted walnut furniture and fine carpets. On the flat roof, were chairs and a table beneath a wide umbrella, where one could take in the passing scene on the lake, and raise a glass or two against the magnificent backdrop of the Himalayas. Small red-painted boats called shikaras plied busily along the shore of the lake, selling fruit, vegetables and other groceries, tailoring services, handicrafts and carpets, to the occupants and owners of the houseboats. Some handed up much weathered letters of recommendation from the time of the Raj; Brigadier so-and-so was more than satisfied with the excellent pair of riding boots; the Hon. Walter Tiddlipush is delighted with the dining table and eight chairs, and so on. I had a full-time cook and a bearer to look after me, and the distinguished and devout Muslim owner of Mona Lisa and two smaller craft would call to take me on outings in his own shikara to the far end of the lake, to a fort, to the Shalimar Gardens and into Srinagar town.

Moored opposite my floating residence, and across a gangplank from the narrow pier, was one of the humbler craft, and I picked up the English accents of the young people living on it. They had no facilities above deck, beneath which they appeared to spend all their time except to emerge now and then to make purchases from a

NOWHERE NEAR GREENLAND

passing shikara. On just such an occasion, while lording it on my upper deck, I deigned to converse with two of them, and they cordially invited me to visit them that evening. I took with me a half bottle of whisky, and below their deck I discovered eight young men and women squatting around a hookah. The interior of their boat was simplicity itself, open plan with a few stools, mattress squabs, and pots and pans, all clean if not exactly tidy, and pervaded by a strong, herbal fragrance. They all hied from Manchester and Birmingham, where they had worked in factories, and took it in turn to return to Britain for a few months to earn wages for the maintenance of their little commune's lifestyle on the lake which, they informed me, cost them each about twenty-five pence a day. They travelled there and back overland via Kabul, hitchhiking and on local buses, along what was then a well-worn, hippy trail. The hookah was passed to me and I took a long pull at the pipe. It was not tobacco! - and the expression of blowing one's mind was instantly made manifest. I made it back to Mona Lisa with some difficulty, crawling slowly across the gangplank on my hands and knees.

While most of this group seemed perfectly happy to spend their days and nights stoned on the boat, with no ambition or interest to see anything more of Kashmir, I had mentioned that the following day I was going to take a taxi to Gulmarg, from which one could hire a pony to climb up though the forest to the snow line, and would be happy if any of them would like to accompany me. A young couple, she recently pregnant, said they would love to come along. Gulmarg had boasted the highest golf course in the British empire, and at its club we had a few drinks, and then with two guides set off on our ponies - two guides, because when we reached the snowline, I wanted one of them to wait while I climbed on up, and clambered about on rocks and snow for a few hours. I rejoined the others for tea back at the golf club, and in the evening we returned to the lake after a thoroughly enjoyable day. While I was in Kashmir, I also went up to Pahalgam and Sonnemarg, where the dark violet eyes of the child goatherds tending their charges at the foot of the glaciers are said to reflect the passage of Alexander the Great nearly two and a half thousand years before.

For another of my departures on leave the charade was somewhat more complex. I was certain something was afoot if things ran typically to form, but I had no inkling of what. However, I was already disappointed, that whatever might transpire, my 'counter charade' had been frustrated, since I had been unable to secure a seat on the Norsup to Vila flight the next day. At the old airfield, the far end of

To Coral Strands

the strip, to which the plane taxied prior to takeoff, was invisible from the little terminal, where all would be gathered to farewell me. My plan had been to park my Land Rover at that far end earlier in the day, to which there was separate road access. Having boarded, I would alight unseen from the plane about to take off, and then drive to the reef at Aop between Norsup and Lakatoro. With the vehicle concealed in the bushes, I would then sprawl out on the reef, complete with the parachute I had made from several bed sheets and lengths of cord. As the convoy of cars, of those who had just seen me off, passed by, I would wave and shout and perhaps stagger about a bit.

So none of that plan came to pass, and I had just finished packing my bags, when two uniformed British Police constables arrived at my house with a properly drawn up warrant for my arrest, signed, of course, by Darvall Wilkins. Handcuffed in the police Land Rover, I was taken to the plantation centre, where a large crowd was already gathered around the shop-house, many of this assembly wearing tricolour turbans and sashes, waving sickles, pitchforks and other weapons, and baying and shaking their fists at me. Upon the raised veranda of the shop, Darvall Wilkins, also in some bizarre, insurrectionary style uniform, unrolled a scroll, read out the wide spectrum of heinous crimes of which I stood convicted, and sentenced me to death. A tractor pulling a trailer, which had been converted with bamboo poles into a tumbrel, then rolled onto the scene, and into this I was bundled under the escort of two revolutionary guards, with whom I fought vigorously, incurring and possibly delivering real scratches and contusions. Meanwhile the tractor trundled along the sea front, past the workers houses and latrines towards the airfield, the crowd loping alongside hurling mud and abuse, which they no doubt found cathartic.

We arrived at the departure point on the airfield, and there stood a full-scale guillotine, complete with diagonal blade, lunette, ropes, platform and a basket for my head. On the platform stood Peter Wright in his resurrected dark brown, mediaeval monk's outfit, holding aloft the large crucifix. Released from the tumbrel I watched, arms pinioned, while the infernal machine was tested with a large, ripe papaw. It worked, and the fruit was perfectly sliced in half. More cheers and jeers from the excited mob. Peter the monk approached, bowing and muttering. Naturally, I was at this point beginning to wonder what safety measures had been incorporated into the guillotine - if any? - and my mind to dwell on those silly, fatal accidents that do sometimes happen. Were things really getting out of hand? However, as my neck was laid upon the lunette, a loud voice mercifully called a halt to the proceedings,

NOWHERE NEAR GREENLAND

and proclaimed with authority that I was wanted in Vila to face more serious charges before a higher court. Boos from the mob, of course, among whom there were now half a dozen amazed passengers who had just arrived on the plane from Santo, and on to which, somewhat battered, liberally spattered and truly exhausted, I was now loaded with my luggage. Lesley was already in Vila and quite wondered why I arrived so muddy and scratched with my clothes torn. But at least I still had my head!

Malekula in the early 1970s was in a poor state of readiness to receive international tourists. There were no hotels, only a few disconnected stretches of barely motorable track along the east and south coasts, and the sole public transport was one dilapidated taxi, driven by a dangerously short-sighted driver named Kaltapan from Tautu village. One day, an inter-island vessel disembarked at Norsup a group of forty or so elderly Germans, the males of whom could well have been survivors of Stalingrad, since few among them were endowed with a full set of limbs. "Take us to the Big Nambas", their leader demanded. It was explained that as there was no road across the island, this would require them to walk through the forest for several hours for which, quite evidently, they were not the best equipped. "Then we will take the boat round to the other side of the island". But, they were told, you will still have to face a long, steep climb of over a thousand feet to reach the village of Amok. So, faut de mieux, they settled on being taken to a nearby beach in the plantation's old five-ton lorry, which earlier that day had been used to transport slaughtered cattle to the abattoir - the practice being first to shoot them in the field, since they were wild and hard to round up. So in a cloud of flies, swaying and clinging to the rattling sides of the truck, these poor people were taken to the beach at Aop. However, as the flies maintained their intimate attentions, they soon returned to Norsup and re-boarded their ship.

Flies were a terrible pest in the New Hebrides, especially during the hot and rainy cyclone season, and particularly anywhere near plantations where there were cattle. Picnics involved a protracted exercise of vigorous arm waving and flapping at the food, and swimming in the sea gave little respite since any part of the body above the surface presented the flies with an irresistible landing strip. Here, and at Champagne Beach on Santo for example, any relaxation was absolutely out of question. Consequently, some years later we imported from South Africa several species of dung beetle, one of which, within ten years or so, had dramatically reduced this scourge by consuming all the fly larvae in cow pats.

To Coral Strands

So our German veterans and their spouses then set off for the north coast of Ambrym, where they had been told they could find natives wearing nambas in the village of Fanla. Eventually, a few of the more able-bodied made it to that settlement, and unfortunately then marched or limped straight into a taboo house, strictly off limits to all but a few local initiates. Following some alarm and excitement, when these hapless folk were surrounded by weapon-waving men clad only in penis wrappers, and forbidden to take photographs, they were permitted after the payment of a hefty fine to make a somewhat disorderly retreat to their ship. There were to be no further adventure excursions of this kind, and this episode possibly did little to promote New Hebrides tourism in Germany.

However, a year or two later, word reached us that the prestigious little cruise liner, 'Lindblad Explorer' which habitually visited the ends of the earth, (until it sank in Antarctic waters in December 2007) for the delectation of a superior and serious class of tourist, was to come to Malekula. These tours included an educational element, and before each landfall, the onboard botanists, zoologists and anthropologists addressed the passengers in the ship's lecture theatre on what they should expect to encounter. Even then, early in the 1970s, fares were in the region of US$200 a day, and some of these cruises lasted for months, so their clientele was largely made up of the rich retired and idle rich, albeit seriously inclined. We learned that the sixty or so tourists and resource persons were to come ashore at Norsup on a Sunday morning. There, they would be shown something of the processing of copra and cocoa at the plantation centre, and then proceed to Darvall Wilkins' thatched courthouse at Lakatoro, where he would endeavour to expound the arcane workings of the Condominium. Following that, they would continue south for some miles down the coast to a coconut plantation where Lucy, the Vietnamese wife of the French manager, would provide them with a splendid seafood lunch.

A week or two before the ship's arrival, and on the perceptive assumption that new arrivals to a country would not think to question the road signs, my artist wife set to work, and other preparations were put in hand for their reception. Meanwhile, the official organisers of the visit made every effort to hire or borrow sufficient vehicles for the excursion. These, of course, included Kaltapan's clapped-out taxi, but also a motley collection of pickups and private cars, mostly very much the worse for wear. However, there were still barely enough vehicles for the visitors, and they would be tightly packed inside.

NOWHERE NEAR GREENLAND

After leaving the Lakatoro courthouse, the convoy reached a road sign reading, 'DANGER, ELEPHANTS CROSSING' and bearing the silhouette of the animal in question. On either side of the road, a wide corridor of bush had been smashed down, and across the road was a liberal scattering of large round balls of 'elephant dung' made up from grass, mud and cow pats. Unfortunately none of the reception committee was there to witness the snapping of cameras or, perhaps, the urgings of the passengers for their drivers to accelerate. Then, a while later, they came to the boundary of Pierre Theuil's Plantation Idéale which, normally demarcated simply by a rudimentary cattle grid and a rusting barbed wire fence against a background of bush, now exhibited an 8ft x 4ft blue on white sign proclaiming 'US AIRFORCE MISSILE TESTING CENTRE. DO NOT PROCEED BEYOND THIS POINT WITHOUT DUE AUTHORITY'. By the greatest of good fortune, Stewart Baldwin, a British volunteer at Lakatoro, possessed a full US Army sergeant's uniform complete with steel helmet. There he stood, chewing gum in heavy shades at the cattle grid, stopping each vehicle in turn, noting their registration numbers on his clipboard, (though some of these vehicles had never possessed such a thing), and peering intently at the perspiring passengers before thumbing them through. Fortunately for them, but understandably, none of the tourists attempted to take photographs. At the southern boundary of Plantation Idéale, another cattle grid and sagging fence marked by a similarly huge sign, but this time reading in red on white 'USSR MISSILE DETECTION CENTRE' and, at long last able to demonstrate the little I had learned from my Russian studies in Auckland, I had contributed a couple of lines in Cyrillic script - almost certainly pure gibberish - punctuated by a lot of large red exclamation marks and a hammer and sickle. Absolutely no-one in sight here so the convoy proceeded nervously onwards.

The next montage on the agenda was Kaltapan's house, a corrugated iron dwelling at the side of the road. Some days previously, we had asked the owner if we might paint it, and though somewhat bemused he had agreed. So this was done with black and white paint, transforming the exterior, as best as we could, into a facsimile of a half-timbered structure of vaguely Elizabethan design and vintage. Lesley had already contrived an elegant inn sign, 'The Cock and Bull', that hung from the cross-tree of a high white post, between the house and the road. The beautifully painted heraldic animals on the sign at least put the word 'cock' into the right context, since 'rooster' is invariably the term locally used for the bird, while the former is entirely anatomical Here we had assembled some fifteen or so of our expatriate community, all dressed in their Sunday best, as appropriate for much cooler climes

To Coral Strands

in former times. Thus, the men all wore suits, and the women long flowing dresses and enormous hats bedecked with flowers. We sat at small tables outside the inn. The 'parson', a New Zealand builder with his collar on back-to-front, moved quietly between us, no doubt mouthing soft platitudes reflecting the sermon he might have delivered in church earlier that morning. Atis, the Lakatoro carpenter from Lamen Island, in a long white apron served us cooling drinks and I lounged at my table reading an ancient copy of 'The Times'.

The motley convoy approached down the long straight stretch of road and came to a halt just short of the inn. Engines were switched off or conked out, and there was silence as crowded heads craned through the open windows of the vehicles, the passengers apparently nonplussed by the spectacle before them. This tension was broken, however, when, timing it just right, Lesley in the largest hat of all and wildly waving a parasol, crashed through the tall grass on the opposite side of the road and joined us, gaily apologising to the company for arriving late. One by one the car doors opened down the line of vehicles, and the, by now hot and dishevelled tourists, certainly unaccustomed to such total invasion of their personal space, red dust, pot holes, broken springs, and the exhaust fumes of ill-maintained motors, possibly pumped to them directly through rust holes in the vehicle's floor, approached our little tableau.

Their initial greetings were plainly hesitant and appropriately formal, given our attire, but the social barrier between us was soon broken by a flood of questions. From one large American, of whom there were many, "Who on earth let the goddam Russians in?", to which he received the reply "Sorry, we are not permitted to discuss that", duly confirmed by the silent nodding or shaking of our heads. And from a German, "Why we were not told that here elephants is?", to which we expressed surprise and puzzlement. To another question, we explained that we gathered here every Sunday after church, which we vaguely indicated was somewhere over there in the long grass. An XXL and profusely perspiring lady asked Atis if she might order a drink. Without hesitation, and with great presence of mind, he replied "Sorry madam, members only", for truly, all we had brought with us had been in three now empty thermos flasks. She relayed the bad news to the rest of the party, "No drinks here guys". So, following a photo session, to which we made no objection and posed in a somewhat exaggerated Edwardian manner, and having assured them there were ice cold drinks awaiting their arrival just a few miles down the road, they crammed themselves back into their transport, and the overladen

NOWHERE NEAR GREENLAND

vehicles trundled off in clouds of smoke.

Before reaching their ice cold drinks, however, they would encounter just one more virtual hazard. A small stream, flanked by high cane, crossed the road at a corner, and its rough, stony bottom could only be forded at very slow speed. Here was strategically placed the last of our road signs, this time depicting the silhouette of a man wearing a pith helmet in a large cooking pot, and reading 'DANGER, NO STOPPING'. We rather hoped that those nearest the car windows would relay this dire information to their compressed companions in the interior and that the more religious among them would be crossing themselves, while others tightened jaw and sphincter muscles as they slowly bumped over the stream bottom. (In fact, not ten miles away to the north, until the beginning of the 1960s, the Big Nambas area was officially closed to visitors, because of continuing, albeit rare, instances of cannibalism).

Once the cavalcade had passed, we set to work to remove all traces of the morning's charade, entertaining the fantasy that perhaps the tourists would believe they had all been victims of mass hallucination. At least on their return, they would approach Kaltapan's house from the unpainted side, and thus not notice the 16th century features that remain to this day. Meanwhile, at their splendid luncheon, Maurice and Lucy le Perronec hosted apparently deranged tourists babbling of elephants, missiles and cannibals. The on-board zoologist, and the anthropologist Bengt Danielsonn who had accompanied Thor Heyerdahl on the Kon-Tiki expedition some years before, were put very much on the defensive for not having done their homework on Malekula. And when much later in the day they diligently sought further information, only to be told that all had been a jape, they were not visibly amused.

Nevertheless, in retrospect, many of the tourists thought it all hugely funny, and we were all invited aboard the Lindblad Explorer that night for a party. But that ship never returned again to Malekula, the tour operators probably believing that the Norsup anchorage should bear a notice reading 'Here be Lunatics'. The Cock & Bull sign was later raised at the thatched terminal building on the old airstrip at Norsup, where Lesley and Peter Wright's brother created a small business and served snacks and cold drinks. Like Peter, his brother was half Fijian, danced a really magnificent tamurai which he performed at parties, and was very gay. Sadly, he was crossed in love a few years later, and at Lakatoro committed suicide with Nivaquine .

To Coral Strands

An early memory I have of Peter and his lovely Wallis Island wife, is of calling on them with Lesley, on the morning of 1st January 1969, to wish them a Happy New Year. We were kindly offered drinks, and then, suddenly from behind, buckets of cold water were dashed over our heads. Then packets of flour were emptied over us. Just a Fijian custom, Peter chuckled, as we blinked through the mess, but in the terrific heat of that time of year it was not so hard to bear. He was a big, cheerful, hardworking man. One pay day in 1974, he had completed paying out wages to the plantation labour, begged a cigarette which he put behind his ear and set off to drive to Lakatoro. As he told it, the cigarette fell to the floor, he bent down to pick it up and the rusty Toyota he was driving crashed into a coconut tree. He was badly injured. The Norsup and Lakatoro doctors were both away, and for political reasons the Norsup airstrip was closed. Frank Palmer's little trading boat was in the bay, and he set off through rough seas to take Peter to Santo hospital, but Peter died on the way. I returned from long leave the next day, and bitterly regretted the loss of a vibrant life and good friend through such a succession of mischances.

The occasion arose, as was its wont to do in our little community, for another elaborate prank when my UN volunteer, Mike Sackett, was due to return to Malekula from Port Vila with Eileen, his newly-arrived fiancee. Darvall and Ida Wilkins had by then made Lakatoro a comfortable posting for contract officers and volunteers alike, with its houses set in botanic garden-like surroundings, backed by virgin rainforest, but with views over the fronds of coconut palms to the sea, and the small offshore islands of Uri and Uripiv. However, for the purpose of this reception, (or deception) it was decided to move Lakatoro to Aop bay, almost equidistant between Lakatoro and Norsup, where for some sixty metres beside the road was a line of five corrugated iron huts, used by the Big Nambas when for short periods they came down to the coast to cut copra for the big plantation. Each comprised a single room, with one window opening, a doorway, a floor of broken coral, and by day as hot as hell. A high flagpole flying the Union Jack was erected, road signs reading LAKATORO and SLOW were put in place at the north and south approaches, and a black and white painted sign, variously reading 'Dispensary', 'District Agent's Office', 'Agriculture', Unmarried Quarters' and 'Police', was nailed above the doorway of each hut. For reasons unconnected with the reception, Darvall had to meet the plane at Norsup, and was able to take Mike Sackett aside and ask him to play along with our joke. Informally welcoming Eileen, Darvall said he would see her later, but unfortunately had an unpleasant official duty to perform later that morning.

NOWHERE NEAR GREENLAND

He then sped off to Aop, changed into his district agent's white dress uniform, complete with sword, gloves, (from which rats had gnawed the ends of several fingers, but now plugged with cotton wool), and white pith helmet, and stood outside his 'office' which contained only two upside-down boxes, his portable Olivetti typewriter on one, and the detritus left behind by the Big Nambas. Ida Wilkins squatted by the roadside cooking something horrible in a large pot over an open fire, beside her the bunch of blackened bananas we had discovered in one of the huts. Douglas Malosu, then the assistant agricultural officer, lay on the coral floor of the dispensary, his heavily bandaged leg oozing mustard and tomato sauce propped up on a box, while Anne Naupa, in a starched white nurse's uniform, hovered over him. George Hart, our tall and gaunt district education officer, splendid in a mini-kilt - of I know not what tartan and made and given to him the previous Christmas by Lesley - instructed a group of local children in the eightsome reel by the roadside.

The tin huts at Aop, Malekula, 1972

A road gang in prison garb, that just happened to include a future president, prime minister and sundry ministers of the country that would gain independence less than a decade later, laboured away with picks and shovels. Several volunteers played drunk atop a pile of empty bottles, while I lay outside the dispensary, legs doubled under me, with walking boots placed over my knees. Just as the scene was fully set, Maxime Carlot, then the assistant French district agent, but himself one day to become prime minister, drove past in his Land Rover, the rapid half rotations

To Coral Strands

of his head suggesting that he was attempting, but failing, to believe what he was seeing. Perhaps the fraught question of 'Why is the Union Jack flying over a French-owned plantation' occurred to him, and quite possibly was subsequently the subject of a confidential note to his superior at Lamap.

Many hands show off George Hart's Christmas gifts

Norsup, Malekula, 1970

As the yet happy young couple arrived at Aop, Darvall greeted them with more formal expressions of welcome than hitherto, as now befitted his official status and splendid uniform. Offering to show them around the station, which he bragged had been created from scratch in a mere seven years, he first introduced Eileen to Ida, by then somewhat smudged by smoke, who offered her a blackened banana which she delicately declined. Darvall then helped the couple with their suitcases over to the 'Unmarried Quarters' hovel, bare except for a few hermit crabs scuttling around in the dirt and coral, and expressed the hope they would be very happy there. Following a, per force, brief tour of his office, they came over to me where I was lying outside the door of the dispensary. I was duly introduced, and Darvall

NOWHERE NEAR GREENLAND

chatted with me about my recent, extensive walking tour on Pentecost, Eileen fiercely fixing her gaze upon my face and away from my awful, truncated legs, and Mike stood directly behind her where he could more easily martial his involuntary facial twitches. Entering the 'dispensary', Mike, seeking catharsis, savagely, and with the wild laughter he had desperately been suppressing, kicked the box away from under Douglas' injured leg. Eileen rounded on him, quite horrified, having witnessed a previously unsuspected sadistic streak in her fiancee's disposition, while poor Douglas groaned on the coral and Anne fussed over him.

At about this point, straw in mouth like some loony, Lesley appeared, cycling so slowly down the road that the bike wobbled and she had to put out a steadying foot every few yards. She joined the drunken volunteers on the pile of bottles, while George explained to Eileen that Scottish country dancing was an essential component of primary school teaching in the New Hebrides, and then whirled off into another reel on the beach - not so easily accomplished in deep sand, and there was some falling about. Darvall then told Eileen he had that tiresome official duty to perform, and it would be better if she stayed with Ida at the end of the line of huts, away from police headquarters. Some months before, Lesley had made a life-size dummy with a most realistic papier-mâché head, very much resembling John Lennon, (though we had named him Bruce), complete with wire frame glasses and a fine pair of papier-mâché hands. We kept him in the spare bedroom where he was sometimes introduced to unsuspecting friends, but when I was away on tour, Lesley would sometimes take him for outings sitting beside her in the Land Rover, usually to the plantation shop in Norsup, which created much speculation and tongue-wagging. He was now to make his first and last fully public appearance.

Darvall marched over to the police shack, and two genuine, uniformed constables emerged from it dragging a reluctant, foot-trailing Bruce to beneath the branch of a Burao tree, to which had already been fixed a rope. Bruce was held upright on a box, and then by the rope which was placed around his neck. Darvall solemnly read the formal sentence of death, "Whereas, heretofore, not withstanding..........etc, etc", the box was kicked away and Bruce dropped. The shock of this short fall caused both his hands to fall off. This farcical denouement broke the spell. I leaped up on miraculously elongated legs and we all crowded round Eileen telling her that it was all a joke. However, the poor girl was quite stunned and remained so for a couple of days, though she and Mike were later happily married and he went on to occupy very senior positions in the World Food Programme, including that

To Coral Strands

of its director in Bangladesh.

Arrivals and departures were the prime occasions for these jokes, so perhaps we should have thought up some wheeze when the Duke of Edinburgh made a royal visit to Malekula in 1972, though we would almost certainly have all got the sack. However, the weather did its best to disrupt his programme, as we were then catching the edge of a cyclone. That morning a plane made a trial landing on the old Norsup airstrip, and a wave of water from the sodden ground broke right over the plane. Not good enough for the duke, but undeterred he made his way up to Malekula, ploughing through heavy seas on the Royal Yacht Britannia. The stone and coral wharf at Lakatoro had been reduced to rubble by a previous cyclone, so a beach landing at Aop was proposed, though we had then hastily to build a track over a culvert of 44 gallon oil drums across a small creek, and with the heavy rain throughout the day this small creek soon became quite a big creek. The duke arrived shortly before dark, and no sooner had the Land Rover bearing him passed over the culvert, then it was swept away. Phew! (No doubt, had it occurred during the crossing, we might, not unreasonably, have been accused of arranging it.) The earlier part of the programme, which had included a doubtless quite fascinating tour of my agricultural station, had had to be cancelled, but eight groups of traditional dancers, all from different parts of Malekula, were gathered on the football field. Lit by flaring bamboo torches, the palm fronds streaming in the wild wind, the scene was indeed dramatic, and the dancing to the beat of great wooden tam tams, the dirge-like singing, and the clatter of ankle rattlers, all accompanying the rhythmic stamping, was absolutely magnificent. The duke also symbolically killed a pig by tapping it lightly on the head with a pig hammer and shook our hands. There followed a cocktail party in George Hart's house while an intrepid few rebuilt the washed-away culvert, and the duke departed safely back to the Britannia and through very stormy seas to Vila.

Hurricanes, cyclones and typhoons are all names for the same phenomenon. Generally incubating near the equator, from which they carry away rising heat from warm seas, they move north in the northern hemisphere and south in the southern, though once they get going their track can be quite erratic. As was Carlotta's in 1969. It did considerable damage to some islands as it moved south, bypassing Efate, where its inhabitants breathed sighs of relief. Then, halfway to New Zealand, it turned right around and moved back north, this time slamming into Efate, and taking the capital by surprise. Lesley and I, visiting from Malekula, were staying

NOWHERE NEAR GREENLAND

at the Lagon Hotel, whose thatch we watched disappearing as from a chicken being rapidly plucked, and in the town there was the scary sight of a sheet of corrugated iron driven deep into the trunk of a mango tree. However, as the normal track of a hurricane is from north to south in these islands, it is useful to know where the eye, or its centre, is located. A useful rule of thumb is to face directly into the wind and point at right angles to your left, and the centre will be somewhere out there. Thus, if the wind is from the east, the eye will be in the north, so look out! If the wind comes from the west, then the hurricane will have passed by to the south, so you will probably be OK - but only probably.

Pastel of Big Nambas dancer by Lesley Weightman, 1969

Nowadays, with accurate forecasting, and satellites continuously tracking the path of hurricanes, their position, wind speed, and rate and direction of the storm's movement, are given every hour on the short-wave station which broadcasts universal time every minute. Likewise, Radio Vanuatu broadcasts hurricane warnings every hour when any are posing a threat to the archipelago, and three red lights in the centre of Vila are progressively lit to warn the inhabitants of the imminence of the storm. There is also much barometer tapping in households during the cyclone season, and in recent years, political correctness has determined that cyclones should alternately be given male and female names.

To Coral Strands

The strongest and longest cyclone we experienced in Malekula, was cyclone Wendy in 1972. It was a vast weather system, nearly a hundred miles wide and moving very slowly south. It took three days to clear us, with the huge eye of the storm passing directly over our island during the second night. As it did so, the wind dropped to a complete calm, the stars came out, and we were in the centre of a great bowl, with lightning continuously groping and flashing around its full circumference, beyond the sea's horizon, and too far away for us to hear thunder. We had no storm shutters on the house, and under the pressure of the wind the glass louvre windows had already let in copious amounts of water, and we were constantly at work with mops and buckets. Cyclones start with light zephyrs that whistle in the mosquito screens. There is sullen heat, high humidity and often heavy rain. Then the gusts pick up in both frequency and intensity, somewhat analogous to birth contractions, until the full storm is upon one, the wind and sea combining in an unbroken roar of sound, from the deepest boom to the highest shriek. There is no sound like it, except perhaps that of a jet engine at close quarters, or a tornado perhaps, and the volume is positively painful, and extremely wearying as it goes on and on. The whole top of the sea comes off as the white horses are whipped away, flung downwind and far inland. There is thunder and lightning, but the thunder is only dimly heard even when right overhead.

On this occasion, the generator which served our few houses at Norsup gamely chugged on and was not switched off that night. We tried playing Wagner at full volume, but could still barely hear it, for this was nature with all the stops pulled out. Tree branches were flung against the house and onto the roof, but we did not hear them. Eventually, quiet returned as the eye passed over us, and we clambered across a debris-strewn hundred yards or so to Monsieur Robert's house. He was a delightful man, standing in for Yves Tanguy, the substantive manager of the plantation, but, as the Irish would say, 'of the drink taken'. Shining our torch through the glass top of his double front door, there he was, right behind it, feet braced against it as he slept in a chair. The door locks had burst under the pressure of the wind almost two days before, and he had been there ever since. We returned from our house with planks of wood, hammer and nails, which we had made ready for ourselves, and Lesley took over some food. We nailed that door shut, checked the rest of the house, M. Robert went to bed, and we hurried home for act two. The eye passed over, and as its trailing edge approached, the gusts started again and slowly gathered in strength from exactly the opposite direction to that of a few hours before. Trees that had been blown one way were now pushed the other, and what

NOWHERE NEAR GREENLAND

had already been loosened up, such as our corrugated iron garage, now quickly flew away. Where we had had louvres shut, we now opened them on the lee side, and vice versa, as the humid heat was stifling and it is wise to equate the air pressure within the house to that of the outside. So heavy was the rain, that even shining a powerful torch outside on the leeward side of the house, all that we could see were dimly thrashing shapes as though through frosted glass. By morning the rain has eased but the wind and the massive seas on the reef still roared. The wet, gleaming coconut fronds streamed downwind from bow-bent palms like green seaweed, later the subject of Lesley's painting. We looked across the storming seas to nearby Norsup Island, and saw that the whole shape of it had changed, with a high bank of sand and coral running in an arc, and creating a new bay.

A visitor to Lakatoro in the early 1970s was Mike Macoun, Inspector General of Police for the U.K. Dependent Territories. Darvall and Ida Wilkins invited Lesley and me to dinner to meet their guest. Also invited was a man called Carruthers and his wife. He worked for the Public Works Department in Vila and was in Lakatoro to inspect some ongoing work. During the dinner, the conversation turned to the Great Train Robbery, which had occurred in England some ten years earlier. I then recounted how shortly after that, I had travelled from Dorset to Scotland with my sister in my new MGB sports car. My sister was navigating and somehow we inadvertently passed through Wales, emerging somewhere near Chester. After a week's holiday in Skye, and then visiting friends in Aberdeen, our arrival into Edinburgh was delayed because the Braemar Gathering was on our route and we visited it for a few hours. As it was too late to disturb my Malayan planter friends in Morningside, we drove through to the seaside suburb of Portabello. There, we found bed and breakfast lodgings with a Mrs. Harris, a widow who had her grandson staying with her for his summer holidays from prep school in England.

What we had not seen were the Scottish newspapers for that day, which banner headlined 'Dragnet Closes In On Portabello'. One of the protagonists of the robbery, nicknamed the Weasel, had been sighted in the area driving a sports car with his girlfriend. A reward of a staggering one hundred thousand pounds had been offered for information leading to his arrest, so there was considerable local interest in spotting him. Mrs. Harris' grandson, who had been hanging around in the hall when we arrived, decided that I was the Weasel and popped round to the local police station with the good news. Oblivious to all this while we slept, the police thoroughly searched my car, and then surrounded the house for the rest of the night.

To Coral Strands

The next morning while I was shaving in the bathroom, there was a heavy knock at the front door, and I heard a voice say "It's about that couple you took in last night, mam", and then the sound of many heavy boots entering the house. I knocked on my sister's door, suggesting she get up, and went through to Mrs. Harris in the kitchen. There she stood trembling, the precious porridge burning, the milk boiling over. "There's some gentlemen to see you in the parlour", she quavered. And there in the parlour stood three very large policemen. However, their faces fell when they saw me, for evidently I did not at all match their description of the Weasel. Nevertheless, perhaps just for form's sake, they asked me where I was on the night of the train robbery, and I was able to show them my passport, which I just happened to have with me, though had not needed for Skye. This showed that I had entered the UK after the date of the robbery, and had in fact been aboard the m.v. Jutlandia somewhere south of Suez. Sorrowfully the police departed, and my sister emerged to ask what all the fuss was about. Mrs. Harris' phone had already started ringing, and when I went out to my car, there were people standing at their front gates all up and down the street. Of the grandson there was not a sign, neither hide nor hair, but Mrs. Harris was lamenting she would never live this down, never, and just wait till she got hold of him!

This was an amusing enough story I suppose, but at the end of it, Carruthers stirred rather uneasily in his chair and looked at his wife. She nodded, and then he told 'his' tale of the Great Train Robbery. On the very night in question he and his wife were on leave in England and waiting for confirmation of a contract that would take him to a new job in Saudi Arabia. They were staying as paying guests at a farm in Buckinghamshire, which, as it transpired, was the nearest habitation to the site of the robbery. Their hosts were a German family and, as might be expected, their activities followed a strict routine for getting up in the morning, greeting their guests, precise mealtimes, going to bed and so on. But on the night of the robbery there had been a lot of unusual activity, lights, the dog barking, a lorry coming into the yard and leaving again, and the next morning there was no sign of the family, though much later in the day one of them came back. They heard about the robbery on the radio, but during the days that followed, when there were intensive searches of nearby properties for the missing millions and any evidence the gang might have left behind, no police came near this farm. Carruthers had thought that if he reported their experience to the police, they might become involved and miss out on the overseas job, and a week or so later they left for the Middle East. Carruthers was clearly glad to get this off his chest, and Mike Macoun was certainly intrigued

NOWHERE NEAR GREENLAND

by the story. And it was indeed a considerable coincidence that guests around a dinner table in Malekula had separately, albeit tangentially, been involved in The Great Train Robbery.

In 1974 there was a second royal visit to the New Hebrides, this time by the Queen and her Consort, accompanied by Princess Anne - newly married to Mark Philips, Earl Mountbatten and others. Having attended the Commonwealth Games in Christchurch, New Zealand, the royal party sailed north on the royal yacht and were to enjoy an unannounced, entirely private day of relaxation on the southernmost island of Aneityum, their official visit not commencing until the following day at Port Vila. Arty Krafft was at that time the sole expatriate inhabitant of Aneityum. A weather-beaten old Aussie, he managed, and somehow kept running, a near-derelict saw mill that processed kauri logs. Later he related to me how on this Sunday morning he was sitting on the doorstep of his little two-roomed cabin, which overlooked the sandy beach of a quiet bay and the small, offshore island of Inyeug. Then a large ship slowly took shape as it came over the horizon, and to his surprise eventually dropped anchor in the waters of the bay. A boat was lowered, and motored its way to the shore. As is customary and polite in the islands, Arty pottered down to the beach in his shorts to catch the rope and welcome the visitors. Having grabbed the rope, he looked up at a woman in the bows and exclaimed "Well bless my soul if it isn't the Queen!". He spent a lazy morning on the beach chatting with the royal party, and was then invited back to the royal yacht Britannia for lunch. Following that, Mountbatten - whose legs he claimed he tripped over - offered him a cigar, and sometime during the afternoon he was lowered over the side into the yacht's pinnace and returned to the beach. As the yacht disappeared northwards around the head of the bay, Arty, back on his doorstep, wondered if the whole day had not been some kind of tropical hallucination. Sadly, he died in Australia about two years later. (The little, uninhabited island of Inyeug, the site of a whaling station in the 1840s, has recently for the sake of tourism been renamed Mystery Island, where cruise ships now regularly disembark their passengers for a day on its fine sand beaches.)

Following their official visit to the capital, the royals continued to the island of Pentecost where they were to witness the Pentecost jump, the ancient and certain mother of all bungee jumping. Commencing at about ten feet from the ground, for the youngest jumpers of six or seven years old, to about one hundred feet for the older and more experienced divers, some thirty males slowly topple forwards from

To Coral Strands

the end of narrow diving boards, custom made for each individual, their fall arrested by lianas tied around their ankles when their heads are just inches from the ground. Three wands support the boards and act as shock absorbers, but are calibrated to break, so that each board, once used, lies flat against the structure of the tower, permitting an unobstructed fall for the next diver. Thus, great precision is required in calculating the height and weight of the diver, the strength of the wands, the length of the board, and the tensile stretch of the lianas; a job for experienced elders. The tower itself is constructed of interlaced wooden and bamboo poles around a tall forest tree, from which branches and foliage have been trimmed. Entirely lashed together with creepers, the top part of the tower is flexible and trembles as the jumpers climb it, and is anyway liable to sway in the wind. Unlike all the jumpers from the lower stages, who can steady themselves as they move to the end of their boards by holding on to the one directly above, the topmost jumper needs great balance and courage to walk out on his slender board, as high up as a ten storey building. Before toppling forwards, legs straight, arms folded against the chest, the divers are at liberty to say what they like, or may simply whistle before plummeting headlong downwards. As the towers are always constructed on a steep slope, over which the soil is thoroughly dug by chanting women between each jump, to soften it and remove any stones, a really good jump consists of rebounding back up the slope as the lianas exert their recoil, landing squarely back on two feet. The whole performance, the skill involved and the courage required, makes the modern form of bungee jumping look tame indeed.

On this occasion, attended by the Queen, the jump was out of season, and the tensile stretch and strength of the lianas was perhaps not so easy to calculate. It is not only important for each board and liana to be calibrated for the individual, it is also taboo for a diver to use a board not specifically made for him. The adult jumpers make their own boards, select and measure their vines for their weight, height and distance to fall, though the little boys receive some assistance with these preparations. In this way, accidents are made rare, and for which no one but the jumper may be blamed. However, this time, when the jump was two thirds complete, a diver decided he didn't want to go through with it. Sensibly, there is no shame attached to this, and an unused board is simply cut so that it hangs vertically. But another diver presented himself, having perhaps been disappointed at not being awarded a place to jump on this royal occasion. His sister, who stood near me on the ground, was moaning that he was breaking taboo and shouldn't jump from someone else's board. Well, he jumped, both vines snapped, and he plummeted

NOWHERE NEAR GREENLAND

hard into the ground. He was carried to a small shelter behind the tower, and I was asked to go and find out how he was. I reported back to the royal party that he was conscious, had drunk some water, and there were evidently no broken bones. I then sought out the American present who had been living for some time at the nearby Lonorore plantation and claimed to be a doctor, but he refused to have anything to do with the matter, and I assumed this was because he feared being sued, American style. (It later transpired the man was a complete charlatan, and had been giving people in the area injections he said would confer eternal youth.) By mischance, Earl Dorney, the Lakatoro doctor, had briefly walked up the coast to tend to his wife who had malaria, so I jogged there to fetch him back. Earl had the man evacuated by air to Vila where he died that night of internal injuries.

In 1975, we awaited the return of Darvall to Lakatoro from his long leave in Australia. The acting district agent Jerry Marston and I decided that this presented another opportunity for a surprise reception, and would comprise three separate components. First, a full size mock-up would be made by Atis of the m.v. Ida's deck. The Ida was Darvall's official touring vessel, named after his wife. On the morning of his arrival, this would be towed out to Decoy Reef, which lay a mile or so off the coast, and which we had so named after HMS frigate Decoy struck it during an official visit a few years previously. There it would be anchored, and laid out as though wrecked. Meanwhile, the real Ida was fortuitously out of sight up in Santo. Even the resident commissioner in Vila was recruited to commiserate with Darvall on the fate of his vessel, telling him he would get the full story when he arrived at Lakatoro, and inevitably Darvall would be looking down as the plane came in low over the reef just prior to landing at Norsup. The second component required me to go into the forest with one of the prisoners on the station and cut down a long, straight tree branch bearing abundant foliage. Darvall's serious veneration of trees had resulted in there being only a single narrow gap between them, through which he could spy the sea from his house, and into this gap we now planted our pseudo tree.

Last but not least, and the most technically demanding, also addressed Darvall's strict insistence on tree conservation. We would record the sound of a tree being cut down by a chainsaw, and play this outside his bedroom window at night. Recording this on the agricultural station, we soon had on tape the sound of a chain saw being pull-started, revved up, screaming through the trunk of a senile coconut palm, and finally the crash and thump as it fell to the ground. A great sequence.

To Coral Strands

The snorting of pigs in their sty nearby, however, afforded us additional inspiration, and by throwing scraps to them we recorded their happy grunts and loud competitive squeals. We set up the tape recorder in the station's little thatched church, some two hundred yards below Darvall's house, having quite by accident discovered that we could transmit our recordings over the telephone wire to the speaker, which we had concealed ten feet up in a tree, and about twice that distance from his bedroom window. The fact that this transmission simultaneously played through every telephone on the station was by-the-by.

Well, as ill luck would have it, on the morning of Darvall's return, a strong southeasterly trade wind blew up, and try as we might we could not tow our version of the Ida out to the reef. We eventually abandoned the deck near the remnants of the Lakatoro jetty, where it was not spotted from the air, and later, Jerry somewhat laboriously explained to Darvall what we had intended. However, the punch line for component two came when Darvall was lunching that day with Jerry, and remarked "You know Jerry, this climate is really quite amazing; there's a tree in front of my house that must have grown fully two metres since I departed on leave", and Jerry expressed himself equally amazed. However, a few days later Darvall noticed that the leaves of the new tree were beginning to wilt and brown, and soon all were dead. He called a prisoner to dig it out, by chance the same one who had planted it. Recounting the true facts of the case, the prisoner laughed and laughed, and so did Darvall, happy now to get his view back.

On the night of Darvall's return, quite late, with the station all asleep, Jerry and I crept over to the church, switched the volume up to maximum, and played the chain saw sequence, again and again and again. The racket across the station was ear-splitting, awakening many and generating hilarity, for word had already spread of our spoof, but Darvall alone slept soundly through it all. We then switched to pigs, their grunts and squeals resounding in the night and echoing back from the surrounding forest, and woe betide anyone who picked up their telephone! More general mirth but, alas, the same result - or lack of it. We laboured on for a second and then a third night, still hugely enjoying our fantasy of Darvall, when daylight came, questioning everyone about the illicit night felling of trees, and searching for the evidence; or, even better, going to the station doctor complaining of hearing pigs up a tree outside his bedroom window, and being prescribed the appropriate medication - no doubt enjoining the medic to keep the consultation strictly confidential. At this time, I was only visiting Malekula from the capital for limited peri-

NOWHERE NEAR GREENLAND

ods, and was required to return there, so I left somewhat disappointed. Ida then returned from Australia, and Darvall organised a reception in their garden to celebrate both their recent arrivals. It was now or nothing, and in the middle of the party Jerry slipped away and played the pig recording. At last we had a result, when Darvall exclaimed "Well that's extraordinary, I do believe there's a pig up that tree!", and all the company fell about laughing.

Over the years, Darvall had created the park-like grounds at Lakatoro from the bush and coconut palms that had once covered them, but managed to preserve most of the indigenous trees. Many of the flowering shrubs he collected on his tours around the islands, and soon I followed suit, bringing back cuttings of many hibiscus varieties for my garden at Norsup which I had laboriously terraced. My long khaki cotton socks, kept damp, proved the best containers for maintaining the cuttings in good shape until I returned home. Bougainvilleas, flowering gingers, frangipanis and cannas, of which there are many, were also highly collectable in the villages, along the paths and in the bush. In the Solomons I was given a variety of hibiscus, not found in the New Hebrides; and planted at Norsup, these seeded and I then took great pleasure in attempting to breed new varieties, in which I modestly succeeded and did the same with cannas. The ease with which cuttings took, and the speed with which they grew was most encouraging. Less encouraging, though, are the frequent cyclones which discourage or prohibit the growing of wind-sensitive trees, such as cashew, Panama cherry, rubber and oil-palm. And in the constant high humidity of the islands, the beautiful Jacaranda tree never makes the magnificent show of mauve against the blue sky, when the whole tree is all flowers and no leaves, as it does in the drier tropics and subtropics, like Australia and southern Africa. The banyan is perhaps the most impressive of all the trees in the islands, and the shade of just one may cover a whole acre. It liberally supports creepers, and epiphytes such as ferns and orchids, and the night-flowering Cirius cactus which literally pops open huge, fragrant, creamy-white flowers just once a year at full moon. This attracts fruit bats in hundreds, and perfectly sets the scene for a tropical version of Dracula. The banyan, which is of the fig family, starts life as an epiphyte on a living tree which it eventually strangles. The aerial roots, which it subsequently suspends from its branches, themselves grow into trunks and the tree becomes massive at the base, well able to withstand most cyclones.

At the lower end of Lakatoro station was the sports field, adjoining the road and agricultural station. A few coconut palms, of which most had been cleared, still

To Coral Strands

stood around the field's perimeter, interspersed with scarlet-flowering Flamboyants, or Christmas Trees as they are known locally, as they are in full bloom at that season. Here we held the first agricultural show in 1970, with farmers bringing in their produce and livestock from all over the district, and it was a great success. There were also coconut-husking, copra-cutting and log-chopping competitions, and Pastor Fred Timakata, later to become President of Vanuatu, won the last of these. In the evening there was a concert on the sports field, when we staged the theatrical drama 'The Great Escape Foiled By Police Sergeant Wilkins'. George Hart was the dangerous criminal, held inside the cage built upon a trailer. Much exaggerated play was made of long ladders, huge saws and ropes, as the rescue attempt by New Hebrideans was made. Lots of slapstick and running about, with Sgt. Wilkins inside the cage at one point, but the escape was finally foiled. The crowd went wild. On another occasion, 'I go Long Pentecost' (He goes to Pentecost) was staged, featuring the aftermath of a sinking touring vessel. This had all its passengers and crew crammed into a tiny dinghy, fighting for biscuits or a more comfortable seat, being ill over the side, singing, drinking, and so on, and then landing on the wrong island. Yet another was set on Ambrym, complete with a miniature volcano which contained concealed bangers and shot rocks into the air. All considered great stuff.

I forget the exact occasion, perhaps it was Queen's Birthday, but the British had challenged the French community at Norsup to a football match. The French District Agency had by then moved up from Lamap to Norsup, so they had ample candidates to make up a full team. The match was to be on the Lakatoro sports field. Unfortunately, there was some breakdown in communication, in that we failed to convey adequately that this was not to be a serious affair, and the French went into serious training. Come the day, our team turned up in bizarre strip, such as silly hats, pyjamas, drag, and I wore gum boots. We gave the French district agent, the rotund M. Lecuyer and captain of the away team, the privilege of kicking off. The ball was already in place at centre field, but it was filled with water. M. Le Delegue took a long run for a mighty kick, and all but concussed his foot on contact. He hopped about a bit but gamely continued. We had arranged that after a few minutes, Darvall would pretend to be injured and roll about on the ground, groaning like a true professional. A stretcher, made up of a Union Jack tied to two poles, would then be rushed onto the field by two volunteers, who would gently roll Darvall onto it; but as soon as they were clear of the pitch he would unceremoniously be jettisoned.

NOWHERE NEAR GREENLAND

All went according to plan. Darvall went down writhing, the stretcher went on, was rushed off, and he was mightily thrown. Perfect, gales of laughter, except that Darvall had really been injured on the field, and further incapacitated by the ejection process. That was the end of the game for him, and he hobbled about with a stick and a sore back for several weeks. We decided to have half time after about ten minutes, and playing in gumboots I was already exhausted. It was quite a long half time, since we had appropriately laid on champagne for the visitors. Eventually returning to the field, a French forward decided to run with the leaking ball, and soccer became rugby. Finally, Monsieur Lecuyer scored a magnificent try between the posts, having run the whole length of the pitch, and then threw up on the touch line. We conceded the game. There was no return match.

George Hart, a very good friend, was nervous of flying in small planes, which we often had to take between the islands. Since my arrival, the planes generally used for this by the local airline had evolved from the three-engine De Havilland Drovers, resembling a small version of the DC3 and retired here from the Flying Doctor Service in Australia, to Piper Aztecs, which had rather too high a landing speed to be safe on the small island airstrips, and finally to the Britten Norman Islanders, introduced in the early 1970s and which continue flying today. These are a high-winged, two engine aircraft with seating for nine passengers. When they were first introduced, one of the pilots described them to me as being cheap, slow and noisy. All true perhaps, however, as they had a stalling speed of only forty-three knots, and empty could take off in less than a hundred yards, they were ideal and safe for local conditions, and so they have largely proved over thirty-five years. I have always enjoyed flying in small aircraft, and though statistically it is more hazardous, one gets a real sense of flying and there is much more to see than from a high altitude jet. Generally flying at between seven and ten thousand feet, the cloudscapes are particularly beautiful. Sometimes the pilot, to relieve the boredom of straight, level flight, would take the plane down to look at whales or an active volcano, and in the case of Ambrym fly around its great caldera, or even flirt with one of the craters. It was an added pleasure to be in the seat next to the pilot, where there is a better view, less noise, and one can take a layman's interest in the instrumentation - altitude, airspeed, bearing, etc. - and even learn the rudiments of flying a plane.

This was the place, I argued that day with the district health nurse Margaret Ponninghouse, where George Hart should sit. We were standing at the old Norsup

To Coral Strands

airstrip, and he was waiting for the plane to fly him to Pentecost, and somehow the question of what to do in the case of a pilot suffering a heart attack had arisen. On the Islander there are duel controls, so up front next to a dead or incapacitated pilot, one could, at least in theory, just take over. However, if one was sitting behind the pilot, it would be necessary first to haul him back over his seat and then clamber over to take his place, or change places with whomever was sitting next to the former pilot. None of these manoeuvres would be easy in the Islander, as there is no gangway, the seats occupying the full width of the fuselage, and there is little space between the top of the seats and the roof of the cabin. Thus, if the passenger sitting next to the pilot was, say, a large lady, option two would be extremely difficult, even dangerous as one of her inevitably flailing legs might easily strike the control column or propel the ex-pilot against it, putting the plane into a terminal dive. Likewise, she might get wedged between the top of the seat and the roof, and time is of the essence in a situation like this. However, let us assume for the sake of argument, that George has somehow gained the controls. Now what? Gain altitude! Get up high, so that you have got plenty of room to make mistakes. You need more engine power to climb, so push the dual throttles forward. These are the yellow topped levers near the floor in the centre of the cockpit. Now pull back slowly on the stick, that steering wheel thing, but not too far or you will loop the loop, and don't take the plane too high or you will faint, and so will all the other passengers; that is if they have not already fainted. Remember, this plane is not pressurised and there are no oxygen facilities. Ten thousand feet will do very nicely. Twelve thou max.

OK. Now assuming you have located the former pilot's earphones, and did not bust the wire when pulling him back over the seat, or whatever you did, put them on and press the little black button on the left side of the steering wheel. This should enable you to talk to the air traffic controller in Vila or Santo. You have no idea what the number of your aircraft is, so just say "This is George Hart speaking." Don't get into the "you don't know me but", routine. Just say "I have taken over the controls of this plane because the pilot appears to be dead, and probably is, and I have absolutely no idea how to fly this thing." They may then ask you to confirm that you are not a hijacker, so do that. Then tell them where you are, flying from Norsup towards Pentecost, or should be if you are still heading east. You will see it as a long, bumpy black line on the horizon, or it may now be right underneath you, if the apparently fatal episode occurred late into the flight, and you are now heading out over the open Pacific, next stop Los Angeles, only you don't have the fuel for that. They may ask you how many p.o.b.; that means passengers on board,

NOWHERE NEAR GREENLAND

so tell them. Do not include the deceased pilot as he is now freight, and strictly speaking you should not include yourself as you are now the pilot. What we think they should now tell you is to turn left, to bring you up to Santo, much closer than Vila, where there is a good long runway, two in fact, and they should tell you how to make a left. If they don't, for goodness sake ask them. We think they should then despatch a plane from Santo to rendezvous with you, and then fly in front of you with the pilot instructing you to imitate whatever he does, finally bringing you to a safe landing. Well, not quite finally, as he must tell you how to feather the propellers, or at least turn the engines off and apply the brakes, otherwise you could run into the back of him or plough into the bush, or whatever, and I think there's a sawmill there somewhere at the end of the runway. Think of the cheers, George, from your fellow passengers, and the crowd running towards the plane across the runway. You are a hero! And the headlines: 'District Education Officer Somehow Flies Plane and Passengers To Safety!'.

And so on, but George is not visibly cheered by this triumphant ending. His plane for Pentecost then arrived, and out stepped a middle-aged, balding pilot. This is not a good omen. Most of the pilots with Air Melanesia are young, adding to their flying hours and experience before moving on to Qantas or some other major airline. So why is this pilot flying here? Well, at least it can't be a health problem, can it? Then what could his problem be? Before we have time for further speculation, George boards the flight and he is sitting up next to the pilot. That's a good start and we give him a thumbs up sign. He later told us he immediately felt some hitherto unfelt sense of responsibility, and took more interest in the controls than usual. The plane took off, and we waved it away. However, shortly into the flight, well before achieving cruising altitude, the pilot began to behave strangely. He was circling his head, first to the left, then to the right, and then leaning right back, then forwards, and then the head circling motions began again. Recounting this later, George said he thought "This is it!", and actually broke into a cold sweat. Fortunately, he did not commence to wrestle the pilot out of his seat, who, he belatedly realised, was merely cooling his bald head in the air jet.

Born and brought up within sight of the great shipyards on the Clyde, and having witnessed the building and launch of some of the biggest ships in the world, George had little confidence in outrigger canoes and other small craft. When nearing the shore in the touring vessel's dinghy, George, replete with nervous energy, would be up in the bows ready to leap ashore with his briefcase bulging with teachers'

To Coral Strands

wages. "Not yet George", we would counsel him as we came in though the breakers, or waited for just the right moment to do so, with our bows already within metres of a steep beach on Paama or Pentecost. "Hang on George", we advised, but apparently in thrall to the call of the land which could not be denied, he would leap into the foaming brine, sometimes actually disappearing, but always resurfacing still clutching the precious briefcase.

Capsizing at Lolowai, 1970

Once, when the Mangaru dinghy was under repair, we arrived off Lolowai, and sang out for an outrigger. George was to go ashore first, and I asked him to wait while I went below for my camera, knowing there was the imminent prospect of an excellent photo opportunity. I have capsized more than once in outriggers, but with George it was a certainty, with his tall figure unbalanced atop the narrow thwarts.

As the diminutive owner of the canoe pulled away from the side of the ship, down went the outrigger and he leant right over to counterbalance it. But he couldn't counterbalance George who had decided to lean the other way. That was my first shot. Second one, with the outrigger now submerged, George, already with one arm and shoulder in the water, briefcase futilely held high aloft. Third photo, George is treading water, gamely smiling up at the photographer, with floating comb and briefcase alongside. He had probably the most thoroughly salt-preserved

NOWHERE NEAR GREENLAND

briefcase in the South Pacific.

Some of the Air Melanesia pilots had a great sense of humour, though this could sometimes tend towards that of the gallows. My wife was sitting next to the pilot on a flight down to Vila, and they landed at Lamap, one of the shorter grass airstrips with tall coconut palms at either end. The remaining seats were then taken and the freight compartment was full. On these small planes, the passengers as well as their luggage and other freight, are all meticulously weighed and recorded on the flight manifest before loading. The pilot decided they had reached the maximum. However, the local agent, Father Zerger, he of the red, back-facing baseball cap, pleaded with him to load just one last item that urgently had to be sent to Vila. There was some protracted discussion, with the pilot suggesting that one of the Father's passengers should be offloaded to make room. Eventually, shaking his head and expressing grave doubts as to the lifting ability of his plane, well don't blame me, etc, the pilot reluctantly agreed to load the extra item of freight. Still grumbling, he taxied the plane to the end of the runway and made a great show of revving the engines. He pushed the throttles forward, folded his arms, and they set off down the runway. Still with arms folded and shaking his head in time with intoning "Heavy, heavy, heavy, heavy, heavy" the plane took off - Lesley swore he did not touch the controls - and shot off over the coconuts. He surely induced tummy cramps in some of his passengers.

Gary Ogg, a tall blond young Australian piloting Drovers when we arrived, exuded confidence and was undoubtedly already a skilled pilot. Indeed, there was a story that he had earlier missed his chance with the large Australian airlines for flying a plane under Sydney Harbour Bridge. One day in 1968, Peter Wright, then the local agent, and I stood by the plantation pigsties to watch him take off empty, i.e., no p.o.b. At that time, passengers and those greeting the aircraft, gathered at the far end of the former airstrip where the plane stood ready for takeoff, and the pigs and flies provided some distraction when planes were delayed. Gary spent longer than was his habit in revving the three engines, waggling the tail and flaps and so on, and then roared off down the strip. The take-off end is marked by a low cliff of some forty feet, dropping down to the road and reef below, and over this Gary and his plane now disappeared from sight. No splash, nothing. Hearts in mouths and for a better view, Peter scrambled onto the roof of his Land Cruiser, and I onto the roof of my Land Rover. Still nothing. Then, suddenly, there was the old Drover, practically standing on its tail, yowling up into the sky. Relief. Then

To Coral Strands

the plane made a steep turn, made as if to land again at the far end, but instead came roaring diagonally across the strip, wheels not three feet from the ground, straight at us! We simultaneously dived from our vehicles, Peter into the ditch, which carried a dark effluent from the pigsties, which I happily missed. The plane skimmed our trucks and clawed through the tops of the coconuts, waggled its wings and flew off to Vila. Quite brilliant precision flying, and we could imagine Gary having a good chuckle - and he would have chuckled more if he could have seen Peter getting back into his vehicle, now blackened and malodorous, closely followed by a swarm of flies.

When they were introduced into service, Gary flew the first Islander down to Tanna. He was to return empty, and Bob Paul, the principal trader on the that island, co-founder of the airline, plane buff, and regular attendant at the Farnborough Air Show, was keen for Gary to show him just what this new plane could do. This was akin to asking a hungry lion to demonstrate stalking a missionary, and might, thereafter, be tempted to exceed its brief. No worries, said Gary, and after carefully checking engines and controls, took off and executed a whole series of steep climbs, turns, spins, and for a grand finale looped the loop. Very exhilarating for Gary and the appreciative spectators on the ground. He then flew off straight and level for Vila and checked his manifest. To his horror he found he had one p.o.b. One little old lady, sitting right at the back. As she had never flown before she probably thought all this was quite normal, though history does not record whether she chose to return to Tanna by boat.

It was on Tanna, some years before, that Bob Paul lost his partner in their new airline, Paul Burton, who failed to lift his Drover out of a steep valley and all aboard were killed. The first crash of an Islander also occurred on that island. At the time, I was looking after the agriculture of Northern District, as well as my own, on behalf of my colleague who was on long leave. Lesley and I would often eat out at a little restaurant in Luganville, operated by the local French butcher. It also had one or two rooms for guests, and here, some of the Air Melanesia pilots chose to stay overnight. Thus we got to know Pierre the pilot quite well. Back in Norsup, a few days after seeing him, Lesley had a very vivid dream in which he crashed his plane. She even said that it crashed in a grassy area. She wanted us to warn Pierre, and I said, well, by doing that you might even cause him to crash, through denting his confidence, and so on. A few days later, the annual Tanna agricultural show was held, and Pierre took an Islander down from Vila. He had with him the British In-

NOWHERE NEAR GREENLAND

formation Officer, who was to take photos at the show, as well as tourists and others aboard. After lunch, they were due to return to Vila, and Pierre took them down low over the White Grass area so that photos could be taken of the wild horses that roam this plateau. Too low, a wing tip struck the ground and they crashed. Two people were killed and Pierre was flung out through the cockpit windscreen. He was to be paraplegic for the rest of his life, barely able to speak or even hold a cigarette.

There have been other crashes since. A newly arrived volunteer of mine, a Canadian, took off from Vila for Santo where he was to be posted. The Aztec aircraft crashed into a coconut plantation barely a minute after take-off. One person was killed and he was badly injured. In hospital, he made me promise not to tell his parents and he made a good recovery. Then the more recent, 1991, Islander crash on Santo, again a plane failing to climb out of a steep valley, this time on the mountainous Cumberland Peninsular where the flight had gone to locate isolated stands of kauri. And more recently still, the crash of an Islander at dusk in bad weather into Mele Bay, from which a few surviving passengers swam for half the night and made it ashore at Paradise Cove.

Some of the larger planes that have served the New Hebrides from abroad were not so reliable. Certainly not the old UTA DC4, on which we arrived. The lavatory on that plane had a concertina door, and it jammed on Darvall Wilkins shortly after the plane had left Santo for Noumea. No lungs could shout loud enough to be heard on that plane, but he was able to force open a small gap at the very top of the door, through which he wiggled his fingers for an hour or so before they were noticed and their significance recognised. The Caravelle that eventually replaced it was a beautiful, much faster and far more comfortable aircraft. I was sitting at the front, near the exit doors, when the plane was held at the end of Tontouta runway in New Caledonia to await a late-arriving VIP. It was very hot in the plane, and the stewardess opened the doors on either side of me. I was then sitting in a pleasant cross breeze, and gazing out at the landscape, when I noticed a cockroach crawling around the door lining, and then another and another. Looking out the other side, there was the same procession of cockroaches marching around that door as well. I was returning from leave in Europe, and I thought, ah, now I really am back in the South Pacific!   A few weeks later, the plane was withdrawn from service, never to return, and I heard it was because cockroaches had consumed the wiring.

To Coral Strands

At that same restaurant in Santo where we had met the pilot Pierre, the butcher's young niece, whose marriage had recently fallen apart in France, came out to stay with him. She was cheerful and pretty, and helped serve at table. One night after the meal, we all drove out to Simonsen's wharf and took turns at pushing one another around at great speed in an old wheelbarrow. It was a hoot! We went home, and she returned to the restaurant where she sat drinking champagne for a while with an overnighting pilot. Then she went to her room and swallowed sixty Nivaquine tablets. She awoke her cousin, and asked him to take her to the hospital, not to be saved, she said, but to save him the hassle of having her die on the premises. They reached the hospital and she expired twenty minutes later. As she was a suicide, the Catholic nursing sisters would have nothing to do with laying out her body, and her uncle wheeled her on a trolley to the hospital morgue. Do would-be suicides so easily hide a decision already taken, or are they quite suddenly overtaken by an impulse, an unbearable depression? I had seen this once before when Pat Freeman, the genial Irish manager of the Musoma Hotel in Tanganyika, danced half the night away, and immediately afterwards shot himself through the mouth with a .22.

During my seven years on Malekula, I was only twice visited by my director, and at no time did I receive any technical advice or guidance on how I might conduct my work, which was great as far as I was concerned, though I would have appreciated more feedback from the monthly reports I submitted to Vila. For the first visit, the then director, M. Thevenin, expressed an interest in walking from west to east across the north of Malekula from Atchin to Espiegle Bay, a distance of perhaps only ten miles but involving crossing quite rugged, thickly wooded terrain. A touring vessel was to meet us on the far side. I had taken this path once before, passing through two long-deserted villages, one named Batarlilip, whose collection of ancient slit gongs still stood, slowly rotting, at rakish angles beside their nasaras, which would not have resounded to the stamp of dancing feet and singing for more than half a century. M. Thevenin arrived at Norsup carrying a heavy movie camera, perhaps only 16mm, but in a thick, old fashioned leather case and with a wooden tripod. With the chief forestry officer, Martin Bennett, two agricultural field assistants and a forest guard, we set off in fine form early one morning, but with the camera equipment soon passing to our local companions. However, by midday things were not going so well, and the director was plainly distressed. By mid-afternoon he was completely exhausted and sat down, saying he could go no further. By this time our slow progress meant that all the water we were carrying had been

NOWHERE NEAR GREENLAND

drunk and we were still some miles from a stream. Our assistants went scouting in the forest and came back in triumph bearing wild oranges. After a while, we started off again, and encouraged our director by saying, just one more hill, the river is close now, and so on, but he konked out and we spent an uncomfortable night in the bush. And it was cold, because we were at some altitude and had brought no extra clothing with us. At almost mid-morning the following day, we reached the boat, which happily had waited for us. We were to have proceeded around the coast to Brenwei, for M. Thevenin to climb up to Amok, film the Big Nambas. and then walk back across the isthmus of the island to Norsup. But, hors de combat, he returned directly to Norsup by boat, and from thence flew back to Vila. Hardly a successful visit, and not one frame was shot with that damn camera.

I did not get many visitors from Vila, and I guess the Deputy Director of agriculture, David Allen, was the most frequent, though he never went beyond Norsup or Lakatoro. J.J. Balmain, however, at one time on the natural resources desk at the British Residency, was really keen to see what went on in the islands. He was a large, jovial, red-faced man in late middle age, of whose good reputation I had heard when I was in the Cameroons, where he had been a popular district commissioner at Bamenda. For work, he always wore a white shirt, voluminous white Bombay bloomers, white stockings, sensible brown shoes, and he carried a walking stick. This time we had climbed up into the hills of north Pentecost to Amatbobo to look at cocoa, yams and other crops, as well as some small cattle holdings. Going up, he was fine, but then it rained and the red clay path became extremely slippery. Having fallen heavily once or twice on the way down, he decided to stay down, punting himself along on his bottom with his walking stick, using it as a brake on the steep bits, and to change direction at the corners. As he gained confidence, and with it speed, his action resembled that of a kayaker slaloming down white water. His natural padding protected him from any injury, and he arrived back at the coast before I did.

However, I put Jim Balmain in the New Hebrides top ten for snorers, scoring equally highly for sheer volume, variety (including whistles, sighs, grunts and snorts) and duration. Sharing a cabin on a touring vessel with this class of performer could be very trying. Jack Barley, captain of the m.v. Navaka, was another way up there on the charts. He had a separate cabin, divided from the main cabin by a heavy mahogany sliding door, which, however, was permanently wedged open. One very black night, rocking at anchor at Craig Cove, on Ambrym, I decided

To Coral Strands

I had had enough of Jack's solo performance, and climbed down from my bunk to close the sliding door. It would not budge, and feeling about with my hand, I discovered the little wedge that had been placed in the bottom track to hold it open. This I prised out, and slid the door across. Except that the door then came right off its tracks, because I had somehow also lifted it. There I was, then, staggering around a pitch black cabin, holding this very heavy mahogany door as the boat rocked from side to side, while Jack persevered with his recital. Nightmare! After some while, I got the door back onto its tracks, but then could not find the wedge to stop it crashing backwards and forwards with every roll of the ship. Holding the door with one hand, and feeling around on the floor with the other, I eventually located this essential little piece of wood, and jammed the door open again. Jack snored on, but by then I was exhausted and fell asleep straight away.

My successor at Lakatoro was another top performer, and mercifully I toured with him only once by boat during the handing over period. In those days, we had monthly district team meetings, when the British administration and some Condominium officers got together to discuss local development issues and problems; how we might best coordinate our use of touring vessels, and assist one another by carrying messages, supplies and salaries to schools, dispensaries, local authorities, and so on. Several of us present had seen previous service in Africa, and we sought to use our experience there to benefit our work in the New Hebrides. In fact, the creation of a district team was an example of this. However, too frequent reference to our savoir faire in another continent, amounted to the 'When We' syndrome and could be extremely wearisome. Those so afflicted were, in fact, called 'whenwees' who, like those with other shortcomings, such as frequent flatulence or pitiless prolixity, liberally dispensed the discomfort around them. My replacement was a mega 'whenwe', who had worked for decades in Uganda, and his contributions at our meetings were invariably prefixed with those dreaded two words. So Jerry Marston and I, after due consultation with Darvall, told Whenwe that Darvall had once undergone a terrible and traumatic experience in Africa, and the very mention of the word 'Africa' could plunge him into acute depression, and even engender suicidal tendencies. We explained that thus far, Darvall had coped very well in masking his reaction to this word, and how much the more we admired him for that, but in due respect to him we should never utter that word at our meetings. And no, Uganda was obviously too close a reference to Africa, and this word should also be expunged from our proceedings, as should Kenya, Bechuanaland, Namibia or any other place we had worked there.

NOWHERE NEAR GREENLAND

This worked admirably, though initially, Whenwe inadvertently let the word slip out a few times. We then all glared at him, Darvall would let his head drop a little over his ancient portable typewriter, and the culprit blushing red lapsed into silence. Though often pressed for details by Whenwe, we claimed, quite truthfully, we had no idea what Darvall's terrible experience had been, though in a manner that clearly indicated we really did. We also invented a district team member who never showed up. This was Brigadier Spilsbury-Braithwaite, DSO, MC, who, we told Whenwe, was involved in infrastructural feasibility studies in the South West Bay area.

Queen's Birthday at Lakatoro, Malekula, 1972

We also concocted a splendid career for him, several years in the Middle East on camels, then behind the Japanese lines with the Chindits, a chestful of medals, and so on. At the beginning of each district team meeting, one of us would present 'apologies from the Brigadier' for non-attendance. We would claim to have met him on tour, or just spoken to him on the radio, recount our bizarre conversations, and always relayed his very best wishes to Whenwe. I have an idea we may have killed him off with Blackwater fever.

To Coral Strands

In 1973, another Director of Agriculture visited, this time accompanied by his young son. My work was first taking me to an anglophone village in Pentecost, and as neither he nor his son spoke Bislama they felt rather excluded, and the boy plaintively asked his father, when are we going to see something French? Later, however, we visited a French cooperative and both visibly cheered up and became quite animated. It was often a problem, with both British and French visitors from Vila, that they spoke little or no Bislama, since it was too easy in the town to get by without it.

So many are the Christian denominations in the New Hebrides, that one was continuously passing from one to another as one progressed through the villages, and for one's touring schedule it was best, for example, to avoid Seventh Day Adventist communities on Saturdays, and Presbyterian or Church of Christ villages on Sundays. It was also prudent not to disclose the church to which one, at least nominally, belonged. At Point Cross in South Pentecost, under close questioning by an elder, I let on that I was a somewhat lapsed, card carrying Anglican. Subsequently, in my slumbers at about five a.m. the next morning, I vaguely heard the village church bell tolling. And sometime later then tolling again, and not realising it was tolling for me, I turned over in bed and went back to sleep. The next thing of which I was conscious, was of someone standing at the open window of my woven bamboo room saying in a tone of urgency "Masta, masta, oli wet long yu ikam long jioch!" (Sir, Sir, everyone is waiting for you to come to church!). When I got to the church, there was the whole village, which had been waiting a full hour for me to come and perform my daily devotions with them. The service lasted an hour and, as always, I enjoyed the singing. This was their daily routine, with another service in the evening, and at least one more in between on Sundays.

Some years before he became prime minister, I attended Palm Sunday matins at Father Walter Lini's church at Nazareth in north Pentecost. The order of service seemed fairly complicated to me, with the large congregation processing around the outside of the church, holding palm leaves formed into a cross, while various whistles, bells and other signals were given, instructing us when to stop, start or turn around. At one point, we were leaving the church, for yet another circuit I believe, when in the porch I saw a 'nasiviru', or rainbow lorikeet, a very brightly-coloured bird of the parrot family sitting on the ground in front of me. I presumed it was a tame bird, and as it was in danger of being trampled I bent down for it to hop onto my hand. This it did, and I stood up, my head unfortunately coming up

NOWHERE NEAR GREENLAND

inside a large bell and striking its clapper which gave out a very loud clang, or it certainly seemed very loud to me within the bell. I emerged, my head still reverberating, to find that the whole procession had come to a stop, not quite knowing what this new signal meant.

A great local character in north Pentecost was Silas Nare, a tall, stooped, rather gloomy and anxious man, who rarely smiled and came from a family of chiefs in that area. Anxious, because he was burdened with problems that defied solution, and which, at least in the case of those to whom he attempted to expound them - and they were legion, were beyond all understanding. He certainly aspired to become a 'big man' in the traditional Melanesian sense of the term, and had built a huge, thatched nakamal to proclaim his status. But his intense preoccupation with his problems prevented him from achieving this ambition, as far as power and influence in his own community were concerned. Some with power spread wealth, others poverty, but Silas spread only perplexity. If only he could sweep these problems away once and for all, and many fervently wished he would, his way would then be clear to advance into those broad sunlit uplands, so to speak. He was a small business man who had inherited a shop, where his father for many years had displayed near the counter his own well-crafted coffin. With laudable civic conscience, Silas had once assisted in local road maintenance with his tractor which, however, had since lain inoperative for many years. Silas always carried with him a well-worn and battered briefcase, which bulged with many small pieces of paper, mainly bills, receipts, credit notes and suchlike, stretching back over many years, and representing the involvement in his affairs of many individuals, businesses, ship's captains, missionaries and the French, British and Condominium administrations. There were also many ancient letters from all the aforementioned, in reply to some written or oral communication from Silas, and every one was couched in similar terms of puzzlement or regret. Somewhere, someday perhaps, the solution, or myriad solutions to his problems, lay at the end of this paper trail - once, that is, it had been sorted chronologically by subject and person or persons involved, and all irrelevant material had been discarded. External to the briefcase contents, one must now add other 'apparently' vital elements, most of which involved his half-brother Luke, who lived down the coast at Loltong, and owned the little hut in which I had sheltered from a cyclone, (though this last piece of information is not at all relevant to Silas' problems). There was, inevitably, a complex land dispute between himself and Luke, and other unresolved questions involving inheritance, reciprocal customary obligations, the rights to chiefly title, as well as a rear tractor

To Coral Strands

wheel that somehow had disappeared in the Luganville area twenty or more years ago.

Silas was an extremely polite man, quietly spoken, almost deferential, and his arrival outside the office door would be as quiet as a shadow falling across the rest of your afternoon. With its limited vocabulary, Bislama is an extremely imprecise language, and even when expounding a simple situation it can take quite a while to get to the point. But with Silas's problems, with their inherent complexities of time and space, huge cast of characters, abstract concepts and conditional clauses, the salient points were so deeply buried that they invariably eluded whosoever strained to grasp them. Seriously compounding this lack of comprehension, were the sundry and seemingly endless small scraps of paper, serially fished from his briefcase - one assumes not randomly, and solemnly handed over as though of great import and moment, and requiring comment. And this latest scrap of paper or document upon which you newly fixed your bewildered gaze, would again seem to have absolutely nothing whatsoever to do with anything that had gone before. Admitting that would merely prompt further obtuse explanation, backed up by more documentary irrelevance. You had hung in and hung in and had now entirely lost the plot, whatever that might have been.

Was there perhaps some school of reasoning or problem analysis of which you remained lamentably ignorant, and thus just couldn't cope? As the scraps piled up, wild thoughts would intrude. Has there ever been a case of spontaneous combustion on a desk top? A careless cigarette perhaps, though blowing the embers into flame would be rather obvious. And anyway, I didn't smoke. The whole experience was absolutely devastating to one's self-esteem. Eventually, defeated again and shaking your head, you would admit to Silas the sheer magnitude of his problems, commiserate with him, and express the hope that everything in time would sort itself out. And off he would go, at once reassured and possibly proud that his problems still beat the best of them. A volunteer, probably at Darvall Wilkins' desperate instigation, once went and stayed with Silas on Pentecost for several weeks to assist him in sorting out his paperwork, and help him move towards some form of closure to his problems. He spectacularly failed. When Silas approaches those pearly gates, I am sure he will at least be asked, very kindly, to leave his briefcase outside.

In 1975, after seven years on Malekula I was transferred to Vila and involved in

NOWHERE NEAR GREENLAND

pasture research for about a year, before being appointed principal of the agricultural school at Tagabe. These were more lateral moves than promotions, and I believe there was some political motive on the part of the French in removing me from Lakatoro, by then the centre for political thought and development among New Hebrideans. And hardly surprisingly, since George Kalkoa, Donald Kalpokas, John Naupa, Kalpakor Kalsakau, Peter Tarakoto, George Kalsakau, Fred Timakata and other future leaders of independent Vanuatu had all been based there, often at the same time, and were in the process of creating first the New Hebrides Cultural Association and then the New Hebrides National Party.

New Hebridean French Police Band, Agricultural Show, Port Vila, 1979

I remember a conversation I had with Donald Kalpokas, in the Cock & Bull at the Norsup air terminal, sometime between 1971 and 1973. I mentioned that in my experience in pre-independence Tanganyika, Julius Nyerere had done well to anchor the grass roots of his Tanganyika African National Union (TANU) in the cooperative movement then sweeping the country in the mid-1950s, just as it was now sweeping through the New Hebrides in the early 1970s. In both countries, these expressed a degree of independence from what had been totally expatriate dominated commerce. My assistant, Douglas Malosu, who eleven years later succeeded me as director of agriculture, was summarily transferred to Ambai in

To Coral Strands

1973 for merely mentioning the word independence at a meeting in Akhamb. Certainly political matters pertaining to independence were discussed with our New Hebridean colleagues at Lakatoro, especially since we knew them socially as friends. Such social contacts were, and still are, rare in Vila.

Meanwhile, our marriage had somehow drifted apart, and Lesley went to South Africa for an extended stay with her relatives, and then took a job in Capetown. However, I visited her there, and we had a great tour in her Volkswagen beetle, driving through the Karoo desert, up through the Transkei where her grandmother had lived, visited the battlefields of the Zulu war at Isandalwhana and Rorkes Drift, met her relatives in East London and Durban, and spent Christmas on a game farm in the Transvaal. We went on to Johannesburg and there had a rather touching encounter. Ten years before, as I have already recounted, I had travelled from New Zealand to the UK on the Greek liner Ellenis, and there collected my mother and Lesley, then my fiancée, and we continued on to Piraeus. In the piano bar of the ship, a middle-aged Polish gentleman in a dinner jacket, soulfully played popular classics on a black, concert grand piano, while his immediate audience sat rapt on barstools around the instrument, their drinks on its closed lid. The pianist accompanied his deeply expressive playing with appropriate body language, leaning stiff-armed backwards, head slowly turning back and forth, crouching forwards, eyes closed, now and then a limp hand poised above the keyboard in anticipation of a plangent chord, or twiddly bit to follow. The piece he played at least once every evening, possibly by popular demand, was the first movement of Beethoven's Moonlight Sonata, to which many of his listeners also swayed with eyes closed, near swooning on some beloved's shoulder beside them. But every night, halfway through the movement he made the same mistake. I knew because this was the one and almost only piece I could play, and knew well.

Then, all those years later while we ate our meal in a Johannesburg restaurant, somewhere at the far end someone began to play the piano. The first movement of the Moonlight sonata. And then the same mistake. It has to be, I said to Lesley. She agreed. When he came to the end of the recital and sat at a nearby table, I went over to him and said, "You wouldn't by any chance be the pianist who entertained us at the Piano Bar on the Ellenis in 1965?" He, of course was overjoyed at the recognition, called for a celebration, and we had several drinks together with his friends, to whom he recounted those halcyon shipboard days.

I then returned to the New Hebrides from Johannesburg and Lesley returned to

NOWHERE NEAR GREENLAND

Cape Town. I did not overly enjoy lecturing at Tagabe and the daily routine of the school, though I took pleasure in managing the agricultural station, carrying out trials on pasture and various crops, as well as propagating cocoa, citrus, pepper and other plants and trees for sale to the public. The FAO vet, a Yugoslav, posted to the New Hebrides to effect control of brucellosis, a contagious disease mainly of cattle which causes abortions, visited the school twice a week to lecture on animal husbandry. He was extremely eccentric - though as mad as a meat axe might more fairly describe him - and took a strong dislike to one student named Reggie, whom he made stand outside the classroom for all his lectures. When exam time came, he set him a separate paper, totally different to that of the other students, which included questions on subjects he had never covered. Thus Reggie was awarded 5%.

He was of considerable assistance to me, however, when the dogs of French neighbours savaged the sheep on the station. These I had borrowed from the Catholic Mission at Montmartre in order to keep down the grass in the citrus orchard. Unfortunately, the mesh wire fence was not buried deep enough, and a whole pack of dogs burrowed beneath it, attacked the sheep and left many dead and maimed. Dr. Petrovic patched and despatched as best he could and took photographs of the carnage. I called on the neighbours and politely asked them to try to control their pets, and meanwhile repaired the fence. Some days later at dawn the dogs broke in again. The station labourers heard the ensuing commotion, rushed out, drove off the dogs before too much damage had been done, but trapped one against the fence and speared it. Not long after, the owner identified her dead dog and strode over to my office. "Bonjour Madame, ça va?" I greeted her. "Ça ne va pas!" she yelled, and then accused me of personally murdering her pet. She decided to take the matter to court, and the whole affair, tiresomely but inevitably, became one of French versus the British. She even got the chief veterinarian, my French colleague, to testify in writing that her dog was incapable of killing a sheep, on the grounds that it was too small. The dog was in fact of medium size, and I remonstrated with the vet that, anyway, dogs hunt in packs; one takes the throat, another a leg, and so on; it is teamwork. He gave a Gallic shrug, and refused to change his testimony. Graeme Mackay, a British magistrate, offered to act for me, and in no time at all the opposition withdrew their case. However, this was an example of true French solidarity when facing an action involving another nationality. I was reminded of the far more serious affair in Santo in about 1970, when the Australian purser of the Burns Philp trading ship Tulagi borrowed without permission a dinghy untended

To Coral Strands

at the main wharf, to fetch something from his ship anchored nearby. The dinghy belonged to the son of a French planter, and when the purser returned with the dinghy, he was beaten to death by the owner and a couple of his friends. The Australian police sent a man over to investigate the affair, but no action of any kind was taken by the French administration against those involved.

Despite, though it seemed to me because of, Dr. Petrovic's strategy to control brucellosis, this disease continued to spread quite rapidly and infect almost every herd of cattle on Efate. Thus he advised that there should be no cattle exhibited at the annual agricultural show that particular year, 1979. By then I was the Director of Agriculture, Livestock and Forestry, and I concurred. And no horses, he added. On this I needed advice, but the horsy crowd, a volatile lot (they still are), had got wind of the matter, and before I could seek expert guidance their representative came banging on my door in the middle of the night to decry this completely ridiculous situation, this shame and a scandal . Had they not been schooling their horses for months and months to leap over jumps and sidestep to music? And what was I going to do about it? Well, next morning I telephoned an eminent animal epidemiologist in Sydney, to ask him the likelihood of this disease being spread to, or by, horses, and his reply was that the risk was minute, that was to say completely negligible. Thank goodness! So instant pacification was effected of the horse lobby, which had collected around my office for breaking news, and subsequent violent demonstrations and horse whippings had been avoided.

However, one cattle owner, an ethnic Vietnamese, believed he should be exempted from the ban and went to see my minister to discuss the matter. He, it was true, did not actually have the disease on his property, but there was the chance that just moving his cattle through an infected area, to and from the show, could risk them becoming infected, which was the reason for the ban on all the herds. Nevertheless, the minister called me to his office to inform me that this owner's cattle should uniquely be exempt from the ban, and that he could exhibit them at the show in the already specified classes. My only small victory in this matter was that we, the show committee, would not provide the prizes. However, the cattle owner then went out and bought all his own prizes, magnificent trophies they were of course, and his exhibits alone were duly judged. We then had the farcical situation of this gentleman smilingly coming forward six times, while the announcer intoned "And the first prize goes to......." ,(and a photo of this illustrious winner, standing proudly by his prize bull, is in my book 'Agriculture in Vanuatu').

NOWHERE NEAR GREENLAND

Shortly after arriving in Vila I helped revive their amateur dramatic society, and wrote a political satire for it entitled 'Robinson's Trousseau'. This involved our castaway, washed ashore with a treasure chest on a Condominium island, where the only black man is an anthropologist researching the curious customs of the British and French. Naturally, each of the powers wants Robinson to 'opt' for their side, so the Resident Commissioners both send their daughter to seduce him, and so get their hands on his treasure.

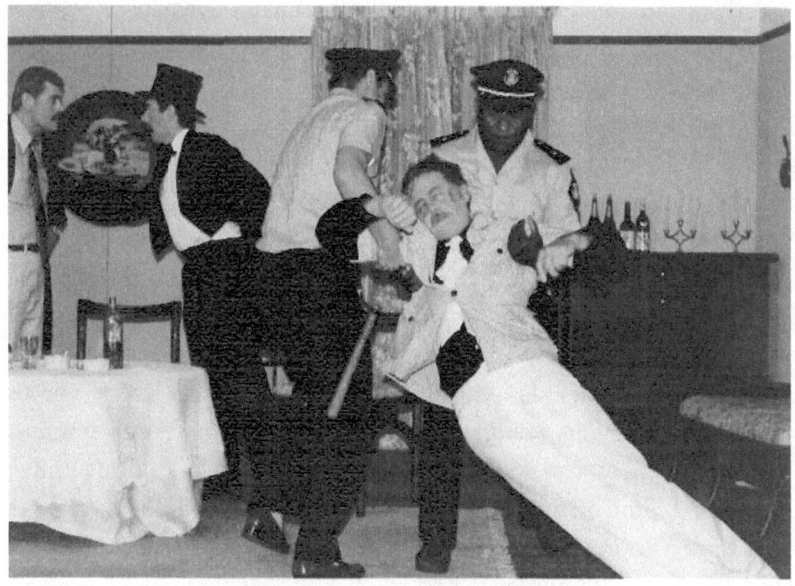

In "Arsenic and Old Lace" yours truly is arrested by
PC Douglas Malosu. Port Vila, 1976.

I tried to interest one or two long time servers at the British Residency to participate, but they considered it far too political and declined. Perhaps the leitmotif of 'Don't upset the French, we want to join the Common Market', which had prevailed for years during the early 1970s, still obtained, though the lampooning made equal fun of the British. Nevertheless, we rehearsed it for a while, but two or three of the principal actors were transferred out of the New Hebrides and the production was postponed indefinitely. Seven years later I rewrote it as a pantomime, largely with the same story, and it was finally staged at Christmas 1982. Regrettably, the script of the original version has not survived.

To Coral Strands

Later I wrote another pantomime, 'Jack Witem Rop Blong Bin' (Jack and the Beanstalk), which included a large and enthusiastic cast of Australians, British, French-Canadians and (as by then they had become) Ni-Vanuatu. Another success was the production of three one-act Chekhov plays, performed together over three nights; one in English, one in French and one which I had translated into Bislama. This was 'The Proposal', whose theme was ideal, since it principally concerned a land dispute, with which Ni-Vanuatu in the audience could closely identify. I also decided to put on an abridged version of 'South Pacific' and wrote away to a friend in New York, Jonathan Donald a successful film maker, to ask if he could find me the script of the original Broadway play staged in 1947. He tracked this down and sent it and we put on the show.

As already recounted, fancy dress parties were an important element of social life in the islands, though it was always a disappointment if many guests turned up in their everyday clothes, either too shy or too dignified to make the transformation, or just plain lazy; so the small minority in costume would then feel self-conscious and silly. And there were those who made a mere half-hearted or token attempt, such as the time when Lesley and I were invited by French teachers to a tramps party at Rensarie on Malekula. As it was our nature to make the very maximum, imaginative effort in matters of disguise and costume for such occasions, we duly blackened teeth, added scars and sores, developed ratty hair, tore clothes, wore boots with soles falling off and carried billycans and grubby bundles on sticks, and of course adopted appropriate deportment and speech. When we duly lurched into the party, there was wild applause and the flashing of cameras. However, all the other guests were very much their normal, casually, even elegantly dressed selves, apart from here and there a small smudge on the cheek, a tiny triangular tear in a shirt, maybe a button missing somewhere, and possibly a patch on a pair of old trousers. And yes, we did feel rather silly for the rest of the evening.

Early in 1977, Lesley and I went on holiday to Kenya. On arrival in Nairobi we booked in at the Norfolk Hotel and hired a 4 x 4 Subaru which we would take to the Masai Mara National Park. Walking along the road near the hotel, we were overtaken by a motorcycle which quickly turned round and came back to us. This was Jean Griffith, who had been a nursing instructor in Vila, and whom I had last seen in Malekula at South West Bay, and was currently working at the Outward Bound school in the Amboselli National Park near Mount Kilimanjaro. Jean, an experienced climber, was now teaching climbing skills, and I arranged to meet up with her in a couple of weeks time at Naro Moru to climb Mount Kenya.

NOWHERE NEAR GREENLAND

In the meantime, we checked in at a large camp in the Masai Mara, where there was a long avenue of tents pitched close together on either side of a paved road. These were similar to the one I had used in Tanganyika more than twenty years before, except that they now had tiled bathrooms and electric light. At the camp's lodge, a comfortable lounge with deep armchairs overlooked a floodlit waterhole, which one viewed through tinted plate glass windows, a chilled drink in hand and emollient, background music playing. Not our scene, and the next morning we decided to check out and look for a simpler style of camp.

Eat your hat out
Lesley & Sandy Macfarlane and author, with Jenny & David Grundy

We eventually located one operated by the East African Wildlife Society. This appeared ideal, a small group of tents, hurricane lanterns and a campfire. Our fellow guests were all Alitalia aircrew. When we came to pay the bill the following day we discovered it was twice as expensive as the previous camp; evidently the limited availability of simplicity made it very costly. .

At Naro Moru I received the news that Jean Griffith could not get away to join me in climbing Mount Kenya. As the ascent of its twin peaks at 17,000 feet demands serious climbing and commensurate skills, there was no way I could attempt this alone, so I had to settle for Point Lonana, about seven hundred feet below the summit. An Australian staying in the same lodge at Naro Moru was keen to

To Coral Strands

accompany me, but after overnighting in the top hut, where I was surprised to see two enormous, scavenging rock hyrax, he awoke with severe mountain sickness and was unable to accompany me further up the mountain.

At Christmas 1977 we held a Twilight of Empire Party at Tagabe. This followed soon after a riot in Vila, which expressed the writing on the wall that France and Britain's going Dutch in the New Hebrides had already reached its Götterdammerung phase. However, the theme was the twilight of any empire, so we had Egyptians, Greeks, Romans, Vikings, Spanish, British, French and even a couple of Nazis! Some years later, my End of the World party celebrated a total eclipse of the sun that had occurred in Vila the previous day, and was in tune with currently dire predictions that happily were not fulfilled. At an Adam and Eve party, no less than four people came as God, which, as host in the same character, I felt was somewhat lese-majesty. And the Eat Your Hat party was a great success. Everyone had to arrive wearing an edible millinery creation. As it was Easter-time, mine consisted of an inelegant, dozen hard-boiled eggs, set in a pastry shape that fitted over my head. But there were many other wonderful and artistic extravaganzas, incorporating fruit, vegetables, meat, peanuts, éclairs, cakes, savoury snacks, etcetera, into their designs. Following the awarding of prizes for design and originality, they were all laid out on a long table and consumed, though prizes were not awarded for digestibility.

I returned from leave to Vila one year bringing with me the latex mask of an incredibly old man, graphically well into his hundreds. Playing around with it with Jerry Marston, we decided that one of us should wear it to a restaurant in Vila. He drew the short straw, and together with the other three of our party, slowly entered the La Mer restaurant, bent double over his quivering walking stick, his head shaking uncontrollably with age. Fortunately, there was a party of some eight Australian tourists already seated at another table, and we heard one of them murmur "Poor old bugger" as we came in. Although there was a small slit for the mouth between the mask's lips, it was not easy for Jerry to eat and, anyway, according to our game plan, and consistent with his frailty, he needed to go the lavatory. While he blundered unaided and half blind around the restaurant in search of the right door, (Jerry could not see too well through the mask), we callously continued talking and laughing, and the tourists were already glaring at us and getting to their feet. One of us finally and rather irritably got up to give him a hand. Jerry then removed his disguise in the lavatory, and exiting unseen by the

NOWHERE NEAR GREENLAND

kitchen door, left the mask, walking stick and his jacket in the car outside. Greeting us as he came back into the restaurant, he asked "Where's grandpa?" We told him, and sitting down at grandpa's vacant place, he referred rather loudly to grandpa's greed, his lack of teeth, the total unsuitability therefore of the food on his plate, and proceeded to eat it all. Time went by. No sign of grandpa. The Australian table had gone very quiet. One of us suggested we should check on him. No, it was decided, he always takes a while, often passes out in the loo. More time went by. We ordered dessert. It was clear the tourists feared the worst, and by now were really hating us. Our next phase was for one of us, finally, to go and look for grandpa, and then return to the restaurant and sadly announce his passing. However, apprehensive of the commotion, or worse, which would inevitably ensue, we confessed to the other table that it was all a joke. Happily, they took it in extremely good part. Jerry then went and fetched the mask, the tourists wore it in turn for photographs and afterwards we enjoyed a number of drinks together.

It was probably with Jerry again that we played an innocent though rather expensive joke on another table of unsuspecting tourists, this time at the Houstalet restaurant. There was, again, a party of eight Australians at the next table, and we were of equal number. It was, and probably still is, Clement the owner's custom, sometimes to offer his guests a complementary liqueur after the meal. This he had already done at the other table and it was gracefully accepted. We then requested Clement to offer them all another complementary liqueur on our own account, but not to reveal our contribution. This he did and he refilled all their little glasses. Before they could call for their bill, we suggested he serve them yet another round, perhaps this time making some excuse such as an anniversary, or serving them a different liqueur that he thought rather special and that they simply must sample. What he said I do not know, but it was all done very decorously and they all partook. By the fourth round there was more than a hint of consternation at the table, though they were not yet at the stage when they just didn't care anymore. "We shall have to pay for this, you mark my words." "What's he doing, is he trying to make us drunk or something?" Another had the theory that Clement was not the owner and was just trying to ruin the establishment. All agreed that such a thing had never happened to them before, ever, anywhere, certainly not, no way! I believe Clement squeezed in "just one more for the road" before they finally asked for their bill, scrutinized it as best as they could it in the circumstances, paid and staggered out. We shared the cost between us and it was well worth the fun. Clement enjoyed it too, though whether there was any subsequent surge in his

To Coral Strands

clientele from Australia I do not know.

Perhaps at a slightly more puerile level (!), also at the Houstalet, Dominique Burgess, then Bob Wilson's fiancé and later his wife, finished her serving of delicious coconut crab, and admired the beauty of the bright, pinky-red crustacean's carapace left on her plate. Did we think the management would mind if she took it, she asked. Of course not, we replied, every coconut crab has one, and they are simply thrown in the dustbin! At that, she wrapped the coveted item in a paper napkin and put it in her handbag. At the end of the meal she visited the ladies room. We then asked Clement, that when she returned to the table he request her to open her handbag.

Atheist at my Adam & Eve party.

Port Vila, 1985

This he did, with extreme politeness and gentility. Dominique, suddenly flushing the same colour as the carapace, complied and guiltily unwrapped the napkin. Gales of laughter all round. "Dirty rotten bastards!" probably thought Dominique, though she was far too polite a girl to say so.

Coconut crabs are now rare on Malekula. When full grown they are huge, blue-grey, nocturnal creatures with soft, fat, turned-under abdomens and two enormous claws, easily capable of snipping off fingers. Lesley and I had been out in our little aluminium runabout boat in Bushman's Bay, and were returning after dark to Norsup. At Black Gate, the boundary between Lakatoro and the coconut plantation, there in the middle of the road, facing us, its claws held high, was the most enor-

NOWHERE NEAR GREENLAND

mous coconut crab we had ever seen. I took an oar from the back of the Land Rover and tried to hold it down while Lesley endeavoured to entangle it with the rope from the boat. It chomped great chunks from the blade of the oar before we managed to secure it safely. We carried it back to Norsup, but found we had no pot anywhere near large enough to put it in, so we put it in the empty bath for the night. In the small hours, we were awoken by a strange clanking sound. I gingerly opened the bathroom door, and there in the beam of my torch was our coconut crab, sitting on top of the gas cylinder, waving its claws in the air not an inch from the rubber gas pipe. It grabbed the towel I hung above it, and I lowered it into the bath which I then half filled with water. I also turned off the gas, just in case. Next day we borrowed an immense cooking pot from Peter Wright, and later shared our superb meal with him and his wife.

Caves have always held considerable fascination for me. This stems from our family visits to Swanage in Dorset when I was a small child, and we would visit the Tillywim caves. These were publicised, at least for children, as pirate caves, though they were essentially created by quarrying from mediaeval times, and their stone was used for building some of the great cathedrals of England. We even now owned a cave of our own on Tenerife. On my first trip around the north of Malekula, I was shown the large cave at Tenmiel. Part of its high roof had long ago fallen in, and a tall tree of the forest now grew up through the hole, its leaves dappling a round circle of light on the cave floor below. There are the silhouettes of spread hands, high on one of the walls, possibly made with lamp black, though whether of modern or ancient origin I could not say. There are also some crude designs lower down, which apparently extend below the current floor level, since raised by the roof fall as well as the natural accumulation of fallen leaves, bat guano and other detritus.

I was then told of a great cave at Tautu, the village next to where we lived at Norsup. This was said to extend for at least a mile under the sea, resurfacing near Bethel on the northern side of Norsup bay. But the legend of this cave was that it received the spirits of the dead, and for that reason none of the living people of Tautu had ever entered it. Chief David, however, was quite happy for me to go inside. So, excited at the prospect, I provided myself with a torch and extra batteries, matches and candles, and a long length of rope in case there should be any serious obstacles to surmount. Leaving a small, silent crowd gathered outside, I entered the cave. After just a few paces, it turned abruptly to the right, and almost immediately I came up against a blank wall. That was it. I checked the rock carefully. Nothing.

To Coral Strands

Just solid rock from top to bottom. Now what? Not wanting to blow the legend, I decided to wait for ten or fifteen minutes before I emerged. When I did, I told the people still anxiously waiting outside, though they might as well have expected I would never re-appear, that "big fela hol ia i go go go, mi mi ting se mi neva save kassem end blong him, mo mi sek sek big wan from mi fraet tumas. Tasdawe me bin kam aot bak agen nao ia no mo" (This big cave goes on and on. I thought I would never reach the end of it, and I was trembling mightily from fright. That's why I came out again). Thus, I hope, preserving the cave's legend.

The scarcity of fresh water was a chronic problem in north Ambrym. When the anthropologist Mary Patterson was at Fonah for the best part of a year, researching kinship patterns, the Burns Philp trading ships Manutai and Konanda would drop off a forty-four gallon drum of water for her every few weeks. Tantalisingly, a large spring of fresh water could always be seen gushing to the surface of the sea only a few yards from the shore, but was always well covered, even at low tide. I had often thought that capturing this water would be feasible, by building a simple caisson around the spring to just above high tide level, but as far as I know this has not been attempted. There are many such springs around Ambrym. Rainfall collected in the great caldera of the volcanoes and on their flanks, percolates down through the ash to the countless tubes and galleries created by earlier eruptions. When the molten lava from these reached the sea it cracked, permitting gravity-fed rainwater to escape upwards under some pressure.

One day, the secretary of the local cooperative society, who was an expert at making intricately carved pig-killing hammers, told me that along the coast a few miles to the west, there was a large cave which was full of water. It was decided this should be investigated, and I came over to Ambrym with Darvall, accompanied by a representative of the water department - a rotund member of the Joli family from Devil's Point on Efate, and somewhere along the way we had collected a couple of volunteers and one of my field staff. With our cooperative guide, we proceeded with the touring vessel to a point on the coast opposite the cave mouth, which opened onto a rock platform a few feet above the sea. In a flat calm, I was ferried ashore in the dinghy with two others, to be joined by three more amateur speleologists on the second trip. Darvall, saying he was not too keen on caves, decided to remain aboard. Arriving on the rock platform, I immediately put my head inside the cave and heard a roaring sound. My first thought was that not only was there water, but a waterfall as well! Then shining my torch inside I realised that the sound was created by the whirling flutter of thousands of bats. The six of us entered the cave, and there from the edge of the rocky downward slope in front of us, stretched a lake of water as far as the beams of our torches could reach. While the bats whizzed and fluttered above and around us, we stepped into the initially shallow water which spanned the full width of the cave, and already we could see smaller tunnels leading off on either side.

On the brink of the Marum crater, Ambrym, 1972

We had brought with us a couple of large balls of string, and in such surroundings it did seem quite possible we might meet a Minator in this labyrinth, responsible perhaps for belching the fire and smoke of the volcanoes three thousand feet above us. However, we decided that for the time being at least, we would follow only what was clearly the main cavern whose roof was perhaps twenty or thirty feet above us. The water very gradually became deeper until we were in it up to our knees. We then realised, as pungent gas bubbles rose to the surface from beneath our feet, that in fact there was only a thin lens of clear water overlying liquid bat shit. It had the consistency of thin porridge, and the stone bottom of the lake was slippery. We ploughed on though the muck, certainly not regardless of the possibility of suddenly loosing our balance and wallowing or even drowning in this horrid stuff. Ahead now, we could see a low mound of rubble at the end of the

To Coral Strands

lake. This we climbed, squelching up in our sodden shoes, and before us again stretched another lake at a somewhat higher level than the previous one.

Soon we were wading waist deep, and the smell was frightful as the gas bubbled up around us. My earlier cries of conserve your torches, only one torch at a time please, now went completely unheeded. Up out of this lake, we again squelched over a barrier of boulders, then down into another one. By now most of us were gagging in the stench, though at this point no-one cried, "enough", perhaps fearful of having to return alone. Sometimes the rock walls on either side afforded purchase to steady our balance, but often fell away as our route was joined by numerous smaller tunnels. Steadily rising in altitude as we progressed, the lakes were also getting deeper, and it became increasingly difficult to keep the glass of our torches clear of this clinging, brown, malodorous sludge. How much further had the bats penetrated? Would we ever come upon that deep lake of pure, clean, sweet smelling water that we so intrepidly sought; possibly millions of gallons of it? However, this vision was progressively usurped by the increasingly more seductive one of being out in the fresh air again, of diving into the sea and ridding ourselves of this filth. Yuck!

Finally, after about two hours of this torture we stood still, almost up to our shoulders in the stuff. Ahead, in the dim brown light of our torches, we could just make out another rock fall, beyond which there was presumably another foul lake. That's it! Ça suffit!, we unanimously decided, turned around and started wading slowly back to the cave entrance. Eventually we emerged into the bright sunlight, which cruelly showed us quite unrecognisable, plastered from head to foot in bat excrement. We dived straight into the blue sea. Absolute bliss. Such contrasts, such instant transformations in life from acute discomfort and degradation to near ecstasy are rare and never to be forgotten. Any sharks there might have been in the vicinity must surely have fled for miles, for we would have repelled any living thing. Clothes and shoes were later all thrown away. There was no way to rid them of the stain and smell, and though when we went back aboard we were relatively clean, Darvall and the crew most discourteously held their noses. Perhaps no exploitable water there, and I am sure no one has been back to that labyrinth since, but, if anyone is interested, there are tens of thousands of tons of liquid, organic fertilizer just waiting to be put to good use and make our planet greener - or that other colour.

Together with the resident commissioner Roger de Boulay and Darvall Wilkins, I

NOWHERE NEAR GREENLAND

once had the occasion to visit west Ambrym aboard the m.v. Euphrosyne, the flagship touring vessel of the British administration's fleet. Father Zerger, formerly of Lamap, and still of the reversed red baseball cap, had been posted to Sessivi mission. He had planned to meet us there with a welcoming choir, but unexpectedly we had landed at Port Vato and now approached the mission from the opposite direction. So eventually we met the Father and choir rushing towards us along the track, whereupon, coming to a stop and completely out of breath, they launched into God Save the Queen, and then the Marseillaise. It was both funny and very touching. Father Zerger loved music, and the last time I saw him was at the Montmartre Mission near Vila, taking part in an Easter performance of Handel's Messiah. He had just returned from Noumea where he had been told he had inoperable cancer, and as he sang his face was transfigured by excitement and joy.

But at the time of that walk along the west coast of Ambrym, Darvall was on the lookout for a gift the New Hebrides might make to the Queen, to commemorate her silver jubilee. The word had gone out, and we met on the path a man who had something to show us. From a small box he carefully unwrapped a shell. A rare golden cowry. It was a fine specimen, and Darvall asked him how much he wanted for it. He thought for a bit, and then said firmly "Seven Thousand Pounds". We all admired the shell, but Darvall very politely declined the purchase and we continued our walk. The current value of such a fine shell was about fifty pounds, but the owner clearly knew little of money or markets. (A Big Namba once asked me fifty pounds for a pineapple.) A minor incident I remember from that trip, was that a Euphrosyne crew member rashly tossed overboard an empty Fosters lager can. "Stop the ship!" commanded the resident commissioner, rather reminiscent of Alan Bates' "Stop the train!", in the film 'The Dresser'. The Euphrosyne duly stopped and the dinghy was despatched to retrieve the offending blue tin.

In the days before the advent of video shops in Vila, there was a splendid drive-in cinema, where at any time during the performance one could walk up to the kiosk behind the ranks of parked cars and collect cold drinks, bags of crisps and other takeaway food. The Australian High Commissioner, Mike Ovington, was a good friend of mine, and had a distinctive large, black, official limousine. On one occasion, which featured the showing of a very spooky film, 'Blind Terror' I think it was, he was parked quite near to my Minimoke. Returning with my crisps and a beer, just as the killer stalked the young blind woman in a dark room, I crept up beneath Mike's door and leaped up with a yell. There were two resounding yells

To Coral Strands

in reply, as the Prime Minister and his bodyguard jumped out of their skins. My profuse apologies to Father Walter Lini that I had mistaken his car sounded rather lame, but at least I was neither shot nor deported.

My house on the cliff above Vila was on the site of a former small coconut plantation, and on what passed for a lawn were six ancient palms, all but one of which would be felled by cyclone Uma in 1987. Returning from leave one year, I brought with me a croquet set.

Ati George & Litak Sokomanu, relaxing with Susie Emmett, Harold Qualao and bodyguard after croquet, Port Vila, 1984

Father Walter Lini, while a theological student, had played croquet, and several times came up to my house for lively matches among the coconuts on weekend afternoons. As there would usually be about a dozen of us, alternative sports of darts and petanque were on offer for those not included in the four playing croquet. President Ati George Sokumano, minister Sethy Regenvanu and Nikenike Vurubaravu also sometimes participated, and when a pause was called to these sporting endeavours, I would appropriately serve tea with cucumber, tomato and egg sandwiches, partaken on pandanus mats laid out in the shade. Competitive croquet is distant from its popular image of gentility played out on vicarage lawns, though inevitably, from time to time, we could not resist the compulsion to dress and act accordingly in 19th century costumes. Given the rustic nature of my 'lawn', local

NOWHERE NEAR GREENLAND

rules allowed us to lay off the length of a mallet when obstructed by the trunk of a coconut, or stuck in a hibiscus hedge, but by sheer luck, we never had a ball propelled over a 300 feet high cliff.

The only other sport I regularly played was doubles tennis, and I took up scuba diving. I also occasionally went sailing. Good friends made in Vila were Tony and Joan Ashford-Hodges. He was a surgeon at the Vila Base Hospital, continuing to ply his skills despite having lost an eye to cancer some years before, and being very short-sighted in his remaining eye. He was an experienced scuba diver, and a short while after he arrived in Vila he purchased a forty-three foot, ferro-cement ketch named the Martinette from a departing New Zealand magistrate. Boats of this kind are basically built by plastering cement over a chicken wire armature formed in the desired shape. Tony intended to sail her back to the UK, travelling via the Solomon Islands to Thursday Island at the north-east tip of Australia, then through the Torres Straits to emerge in the Indian Ocean, and then through Suez and the Mediterranean to Great Yarmouth in Norfolk. The boat first required much work and a considerable addition of equipment to make it seaworthy, safe and comfortable for that long voyage. Both Lesley and I assisted with this in small ways, sand papering, painting, lifting and suchlike as required.

When all was nearly ready, we went for a trial run up to the north of Efate, and Lesley joined them for a sail down to Tanna, but they were turned back by high winds and heavy seas. Tony and Joan had the tendency to countermand each other's orders in tones of unimpeachable authority, so sailing with them did not lack dramas, such as extremely close encounters with reefs, persons all but knocked overboard by the boom, and a fire in the galley. For their voyage to England, they had with them their daughter as well as four others, including a young couple who were to be married under an old law of the sea, which permits the captain of any vessel, which has not touched land for forty-one days, to carry out this office. We waved goodbye to them from Vila sea wall, and then drove out to Devil's Point to watch the Martinette finally disappear under full sail over the horizon to the north.

The Torres Straits between Papua New Guinea and Australia are notorious for strong tides and the hazard of reefs that lurk around the many tiny islands that sprinkle this long passage. Arriving one day off a small islet, they dropped anchor and went ashore for a picnic. Meanwhile, the tide went out and impaled the Martinette on a pinnacle of coral that lay directly beneath her. With the hull pierced,

To Coral Strands

they hurried to beach the yacht before she sank. A long trip was then made in the dinghy to obtain bags of cement to patch the hull. However, despite their efforts over several days, they were unable to get the patch to bind with the rest of the hull, whose cement just crumbled away around it, so the Martinette was abandoned. With some difficulty, the ship's company made its way back through the straits to Cairns, where Tony worked as a surgeon for a few months to accumulate funds to fly them all back to the UK.

A year or two later, when I visited Tony and Joan at their former Victorian vicarage home near Great Yarmouth, Tony was fitting out a new hull, this time made of steel, on the tennis court. He later invited me to join them on a voyage to Turkey, but since by then I was working in Malawi I was unable to do this. However, after reaching Turkey they proceeded on down through Suez into the Red Sea. There they inadvertently put the boat hard onto a reef at nearly high tide, to find themselves marooned on a pond, surrounded by coral on all sides. Only by throwing everything removable overboard to lighten ship, were they able to get off again, and the boat returned to England as deck cargo on a freighter sailing from Djibouti.

There are quite a number of active volcanoes in Vanuatu. Currently eight, if you count Matthew and Hunter in the far south, until recently claimed by the French, but part of the same volcanic chain that has formed, and is still forming, the Vanuatu archipelago. Also included is the underwater volcano in the Shepherds group, whose half dozen small islands are the remnants of Kuwae island, blown to smithereens by a gigantic volcanic explosion in 1452. The two thousand feet high horseshoe of Uruparapara in the Banks Islands is evidence of an earlier great explosion, its deep bay the legacy of that volcano's crater. Some of the now dormant volcanoes in Vanuatu may burst back into life at any time, as in the 1950s did mile high Lopevi whose three villages, one named Tomato, were evacuated, and the island remains uninhabited to this day.

In the early 1970s, the felicitously named French vulcanologist, Dr. Blow, advised the total evacuation of the island of Gaua, in the Banks group. There, the active volcano, whose cone rises from the side of a deep lake two thousand feet above sea-level, was entering an eruptive phase, and there was the prospect of the cone fracturing, and water entering the vent to cause a Krakatoa-like explosion. However, the eruption passed off without the feared calamity, and after a year the entire population was returned to the island. Mount Gurumati on Vanua Llava, also in the

NOWHERE NEAR GREENLAND

Banks islands, though currently quiescent has a number of roaring fumaroles which vent many tons of pure sulphur around its summit. This sulphur was exploited by a French company employing convict labour until the 1920s, and the concrete base of the pylons, that once supported a cableway taking the sulphur down the coast, can still be found in the bush.

Jimmy Jones at the Crocodile River. Vanua Lava, 1980

From this volcano flows the Sulphur River, whose temperature is that of a very hot bath, (as I found out when I and a friend fell into it while climbing up through its gorge in 1980), and where it meets the sea in a small delta, the patina on the sulphur-washed pebbles makes them shine like gold nuggets. Nearby is the Crocodile river, where Jimmy Jones shot a twelve-foot crocodile on New Year's Day in 1973, and this is perhaps the farthest point south reached by estuarine crocodiles in the South Pacific.

In the interior of Vanua Lava are two crater lakes, one of which I have visited twice, in 1973 and 1980, the second time descending into the crater and camping by the lake. The approach is through miles of dense cane and bracken, and the only practical way of proceeding is to flatten them in front of one. Cutting it is just as slow, and one is then frequently speared by the cut ends of the cane. Time did not allow

To Coral Strands

us to trek to the smaller second lake, quite near as the crow flies, but very far as measured through the cane, which to the best of my knowledge has not been visited for more than a century. The interior, forest clad slopes of these craters, enjoy their own microclimate, and support a very different flora from the surrounding countryside, and should prove interesting sites for investigation and collection of small fauna as well.

Jimmy Jones, wiry and narrow-hipped with the gangling walk of the cowboy he once was in New Caledonia, lives on the small island of Pakea off the south-eastern corner of Vanua Lava. It is the cliché one imagines for a small, tropical Pacific island, rimmed by golden beaches, backed by fine stands of Pacific teak, and encircling a turquoise lagoon abounding in mullet. Son of Frank Jones, a Welshman who had acquired the island from the Whitford family in payment of a debt, and of a local woman from the Banks Islands, Jimmy lives there with his wife Violet and a handful of labourers. The latter harvest coconuts and make copra for themselves in lieu of wages, thereby keeping the rough pasture clear for a small herd of cattle, and regularly assist Jimmy in harvesting fish and crustaceans from the sea. A few years before independence, he was cheated of his inheritance of the coconut plantation on the mainland by a Belgian who acquired it for a pittance from his senile father in Sydney. Stocked with cattle and horses and producing copra, Jimmy had from there gained most of his living, and since that time, (at independence the plantation was returned to its customary landowners), he has lived a life of semi-frugal subsistence on his small piece of paradise. In 1972, Pakea was one of the islands struck by cyclone Wendy, and his daughter born shortly afterwards was named after it. The storm also cast ashore forty-three golden cowries, which the supercargo of the 'Konanda', a ne'er-do-well Australian, bought from him for a small fraction of their worth. Jimmy is now tired of his small island isolation, and plans to move to a plot of land he has on Gaua, though the reduction in isolation will be entirely relative.

The twin volcanoes of Marum and Benbow, sitting in a twelve kilometer wide caldera and ash plain in the centre of Ambrym, are currently the mightiest and most active in Vanuatu. Their plumes throw ash high into the atmosphere and regularly fertilize the soils of Malekula many miles downwind, from which island at night one can see a pulsing pink glow reflected by the clouds above them, and their smog can reach as far as Santo. The grey, moonlike plain provides a shortcut which I sometimes took when walking between the north, west and south east villages of the island, strategically perched as they are on its coasts and extremities,

NOWHERE NEAR GREENLAND

as far as possible from the violence of the volcanoes. An article in the National Geographic Magazine in 2002 described an expedition to these volcanoes the previous year, and spoke of its German and American members 'hacking their way through jungle' on their way to the ash plain from Port Vato. On this route, downwind of the volcanoes, and constantly subjected to falls of ash and acid rain, there are only sparse grass, ferns and stunted Casuarina trees. No jungles, nor are there any on Ambrym. One is reminded of Kal Muller's "rumours of people in the interior", in that same publication years before. This recent expedition describes in machismo terms its part descent into an active crater, which I had once made in my tennis shoes, and the subsequent, entirely predictable falling-out with the local porters, who clearly would not have appreciated the bragging, gung-ho approach to their feared and venerated volcano, often closed to visitors in order to pacify it.

The most accessible volcano, and frequently visited by tourists since Australian Aid paid to build a road almost to its top in the 1980s, is Yassur on Tanna. It can be relied upon to make a loud bang every few minutes, throwing fire and glowing lava many hundreds of feet into the air, and best seen to advantage after sunset. These lava bombs flatten out like grey cow pats when they land around the rim of the crater, and can seriously injure or kill anyone who has not heeded the direction of the wind. Approaching the rim, when a heavy brown sulphurous gas is pouring over it, to the accompaniment of bangs, flashes, streams of ascending fire in the sky and the whiz and patter of falling lava, one experiences what must be a fair semblance of the far more deadly son et lumière of World War One. In 1789, Captain Cook landed nearby at Port Resolution, though subsequent eruptions and tremors have moved some yards inland the exact point where he anchored his ship, and only in the past two or three years has the calm mirror of Lake Siwi entirely disappeared from the ash plain beneath the volcano. All is movement and change in these geologically young volcanic islands, beneath which the Australian tectonic plate continues to subduct, thrusting them up and adding to the lava and ash in the island building process. Thus are found coral reef terraces thousands of feet above sea-level, and in 1965 the whole of Malekula rose up one meter on its eastern side, and half that on its western side in a shaking that lasted for several days. Pierre Theuil claimed that his Plantation Idéale gained some twenty hectares from this uplift, and on the agricultural station at Lakatoro, I was able by 1970 to plant sweet potatoes on former tidal mud flats that had once been the preserve of mangroves. With such upward movements continuing, they will more than keep pace with the currently predicted rise in sea levels associated with climate change.

To Coral Strands

My work did not take me often to Tanna after I had become director, though I had several times been as a tourist to visit the volcano and the wild horses on the White Grass plateau. I regret that I never witnessed a 'toka', the most spectacular of all the traditional dances performed in these islands, attracting hundreds of performers in very colourful costumes and facial decoration. The dance is performed in successive villages only once every few years, and is accompanied by bounteous gifts of food presented by the visitors from surrounding communities. Tanna is too far south for coconuts to be productive, and though amply self-sufficient in food production, growing magnificent yams in its deep volcanic soils; it exports little. An exception was vegetables, notably potatoes but also garlic and onions, whose growing and exports to Vila were largely the result of a French initiative in the late 1970s, but sadly this trade has all but disappeared, and the capacious cold storage facilities are long abandoned and now derelict.

Early European settlers, mainly British and Australian, had successfully grown arabica coffee there from the 1870s, though later they were all murdered or driven out by the local people, inevitably in disagreements over land. However, some remnants of coffee remained on the island, where they had flourished and were entirely free of disease. On this evidence, it was decided in 1980 to establish a coffee plantation on the plateau, under the management of the Commonwealth Development Corporation, to which out-grower smallholders would also contribute their crop for processing. And though the coffee performed well, the volcano performed even better, regularly showering the plantation with highly acidic ash during its formative years. CDC eventually pulled out, but there is now a significant production supplying domestic use, and a limited export of high quality, certified organically-grown coffee by the Tanna Coffee Development Company. Certainly with all that wholly natural inorganic ash, (which in this context qualifies as organic!) there will never be a need for artificial fertilizers.

I had also passed through Tanna on my way to the small islands of Aniwa and Futuna, the latter originally settled by Polynesians from an island of the same name a thousand miles to the east, and now supporting a mixed Melanesian and Polynesian population of a few hundreds. The island is an old, eroded volcanic cone rising straight out of the deep, with no beaches and of difficult access up a cliff by means of a series of ladders, the bottom-most of which one must grasp from a heaving dinghy. The island is like a tall hat, with its villages scattered around a narrow

NOWHERE NEAR GREENLAND

brim. Its crown is a diminuitive plateau of old reef limestones nearly two thousand feet high, often in cloud, where the people have their principal food gardens and grow yams, taro, plantains and other vegetables. Livestock here are limited to a few penned pigs and many chickens, for cattle would soon break their necks. Drainage from the plateau is down a steep, vegetation-choked crater at its centre, where I was told that if you throw a stick down it will later emerge in the sea.

The neighbouring island of Aniwa, on the other hand, is almost flat with the largest lagoon in Vanuatu. It exports several tons of sandalwood every year, though most of its stands were decimated in the rush for that fragrant product in the mid-19th century. However, mandarin trees have spread and been planted over much of the island, and their fruit exported to Vila is now a major source of revenue for its inhabitants. I travelled there in a small boat, with an outboard motor hired from Whitesands village on Tanna, a crossing of some fifteen miles. Returning a couple of days later, the motor died halfway across, and it was a full hour before we got it going again. Less than a month later, the senior cooperatives officer in Santo, Mark Abner who was from Aniwa, also set out to return to Tanna in the same boat, and he and his companions were never seen again. There is always some risk travelling between the islands in this manner, generally with no paddles, no sail, no lifejackets, no flares, no provisions. I had also crossed in a similar craft from Lolowai on Ambai to north Pentecost, with Mary Lini when she was engaged to be married to Walter, Vanuatu's first prime minister. However, during my years in Vanuatu, lost boats and their occupants have sometimes made landfall, weeks or even months later, in islands far away, including the southern Solomons. Such unintended landfalls have no doubt contributed to the settlement of the Pacific islands over thousands of years.

Among the islands to the south of Efate is Erromango. It was once known, particularly in missionary circles, as 'Erromango of the Martyrs' because so many churchmen were killed there in the 19th century, most of them immediately upon landing on the beach. These included John Williams, who was the first to bring bananas to the New Hebrides, particularly the Cavendish variety which he had obtained from the English duke of that name when visiting his greenhouse in the UK. However, he did not have the chance to take them out of the box in which they were stored on board before he was killed. They were eventually offloaded in Samoa and planted, and many years later were brought back to the New Hebrides by other missionaries, when they were given the name of banana Samoa. Erromango, like

To Coral Strands

all the islands in the New Hebrides, and indeed throughout the south Pacific, suffered massive depopulation through initial contact with Europeans, who brought with them diseases to which the local people had no resistance, such as measles, smallpox and tuberculosis; this decline was exacerbated by the forced recruitment of labour for the cane and cotton fields in Fiji and Australia, and to some extent by the demon of alcohol.

Aneityum, the southernmost inhabited island, also once supported a considerable population, which developed in response to demographic pressure on the land a sophisticated irrigation system for intensive taro cultivation, employing stone-lined and ravine-spanning canals. But successive epidemics reduced its population from many thousands to just a few hundred, so this intensive system fell into disrepair. Lying just north of the Tropic of Capricorn, these southernmost islands enjoy an almost subtropical climate, too cool for coconuts where they can not be grown commercially, and their major natural resource for income has been the hardwood kauri, and Tanna has its coffee. Today, tourists arriving by air and on cruise ships, are making an increasing contribution.

In 1977, at the end of two years teaching at Tagabe, with a year to go to see through my set of students, and on the very day I was to proceed on long leave, I was handed an official paper in French announcing my 'fin de carrière'. When I asked my director what this meant, he shrugged his shoulders, pouted, half raised his hands in the air, and said I could come back if I wanted to but would have to pay my own passage. So I called his bluff and did just that. My director was a small, bald man from Calais who had once trained as a professional clown. I did not get on very well with him, and he often expressed himself as 'étonné' by my actions or informed me I was 'incorrigible', though I greatly admired his amazing range of facial expressions, and quite brilliant imitations of a shambling ape, and suchlike. And when he pronounced the word 'bon', which somehow was never in direct reference to my work, he would first blow out his cheeks and then let the word come out with a soft pop. Unfortunately, when I took over from him he had removed all references to me from the confidential staff files, which I am sure would have made most interesting reading, since I was certainly politically suspect as far as he, his predecessors and fellow countrymen were concerned.

During that final year at Tagabe, I received a large envelope from South Korea bearing an impressive number of stamps from that country, and inside was a letter with

NOWHERE NEAR GREENLAND

an ornate letterhead promoting some product or other. By coincidence, at the same time, lying on my desk, was an odd joker card I had mixed up with my own pack of cards, following a game of racing demon patience with Martin Bennett, the chief forestry officer, and his wife at their house a few days previously. It was there to remind me to return it to them, but somehow I now had the idea to effect this in an indirect manner. With the help of the photocopier, I changed the letterhead of the Korean enterprise to that of the office of the general manager of a major plywood manufacturer in South Korea. In the letter, I stated my company's interest in establishing a large-scale plywood manufacturing plant in the New Hebrides, perhaps on the island of Espiritu Santo, which I understood had the most extensive resources of suitable timber for that purpose. Eight of us would therefore come on an investigative mission, arriving on such and such a flight for a period of one week. We would naturally greatly appreciate it if the chief forest officer himself would meet us on arrival, accompany us on our mission, and most kindly make all necessary bookings for hotel accommodation in Vila and Santo, and for all internal flights. I added that as chairman of the company, the prime minister of South Korea would be in the party in an entirely private capacity, in which case there was to be absolutely no publicity concerning his visit, nor any official receptions or suchlike functions. Samples of the quality and grade of plywood we were interested in manufacturing, would be sent shortly under separate cover. Yours very sincerely, etc. Transferring some of the Korean stamps onto a new envelope, I placed it in Martin's mailbox at the department headquarters.

I had timed the arrival of the party for a week later, and during the interim I saw nothing of Martin nor heard from him. However, he had gone ahead and made the necessary bookings, and on a strictly need to know basis, discreetly informed our director and the British Resident Commissioner of the visit. Doubtless this information would have been passed by one or the other to the French Resident Commissioner, and probably discreet security arrangements were put in hand. On the morning of the scheduled arrival of the Koreans, I placed the joker card between two small oblongs of plywood, put it in an envelope bearing the remainder of the Korean stamps, and placed it in Martin's mail box. No covering letter. The surprise was complete, and Martin took the joke extremely well and roared with laughter over the phone; though he was of course busy making hotel and flight cancellations, and informing our superiors that the visit had at the last moment been cancelled.

Towards the end of that year, I was visited in my office at Tagabe by an American

To Coral Strands

civil engineer from San Francisco, who was in the process of buying the two thousand hectare Jean My plantation on Santo. He sought advice about the planting and upkeep of cocoa, coconuts and coffee, as well as on cattle management, of which he admitted he knew absolutely nothing. Rather a broad request, but I gave him some literature and notes to get on with. A week or so later, having been up to Santo, he came back again and asked me if I would visit his plantation during weekends, to help him further plan and implement some activities there, and draw up and cost a development programme and its projected returns. I said I would, in return for the airfares only and my meals while I was there. Then about a month before the end of the school term, and my putative final departure from the New Hebrides at the end of November 1978, he asked me if instead of leaving I would work for him full-time, and he offered me a fair salary. I agreed to this, and the department duly held a farewell party for me, at which the director was no doubt happy to at last present me with some outstandingly modest parting gifts. During this last year, when the New Hebrides had been granted self-governing status, Thomas Reuben Seru of Hog Harbour, a member of parliament in the new Government of National Unity, had also been coming to me for advice, chiefly regarding cocoa planting. On my departure from Tagabe I wrote him a brief letter saying that if at any time in future I could be of assistance to him or the New Hebrides government, I would be very happy to give it.

I then moved up to Santo and into the Jean My house, a highly original building constructed in 1938 in the form of an octagon. Its large, high-ceilinged, central room gave on to screened verandas at front and back, and subtended three rooms on either side. The back veranda looked over a patch of rough grass on to the coral foreshore and the sea. However, somewhat detracting from the aesthetic pleasure of this aspect, were the accumulated bleached bones and scattered skulls of cattle that had been slaughtered in the very basic abattoir only yards away from the house - and unfortunately upwind. A further disadvantage was the siting of the bucket shower and latrine. This, though quite near the house, was on the far side of a stockway through which cattle and horses, desperate to quench their thirst, would thunder en masse on the way to the water troughs. Thus, when running this gauntlet with towel or toilet roll in hand, it was prudent to be alert for the sight and sound of any fast-approaching stampede. These animals were the more fortunate ones on the property, for when I visited one of the large, distant paddocks adjoining the forest reserve, I found a dried-up stream bed, littered on either side with dozens of shrivelled carcasses of cattle that had died of thirst. Water supply to other areas of

NOWHERE NEAR GREENLAND

the plantation depended on its delivery by tractor and trailer, which was evidently neither sufficient nor timely enough to prevent further losses. Admittedly, that year there had been an exceptional drought during the cool season, but its occurrence was enough to disprove Dr. Valin's pronouncement to me years before, that cattle in the New Hebrides did not need to be supplied with water because there was always enough in the grass.

The front veranda of my house overlooked a series of decrepit buildings, including the copra and cocoa drying beds, this time happily downwind because their hot air pipes had long since rusted through, and both products were in effect smoked. The wood smoke and aroma of the cocoa beans and copra filled the adjoining corrugated iron garages and workshops which served for the housing and maintenance of the clapped-out vehicles and machinery that had accumulated and corroded there over the years. Fortuitously, the hovels housing the plantation labour were out of sight, but not out of mind as far as I was concerned, and I made the building of new quarters a priority. Woven bamboo walls and partitions, as found in all of the islands' villages, are aesthetically pleasing, cool and cheap. So I renewed my long acquaintance with Jimmy Stevens at Fanafo, whose centre was not far from the plantation's boundary, and asked if he would prefabricate woven bamboo sections for the proposed housing. At that time, the plantation recruited most of its labour from Fanafo, and would be needing many more to prune the old coffee and thin out its shade trees, as well as for planting coconuts, cocoa and more coffee - that is if my development plans were to be realised.

As I now belonged to the Santo planting community, I attended a meeting of the Syndicat Agricole. This was made up entirely of French or part-French planters, many of them unreconstructed nineteenth century thinkers as far as their views on natives were concerned, (one in south Santo had prominent warnings of mantraps posted around his boundaries, which he regarded as a sporting concession to the unwary trespasser). Now more anti-British than ever, with the dread prospect of independence no longer beyond the horizon, my reception at the meeting was palpably chill, and my feeling that I was regarded as an English spy was, I am sure, well founded. A francophone friend who had been at the meeting later told me that some of the planters averred that they could never, ever forget my part in 'les événements' in Vila in 1977. This was passing strange because I had spent most of that day at Tagabe, teaching Claudia Huffman to drive, and had only ventured into Vila that evening, long after the shouting and tumult had died. However, their need

To Coral Strands

to believe in my riotous, anti-French participation clearly revealed their general attitude towards me and anglo-saxons in general.

Recalling the truly memorable driving lesson on that day, Claudia was at the wheel of one of my two Mini-mokes, and in the back we had a neutral observer, David Friend, a cocoa specialist from the Solomons who had come to advise the department of agriculture on the development of that crop. After making excellent progress, driving around the agricultural station which provided an ideal and safe location for this exercise, though still frequently punctuated by Claudia's Colombian screams whenever she incorrectly anticipated being unable to make a turn, miss a tree, or pass through a wide gate, we approached my car port, at the front of which was parked my other Mini-moke. Claudia perfectly changed down into low gear, but somehow simultaneously contrived to heavily depress the accelerator pedal, and we slammed into the back of the other vehicle. More screams, and analogous to the principle that you should immediately remount after falling off a horse, I softly persuaded her to back up and try again. The result was almost the same, except that this time the resulting collision was regrettably and decidedly more powerful. Kirk recorded his wife's achievement on film, David was in paroxysms of laughter, Claudia was screaming fit to bust, and I decided at that point, not to invoke Robert the Bruce's dictum, that if at first you don't succeed, try, try again. Twice was already enough!

Subsequently David had an exciting visit. We flew up to Norsup the following day to look at cocoa on Malekula. As we approached the francophone area of Wala-Rano, we were stopped at a road block and ordered out while our vehicle was thoroughly searched for 'bombs'. (Tear gas had been employed during the riot in Vila the day before.) Though the people concerned had known me for years, and one did express a small measure of regret at the inconvenience, the power of propaganda, presumably transmitted by radio the previous night or that morning, was manifest.

We stopped at the Catholic mission, and there I was hectored by my old friend Father Soucy, who wanted to know how I would like it if the IRA raised its flag over the centre of London? For him at least, the religious divide between anglophone and francophone politics was paramount, and it was Protestants versus Catholics again, and this was no longer the same Father Soucy I had known for years as a friend.

Meanwhile, back at Lakatoro, Jerry Marston, now the British District Agent,

NOWHERE NEAR GREENLAND

awaited a threatened attack on the agency by the forces of francophonia. He therefore seated himself alone at a small table in the middle of the sports field, where he could clearly be seen from the road, in the hope that he could forestall any attack on the agency through the power of persuasion. A cavalcade of vehicles bearing heavily-armed men duly approached, the rear brought up by a French gendarme. However, it drove straight past, heading for the village of Lingarak, where the rainbow banner of the National Party had been hoisted, and the flagpole was surrounded by armed men ready to defend their flag. With serious bloodshed the likely outcome of this armed confrontation, Chief Rion of Litzlitz said "Let them take the flag, it is only a piece of calico, and not worth a life", so they withdrew and their flag was captured. (Chief Rion, was only months later struck on the head by a small piece of wood flying from a tree being felled, and died on the spot.)

Back on the American's property on Santo, seeking a solution to the problem of water for the cattle, I ventured into the extensive undeveloped part of the property still largely covered in rainforest, but with enough grassy glades therein to feed the sizable number of feral cattle which had escaped the plantation and happily dwelt therein. One-way gates, essentially corridors of bamboo poles, wide at the forest end and narrowing at their exit into the plantation, had been built along the boundary of the reserve to entice cattle back into the cleared pastures. But the wild cattle were far better off where they were, so it tended to be only bulls passing through when they sensed cows and heifers on heat. About a kilometre into the forest, I found a permanent stream which at one point flowed steeply down over rocks, and I judged this an ideal site to install a hydraulic ram pump, which is powered entirely by the pressure of falling water. The height it would need to pump was small for a ram, which can lift water many hundreds of feet, and just within the developed plantation, this water could then be fed by gravity all the way to the waterless paddocks and beyond. With a gang of labour, I set out to cut a trace which the pipeline would follow through the forest. Hacking away with my bush-knife, I cut into a tree which exudes a dark poisonous sap - hence the name of 'goudron', meaning tar given to it by the French, and almost immediately my bare right arm developed large blisters. Years before at Lakatoro, I had encountered the same problem when I stacked dry wood from the forest along my arm to carry to a barbecue. I needed antihistamine, so I left the work gang and drove the twenty miles or so into Luganville.

The British doctor there gave me an injection and some tablets, and said to be care-

To Coral Strands

ful when driving as they could make me drowsy and slow my reactions. I know, I know, I replied, I've had this sort of thing many times before, and drove and then walked back to the ongoing work in the forest. A short while later, a Pacific boa, the non-venomous constricting snake of the islands, dropped down from a tree. The work gang promptly disappeared into the forest, the crashing sounds of their progress fading away in proportion to their speed and distance. As is my wont, though in this case shouldn't have, I went to pick up the snake just behind its head, quite forgetting the doctor's caution, and the snake zapped me on my thumb. (My third snake bite, but the first non-poisonous one.) Non-poisonous, yes, but snakes have a dirty bite, and what I now needed was an anti-tetanus jab. So off I set again for Luganville, already practising what I would say to the doctor: "Sorry to bother you again. You remember what you told me about slowed reactions? Well, it was like this……..". Or maybe I should just look for another doctor.

Gus, the owner of the plantation, returned from America with his wife, their charming daughter Clarisse, who was a bank manager in San Francisco, her husband Chuck who was an aircraft engine mechanic, and their small child. Clarisse, Chuck and child would stay at the 'ranch,' as her father liked to call it, (and would I please choose some good cows horns to mount around the wooden walls of the lounge room), and he and his wife would just visit from time to time from the US. Clarisse would do the figuring, I the crops and livestock and Chuck would get the cars and tractors working again. Chuck, a very large man of few words, from thenceforth was only to be seen zooming around on his back between the wheels and junk in the workshop, on one of those mini-wheeled boards that garage people use, or at his appearances at mealtimes. The owner stayed on for a while walking around the property with me, drawing up the development programme and installing a bath and lavatory in the house, so his daughter and her baby were now much less likely to be trampled by a bovine stampede.

A month or so later, Lesley was in Vila and went to meet Gus and his wife returning again from the United States. The wife was first through customs with her suitcase, and suggested that she and Lesley go ahead in a taxi to the Hotel Rossi, as Gus had brought many things for the ranch and would be a while. They set off, but when only halfway to town they heard the siren of a police car behind them, and looking round saw the police signalling for them to stop. "Go faster, go faster", Mrs Gus urgently ordered the driver, who was beginning to slow down. "What are you doing?" asked Lesley, "this is not Chicago, of course he must stop!" Thus the Key-

NOWHERE NEAR GREENLAND

stone Cops scene was curtailed, and they were ordered to return forthwith to the airport. There, customs had discovered handguns inside Gus's luggage, and now wanted to see inside his wife's suitcase which had been waved through inspection without opening. There was a handgun inside her suitcase too. Fortunately for them, they had previously opted to answer to French jurisdiction. Gus remained in Vila until the matter had been sorted out, and he was fined and the guns confiscated. When he arrived back in Santo he was most indignant at all the fuss. I patiently explained that in most countries of the world handguns were the attributes only of crooks, the armed forces and police, and even in the latter case their use was often severely restricted. I desisted from telling him I thought Americans' general attitude to guns was hopelessly juvenile, and not at all as manly as they imagined. I discovered at about this time he was, anyway, a member of the John Birch Society in the USA, an extremist right wing organisation, very much into guns and libertarian ideology.

Gus was very friendly with the Belgian who was temporarily living in Jean Ratard's former and, for the New Hebrides, palatial plantation house on Aore, and together they were involved with the real estate company in Hawaii that was advertising New Hebrides plantations there and in mainland USA. They in turn were associated with Michael Oliver and Eugene Peacock, who had long been involved in speculative property purchases, scams and loony libertarian ideals and deals in the Pacific and Caribbean. Previously, this Hawaiian company had succeeded in arranging the sale of Rene Thevenin's plantation at Lonorore on Pentecost to Joel Nevels of California. The latter was eventually deported for using a hand gun to scare off local people using their traditional paths to cross his land, though not before his Hawaiian lawyers had drawn up for him a highly ornate document, shown to me by Darvall Wilkins, proclaiming 'The Independent State of Lonorore'! His case was not improved by his having given long term lodging to the quack American doctor who administered eternal youth injections.

The real estate agent came over from Hawaii, and Gus invited me to go over with them and the Belgian to the Valesdir plantation on Epi, then being managed by Dick Kerr. I was to make a survey of the property and supply the information they needed on crops and livestock which they would include in a brochure to market this property in the United States. I duly made the inspection, noting in my report the broken fences, semi-wild cattle, weedy, overgrazed pastures, senile coconut palms, abandoned coffee and sparse cocoa. Hawaii were quick to produce a glossy

To Coral Strands

brochure, which attributed to me, their 'agricultural expert' a really glowing description of the bounteous crop and livestock assets of the plantation. But this is completely untrue, I complained to Gus. Ah, he explained, Americans expect real estate agents to exaggerate, and if you make a factual description of a property, prospective buyers will believe it to be much worse than it really is!

Cyclone Jean strikes the Jean My plantation Santo, 1979

By January 1979, I had already made up my mind to quit this employment. Not only would I and my wife be judged by our association with these people, (my wife in the airport incident, for example), but with the New Hebrides moving rapidly towards independence, they were the wrong people in the wrong place at the wrong time, their incomprehension of the local scene, and the commonly held values of the country, being almost total. Then a most timely message was relayed to me by Lesley, that Thomas Reuben Seru, by then the Minister of Agriculture and Natural Resources in the Government of National Unity, and his first secretary Barak Sope, needed to speak with me on a matter of some urgency.
I flew down to Vila and accepted their offer of the directorship of the Department

NOWHERE NEAR GREENLAND

of Agriculture, Livestock and Forestry. I was told that this tenure would extend only until independence, scheduled for the following year, when the post would be localised, though as things turned out, I held it for more than five years.

I returned to Santo and started to pack my things, though fortunately most still remained in their crates in Vila. All the American family were then back in the States, so in the middle of a cyclone I recorded a tape for Gus, tending my resignation and giving him my good news. I handed over to the assistant manager, Monsieur D'Ambreville, and within a few days travelled down to Vila.

André Pilecki plans the layout of his new Coffee and Cocoa research station Santo, 1982.

I then went to see the personnel officer at the British residency to ask if a contract for me could be arranged with the UK Overseas Development Administration. He received me most rudely, barely looking up from his work, with "What do YOU want?", but later became more gracious when he realised that a senior post, hitherto always reserved for a Frenchman, had been secured by a Brit. He also later obtained for me a refund of the airfare I had paid to return to the New Hebrides the previous year. Meanwhile, my former director had rapidly departed for France, no doubt handing over to me being too bitter a pill to swallow, though his facial contortions and stomach clutching, possibly prompted by the occasion, would have been a

To Coral Strands

farewell performance well worth seeing.

With the coming of independence, there was now the prospect of development aid coming from more than just the traditional sources of France and Britain, so I busied myself with identifying suitable projects, and recruited two economists to work with the department and ministry to assist in the drawing up of proposals.
Thus, over the next year or two, funding was secured for a national copra improvement programme, cocoa development, the quarantine service, coconut planting, smallholder cattle development, industrial forest plantations, root crops development, and others. I invited the French to consider developing their IRHO (Institut de Recherche pour les Huiles et Oliageneux) coconut research station on Santo as a regional centre of excellence, and to bring in the related IRCC (Institute de Recherche pour Café et Cacao) to assist in the research and development of coffee and cocoa.

For some years I had been on the Vila Agricultural Show committee, and was now on the national development council and various other committees, and perhaps on the strength of this, I was invited early in 1980 by Prime Minister Father Walter Lini, to form an independence celebrations committee. This would prepare for the day, as yet unknown, when Vanuatu became a nation. I invited on to the committee representatives of the commercial sector, government services and the churches, and the British and French residencies were each requested to provide an observer, principally for liaison purposes. This committee would make proposals to government on what the celebrations should comprise, who should be invited, locally and from overseas, and organise all the logistics of transport, accommodation, invitations, catering, publicity and so on.

The committee decided that the core events should be the lowering and raising of the national flags, symbolising the transition from the Anglo-French Condominium to the new independent republic of Vanuatu, a presidential breakfast, a state banquet, and a traditional ceremony presided over by the National Council of Chiefs. First we needed advice from the two residencies concerning the lowering of their flags, bearing in mind that the Condominium was unique, and that none of the many celebrations, marking the independence of their former colonies, protectorates or trust territories, had been shared with another departing colonial power. Would, for example, the British and French flags be lowered together, with their respective national anthems played simultaneously, symbolising perhaps the

NOWHERE NEAR GREENLAND

discord which had so often existed between them? With both powers' long established touchiness over precedence, and the precise height of competing flagpoles, this surely promised to be a thorny issue. However, the charming French submarine officer, Yves Leborne, as liaison officer for his residency - and who soon would marry a secretary from the British residency, brought the reply to our next meeting, that on such occasions the French never lower their national flag at a public ceremony. This now meant, in effect, that neither could the British, so the soon to be former colonial powers made separate arrangements to lower their flags on the night preceding independence, the British at the resident commissioner's house on Iririki Island, and the French at their equivalent on the mainland.

Soon after came the question, where should the flag raising and attendant ceremony take place? The obvious, sufficiently large open space near the centre of town was the British Paddock, best known, hitherto, for its cricket matches. This was duly proposed. The response from the French Residency came back: British Paddock! Non! I then suggested, well, suppose we now rename the paddock; say, for example, Independence Park? This, thank goodness, was accepted, and we now had a site where the required stands could be built, a single flagpole erected for the Vanuatu flag, and the precise places for prayers, slit-gongs, bands, choirs, scouts, marchers, counter-marches, etc., could be mapped out.

About seven weeks before Independence, by then scheduled for 30th July 1980, Professor Ron Crocombe of the University of the South Pacific presented Father Walter Lini with a copy of his Institute of Pacific Studies latest publication. This celebrated the independence of Kiribati, formerly the Gilbert Islands. We must have a book like that, said the prime minister. "But who will take that on?" asked Ron. "Barry Weightman will", replied Father Walter. Ron Crocombe promised that the IPS would publish it in time for independence, provided we got the draft to him some three weeks before, which left me just a month to complete it. I immediately wrote or spoke to about a dozen people, inviting each to contribute a chapter appropriate to their knowledge of the subject: politics, religion, law, education, medical services, agriculture, commerce, communications, fisheries, and so on. I had hoped to have equal numbers of British, French and ni-Vanuatu contributors, particularly as the book was to be published in three languages, each in one of three columns on every page. However, most of the French or francophones I approached, including Father Lemang and Vincent Boulekone, whom I had selected for church and law respectively, declined, probably because I was British

To Coral Strands

and they were not happy that independence was to be celebrated under an anglophone-led government.

The prime minister would write the preface, and in pretty quick time the contributors set to work. I had indicated the number of words required from each; however, most of the submissions were markedly under the target given, a few were wildly over, while some writers were clearly out of practice at expressing their thoughts on paper. One way or another, with time running out, I had a major rewrite job on my hands, and just hoped to get away with it without creating feelings of lese-majesty or being accused of misrepresentation. I trawled round my friends, and the archives of the local French and British information services, for photographs to illustrate the chapters. These would also play an essential part in filling up blank spaces, since the relative succinctness or otherwise of the three languages was reflected in the length of their columns, those in French being twenty per cent longer than those in English, and those in Bislama being twice as long again. And now I had to find translators, so that each contribution could be presented in all three languages. Finally, with a few days to spare, the chapters and the photographs were rushed to Fiji where their technicians set to work on the layout. Then galley proofs were returned, checked and sent back again.

The first bound copy of 'Vanuatu' arrived and I took it to show to the prime minister. He opened it, only immediately to find that the first, full page photograph in the book showed him signing a document with his left hand. The photo had been printed back to front! An urgent phone call to Fiji turned it round the right way, and just two days before independence, boxes of the book were flown to Vila, where each official guest at the celebrations was to receive a copy. Of much less importance was that my photograph of a 'mahe-mahe' fish being gaffed aboard the m.v Rocinante was printed upside down, and that the photo showing Pastor Fred Timakata hacking his way through a coconut log to victory at Lakatoro was wrongly captioned, and these minor errors have remained uncorrected.

At this time, it seemed the French were bent on spoiling the smooth transition of the New Hebrides Condominium to a Vanuatu republic under an anglophone government, since they were then tacitly supporting secessionist movements on the islands of Tanna and Santo. The former ended in a brief but fatal skirmish, but on Santo where Jimmy Stevens had proclaimed the Republic of Vemerana, the situation was more serious, and the minor hostilities of what the foreign press

NOWHERE NEAR GREENLAND

dubbed the 'coconut war', had opened. During this period I was from time to time on duty in the operations room at Vila police headquarters, and in touch by radio with the m.v. Euphrosyne engaged in the evacuation by sea of British nationals from South Santo. I was also fielding questions from the world's press, and sometimes agreeing to speak live on their radio programmes. Chief geologist Sandy Macfarlane had been on the m.v. Euphrosyne, and when he got back we had a lively party at his house on Independence Park. A late, international telephone call came through for Sandy from 'The Scotsman' in Edinburgh. Would he please describe the present situation in the New Hebrides? "The situation", shouted Sandy, above the surrounding din, and taking in the roomful of merry makers, "is fluid, very fluid", and that is about all he managed to say before he hung up. (The international press later made a mischievous joke of the bislama words in the new national anthem 'yumi, yumi, yumi', pronounced you-me, you-me, you-me – simply meaning 'we' – and not yummy, yummy, yummy, and definitely not alluding to any former cannibalistic tendencies.)

Final preparations for the independence celebrations went ahead. We had been asked to invite both Fidel Castro and the King of Spain, but in the event neither was able to come. A Chilean admiral, one of Pinochet's men then serving as his ambassador to New Zealand, practically invited himself. We referred this to the prime minister and it was agreed he could come. So, on the seating plans we were already drawing up, we sat him next to the ambassador from the Soviet Union. The regional director of the World Health Organisation, based in Manila, Dr. Nakajima, later director general of WHO, also wrote to say he thought he should be invited, so he too was sent an invitation. As there were about twenty church denominations officially present in the New Hebrides, invitations to their regional representatives, such as the Papal Nuncio in Wellington, the Archbishop of Melanesia, and so on, greatly swelled the overseas guest list. Meanwhile, the government was building a VIP lounge at Bauerfield airport to receive the distinguished guests, hostesses were recruited, trained and dressed to receive them, a fleet of cars was organised to take them to their hotels, and folders were prepared containing their individual invitation cards to the official events, as well as background information on Vanuatu, and other goodies and handouts such as the book 'Vanuatu', hot off the press from Fiji.

Fiji sent two protocol officers, two charming and elderly 'ratus', to assist us and Vanuatu's fledgling foreign affairs department in making sure that dignitaries did

To Coral Strands

not get their noses put out of joint. Nikenike Vurubaravu, of newly created foreign affairs was assigned to work directly with us. David Browning stepped smartly forward to assist with the military side of the celebrations and work with a brigadier just arrived from PNG, and Coco Browning took charge of the media. Father Brian Macdonald Milne on our committee liaised with the various churches to plan the ecumenical service and blessing at the flag-raising ceremony, the prayers at the Presidential Breakfast, and so on. The Vanuatu national anthem had been composed, and sheet music printed. The national flag had been designed and a few big ones manufactured, several thousand small flags were despatched for distribution in the islands, and an entrepreneur donated several hundred Vanuatu Independence golf umbrellas. Taking time out from the hectic scene in Vila some weeks before independence, I assisted, aboard the 'Rocinante', in the distribution to the Banks and Torres Islands of those flags and the words and music of the national anthem. This was the only time I visited the beautiful Torres Islands, and it was great to see their people's enthusiasm and involvement in preparations for independence in these isolated outposts of the fledgling republic.

Two or three days before Independence Day, overseas guests began arriving on scheduled flights. We knew exactly which guest would arrive on which flight. A hostess was assigned to each one, and specific cars in the fleet stood by to carry their particular VIP to the hotel where their accommodation had been arranged. Then, unexpectedly, Dr. Nakajima arrived two days ahead of schedule. He was most irate to see other guests whisked off while he was left stranded without a vehicle. A thousand apologies. His personal folder was located and given to him, and a car summoned to carry him to his hotel. The next day, the representatives of the royal families of Samoa and Tonga arrived on the same flight. All went well at the airport, but on the way to Vila the car carrying the Tongan royals overtook the Samoan royals, arrived at the hotel out of sequence, and were given the wrong rooms. A right royal row then threatened between these regal houses that did not always enjoy the best of relations. But somehow it was all settled, at least down to simmering level.

Then the day before independence, horror of horrors, a second Dr. Nakajima with identical initials to his name arrived, and was extremely irate and insulted that no preparations had been made for his reception. Informing him that he had already arrived two days previously, merely served to enrage him further. Phoning the airport, and then checking with our hotel bookings schedule, I found that due to a cancellation we could at least offer him a hotel room until the matter had been

NOWHERE NEAR GREENLAND

sorted out. I then rang Gordon Haines, working for British special branch and better known locally as 007, to suggest that we might have an impostor on our hands and possibly a security threat to VIPs, since these were still the days of the Red Brigade in Japan. Could he find out which was the real Nakajima? He came back to me later in the day. The second Dr. Nakajima was our Dr. Nakajima of WHO. The first Dr. Nakajima was also a bona fide Nakajima representing radio ham operators in Japan, nothing at all to do with the independence celebrations, and had come to attend a meeting of fellow ham enthusiasts in Vila. Fine, but our problem was that Nakajima One now had the folder with all Nakajima Two's official invitations, including the much coveted presidential breakfast of extremely limited issue, as well as all the other goodies and handouts.

We now had to get these back, and this was Nikenike's very first diplomatic mission. However, Nakajima One displayed limpet like qualities, clinging to his superior room and the precious invitations; but at length, as a result of Nikekike's diplomacy, he reluctantly relinquished them in return for an invitation to the flag-raising ceremony and a place on the grandstand. A British representative of local ham operators later rang me up to complain loudly of the cavalier treatment meted out to their Japanese ham delegate. This was just too much and I hung up.

The evening before independence, I attended an investiture and lowering of the Union Jack on Iririki Island to the music and last post played by the band of the Royal Marines, white under the moon in their solar topees. And Sandy Macfarlane played a solo lament on his bagpipes. Somewhere across the water, out of sight and sound, a similar though less elaborate scene was being played out at the French Residency.

With the highly unpredictable, acceptably flexible, 'Pacific time' in the islands, it is rare that things go like clockwork, but so went the celebrations next day in Independence Park. The sun shone, the bands played, the priests and people prayed, the flag hit the top of the flagpole at the split second of noon, the guns and drums boomed, the planes flew past, the troops paraded and speeches were made. That night at the Independence Banquet, President Ati George Sokomanu handed out Independence Medals, and Fiji's Prime Minister, Ratu Sir George Kamisese Mara, made a fine speech. But towards the end of the banquet, the serving US Ambassador in another Pacific nation, an ethnic Greek - by some if not happy coincidence named Condom, who was to be accredited to Vanuatu, approached the independ-

To Coral Strands

ence committee's table in an inebriated fury. His complaint was that he had not received an invitation to the presidential breakfast on the morrow. However, this we had been instructed, was strictly for heads of delegations only, and James Mitchener was President Carter's official representative, not him. Hence no invitation. For some reason he picked on Coco Browning as being personally responsible for this perceived slight, and had her in tears.

The next day at the Vila agricultural show, I was assigned to attend the Duke of Gloucester, who had represented the Queen at the celebrations. I had felt that having the show as part of the celebrations was rather overloading the programme (and us!) however it went well. The Duke was knowledgeable of things agricultural, showed an interest in the livestock and entries of tropical crops hitherto unknown to him, and enjoyed the rodeo, barrel races and other horse events.

The day after that I departed on leave. I had arranged my hotel booking at Kuta beach in Bali through Burns Philp's local travel agent. I was really quite fatigued by all this recent activity, and was looking forward to a week's good rest there before continuing to the UK. Flying via Sydney to Jakarta, I there boarded the Garuda flight to Den Pasar on Bali. The flight was packed, because it was an Indonesian public holiday to be followed by a long weekend, and the plane was filled with the eye-watering smoke of 'kretek' cigarettes, which are a mixture of cloves and tobacco. It was already late in the evening when the plane arrived, and I took a taxi to my hotel. But they had never heard of me, and the hotel was booked out solid. No hope of a room. Somehow the booking has not been made. So I set off in the taxi to find alternative accommodation. Everywhere was full. About two hours later, with both taxi driver and myself by now exhausted, we came back to the original hotel. Having spoken fluent Malay for five years, I followed the ensuing conversation without difficulty. This approximated, "In the names of all Hindu divinities, please, oh please find something for this man so that I can go home to my wife". "Well", said the night manager, "we do have a little room that is used once a month by our accountant who flies down from Jakarta. It's not really a room at all, because this is where we store all our sheets, pillow-cases and table-cloths, but its the best we can do. And in two days time we can offer the tuan a chalet on the beach". "Yes, thank you", I said. And "Yes, yes, bagus, sangat baik", said the taxi driver. The manager was absolutely correct. It was not a room; it was a linen closet. It had one tiny window high up on the wall, a camp bed and a door that led directly into the restaurant. But I was very grateful for even that, and in the early

NOWHERE NEAR GREENLAND

hours of the morning, surrounded by stacks of linen, fell fast asleep.

Waking rather late, wearing only my lavalava and still somewhat disorientated, I threw open the door of my closet to be greeted by the startled looks of guests having their breakfast. I retreated rather hastily, closing the door, and they must have wondered what it all meant. I dressed, then with towel and toothbrush re-entered the thankfully now empty restaurant.

With what was left of the morning, I went to lie on the beach under my newly acquired Vanuatu Independence golf umbrella. I was awoken from my doze by an exclamation of surprise, and an upside-down head joined me beneath the umbrella. It was that of a good friend from Vila, amazed to find that only three days after the event, Vanuatu's independence had reached Kuta beach. She and her Canadian boyfriend had also just arrived from Vila. That evening we went for a meal at a restaurant, and were intrigued to find magic mushroom soup on the menu. Why not, we decided, let's just try it, so we ordered a bowl each. After ten minutes or so we agreed we all felt absolutely normal. Perhaps it was just ordinary mushroom soup after all. Anyway, it had been very tasty, so we each had another bowl and went on to order the next course.

I then noticed that my friends' faces appeared decidedly odd. Her eyes had drawn so closely together she was now practically a Cyclops, and his ginger hair was now tinged with green. They stared intently back at me, and what they saw was evidently a source of some merriment to them. Soon we were all laughing. The rest of our meal, probably a simple one, became a banquet, and heads bent low over our plates we exclaimed at the sheer beauty of the boiled rice grains, the awesome symmetry of the cubes of pork, the vibrant green of the Chinese cabbage, their subtle harmonies and yet self-respecting individuality. Pushing gently with our chopsticks, we could create Euclidean patterns of profound significance to us, and modify the existential relationships between the rice, pork and cabbage; and when we ate them, their taste was transcended into delectable colour and music. Why had we never noticed such things before? We walked down the road towards my hotel, and found that the empty restaurant outside my room had been transformed into a glittering temple, and for a while we stood stunned to silence by the sheer beauty of it all. Then we lay on the beach at the very point where our planet meets infinite space and became totally absorbed in the night sky.

To Coral Strands

Returning to Vanuatu after leave, I now served a new and dynamic Minister of Agriculture, Sethy Regenvanu. For many years, the agricultural stations at Santo, Lakatoro and Tagabe had sold breeding cattle at subsidised prices, mainly Illawarra and mostly to small farmers. The national herd, the great majority of which grazed under coconuts in the plantation sector, was a mix of many breeds, the original foundation of which were Jersey cattle introduced in the 1850s. Subsequently, and for a hundred years, apart from Herefords, the other breeds introduced were also of dairy or so-called duel purpose types. The need now was for beef cattle, since the plantation sector, with ageing coconut palms and poor returns from copra, was rapidly evolving into a beef based industry.

Breeding stock of the right type to boost the beef industry
Port Vila, 1983

Further, the general lack of a roads, electricity and refrigeration limited the sales of milk to the small urban communities of Luganville and Vila. (In the early 1980s I was invited to inspect a newly installed, ultra-hygienic automatic milking parlour at the SDA mission on Aore, which had for some time been supplying milk to Luganville. All was spotless, the milk passing through transparent tubes from the milking machine cups on pre-washed cows' udders right through to the dairy where a pile of clear plastic sachets were ready to fill with milk from a gleaming spigot, before heat sealing for sale in the town. There, the dairy attendant gave each sachet a sharp shake to open it up before placing below the spigot. Alas, more times than not, the sachet did not sufficiently open, so he blew into it. Many a slip

NOWHERE NEAR GREENLAND

twixt cup and lip!)

The introduction of Charolais beef cattle from France in the 1960s had proved something of a disaster. Not only had brucellosis been introduced with them, but they are a very large breed, and when bred with local cattle which are relatively small, there were many calving problems. They also suffered from arthritis, did not acclimatise to heat, required a high level of nutrition, and with each succeeding generation became smaller and smaller as they adapted to local conditions. To boost the beef industry, we now decided to buy a large property outside Vila, which would produce breeding stock of the right type for sale to ranchers and farmers. We brought in an animal geneticist from South Africa, who recommended that for our climate and intended purpose, we should cross our existing herds of pure Limousin and Charolais with the Zebu and Africana breeds, and stabilise the resulting crossbreed with the right proportions of each. However, before we had even commenced this programme, there was an outcry in the New Caledonian press that had got wind of it. The essence of this was that the nationalistic anglo-saxons, of whom in this instance I was their leader, were planning to destroy the pure French breeds by crossing them with lesser breeds, (Doctor Valin had told me he just could not stomach any beef that contained Zebu blood), and thus sabotage the good work of their countrymen over many years. Was it not a shame and a scandal, and so on. Nevertheless, this breeding programme was a considerable success for the growing beef industry over a number of years. We also decided to stimulate beef, cocoa and coffee production by establishing large projects for each: cattle on Santo, cocoa on Malekula and coffee on Tanna. This would provide investment and jobs for three of the then four districts of the country. The fourth, in proximity to Vila, was already benefiting from the creation of the financial centre with its offshore banking facilities, and tourism.

Following the rebellion in Santo, many plantation owners and their overseers left, most of them going to New Caledonia, leaving their properties unmanaged. At independence, these all reverted to their customary owners, but because much of this land had been alienated to Europeans for up to one hundred, years it was now difficult to trace the original, indigenous owners. So, until this could be done, and with the land being held in trust by the government, we set up a plantation management service to take care of these properties, and prevent the loss of valuable livestock and other assets. We also looked at the feasibility of amalgamating a number of these largely abandoned plantations in the South Santo area to create one large beef-producing unit. This was done, and a lease was initially awarded to an Australian company. The subsequent history of this project has been chequered, largely due to local squabbles and politics, but over the years it has substantially contributed to the beef industry.

Children at Coffee Nursery on the island of Tanna, 1984.

On Malekula, the Commonwealth Development Corporation (CDC) was invited to carry out a feasibility study for the establishment of a large cocoa plantation on the former Verteuil concession, on the north west coast of that island. This was done, the forest cleared and about a thousand hectares of cocoa were planted. However, the young cocoa suffered from particularly dry years, more so since it was in a rain shadow on the drier side of the island, though once the cocoa had got its roots down to the water table, growth and yields picked up. But by that time CDC had decided to pull out, and management, answering directly to government, was for a long time intermittent and indifferent, chronically suffering from shortages of labour and capital to repair cyclone damage, maintain buildings and generally upkeep the plantation. However, in recent years the property has returned to good, professional management and, one hopes, to better prospects. The story of the CDC nucleus coffee estate and out-grower programme on Tanna has already been told.

Kava was also by now being popularised, with an increasing number of kava bars

NOWHERE NEAR GREENLAND

opening in Vila, and its general promotion throughout the country as a cash crop for export and domestic use encouraged research into its many different varieties, very many more in fact than anywhere else in the Pacific. It was also recognised that its more general use had contributed to a considerable reduction in public drunkenness and alcohol-fuelled domestic violence. In Vanuatu, kava is drunk only in the evening, generally between five and eight p.m., and it was becoming the social habit of civil servants and other office workers in the urban areas to drop into a nakamal for a few shells before returning home.

As director of agriculture, I had to ration myself in the number of overseas trips I took in response to invitations from international bodies, to attend workshops, symposiums and conferences. Vanuatu, with only three or four senior officers who might benefit from attending them, and one might hope pass on what they had learned to further the country's development, would receive almost as many invitations as, say, India or China, who could field countless thousands of suitable candidates. Thus, I let the Winged Bean Conference at the Hague pass me by, similarly potatoes in Peru and cucumbers in Chile. However, I did attend a meeting and study tour on coconut timber on Mindanao in the southern Philippines. Vanuatu had many ageing coconut plantations which were fast evolving into cattle ranches, and nuts were often no longer harvested from beneath palms progressively thinned out by age, lightning and cyclones, the fallen trunks of which just lay and rotted on the ground. Here was potentially a considerable resource to be exploited. The Philippines, the largest producer of copra in the world, had already created a thriving industry based on coconut timber, since, with the palms reaching the end of their economic life at around sixty years of age, there was always a plentiful supply of old trees. However, the milling of coconut timber requires special techniques and equipment. Not only does the density of its wood vary from the outside to the inside of the trunk, but also from the base to the top. And the wood is also full of silicate crystals that blunt a standard circular saw blade in seconds. It must also be treated with a fungicide immediately after milling, since in hot, humid climates mould can rapidly penetrate and discolour it.

We went out into the field with an armoured car at either end of our little convoy, because the Moro Liberation Front, a Muslim separatist organisation, was most active on Mindanao. There, with armed guards encircling us at a respectful distance, we saw a mobile unit of bulldozer, sawmill and timber treatment cylinder at work on a plantation. Later, we were shown all the products made from the timber, ranging from complete houses, furniture, wooden bowls and ornaments to tool handles.

To Coral Strands

Because coconut wood has exceptionally long fibres, it makes excellent and slightly flexible handles for axes, hammers and garden implements. Back in Vanuatu, we did try to attract commercial interest in our resource, particularly around Luganville and Vila where there was a large concentration of ageing coconut palms, but with no success and it has since all but disappeared.

I also went with Iolu Abbil, then first secretary in my ministry, to Sri Lanka to discuss the setting up of a South East Asian & Pacific organisation to represent the coconut industry. After the meeting, we had a couple of days free before we could take our flights home, so we took a taxi up to Kandi, and then on up into the high tea country around Nuarellia. Here my stepfather's father once had a coffee estate, but with all his neighbours he went bankrupt towards the end of the nineteenth century when coffee rust moved in and wiped out the industry.

It was only then that tea planting was promoted in Ceylon, for which that island later became famous. But what Iolu will remember as infamous, was the hair-raising journey we had back to the coast with an insane taxi driver. Iolu was moaning on the back seat with his eyes shut, rolling from one side to another as we screeched first left and then right around corners, while up front I repeatedly entreated the driver to slow down. We eventually got down safe if not entirely sound, and I imagined the driver later consulting a colleague, "What is meaning slow down?" And on being told he had confused this phrase with 'speed up', musing "Ah, only now am I understanding why they were shouting and shouting".

There was also a trip to Bangkok to discuss coconut research, only that time there was not even a half day available to play the tourist. However, near the FAO headquarters where the meeting was being held, there was an excellent seafood restaurant on a boat moored on the klong. This specialised in 'steamboat' cooking, an oriental variant of fondue whereby one added the raw materials of fish, prawns, eggs, meat, vegetables, etc., to the charcoal operated utensil on the table. I did, however, venture into the city's night spots one evening with George Lepping, my fellow director of agriculture from the Solomons,. When I saw his name mentioned some years later, he had become Sir George Lepping, Governor General of the Solomon Islands.

Following independence, a number of charlatans descended upon the government to sell them one spurious scheme after another. Those of colour were initially given more credence than the white variety, for not only were they a novelty, the Ni-Van-

NOWHERE NEAR GREENLAND

uatu having been ruled and advised by whites for nearly a century, but it was also now politically correct and sometimes justified to treat them as equal to the task. Those coming from the United States of America had assumed that after so many years of colonial tutelage, the level of ill-feeling based on race would be as high as in their own country, and must have been surprised and disappointed to find that this was not at all the case, and was not there to exploit. One self-styled doctor presented as his own a lengthy proposal concerning the purchase and operation of a floating oil mill. This ship would progress from island to island buying whole coconuts. Aboard, they would be de-husked, cracked open, the shell and coconut water recovered, and the oil extracted from the flesh of the coconut. By-products of the operation would include coir for matting, shell to produce carbon for gas extraction, coconut water for bottling and coconut cake for cattle feed.

The paper was passed to me by the council of ministers for comment. Firstly, the ship was huge, of many thousands of tons employing hundreds of workers aboard, who must process a minimum of 50,000 nuts a day. Since, apart from Vila and Luganville, there were no wharves in the islands, and in many cases lightering would not prove practicable, perhaps nets could be spread between the masts of the ship and the nuts fired into them from batteries of catapults ashore? During this bombardment, the workers would of course be kept out of harm's way below decks. Secondly, the production of bottled coconut water was given as twenty tons a day which, in the certain absence of export potential, would keep the whole population of Vanuatu hard at work swallowing it. Somehow, the whole scale of this operation seemed way above the capacity of Vanuatu to support it. More careful examination of the seventy page proposal revealed that the word 'Vatu' appearing before each detailed costing, was in slightly different type from the rest of the document. Then on one of the last pages the word 'Pesos' had not been substituted. This was, in fact a pirated proposal for the Philippines which exports some three million tons of copra a year, about forty times that of Vanuatu at the time.

I also had to resist, incurring some ministerial displeasure, a proposal to establish an oil-palm industry on Santo, this time from Malaysian and local political interests. Oil-palms occur naturally within five degrees of the equator and have absolutely no resistance to cyclones, as had already been demonstrated in a long-term trial at the IRHO research station on that island. Unused to changes in day length, production would also dip significantly during the cool season, rendering the operation of the factory uneconomic for that period, as its capacity would have to be for peak input of the crop. And, as the minimum viable size of an oil-palm plantation is many thousands of hectares, it would prove impossible to locate locally the large number of labourers required. So this one too was a non-starter. (At the time of writing this, more than twenty years later, I find myself again opposing - now in a private capacity - another proposal to develop an oil-palm industry in Vanuatu, this time with Chinese sponsorship; their paramount interest is surely in the hardwood timber from the 10,000 hectares of rainforest that would have to be clear-felled for the project).

Then there was the Indian guru who suggested that Vanuatu's gross imbalance in trade was due to imports principally to supply expatriate needs. I was called upon to participate in a debate on this hypothesis in the parliament chamber. Happily, he used for his prime example the importation of rice. The depth of his ignorance was such that he was quite unaware that rice was the main convenience food of the ni-Vanuatu population, which fact I then pointed out. It was also the staple of the resident Chinese ethnic minority. With regard to expatriates, hardly any of my acquaintances, with the obvious exception of the few Chinese and fewer Indians, would eat rice even once a week. As for myself, until I was an adult I had never eaten it except as rice pudding at school.

Armand Baudouin, a personable Canadian geologist and gold prospector working on Santo, one day found himself and his girlfriend on the lower course of the Jordan River where it flows north into Big Bay, and thought this might be a good site for an irrigated rice project. I went up to have a look at it, and as it seemed to have potential, I managed to secure funding for a feasibility study. This was carried out by a German company, but their ground survey found that without costly engineering, less than a thousand hectares could be irrigated simply by gravity feed. The cost of road building to the area, the lack of any significant resident population, a sub-optimal potential number of crops per year, less than ideal hours of sunlight at this latitude, and likely pest and disease problems, were other negative factors that resulted in such a scheme not being pursued. Nevertheless, I was grateful to have had the opportunity of visiting where the Portuguese navigator de Quiros had landed in 1606, and of swimming in the Jordan River.

Then, one day, a large delegation from the People's Republic of China arrived to discuss aid to the agricultural sector. If there is something the Chinese know about, and in which they can instruct the world, it is rice, and particularly rice as grown

NOWHERE NEAR GREENLAND

by a billion smallholders. They proposed to send a mission to Tanna to look at the potential there for smallholder rice production, and to ask the people if they would like to grow rice. It was my view that rice would grow perfectly well there, but that it would not be a simple matter, and probably unwise to ask the people who had limited land on which to grow food crops to abandon their traditional cultivation of yams, taro and other root crops and grow rice instead.

Rice would also require full tillage of the land, rather than the digging of individual planting holes, which is the traditional and familiar method of cultivation. The popularity of rice lay in it being a relatively cheap convenience food. Short of something for a meal? Just pop down to the local shop and buy some rice; and it stores well. The mission arrived, went to Tanna, and returned delighted to report that absolutely everyone they had met there wanted to grow their own rice, rather than having to buy it in a shop. They therefore proposed a mass rice-growing campaign for the whole of Tanna. I countered with a more cautious proposal, along the lines of a pilot project, whereby it would be grown and demonstrated in two limited areas that would favour success, and if farmers elsewhere were interested, the project could be expanded to include them. Several Chinese rice technicians worked away for two or three years in the selected areas, and reluctantly came to the conclusion that the really strange people there didn't want to grow rice for themselves after all. (As I write this, the Chinese are back revisiting this mystery. How can there be a people who don't want to grow rice?)

Fortunately, the current, general and relatively low level of population, compared to the availability of land appropriate for agriculture, will enable the people to continue their traditional methods of cultivation, which are ecologically sound and productive, for at least some years to come. This will depend on significant areas suitable for food production not being leased to large scale enterprises for beef and cash crop development, and, at least on Efate, extensive real estate speculation and development around the coast not depriving local communities of essential garden land.

From the time of my first arrival in the New Hebrides until I departed Vanuatu, there was never any shortage of people arriving new to the islands and exclaiming "Why on earth don't you grow, or produce or improve so and so?", as though no-one before had had the wit to think of it. An obvious and continuous target for improvement has been the small, rather scruffy chickens typically found in the villages. These scavenge and are not routinely fed by their owners. They make good mothers, are fiercely defensive of their chicks, resistant to disease and are well suited to the climate, probably because they have interbred with the wild *Gallus gallus*, the ancestor of all domestic chickens, whose roosters from time to time wander in from the forest to fraternise with village hens. The would-be improvers soon find that under typical village conditions, the modern hybrids created for high egg production or meat growth just cannot cope. Eggs, anyway, are not much eaten in the islands, because the hens are on free range and lay clutches of eggs in secret places around the village and in neighbouring fields. Eggs are looked upon as embryonic chickens to replace the present generation of birds. Well, why not pen the chickens? Under the agricultural loan scheme, many farmers took out loans to do just that, believing this to be an easy option, only to find they were then locked into a daily routine of feeding and watering that was incompatible with traditional village life and the uncertain local supply of feed. Whole villages like to go off for days to attend a church assembly, a funeral or a wedding, and if penned hens do not get regular meals and the same feed every day they tend to stop laying.

An agricultural volunteer working with me at Lakatoro spent the best part of two years devising a layers' ration that could be made up from local ingredients such as coconut and taro, though the protein component of meat or fish meal would always have to be purchased from trading vessels, or ordered from Vila or Luganville to be delivered by ship or plane. Not so simple, not so cheap. A compromise solution was to let the hens out at midmorning to scavenge, by which time some eggs might have been laid, but this still imposed a daily routine on the owner. To the best of my knowledge, not one of the many who took out loans to produce eggs for sale in the villages succeeded. However, we did find that the old fashioned Rhode Island Red breed, when crossed with local chickens produced a larger bird with the right characteristics for village survival. But as this breed was progressively superseded by the hybrids of the modern world, it became something of an antique collectors item, and increasingly difficult to locate an overseas supplier of day old chicks for subsequent distribution to local farmers.

Again, the local pig - probably introduced into the islands with the arrival of the first people three or four thousand years ago, and the only domesticated mammal there until the first dogs were brought in, possibly at the beginning of the 19th century - is well adapted to survival, both in the villages and in the wild. Having a cult status in traditional society, whereby the ceremonial killing of pigs confers

NOWHERE NEAR GREENLAND

rank upon their owners, these animals are carefully tended, particularly when their top incisors have been removed and their tusks grow back through their lower jaws to form a complete circle, or even two circles, so prized as prestigious body ornaments. Continuous efforts have been made to 'improve' the local pig, the most successful with the mainly black Berkshire breed, since white-skinned pigs suffer severely from sunburn, and this has proved useful where isolated pig populations have become inbred. A cautionary tale comes from Haiti, where because of an outbreak of swine fever among the local pig population, the US government - fearing the proximity of that disease to their own country - paid to have them all slaughtered and replaced with a far superior breed supplied from the States. Within a year or so all the latter had died from sunburn, heat stroke and other stress-related disorders. The US then had to purchase as replacements thousands of pigs from the Dominican Republic, whose characteristics were similar to the now extinct Haitian pigs.

In 1985, James Mitchener, together with his Japanese-Hawaiian wife and secretary, visited Vanuatu for the last time. It would also be his first return to Santo for very many years, the island which he knew in World War Two, and some of whose colourful characters had inspired his 'Tales of the South Pacific', and by derivation the play and musical 'South Pacific'. I was able to give him some information on who was still in Santo and who had passed on, when he and his wife spent half a day with me at my house overlooking Vila harbour. He was much taken up with words, and spent some time exploring them in my Collins English dictionary which he compared favourably to Webster. I showed him the book commemorating the 1947 Broadway play production of 'South Pacific' that Jonathan Donald had sent me from New York five years previously, and he was fascinated to read the names of the original members of cast and see their photographs. It became a "I wonder whatever happened to" session between him and his wife. He inscribed the book "It was a pleasure to find this book here where it all started". However, with most of my possessions, it suffered in cyclone Uma in 1987, and when I finally received it in England it was still wet and so badly damaged I threw it in the dustbin. But after several days I relented, fished it out, dried it out, and I still have it. In Santo, James Mitchener found an old lady living on hard times on whom he had based one of the characters in 'South Pacific', and he generously left her a useful sum of money in the bank account he opened for her.

In 1984, Douglas Malosu had returned from Reading University in England and

To Coral Strands

took over from me as Director of Agriculture, Livestock and Forestry. I was then made an advisor to the minister, Pastor Jack Tungan Hoppa from South East Ambrym, and we were relocated to the top floor of Lo Lam Building, whose lift never functioned but whose stairs provided good daily exercise. However, not long after that, the annual congress of the ruling Vanua'aku Party voted in favour of the immediate termination of all expatriate advisors' posts, the feeling being that these were a manifestation of neo-colonialism that compromised the independence of the country. I still had some eighteen months of my contract to run, and at the suggestion of the Overseas Development Administration's regional agricultural advisor, based in Suva, I was requested to stay on to write a book about agriculture in Vanuatu, of which by then I had an experience of sixteen years. Asked how long I thought it would take me to write this book, I said I could probably produce a 'pop up' book in about two weeks. But if it was to serve its intended purpose, which was to provide definitive background information and serve as a guide to donor agencies, future investors and those involved in the natural resources industry, the necessary research and writing would probably take me at least eighteen months to complete. In the event, it took me twenty months.

I decided to give the book an historical perspective, not only because it interested me to do so, but because I had found many ni-Vanuatu were totally unaware of the origin of many plants and animals that contributed to their daily lives, believing that most were indigenous to the country. It was also useful, I thought, to list all those crops that had been attempted since the nineteenth century, and to follow their success or failure up to modern times. From my experience, people constantly arrived in the islands proposing to try this or that crop, unaware that this had already been done, possibly several times over with no good outcome. There was also some romance and often humour attached to these early introductions, the first cattle, the first goat, of missionaries battling away with arrowroot and maize while endeavouring to keep the indigenous pigs out of their churches; the first planters of coffee in Tanna, massacred or fled to Efate. De Quiros planted a small garden in Big Bay, Santo, in 1606, and this would almost certainly have included maize and cotton and possibly sweet potato and beans. But he made himself so unpopular with the people he encountered there, particularly through stealing their pigs, that the garden was deliberately destroyed immediately after he left, and it was to be more than two hundred years before these crops were introduced again.

The legends concerning the origins of kava, coconuts and yams, of which I collected

NOWHERE NEAR GREENLAND

and recounted just a few, are also colourful and strange, and vary from island to island, and certainly deserve further collection and recording before they are lost. My research was limited to what I could find in Vanuatu, whose formal archives were neither easily accessible nor well ordered, and many of those in the Department of Agriculture had either been thrown away, or chewed into brown fragments by cockroaches in the dank basement where they were stored. Had time and funding been available, I should like to have furthered my research at libraries and museums in Sydney, Noumea and Paris, though I was able to locate useful information and photographs in the Royal Commonwealth Society and Royal Geographical Society libraries in London.

In 1981, I had moved out of my four-bedroomed house at Tagabe, in order to make room for the new Quarantine Officer, Bob Weller, arriving from Australia with three children, and thenceforth lived in a small house perched on top of the three hundred foot cliff above Star Wharf. Not only was this the highest house in the immediate area of Vila, but it enjoyed a magnificent view of the town, harbour, offshore islands, the sea and distant hills. Twenty years later I was able to buy this house and now live there for several months each year. Less convenient was the fact it was higher than any water tank in the town, and water had to be boosted up to my house by a dodgy pump halfway down the cliff, demanding frequent clambers down to it. There was also no telephone, a lack that I could happily endure since, though fully appreciating their practical use, I have never welcomed their shrill summons, the precedence they claim over whomever one is with or whatever else one is doing, the wrong numbers, and my complete inability to focus my hearing on what is being said if there is the slightest background noise. My current mobile shrills with lunatic, electronic Bach.

However, also in view of the house, a mile or so away, is the Lo Lam building in the centre of Vila's business district, and while writing the book on agriculture I was reluctant to lose time and the very slender thread of my thoughts by having to traipse into town every day to check if there was mail for me. But while visiting Hong Kong in 1982, I had purchased a telescope, and every morning I trained it on the top floor office window of my colleague Martin Fowler in that building. If mail or a message awaited me, Martin sellotaped an orange disc to the window and down to town I would go. The system worked perfectly for nearly two years.

I left Vanuatu in February 1986, a few days over eighteen years after I first arrived

To Coral Strands

in the New Hebrides. Not only had I been privileged in this time to visit and explore the mountains and shores all of its inhabited islands, and some of the uninhabited ones, but I had witnessed and taken part in its rapid evolution from the intriguing and unique status of a Condominium, to that of a small independent republic in the Commonwealth. By nature, and in my profession, I have always been a generalist, with a keen interest in the many elements of nature that surround us, knowing a little about a lot of things, while trying to make some sense of the whole.

At least in the New Hebrides and then in Vanuatu I had the opportunity to know the whole, almost in terms of an extended family, its interests and values, the interaction of its people within and between the islands, and with the outside world. The small size of the country meant that one knew all the major players involved in this transformation, whether political, economic, social or spiritual, could see all round them, and follow their moves as though watching some complicated game.

Unhappily and sadly inevitably, then progressively followed over the last twenty years the widespread corruption of politicians, their deception of the people, their incomprehension of disinterested public service, their naivety exploited by conmen, their self-importance easily flattered and integrity compromised by gift-laden overseas trips, which have allowed the development of major projects against the national interest. The simple and no doubt all too common ploy of one notorious corrupter, has been to tell ministers and other government servants, that since they would not enjoy their exalted positions and salaries for ever, they owed it to themselves and their families to accept something extra, a little gift against that future rainy day, in exchange for a small favour of course. One by one he picked them off and then went into politics himself to manipulate from the inside, from the top, buy the voters. Inevitable, given the subsequent history of possibly every newly-enfranchised state in the twentieth century. And it would have been naive to expect otherwise; and one can always say "Well, at least it's not as bad as so-and-so", citing another country afflicted by greater poverty, ignorance, epidemics, disorder, crime and corruption. But disappointment is commensurate with expectation, and one had hoped for so much better.

On the plus side, there is still a far greater civility among the people in Vanuatu than in most developed, supposedly civilized countries; less pollution of the air, land and sea; a greater proportion of unspoilt pristine nature and a more sane pace

NOWHERE NEAR GREENLAND

of life. And, as always, one is heartened and encouraged by the common decency of the great majority of the people, and trust that in the long run they will prevail. Vanuatu has recently been judged the happiest little country in the world, and those of us that still live there and have experienced many other countries, believe this. Nowhere is perfect; it's all a question of relativity.

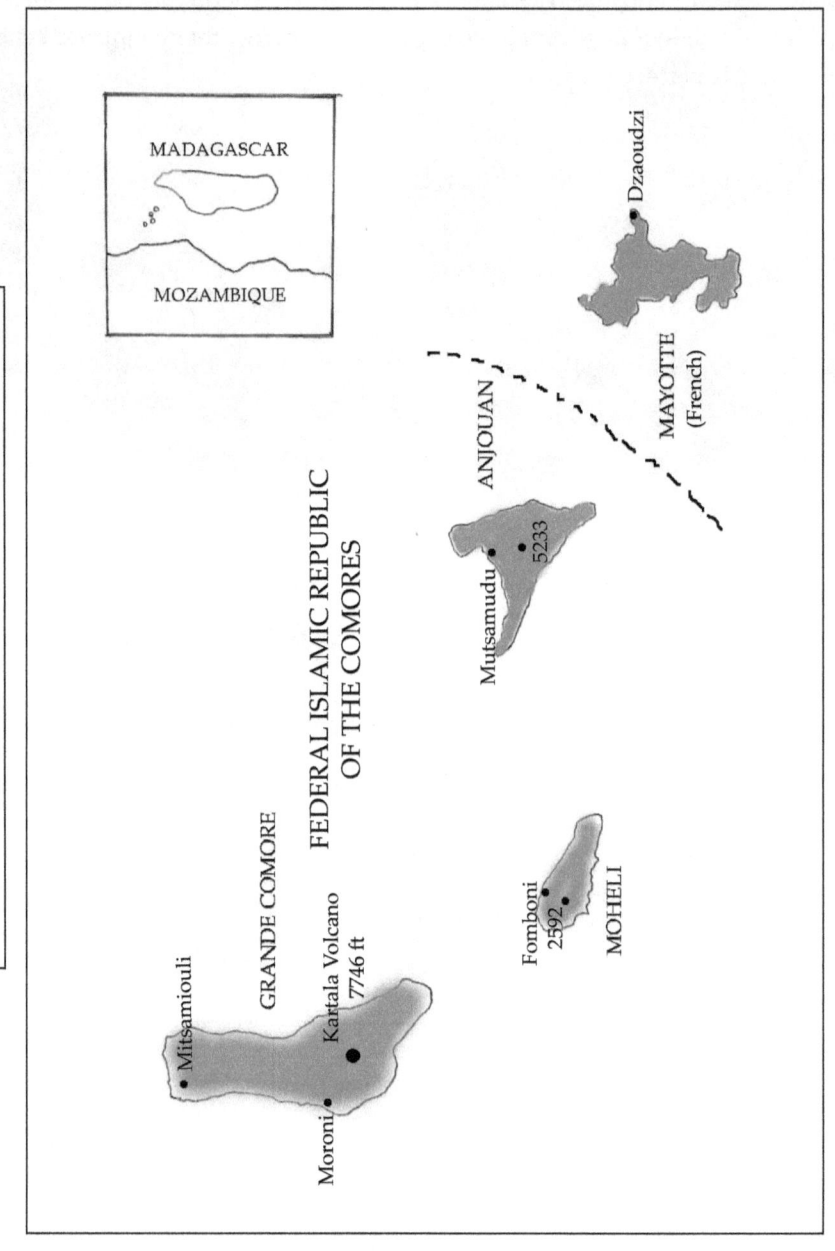

NOWHERE NEAR GREENLAND

COMOROS, COFFEE AND KAVA

In 1979 I had bought a small cottage in the northern Wiltshire village of Chilmark in which to spend my leaves from overseas. The original building dated back to the 14th century, but in early Victorian times it had been enlarged, refaced in stone with red brick around the windows, and the thatch had been replaced by tiles. It was on the main and only street of the ancient part of the village, down which ran a winterbourne - a stream which in chalk country flows only during the winter months, though here there was usually at least a trickle of water for most of the year. One great advantage was that little traffic came through the village, the main road between Salisbury and Hindon being some hundreds of yards away beyond the Norman church, and ran past the scarcely less venerable, but likely more venerated Black Dog Inn. However, one large disadvantage for me, having always preferred to spend most of my waking hours out of doors, was that when a previous owner had moved next door into what had formerly been her parents' farmhouse, she had taken the back garden with her. This left me with only a tiny front garden, separated from the road by a very low stone wall, and sitting in it somewhat obliged me to pass the time of day with every passer-by. I did have hopes of buying the back garden from the old lady, and she was not against the idea, but her children, already scattered across the county, did not agree. However, for now it sufficed for my leaves, and any insipient claustrophobia was relieved by taking long walks along ancient tracks and bridle paths, and through the many de-

The Comores, Coffee and Kava

ciduous woods of that part of Wiltshire. Later I would need something with more space of my own around it.

This time, in February 1986, I came home to it from Vanuatu, but was already keen to take off overseas again. The former chief forestry officer in Vanuatu, Martin Bennett, was now in the Federal Islamic Republic of the Comoros Islands, working there as a forests adviser, and he informed me that the Food and Agriculture Organisation (FAO) of the United Nations was recruiting a senior adviser to represent it in these islands. I duly applied to FAO, went to Rome for an interview and was told I had the job. But then came a delay of eight months, while the UN administrative mills strove mightily to surpass God in grinding exceeding slow. In retrospect, I should have accepted another long term contract that was offered during this interim, but I hung in for FAO and duly flew from Nice to the Comoros Islands in November 1986.

The diminutive flyspeck I had seen on a map grew into the shape of an elongated leg of lamb as we approached the island of Grande Comore, the largest of the three islands that today comprise the Comores, as they are known by its largely French-speaking population, though the indigenous language is akin to Swahili. First settled by Arabs more than a thousand years ago, as they progressed down the east African coast from their colony in Zanzibar, the population of these islands at the northern end of the Mozambique Channel is today largely made up of Bantu people, subsequently imported as slaves from neighbouring Tanzania and Mozambique. To the south of Grande Comore lie the other two islands of the republic, Anjouan and Moheli, and between them and the northern tip of Madagascar is the island of Mayotte. Formerly part of the Comores, the population of Mayotte is largely Malagasy and, unlike the Muslim majority professes the Catholic faith. In the 1960s, the French colonial masters of the Comores held a referendum for the people to decide whether they wanted independence, or to become part of France as one of its overseas territories, such as New Caledonia, Tahiti, Reunion, Guadeloupe, etc. This decision was made island by island, rather than by a majority of the population of the islands as a whole, and Mayotte, predictably, and to its huge and lasting benefit, voted against independence.

The island of Grande Comore is dominated by the active 7,700ft high Khartala volcano, at the base of whose western flank is the Comores' capital Moroni and its very modest seaport. I flew in with a heavy dose of influenza, and there was no-

NOWHERE NEAR GREENLAND

one to meet me at the airport which stretches beside a shoreline of black basaltic rocks twenty miles out of town. Typically for FAO, as I was to discover in my office there a week later, I received a telegram from Rome announcing my arrival. With a high temperature and feeling close to dissolution, I asked a taxi driver to take me to the nearest decent hotel. I retained no impressions of that ride, other than remarking the electrocuted, blackened and putrefying corpses of fruit bats, still dangling by their feet from the power lines at frequent intervals along the length of the road. The taxi deposited me at the Hotel Coelacanth, named after the fish that emerged from prehistory when it was first caught and identified in 1939, and still lurks at considerable depth in the waters around the Comores.

Traffic flow interrupted on Grande Comore, 1977

I crashed there for two whole days, and only on the third morning arose to make contact with the outside world. My FAO car and driver came to collect me, and I duly presented myself to the rotund and cheerful Minister of Agriculture, nicknamed Mamadoo. He was very black, unlike the president and the rest of his cabinet who were largely Arab by descent. I was to advise him, as well as supervise and manage other FAO personnel and projects in the Comores. The Director General of Agricultural Services had his own French adviser, a very bright young Frenchman named Dreyfus, but I was to assist and advise on the reform and re-

The Comores, Coffee and Kava

structuring of those services. I rented a house in the centre of Moroni, there being little choice available, and was considerably and constantly disturbed by the noise of my near neighbours, the barking of stray dogs scavenging in the dirty streets, and of their better fed but frustrated relations confined behind security gates. The close proximity of three mosques, whose highly amplified first calls to prayer commenced in the very early hours of every morning, was also not conducive to sound sleep. I have friends who take comfort in the noise and bustle of humanity around them, but I am not to be numbered among them. However, once my flu had subsided and my sense of smell returned, I became aware that, even in the town, the night air was redolent with the scent of ylang-ylang, the most heavily perfumed flower in the world, whose essential oil is distilled in the Comores and exported to perfume makers in Grasse, in southern France.

I took off on a familiarisation tour of the islands, visiting the many centres for agricultural development that had already been set up with FAO funding and assistance, and meeting local and expatriate staff. On Grande Comore, typical of small islands that have grown from volcanoes, its communities were scattered around the periphery, most of the interior plateau being covered in a rubble of lava, and scarred by craters that had even recently popped open like bursting boils. Here, as on the other two islands of Anjouan and Moheli, cassava had already become the staple food, since it will still grow and produce a crop on infertile and exhausted soils, and the generally miserable condition of the maize here, stunted with leaves exhibiting every kind of nutritional deficiency, gave visible testimony to how impoverished the soil had become. This, because the rural population had increased to the point when it was no longer possible to fallow even a fraction the land, by which traditional means the fertility of the soil could be recovered for future cropping.

The very beautiful island of Anjouan, born aeons ago as an active volcano, has a high rounded summit, indented with a crater lake and ringed by the remnants of rain-forest, among whose high branches, already rare and besieged lemurs still leaped and called. Before the colonial powers had quite decided to whom Anjouan belonged, it had an English consul, but he was sacked by Queen Victoria in the 1850s for still owning slaves. Now, recently independent after a hundred years of French administration from their nearby colony of Madagascar, the island was under concentrated assault from its human population. Here, FAO and CARE International projects were desperately trying to educate the population to adopt soil

NOWHERE NEAR GREENLAND

conservation measures, to halt massive, widespread and increasing soil erosion, and prevent the disappearance of the last of the rain-forest. Dry-land rice was the most prestigious food crop, but yields were plummeting due to soil degradation. I visited yield trials, and demonstrations of rice grown with and without fertilizer, which had been repeated on Anjouan without cease for more than twenty five years, initially by French researchers. But there had been absolutely no uptake of fertilizer by farmers due to its high local price, and because there would still be no surplus for sale to recoup the cash outlay, once the needs of extended family members had been satisfied; so a quarter of a century's research remained of purely academic interest. Even earlier than that, vetiver grass had been planted in lines along the contours of the steep, cultivated rice fields in an attempt to halt soil erosion. This grass, originally from India, is tough, wiry, inedible to livestock, competes little with adjoining crops, and a perfume can be distilled from its essential oil. Farmers had been paid to plant it, but this activity had never progressed beyond being a demonstration in a relatively small area, because no-one had been sufficiently convinced to plant it on their own account. There were now wide gaps in the strips of grass where they had been trampled by cattle, and soil was still being washed liberally down the hills. I was moved by this situation to write a paper entitled 'La Crise en Anjouan', emphasising the urgent need for large scale soil conservation works, but as far as I know it failed to inspire the desired response.

An attractive feature of some areas of Anjouan were the groves of clove trees. This is a small tree, and at certain times of the year, when it is putting on new leaf, it exhibits a bright golden crown. The biggest market in the world for cloves had been Indonesia, which imported some thirty thousand tons a year, largely to mix with tobacco for their local cigarettes, or kretek. Unfortunately for the farmers of Anjouan and elsewhere in the world, Indonesia had made huge plantings of this spice, and was now looking to export as much as it used to import, so the bottom had fallen out of the market and farmers here were chopping down the clove trees for firewood. Nevertheless, a few farmers continued to harvest for the local market, and the freshly picked cloves, pink and orange in colour, were spread out like fragrant carpets at the roadside.

Some years previously a cordon sanitaire had been created around the remains of Anjouan's rain-forest with the hope of preserving it, but timber lorries were still to be seen loaded with its rare and fast disappearing hardwoods. Corruption was so widespread in the Comores, from the very top to bottom, that there were no means

The Comores, Coffee and Kava

of stopping such activities. One local tradition, stemming from ancient times, was the *grand marriage*, whereby a married couple would save, beg, borrow or steal for years in order to accumulate the wherewithal to enact this custom. This involved inviting hundreds of guests to a feast that demanded the slaughter of dozens of cattle and goats, innumerable chickens and the serving of huge quantities of rice and other local and imported food and drinks.

Cloves drying by the roadside on Anjouan, 1987

While I was there, the Minister of Health held his *grand marriage* on his small home island of Moheli. For that purpose, which included ferrying his guests by air from the other islands, he spent the entire budget allocated for the evacuation of critically ill and injured persons to hospitals in South Africa. The devout wish of the people to perform the haj at least once during their lifetime, was a further motive, if not justification, for begging, borrowing and stealing.

The third and smallest island of the federal republic is Moheli. It has just one small

NOWHERE NEAR GREENLAND

town, the majority of whose inhabitants it seemed, used its beach front as a lavatory, and not all of whom were sufficiently public spirited to make their deposits below high tide level. The island was low and rather flat, with no redeeming features, though it did have some excellent vanilla growing on farmers' smallholdings. Unfortunately, neither the vanilla flowers nor the green pods have any scent at all, which otherwise might have countered that island's less pleasant odours. One meeting I attended there included the UNDP resident representative. He was unable to return to Moroni in the French army helicopter provided for him, and I took his place as the only passenger. The pilot asked if I would like to take a close look at the Karthala volcano. Another no brainer! I had climbed it the previous year, but this would provide a quite different perspective. So we rose to over 9,000 ft, came in low over the caldera and its ash plain, and then descended into the crater itself, which is perhaps a thousand feet deep.

On the edge of Khartala crater, Grande Comore, 1987

Though there was some activity at the bottom, I was glad not to see rocks going up past the windows. Then we climbed vertically out again and skied down, as it were, just over the tops of the trees to the bottom of the mountain, sea level and Moroni; a very exhilarating experience.

One day, my secretary presented me with a huge bill for stationery, which she said had been left unpaid by my predecessor more than a year before. Why had there

The Comores, Coffee and Kava

been no reminders, I wondered, as I placed it in my in-tray. Searching the accounts' archives after she had gone home, I found that another invoice had been paid for a large amount of stationery from the same shop on almost the same date as the newly discovered one. Clearly she had some scam going with the stationers whereby they divided the money between them. I left the invoice in my in-tray to be covered up by incoming mail, but every morning there it was back on top again! Eventually I told her I was not going to pay it because I didn't believe it. Meanwhile she had wisely decided to emigrate with her six children to France, which thanks to her Malagasy ethnicity she was entitled to do, and where she would be eligible to receive all the social service benefits of that country. A hanger-on around the government compound, a ne'er-do-well and notorious creep named Bourhane, came to my office to tell me that everyone was contributing towards a farewell gift for my secretary, and that as her employer it was incumbent on me to make a particularly large donation. The gift, he informed me, was to be a gold necklace from one of the goldsmiths in town. I told him that whatever contribution I made would be from my own pocket, and not that of FAO, though I did not tell him I was not keen on giving anything at all, having just caught her out over the stationery scam. And what was the value of the proposed gift, I asked him. On quoting the equivalent of many thousand pounds sterling, he noted my shock and incredulity and said that if I did not believe him he would borrow the necklace from the jeweller and bring it to show me.

This he did the following day, and it was indeed a most impressive, heavy and intricate creation in solid gold. I told him that as far as I was concerned such a gift was out of the question, and gave him a sum which I said should go towards buying something far more modest. He was most put out by my meanness, and then proceeded to display the necklace on a fund raising tour of all the government offices. I informed Kassim, the director general of agricultural services, of my disquiet and he said he would instruct Bourhane to buy something of considerably less value.

The day soon came for her departure, and before many assembled government staff, I made an appropriate speech thanking her for all her hard work over the years, etcetera. Kassim then said some nice things before presenting her with a gift-wrapped box. On opening it she gave a feigned scream of delight and surprise as, to loud applause, she dangled before us the very same gold necklace. After the ceremony, I was told, she handed it back to her friend Celestine, the FAO librarian

NOWHERE NEAR GREENLAND

and fellow Malagasy, to whom it belonged, and was happy to take the cash it had raised back to France. No doubt Bourhane got something out of it as well.

While I was there, a newly arrived Peace Corps girl was utterly staggered by the huge electricity bill she received for the first month in her rented house. It was way beyond her monthly allowance. Someone who had been in the Comores for rather longer suggested that she should turn off the power at the mains that night and observe results. This she did, and out went all the lights in the neighbourhood that had been connected to her meter. Similarly, one month I noted a dramatic increase in my office phone bill. I went down to the post office to obtain an itemised account, and found that there had been many calls to Paris I did not recall making. Some time later, I was working out of hours in the office, when the phone on my desk starting making a faint tinkling sound. I lifted the receiver to hear my minister talking at length to a lady friend in Paris. Though his own office was about three miles from mine, he had had telecommunications install a link so that his calls could be debited to my phone. I forwarded the bill to him without comment, and there was no repeat of the problem.

The regional director of FAO, John Phillips, was based in Nairobi, and I had occasion to visit him there a couple of times, and once he came to the Comores. On one such visit to Kenya, I stayed a weekend with my old friends John and Valerie Armitage, on whose farm I had worked during the Mau Mau rebellion, and who had now retired to a fifty acre property on the southern shore of Lake Naivasha. Their near neighbours had been the Adamsons, of Born Free fame, but by then both had separately been murdered and their house turned into a museum. Also close to them was the Naivasha Yacht Club, where Lord Errol of the Happy Valley set, had been its commodore in the late 1930s, and was subsequently mysteriously murdered. During my stay, John suggested we visit nearby Hell's Gates, an actively volcanic area at the far end of an impressive gorge. Valerie was friendly with a colony of rock hyrax that lived on a granite outcrop on the way to the gorge. She took with her a bag of stale bread crusts, and we stopped to feed them. Valerie was throwing them crusts while I squatted, my empty hands dangling. John had just remarked that hyrax are very short-sighted, when one of them darted forward, and with its razor sharp teeth took a sizeable piece out of one of my fingers. Not long before, John had shot a rabid dog in his kitchen. Though a complete stranger to the property, this interloper was not confronted by John's own dogs, who instead had given it a wide berth, apparently sensing that death lay in its teeth and saliva. John

The Comores, Coffee and Kava

had also recently lost two cattle to rabies, so after I was bitten by the hyrax, he suggested I should commence a course of anti-rabies injections, starting at the Nairobi General Hospital the next day. This I did, finding the staff there most efficient and friendly, and took the rest of the four-month course of injections back to the Comores, where they were administered at a mission hospital.

When John Phillips visited Moroni, we gathered with our FAO colleagues and friends at a restaurant a short way out of town. This was frequented by foreign mercenaries, mainly French, German, Belgian and South African, and their notorious veteran commander Bob Denard. A few years before, they had ousted the first president of the independent Comores, and later assassinated the second, Ali Soilih, probably at the behest of the French government as he had embarked on a brutal and highly eccentric rule. He was replaced by Ahmed Abdullah Abderamane, or 'A cubed' as he was nicknamed by one expatriate wag, whom Bob Denard also assassinated not long after I had left the Comores. That night in the restaurant, the mercenaries were singing lusty songs, and John, who has a great voice and with his wife sings regularly in Cornwall choirs, led us in ballads and ditties of our own, such as Clementine, the Good Old Duke Of York and The Foggy Foggy Dew. It became quite a contest, but with both volume and quality on our side we prevailed and the mercenaries left the restaurant, somewhat miffed I thought, but without firing a shot.

The seven-year-old son of my houseboy was run over by a drunken army driver, and his leg was badly fractured. It was subsequently and disastrously set by a drunken Belgian doctor at the Moroni General Hospital, a fact that became only too obvious when the cast was removed six weeks later. I took X-rays of the crooked leg to the South African Chargé d'affaires in the Comores, one of the few countries in black Africa that had retained diplomatic relations with the apartheid regime. As the Minister of Health had spent all the money that might have been used for his evacuation and treatment, the South African agreed to underwrite all the costs, and the young boy returned from Johannesburg three months later with a straight and fully functioning leg. As a result of this incident, I had had the opportunity to visit the Moroni hospital, which was wretched in the extreme, filthy, and its once-white walls now black. Thus, when I developed an abscess on a wisdom tooth, I was not too keen to have it treated there. The local UNDP representative, Kevin McGrath, who coordinated matters for the UN agencies, said that to authorise my treatment outside the Comores he would require a chit from the dentist who op-

NOWHERE NEAR GREENLAND

erated from the hospital, certifying that he could not carry out the work himself. I then attempted to contact a great friend in Malawi, the chief anaesthetist at the Queen Elizabeth Hospital in Blantyre, to ask if I could have the treatment done there. Malawi, under President Hastings Kamuzu Banda, was another country that had maintained official relations with South Africa, and there was a once a week South African Airways flight between Moroni and Lilongwe. However, as an outworn colonial legacy, all international telephone calls from the Comores were still routed through Paris, even though, as in this case, the recipient country might be close by. This phone link was also tenuous in the extreme, and one might wait for days to succeed in making a call, the local operator insisting the whole while that "Paris ne répond pas". When I eventually got through to Blantyre, I discovered that by shouting my friend could just hear me, whereas I could hear almost nothing at all. Eventually, yelling my question as to whether I could get dental treatment there, and instructing him to shout back at his loudest possible just one word, yes or no, I very faintly detected the word 'yes'. Meanwhile all the neighbouring government offices had banged shut their doors and windows.

I then reported to the dentist at the hospital. It transpired that there were actually two dentists who shared a large room, half-divided by a partition. The approach through the grimy corridors of the hospital had hardly raised my expectations, so I was not overly dismayed by what I found. With numerous deep pits in the floor and walls, it appeared as though one or more hand grenades had exploded within the clinic, and several of the ceiling panels were hanging or missing. Nestling in the holes in the floor were old swabs and tissues, with here and there the glint of a needle. Pipes festooned with grime hung from the walls, from which they had apparently been gouged with crowbars, and a single tap dripped into a cracked and stained porcelain basin. Incongruously, what seemed to be two brand new, state of the art dentist's chairs, gifts from Germany, stood gleaming among the litter, one on either side of the partition. Called to the farther part of the room, I explained to the Comorian dentist that what I really needed from him was a note to say that I should have the extraction done elsewhere, and that to replace the missing tooth I might, anyway, need some sort of denture which could not possibly be made here. To all this he was perfectly agreeable, but said that he should first make an X-ray of the infected tooth. The fine piece of apparatus attached to the chair was focussed upon my cheek, and following a buzz and a click, the dentist asked me to wait on the far side of the partition until he had the developed the negative. So I went and sat on a bench which faced the other chair. In this a young man sat awaiting atten-

The Comores, Coffee and Kava

tion, while around him had gathered a crowd of friends and relatives, or perhaps merely interested spectators. Eventually a man in a decidedly off-white gown, whom I took to be the dentist, arrived and started to wash his stainless steel instruments under the tap. Aha, I thought, some hygiene at last. But it was not to be, for he then took a cloth, that was so black it had gone green, to wipe them. Not unhappy to miss the ensuing performance, the anticipation of which was making my abscessed tooth rage all the more, I left clutching my jaw, the X-ray and my precious signed exit chit from the dentist. I flew the next day to Lilongwe, the capital of Malawi.

I was met there by my doctor friend from Blantyre, Paul Fenton, and his wife Joan, whom I had known in Vanuatu. The five-hour car journey down to Blantyre, with which I would later become very familiar, runs for fifty miles or so along the frontier with Mozambique. The left hand side of the road is Malawi with life going on as normal, small shops busy with their customers, farmers tilling their fields, children playing, old folk gossiping. The right hand verge of the road is Mozambique, with every shop-house along it blackened by fire or destroyed; and where there had once been fields there was now only tall grass and encroaching bush, and not a hut or track to be seen this side of the horizon. The civil war between Frelimo - the army and supporters of the Mozambique government, and Renamo - a rebel army funded by South Africa and the United States for the overthrow of Marxist president Samora Machel, had dragged on for years and would continue for some time to come. Not long before, a Malawi civilian plane flying between Blantyre and Lilongwe had unwisely taken a short cut across Mozambique territory, and been shot down by a SAM missile, killing everyone aboard.

My raging tooth was successfully extracted by a British dentist at the Queen Elizabeth Hospital in Blantyre, which displayed an infinite improvement in hygiene over its counterpart in Moroni, though its corridors were already lined with recumbent AIDS sufferers. By that year, 1988, the incidence of AIDS in the Blantyre urban area had already reached over thirteen percent of the sexually active population, and some five years later it had climbed to thirty percent.

I flew back to Moroni the following week, and a short time later managed to inherit a rented house from an FAO colleague who was leaving the country. This was on the coast a couple of miles out of town, and the garden stretched down to a jumble of black basaltic rock that formed the shoreline. The calls to prayer and the noise

NOWHERE NEAR GREENLAND

of traffic were now distant, and I had only the sound of the sea, to which I had long become accustomed in Vanuatu. That was until the screech owls came into their breeding season. This occurred shortly after I had taken a brief spell of leave in the UK, where I had received the shocking news that Lesley had died of a heart attack in Ghana. She had been with her partner and their two young children in a remote town, and he, also an agriculturist, had left to do field work. She suffered acute chest pains and reported this to the local dispensary, where she was dealt aspirin and castor oil. Back home she was resting, with the children playing in an adjoining room, when she suffered a massive heart attack. Lesley died trying to reach her children; she was forty-four years old. I then entered a period of profound grief and depression, not hearing a word of a meeting I attended in Rome. Back in the Comores, the screech owls with their courting territory at the end of the garden emitted a loud, rasping hiss every few seconds all night long for weeks on end, while the waves of a near calm sea thudded sullenly on the shore. This was a very bad time for me.

I received a telegram from Rome one morning, (FAO knew that it was useless trying to phone via Paris), to say that two 'experts' from headquarters were to arrive next week; only that was today, and would I make all necessary arrangements for their accommodation and internal travel. It happened that a major conference was being held in Moroni - I believe by Les Amis de la Francophonie, or some such, and the two good class hotels were full. I therefore phoned a very clean and pleasant rest house just out of town, booked them in there, and sent my driver off to meet them at the airport, with the instructions that he take them to the rest house and I would see them the next morning. The driver returned with two disgruntled experts and their suitcases in tow. Both were Italian, one a middle-aged man wearing a ginger-coloured Harris tweed hacking jacket, somewhat unsuitable for the climate perhaps, but certainly original, and the other was a tall, very thin youth, so pale that he looked as though he had spent all his life underground, and he never once spoke a word within my hearing. I thought, where do they get them? The rest house was most unsuitable, the older man complained. I explained the situation, but he said that if that was the case they would find their own accommodation. Well, good luck, I replied. And would I please book them a flight to Anjouan the next day, inform our agronomist there, and instruct her to meet them at airport. Somewhat short notice, but I would do my best, and off they went with my car and driver. He eventually returned to say they had booked in at the Karthala, a notorious flea pit and short-time knocking shop. So be it, I thought.

The Comores, Coffee and Kava

At least the phones within the Comores were not routed via Paris, and I managed to contact our agronomist, a pretty but tough young Dutchwoman. I mentioned the name of the elder of the 'grain experts', as they claimed to be. She wailed loudly and then fulminated. This was the same idiot who the previous year had given her an envelope of sorghum seeds to try, and the emerging plants developed a disease never before seen in the Comores. "He's all yours" I said, "and please book him into the Mitsoumoudu, the best hotel on Anjouan". Next morning, the awful twosome came to collect their tickets.

Coastal scene overlooking the the airfield on Anjouan, 1988

They had clearly had a terrible night, the pale boy was now blotched and both were scratching, but off they went. I later heard that they had turned down the room booked for them in Anjouan, too expensive they said, and again went looking for themselves in the town. The room they rented had a single bed and an entire but completely dismantled Volkswagon strewn over its floor. Our agronomist refused to accept another envelope of seeds, told him off about the previous one, and the next day loaded both back on the plane to Grande Comore. So they now had time to kill. I asked would they not like to meet agronomists here, look at some research plots, visit a few farmers' fields perhaps? Not on your life; instead they wanted my car to take them to the Galawa hotel, with the very best beach, at the farthest extent of the island and about forty miles away. It should then come back early the fol-

NOWHERE NEAR GREENLAND

lowing morning to take them to the airport. Niet, I said. I had in my house the very pregnant wife of a Belgian colleague who had been on the same plane as them from Anjouan. I had to drive her to the airport the next morning, in the ardent hope the airline would carry her. My car would take them to the distant hotel, but they would have to take a taxi to the airport the following morning. Sour faces and shaking heads, but off they went.

Planting trees on Grande Comore, 1988

Less than halfway to the airport early next morning, a car approached, flashing its lights. Out jumped the elder grain expert. "Yesterday your driver stole one hundred US dollars from my jaquette anglaise", he yelled, with ethnically linked gesticulations. He had called at the UNDP office the previous afternoon to bid goodbye to the resident representative - though goodness knows why, unless to claim some allowance or other or complain about me, and had left his side-pleated, ginger tweed hacking jacket in the car. On returning from the UNDP office he had asked my driver for a piece of paper on which to write a note. The driver took out his wallet, found within it a suitable scrap of paper, and hawk-eye grain expert just happened to notice it also contained a US$100 bill. When he went to pay the hotel bill this morning his own note was gone, stolen by my driver! Strange, I said, that having spotted the other bill he did not immediately then check his jacket. And, no, of course I did not doubt his story, as grainy started jumping up and down, and I promised to investigate the matter thoroughly. But now we must rush to the airport. The prospect of them missing the plane was too frightful to contemplate, and my

The Comores, Coffee and Kava

pregnant passenger was already becoming agitated, threatening an almost equally unwelcome outcome. Fortunately there was no room in my car for them, and their taxi turned around and sped off ahead of me. I engaged the clutch, whereupon it, or something, broke, and I roared all the way to the airport in second gear. These people, I thought, really spread disaster in a wide radius around them. We just made it to the plane in time.

Back at my office I called in my driver to discuss the matter of the note. Yes, it was true he did have a US$100 bill in his wallet, but this had been sent to him a few days previously by his brother in Dunkerque. He then went home and produced for me a letter from his brother saying he had enclosed US$100. I then telegrammed the details of my enquiry to the grain expert in Rome. For his part, he submitted to FAO an official complaint of my behaviour and general lack of proper respect and hospitality, and for siding against him with my thieving driver, etc, etc, copied to UNDP and me. I did not deign to reply, but I then thought, even with all the perks and a pension, I really do not want to work for FAO.

One of my assignments was to advise on restructuring the agricultural extension service. This involved establishing reporting systems, responsibilities, linkages, co-ordination, lines of command and so on. The extension service's task was to research the needs of local farmers and develop strategies to assist them, including testing and demonstrating new crops, new varieties, soil conservation, pest control, crop processing, storage, and marketing. There were several dozen field extension workers who had direct contact with farmers, and they operated from well-equipped information centres on each island. They in turn, were advised by subject matter specialists, in such fields as livestock, agronomy (research), pest and disease control, etc. However, the results from all this had proved meagre in terms of improving the lot of the farmer. Morale among extension staff was low, cooperation between subject matter specialists was imperceptible, there was almost no reporting and, in short, something needed to be done about it.

Thus I held many meetings with the Director General of Agricultural Services and his senior officers and specialists, and on a large blackboard in the meeting room, organogram after newly-proposed organogram was chalked up, discussed, amended, rubbed out and, after someone had been sent out to find more chalk, started anew, this time with perhaps more or less boxes and direct linkages, or wandering dotted lines in different colours. However, progress was being made and

NOWHERE NEAR GREENLAND

consensus was close, but I then made the cardinal mistake of informing Rome of this. The man who had originally set up this extension system some fifteen years earlier was a Monsieur Grison. Though now in retirement, word had evidently leaked to him, from former colleagues still at FAO headquarters, that his precious structure was now being tampered with. In a master stroke, Rome decided to take M. Grison out of mothballs and send him on a mission to the Comores, ostensibly to assist me in the restructuring of the extension service, but in reality, at least as far as he was concerned, to defend the status quo with his every remaining tooth and nail.

The elderly gentleman, accompanied by his wife, duly arrived in Moroni, delighted to be back again after all those years. Did I not know, he modestly informed me at the small dinner party I gave for him, that his extension system, as established in the Comores, was unique in the world? This did not unduly surprise me. At our first official meeting, attended by M. Grison and all those who had been involved in the drafting process, the most recent version of the organogram, now nicely laid out in coloured inks on paper, was pinned to the blackboard, and Director General Kassim himself started to explain it. Meanwhile, grey eminence Grison was turning a healthy shade of pink, and then an alarming purple. Non, non, non, non, non! he eventually cried out, that will not do at all! To explain why not, he pinned to the blackboard his own organogram, which he had thoughtfully brought along with him. Silence while we all studied it. Then someone ventured, but that's exactly the same as the one we are trying to change! It would be more true to say that the meeting soon broke up in disorder, than to say it was adjourned, since a number of papers were tossed into the air and chairs clattered over as their former occupants abruptly stood up. M. Dreyfus wanted to know why M. Grison had come at all. M. Grison looked to me, as an FAO colleague, to defend his point of view. So I suggested he make a field trip to Anjouan with his wife, to see things for himself on the ground, and talk with extension staff and farmers there. While they were appropriately shocked by the erosion and general degradation of that island's land, which had occurred over the past fifteen years, he still stuck to his guns. There was absolutely nothing wrong with his system, the problem had to be with the people implementing it, which of course, was at least partly true. Nevertheless, M. Grison ceased attending the meetings and a consensus on changes was quickly reached. He returned to Rome and France highly dissatisfied with the outcome, for something unique had been lost to the world.

The Comores, Coffee and Kava

I had by then made up my mind to leave FAO, something that was rarely done given the security of tenure, the excellent salary, the UN passport, business class travel and the prospect of a pension. But I was not cut out to be a part of a massive bureaucracy, to keep my head below the parapet, and docilely go with the flow. I had also become involved in a silly spat between two divisions of FAO, one of them my own, between which relations were chronically fractious. In this particular argument I had sided with the locally-based representative of the other division, for which I did not earn brownie points in Rome. All very tiresome and diverting from the main task of trying to improve the lives of poor farmers.

Well, maybe not 5th Avenue exactly. Anjouan, 1992

There were many able people within FAO, such as John Phillips, who, despite the constraints of the organisation, were able to make a very positive contribution towards the latter aim. However, I found it overly demanding to maintain a good working relationship with the even greater number who were clearly, in the modern term, 'not fit for purpose'. So, in April 1988, just eighteen months after I had first arrived in the Comores, I resigned and returned to my cottage in Wiltshire.

That spring I decided to look for somewhere to live with a little more space around it than afforded by my cottage. With my sister Jill, I looked at a number of small farm properties in south-west Wales, all muddy and depressing, and saw nothing

NOWHERE NEAR GREENLAND

I liked within my affordable price range. I then fruitlessly repeated this exercise in Cornwall, all of which properties had quite evidently been the subject of estate agents' trick photography, and the vendors' dreams of dizzying wealth.

I had earlier registered my name and CV with a number of consultancy companies which recruit expertise in a wide number of fields to undertake long and short term assignments in the developing world. I was soon contacted by an Australian company, which was assembling a team to draw up a five-year, national coffee development programme for Papua New Guinea. On this three month mission, funded by the World Bank, I would be the programme planner accompanied by a coffee agronomist, and for the last two weeks we would be joined there by an economist and a marketing expert.

In August 1988 I travelled out to PNG via Vanuatu, where I stayed for three weeks compiling the index for my book 'Agriculture in Vanuatu', which would be published the following year. In Port Moresby I met up with the coffee agronomist, an elderly, genial, pipe-smoking British boffin in voluminous khaki shorts and matching stockings, and we had a meeting with the resident representative of the United Nations Development Programme to discuss our mission. While still in the capital, I was invited to dinner by Sid Palmer, former Assistant British High Commissioner in Port Vila, and now in a similar post there, who lived in that dangerous and unattractive city, behind high walls, security lights, guards, dogs and alarms. He showed me the strongroom at the centre of the house, to which the family might retreat in case a band of thieving, murderous and rampaging rascals breached all the other defences. The resident expatriates maintained a self-imposed curfew, and any trips to the beach at weekends could only be made in convoy. Such was their poor quality of life. The chronic problem was, and apparently still is, that young highlanders, high on testosterone, spiritous beverages or drugs, would come down to Port Moresby and other coastal towns, attracted by tales of bright lights, the prospect of work and the promise of sex unconstrained by the strict mores of their village societies. Largely uneducated, most would fail to get work, and penniless, would then join with gangs of other highlanders who sustained their economy through crime, and their male pride through rape. Per head of population, Port Moresby was the rape capital of the world

After two nights, we flew to Goroka, (there being no road connection between the highlands and the coast), a provincial capital seven thousand feet above sea level,

The Comores, Coffee and Kava

where we checked into the Plume of Feathers hotel, with our workplace in nearby government offices for the next three months. We were to look at the present state of the coffee industry throughout the PNG highlands, which produced most of that country's high quality exports of arabica coffee, but also to make several forays down to northern coastal areas where there were smallholder plantings of robusta coffee, more generally used for blending and instant coffees. We visited the coffee research station near Goroka, and met a young French agronomist who had very recently been posted there. However, on the following Sunday morning he was driving to mass, when around a corner he met a drunken motorcyclist bearing down on him on the wrong side of the road. The motor cyclist was killed in the ensuing collision, and the French embassy arranged for the researcher to be flown out on a chartered plane to Australia that same day, mindful that in PNG the customary tradition of 'pay back' can swiftly be carried out by the extended family, or 'wan toks', of the deceased and injured. Not long before we arrived in Goroka, two government officials in a Land Rover had been stoned to death there, immediately after running over a child on the airfield. And shortly before we completed our mission, an Australian pest control adviser ran into and injured the young son of the ANZ bank manager in Mount Hagen. He too was immediately evacuated to the coast. Thus, drivers in PNG need to take pedestrian crossing signs very seriously, since for them they could literally prove a death trap - perhaps a good training environment for drivers from, say, Italy or Greece.

We had been warned that it would be wise to impose a curfew on our driving schedule, since there was a greater likelihood of meeting 'rascals' on the road during the evening hours, or in the very early morning. A tree branch across the road was sufficient for these predators to halt a car, rob and possibly kill its passengers, and it was risky to suffer a breakdown at any time. In talking to the local people during the course of our work, and particularly to coffee plantation owners who were often white or of mixed race, we sensed a palpable undercurrent of violence, with their frequent references to fights, thumping someone and general drunken mayhem. Their fear of attack was expressed in defiant statements such as "Just let them come, we are ready for them", and one planter we met, a direct descendent of the pioneering Leahy brothers, allowed that the highland people had 'very short fuses'. It was as though this smouldering and sporadically erupting violence was a never-concluded deadly game, involving protracted premeditation, surprise, rapid reaction and revenge, so that the whole population was poised either to attack or defend at any time.

NOWHERE NEAR GREENLAND

It had been with considerable cunning that a young Australian woman helicopter pilot had been raped and murdered at about this time. Soon to leave the country, she had advertised her car for sale. A couple of highlander men attended by a woman requested she accompany them on a test drive, and at a suitably remote spot she was assaulted and killed. The first manager of the CDC's Metenesel cocoa estate on Malekula in the 1980s was later transferred to an oil-palm plantation in Papua New Guinea. He was addressing a gathering of labour to explain the details of the settlement of a strike, when one of the workers suddenly sprang forward and speared him to death.

In the course of our investigation of coffee, its extent, health, age, yield, profitability and ownership, we travelled extensively throughout the five highlands provinces, every route a scenic one, often rising to the cloud base where cold, grey mist streamed just above us through the moss and lichen-covered treetops; then on up into the chill fog of cloud itself. Rising higher into clear sky, the cloudscapes, now revealed beneath us, created a white ocean that surrounded isolated peaks and distant mountain ranges, or merely threaded the bottom of deep valleys with a thin white shroud. The immediate, intensively cultivated landscape typically featured treeless hills covered by the dark green carpet of sweet potato fields, the staple crop. A rough chequerboard was created by the boundaries of these food gardens, scattered among smallholdings of neatly ranked coffee bushes, and fallow, abandoned plots reverting to woodland and forest. Far from these roads, dark billows of dense, undisturbed rain-forest broke the skylines, and stretched away under cloud shadows to distant horizons. This was home to hundreds of species of birds, including the bird of paradise, and the male bower bird that decorates a sophisticated nest with flowers, berries and shiny objects to woo a mate. Also found here are the world's largest and loveliest moths and butterflies, myriad epiphytic orchids, and dozens of species of snakes which thrive and writhe in this green immensity. Twice we descended the wide Markham Valley, which stretches from the highlands to the port of Lae on the north coast, driving down past lush, beef cattle pastures and extensive fields of maize, and on down to coconuts and mangoes, and a return to tropical heat.

At a distance, the small scattered villages could be distinguished more by the trodden red earth surrounding them than by any feature of buildings, which for the most part consisted of widely separated thatched huts with walls of woven bamboo or crudely fashioned wooden planks. Closer acquaintance was best avoided,

The Comores, Coffee and Kava

certainly on the cold and rainy days we happened to visit them, revealing to us a far from idyllic scene, with the ground slick with pig and human ordure, and the damp and drab inhabitants foul-smelling in breath and body - unlike in Vanuatu where villages are scrupulously swept clean every morning, and the daily routine of washing in the sea or streams is deeply instilled. We passed through Enga Province where villagers had recently discovered rich deposits of alluvial gold, and would make their way to a bank in Mount Hagen with bottles full of it. Men would buy a truck, load it high with beer and then drive back to their village. Children too young to drive bought cars straight off showroom floors and hired drivers to take them home.

While there are a few large estates, nearly all the coffee in PNG is grown by smallholders, of whom we visited dozens, assessing the varieties grown, pruning systems employed, general care, and disease status. Arabica coffee under stress, particularly at lower altitudes is prone to the yellow fungal rust known as Hemilia vastatrix, and it was this disease that destroyed the coffee industry in Sri Lanka towards the end of the 19th century. Once, travelling through Southern Province, we were driving down a long hill when we began to overtake plumed warriors in full war paint, carrying spears, axes and bows and arrows. We stopped, rolled down the window, and addressing the nearest of them in pidgin English, I asked if it was alright for us to continue on down the road. Yes, yes, no problem, he replied, but after you cross the bridge at the bottom of the hill, tell those rubbish people on the other side of the river that we are ready for them. If there was anyone on the other side they must have been well concealed, for we saw no one, and had anyway already decided to avoid being shot as the bearers of ill tidings. A few weeks later we came across another war party in Highlands Province. This kind of tribal warfare is endemic, a few men are killed, huts are burned, crops destroyed, pigs abducted and women raped. Their payback system perpetuates and re-ignites these smouldering hostilities, whose traditional causes are disagreements over land, pigs and women, just as they have been in the New Hebrides, and probably throughout Melanesia whose people largely share common values and customs.

Except for a tenuous trade in cowry shells, sometimes in exchange for bird of paradise plumes, there was practically no contact between the two million highlanders and the far distant coast until the Leahy brothers landed their biplane among them in the early 1930s. However, the vines of sweet potato, which over a period of a millennium or more were carried from their South American homeland, island by

NOWHERE NEAR GREENLAND

island, westward across the Pacific Ocean, found their way up to this remote interior some hundreds of years ago, and have long since provided the staple food of the people, supplemented by yam, taro, banana, cassava and plantain, and many edible leaves such as pumpkin and hibiscus.

Back in Goroka, towards the end of the assignment and drafting our report, I was having some difficulty in phoning a friend in Port au Prince, with whom I was soon intending to stay before going on to Colombia and then back to England. This was as a result of the time difference and the ramshackle phone network in Haiti. However, communications with the outside world had not consistently proved problematic, because a few days earlier I had been to see the local agent for Air New Guinea who operated out of a small thatched hut on the outskirts of the town. I needed to know what airline and flight I might take from Port au Prince to Bogota on a particular date. I was not optimistic of obtaining such precise information any time soon, but the agent tapped a few keys on his computer and within seconds I had the departure and arrival time of an Air Surinam flight from Miami, and was immediately able to obtain a confirmed booking! With continuing problems in contacting Haiti, I decided to ask my sister in Wiltshire to relay my message. While on the phone, I had a long, animated and amusing conversation with my mother, whose ninety-third birthday was in two days time. Just a few hours later, shortly after opening her greetings cards, she died of a stroke, her mind and hearing acute until the last hour of her life.

At Miami airport I exchanged some money at the bank, but when my flight was called some time later, I could find neither passport nor ticket. Having survived a panic attack, I retrieved these from the counter at the bank where I had left them in full view of dozens of subsequent customers. As almost unbelieving I picked them up, the bank teller winked and made the gesture of cutting his throat; by which time I was already a believer.

The Surinam plane was full, but I was the sole passenger to alight at Port au Prince. All those customs and immigration officials and armed police just for me! - and Graham Greene was right at my shoulder. Fortunately my friend Christy was there to greet me, and we drove back to her house at Petionville, an affluent suburb high above the city, from which distance it looked elegant, curving round the bay, and at night pretty with twinkling lights. Close up by day was ugliness and poverty, amid which the people celebrated life. The buses painted in a rainbow of colours

The Comores, Coffee and Kava

growled and belched black smoke, the crowds swirled and jostled, and a man lay dead in the gutter, burned and apparently electrocuted. We drove to Sans-Souci, the palace ruins of Henri Christophe, the first emperor of independent Haiti, and climbed the steep track to his immense fortress, the Citadelle Laferriere, where, in the centre of an acre of flat roof, behind the high ramparts, he blew himself up in 1820. We drove west to the little Ile à Vache, swam and stayed in a nearby town where we met a Colombian girl, a volunteer with a club foot who was working with the local poor. When she learned I was leaving the next day for Bogotá she

Ahee! Claudia Huffman's mother serves me another delectable dish. Bogota, 1992

asked if I would carry gifts to her parents. She reappeared in the morning with her small parcels and her father's name and telephone number. I arrived in Bogotá, a high altitude, temperate city set amid pine tree-clad hills, and was met by Kirk and Claudia Huffman. Claudia's mother was a celebrity television cook, and as we would be staying in the same building, Claudia asked her mother to pull out all the stops in her preparation for me of traditional Colombian dishes. This she did with gusto, employing many species and varieties of fruit and vegetables, some of which had not been commercialised outside South America and were quite un-

NOWHERE NEAR GREENLAND

known to me. One highly spiced dish Claudia called Aheee! - for obvious reasons. And she screamed when I gave her the name of the person for whom I carried presents from Haiti, for it was none other than the lord mayor of Bogotá, a very important person indeed. He invited us over to dinner at his well-guarded mansion, and the next morning with an armed escort we visited the packing plant of his vast cut flower enterprise. Every day, cargo jumbo jets leave Bogotá for Europe carrying roses, carnations and orchids.

Returning to England at the end of 1988, I soon renewed my quest for somewhere more spacious to live, the essential requirement being that there should be more space outside the house rather than within it, and this time I took my search to France. In January 1989, I went skiing with Christy at Val d'Isère, and she obligingly agreed to accompany me afterwards for a week's house hunting in the Dordogne. I had already passed through the area a couple of times by train from Paris to Barcelona, en route to visit the Huffmans in Ibiza, and had been rather taken by its generally rolling and well-wooded landscape, somewhat reminiscent, I thought, of parts of Wiltshire. So we hired a car in Perigueux, with the intention of visiting properties for sale in the towns and villages of the area, but in the event were taken everywhere by the estate agents of that city, against whose windows we had pressed our noses. I had expressed a particular interest in looking at water mills or riverside properties, having since childhood always indulged in messing about in streams, damming and diverting them, rounding up their minnows, and bombarding with stones the frail craft I had created expressly for that purpose. Fortunately there was no shortage of such properties, though they ranged from little more than heaps of ancient stones by long dried-up millstreams, to cavernous and sinister relics of the industrial revolution, to twee over-renovated buildings, complete with pseudo revolving water wheels and eternally-fishing garden gnomes. However, within five days we had been shown two properties which exactly suited my pocket and taste for the ancient.

The one I chose was a former water mill in some state of dilapidation, which had been left empty for more than a year by the proprietor who was the leading light of the local communist party. The entire ground floor of the main building had been divided into pens for raising pigs, as well as raising ducks and geese for pâté de fois gras. There were many ramshackle outbuildings tacked onto the mill for housing chickens, rabbits, discarded machinery and the rusting cadaver of a car, and by all appearances whatever had been discarded or fell from this comrade-owner's

The Comores, Coffee and Kava

hands - wire, plastic, bottles, cans, tools, twine and fused power tools - was left to choke the mill stream or litter the ruins of the garden. When later I met him, he boasted that formerly there had not been a living blade of grass on the place, every last one having been consumed by his two thousand ducks, leaving only mud and bird poo behind. The good news was that the mill already had an indoor lavatory; the bad news was that it emptied straight into the now stagnant millstream directly beneath it. Nevertheless, it was a solid seventeenth and eighteenth century building on much earlier foundations, with limestone walls over two feet thick, and enjoying a delightful prospect of the modest Nizonne river and its water meadows. Four hundred yards downstream, the 12th century tower of a chateau rose above woods of ash, oak, chestnut and elm, providing the only visible evidence of other inhabitants in the valley.

On completion of purchase ninety days later, I commenced demolition of the pens and appendages, and immediately installed a septic tank, much to the delight of my neighbours downstream, whose lake had for years been fouled by raw sewage and the effluent associated with intensive pig and poultry production. During later renovation, I was to discover the massive limestone blocks of an earlier building, and beneath what was to become the dining room, a coin of the Roman emperor Vitellius, the immediate successor of Nero, minted in Spain in AD69. I would also find blocked and sealed caves in the low limestone cliff against which the mill had been built, that had apparently provided prehistoric dwellings. Over the next dozen years I would gain enormous pleasure in the heavy duty exercise their excavation provided, as well as from digging out the millstream down to the bed rock, from which it originally had been hewn, finding mediaeval coins, pottery, boars' teeth, oyster shells, thousands of hand-forged nails, a pair of ancient dividers and a stone cannon ball and shot. These latter were probably relics of the Hundred Years War, during which many of the chateaux in this part of Aquitaine were successively occupied and besieged by the English and French.

In September of 1989, I went on assignment to Fiji for two months, to assist in drawing up a five-year development programme for eight outer islands. Our team comprised a Cockney economist, a Scots fisheries consultant, and myself as the agriculturalist. The work entailed visiting islands seldom or never visited by tourists, and still strong in the traditional Fijian way of life. We travelled between the islands on a government touring vessel of several hundred tons, built rather like a small tramp steamer. Our three Fijian counterparts were all former or current,

NOWHERE NEAR GREENLAND

international rugby players, but on this voyage they took their exercise in the daily hand-peeling and grinding of dried kava roots, to present to the chiefs whose villages we would visit. On arrival at a village, the chief would formally accept our gift, and then, as we sat cross-legged in the meeting house, ceremoniously serve us with his own kava from a massive 'tanoa' or kava bowl. Following the kava, we would then listen to a presentation of his ideas and those of his advisors as to what they perceived as priorities for the development of their island. These included the need for infrastructure, such as roads and wharfs, the exploitation of forested areas, crop diversification, livestock development, fish aggregation devices, and more frequent shipping to transport their produce to the urban markets of Fiji.

Le Moulin de Connezac, Dordogne, France. 1991

Such was the demand for kava at that time, the high price paid to producers and the traditional skills of the local people in growing it, that we recommended that kava should be a major focus for development on all eight islands. As we were visiting several villages a day, and at each one were required (and happy) to participate in a kava-drinking ceremony, we felt especially qualified to make this recommendation, as well as being somewhat stoned when we returned to our ship each evening.

The Comores, Coffee and Kava

One dark and stormy night at about 2 a.m., when we were travelling between islands through exceptionally heavy rain, our ship ran onto a reef. We were almost thrown from our bunks by the impact, and the ship immediately adopted a heavy list to port. The economist, no seafarer, with whom I was sharing a cabin, asked me in some alarm if we were going to sink. "No", I said, "We are fine as long as we stay on the reef", and in a show of what I hoped was a reassuring, nonchalant calm, with the list tilting me cosily against the hull, I pretended to go back to sleep. However, as his bunk listed toward the centre of the cabin, he had to abandon it, and went aloft in his lifejacket to seek further reassurance. At dawn next day, two members of the crew swam around the hull to assess the damage, and it was judged safe enough to winch the ship off the reef with its anchors at the next high tide. Nevertheless, we had sprung a couple of plates, and with pumps working full tilt we returned to Lautoka for repairs. It was a full week, during which time we started writing our report, before we could put back to sea again.

NOWHERE NEAR GREENLAND

SIR, THE HIPPO

At the end of that year I was offered and accepted the job of managing an EC-funded 'food for work' programme in Malawi. I was to be stationed at Senga Bay on Lake Malawi near the small town of Salima. The garden of my house went right down to the sandy shore of this longest and deepest of the Great Rift Valley lakes, beyond the far side of which, forty miles away, I could see the long line of hills linking Malawi with Mozambique. Small boats put out every morning to fish for tilapia, that most succulent of freshwater fish, and fishermen came into the garden to sell them to me. Other sardine-sized fish were also netted and laid out on low, woven bamboo platforms to dry in the sun, but fortunately at least a mile away, so that their pungent, somewhat rotten smell did not waft as far as my house. A feature of this lake, like that of shallow Lake Victoria, is that lake flies, much smaller than a mosquito, hatch out from the surface in countless millions, their black columns rising high above the lake like tornadoes. Not far along the lake shore lived an Englishman named Stuart Grant who harvested cichlid fish for export, principally to Germany and Japan, where they were destined for fresh water aquariums. Many varieties of these small, colourful fish, which after spawning their eggs guard them in their mouths until after they hatch, are found in this lake, very many more than in Lake Victoria. Grant had teams of local collectors working for him around the lake, but the development of his business had reached the point where most of the fish he supplied were now bred in large concrete tanks near his house, also used for multiplying the rarer varieties in order not to deplete

Sir, The Hippo

the biodiversity and numbers of those in the lake.

The food for work project I had come to manage was still in its pilot phase and involved just two villages near the lake. These had been chosen for their relative poverty, which in Malawi means very, very poor, and in principle the poorest households in these villages received five months rations of maize flour, beans and cooking oil a year over a period of two years. However, when I looked into the records of this food distribution I found that the situation of the one hundred families receiving this assistance bore no absolutely relation to their economic status. In fact, surprise, surprise, most food had gone to the relatives of the village headmen, rather than to those with insufficient means to support their families. Female-headed households are often the poorest, as they lack sufficient labour and available time to provide for their children and elderly, once they have drawn and carried water, cut and carried firewood, often for miles, as well as cooking and generally caring for their dependents in sickness and health. Though this was supposed to be a food for work project, there was in fact no work component, and while it ostensibly sought to break the cycle of poverty, there was no evidence it was doing so since it did not address the causes of poverty. These had everything to do with the exhaustion and erosion of the soil on their very small plots of land, and chronic ill-health due to water-borne diseases and poor sanitation. The traditional means of restoring the fertility of the land by letting it lie fallow, had long been abandoned because it could barely support the people even when all of it was cultivated every year.

The rural population had increased nearly six times in just two generations, and with little development of industries as alternatives to subsistence farming, the land had been overwhelmed, and the people had no option but to live in considerable poverty. The average fertility rate at that time, in other words the number of live births per woman, was six point seven, of whom approximately half died before reaching the age of five, largely from diarrhoea, malnutrition and malaria, but also cholera. Nevertheless, the national population was still doubling every eighteen years. The average area per household available for growing crops was a little over half a hectare, of which almost all was planted to food crops, including maize, cassava, pigeon peas and sweet potatoes, none of which, incidentally, are crops indigenous to Africa. For years, the government had subsidised the cost of fertilizer, for which low interest loans were available to farmers' clubs, whose individuals stood guarantee for repayment. But national uptake averaged only ten per cent of

NOWHERE NEAR GREENLAND

households, because even with the application of fertilizer there was no surplus production to sell, so no income from which to repay loans. Crop failure due to drought was also common, so there was also a high degree of risk attached to the loan. Some sixty percent of the rural population in Malawi was dependent on food aid, mostly in the south where demographic pressure on the land was highest. This situation contrasted dramatically with that of only ten years previously, when Malawi was a net exporter of food crops. But with the population increasing by a third of a million a year, there was no longer spare land to accommodate and feed them.

Communal Tree Nursery. Malawi, 1992

There were funds available for me to expand the project beyond the original two sites, so I scouted for villages further afield that combined the problems of limited and eroding land, and a polluted or distant water supply, which together were enough to cause extreme poverty exacerbated by ill-health. Cholera was not an infrequent visitor to many of these villages, where stream and spring catchments were fouled with human excrement. The EC eventually agreed for me to include a public health component in the project, which would allow me to build protected wells and organise the provision of a pit latrine for every household. The deal with the villages was that I would choose the site for the well, and the community would

Sir, The Hippo

dig it and fire the mud bricks to line it. The project would provide a mason to construct the lining, as well as a hand pump to lift the water, so that the well-head could be capped and sealed. Dirty buckets thrown down to haul up by hand would be a source of pollution, and in one case a neighbouring village, jealous of the new well, threatened to poison it, resulting in an immediate return to the original polluted source. I had decided I would choose the well sites myself, since in an early instance the headman of a village located it next to his house, which happened to be on top of a hill, and many days were wasted digging a very deep, dry hole. For the pit latrines, each household would dig its own, with the project supplying a cast concrete top with a keyhole shaped hole and lid.

To control the erosion, the project encouraged the planting of hedges at intervals on the contour. These comprised various leguminous species which would fix nitrogen in the soil, and provide prunings for a nitrogenous mulch, which would also boost soil fertility and conserve moisture. Drought is of frequent occurrence here, and there is absolutely no prospect for irrigation or a piped water supply over the steep land many hundreds of feet above Lake Malawi, and there are no rivers in this generally rugged terrain. Not only has intensive agriculture and widespread deforestation caused the accelerated, surface run-off of rainfall, washing away the topsoil, but has also resulted in falling water tables and the drying up of springs, because little precipitation percolates down to the aquifer.

One Sunday afternoon, my cook returned from his village with his sixteen year old daughter. She had been looking after his father who had just died there of cholera. She soon took sick, and the cook fearful it might be cholera was afraid to inform me. However, he eventually asked me to take her to the small hospital in Salima just a few miles away. She clearly had a high fever, was already in a coma and breathed only intermittently. There were no staff to be found at the hospital, so we lifted her out of the Land Rover onto a trolley where she very soon died, and we drove her body back to the village for burial. She probably had cerebral malaria, to which my wife's father succumbed after surveying a site for a hotel on Lake Malawi in the 1950s. I then thought of Lesley who had also died in Africa where, following a heart attack, she was offered just aspirin and castor oil at the local dispensary.

As the number of my project sites increased, particularly in the south of the country where high population pressure, and scant prospects of employment, beyond sur-

NOWHERE NEAR GREENLAND

viving on subsistence agriculture, had promoted general poverty, it became practical for me to move up from the lake and live in the capital, Lilongwe. I had, anyway, increasing need to visit the delegation of the European Commission there, and, somewhat reluctantly, the Ministry of Agriculture, through whose employees I worked in the field. I do not recall ever meeting any villagers who carried a spare ounce of flesh; all were lean and wiry and many were malnourished. So I was particularly averse to seeing the contrasting corporeal display at the ministry, where obese and bejewelled women wobbled around on high heels, and their fat bosses sat behind big fat desks in three-piece suits.

Eroded farmland, South Malawi - 1992

President Kamuzu (Taproot) Hastings Banda had once decreed that all civil servants should dress like English gentlemen, so presuming to include myself in that latter category, meant I also had to conform to this code, at least when visiting the ministry. The Minister for Education having heard that I was into tree planting for the benefit of the land, (as opposed to the forestry department which persisted in the promotion of eucalypts that drain water and nutrients from the soil and are a disaster for any crops planted nearby), invited me out to his large estate to advise him on where and what trees should be planted. When we arrived, he called his labour to attend, and they emerged in rags from pitiful hovels to be berated for the

Sir, The Hippo

recent death of a goat, for which they would be fined. They had been hired from far away villages, were almost certainly miserably paid, and would not have the wherewithal to return home. When I told the minister the project could not freely provide and plant the trees for him, he lost all interest in the idea.

President Banda at this time was already in his nineties and, surrounded by sycophants, was increasingly divorced from reality. Once a year he was transported to a particularly bountiful crop of maize, where he would routinely declare a 'bumper harvest' for the country, despite widespread evidence to the contrary. However, under his autocratic leadership, the roads were maintained in good condition, electricity and water supplies in the towns were regular, traffic lights functioned, the law and order situation was generally good, and the country was safe for tourists - positive elements that have become increasingly rare in sub-Saharan Africa. However, outspoken criticism of his rule and one party politics was creating a growing number of political prisoners, and there were increasing reports of their torture and murder. In the light of this, a group of bishops one Easter decided to publish a long pastoral letter openly critical of the president, something unheard of in recent years and it created a sensation. It was immediately proclaimed a criminal offence to be even in possession of this letter, and there was an atmosphere of general alarm. A friend had passed me a copy, and I went to post it to my sister in the UK from the post office in Mangochi, at the southern end of the lake. The clerk took a look at the rather fat envelope, for which I had requested stamps, asked me to wait, and disappeared behind the scenes; so I drove off, stamped it myself and posted it elsewhere.

The worst of Banda's prisons was said to be at Nsanje in the Lower Shire, where he had a palace but never visited it – understandably, since there in the very south of the country, and only a few hundred feet above sea level, it was fiercely hot and humid. I stayed just once in that small town's primitive hotel, lying on a mattress black with the dried sweat of others, into which my own sweat soon dissolved and mingled, giving out a heavy and sweet musky odour. Mosquitoes poured in through the room's barred window space and the gaping holes in the net over my bed, so that what with the pong, their ping and the stifling heat, sleep entirely eluded me. Not far from the town, the single track railway line which had once linked Malawi with Mozambique disappeared into long grass at the border, and the long-disused, rusting rails sagged over gaps, once spanned by bridges that had crumbled away.

NOWHERE NEAR GREENLAND

Rural agricultural development centres were scattered throughout the country, and their staff assisted me in implementing the project in the areas they covered. Once, looking for them in the Lower Shire, in an area new to me and my local counterpart, we drove too far down a narrow track and over the unmarked border into Mozambique. This led us straight into the camp of Renamo rebels, heavily armed and in ragtag uniforms. They were fighting Frelimo, the regular army of their government, and often based themselves on or near the Malawi border, across which they could retreat if pursued.

In the Renamo Camp, Malawi-Mozambique border, 1993

We got down from the Land Rover, and shook hands with the men who soon gathered around us. My counterpart spoke Chichewa which they understood and explained, that we were with the Ministry of Agriculture looking for our field workers in the area. I was offered a chair on the veranda of a small hut, and I picked up from a table a bible in Portuguese. The combination of the bible and my pointy beard gave a latecomer to assume I was a priest, and he asked if I would confess him. I disabused him of this deduction, and asked if I might take a photograph of the group. One who was apparently less equal among others, said that he would have to ask the 'commandante' and went off to find him. Oops, I thought, I have probably made a mistake here, but he returned with his commander who was per-

Sir, The Hippo

fectly happy to pose for a photograph with his men, which they did with a great show of their weapons. Two or three asked for a lift back down the track in the direction of Malawi, to which I agreed, but thought it would be prudent for them to leave their guns in the camp, lest I stand accused of facilitating a small invasion. I had the photographs developed in the UK, because we would have been in serious trouble if the Malawi authorities saw them.

President Banda also had a strict code of dress and appearance for visitors to his country. Women alighting from international flights, or arriving at border crossing points, were not permitted to exit immigration and customs controls wearing trousers or shorts, and thus they might emerge sporting a towel, or any old piece of cloth around their loins. Similarly men with long hair had it shorn on the spot, and I remember seeing a whole heap of mixed blond, brown and ginger locks on the floor at a crossing point on the border with Zambia. The president's official hostess was named Caroline, and it was forbidden throughout the country to play the popular tune 'Sweet Caroline', since it included a line about dallying with her in the afternoon. Whenever he made an official visit to a town, he would be greeted and entertained by a group of women dancers, who gyrated , sang and ululated, and on the back of whose tight skirts, over ample behinds, was the smiling, coloured photographic imprint of Kamuzu Banda's face.

At this time, there were well over a million refugees from Mozambique living in two or three large camps in southern of Malawi, and along the main road from Lilongwe to Blantyre the refugees sold large tins of cooking oil, kettles, hurricane lamps, thermos flasks and other handouts they had received from the United Nations High Commission for Refugees. Some refugees had lost limbs to land mines, and while I was there a team of three Norwegians came through to demonstrate the different models of mines they were likely to encounter. These included one whose trigger had a momentary delay, so that it would explode between the legs of the person who stepped on it. The ingenuity of man!

The spread of my project villages across central and southern Malawi, eventually to total ninety-seven before I left, gave me the opportunity to spend nights in nearby game parks One of these, Liwonde, is a small park bordered on the west by the Shire river, which at its northern end widens into Lake Malawi, for which it is the outlet. Every dawn there is spectacular flight of cormorants flying fast and low upstream to the lake, and hippo that have been grazing and rooting in fields

NOWHERE NEAR GREENLAND

overnight make a run to return to the water before the sun comes up, sunburn being a serious concern for these two ton amphibians. The small brick, two bedroom chalets here are separated from the river by only a narrow path, and having stepped out to witness the dawn flight of the birds, I had only just withdrawn inside when a hippo purposefully trotted past at twenty miles an hour and launched itself into the river. There are many lion here, and some like to sprawl along the branch of a tree, their four legs dangling on either side, and with my sister I once drove under one that was on an acacia branch over the road. On another occasion I came across a Range Rover that had ventured off the road and was hopelessly mired in deep mud. The three Korean occupants told me their compatriot driver had set off on foot through the well-wooded bush to the park camp some considerable distance away to summon help. After two or three miles I caught up with him, and not wishing to be complicit in feeding the lions I offered him a lift.

Kudya Discovery Lodge (Hotel Hippo!!)
on the Shire River, Malawi, 1992

Immediately opposite the park, on the far bank of the river, was the Kudya Discovery Lodge, and I would generally stay there in preference to the park, because rather than having to cook for myself, excellent meals were provided and there was a well-stocked bar. The main lounge area of the hotel was a large semicircular room, bounded on three sides by a series of wide arches giving onto a lawn that ran down to the river. At this time, I had a volunteer assisting me with the project, a graduate from Oxford University and longtime friend of my younger sister, Sally.

Sir, The Hippo

One evening, with her back to one of the arches, she was using the wall-phone to speak to her mother in England. I happened to look up from the far side of the lounge, and saw that a large hippo was standing directly behind her; so I called out "Pippa, there's a hippo behind you". Glancing round she then yelled into the telephone "Mum, there's a hippo behind me", perhaps one of the rarer sentences spoken over the phone! There were two other instances of hippo coming into the lounge while I was there, and which, despite their weight, have a totally silent approach. A party of three Americans were drinking in low armchairs beside one of the arches. A hippo sidled in behind them and ambled slowly past. After it had gone safely by, one of them quipped "My God, I'll never touch another drop", drained his glass and immediately called for another. On the other occasion I was sitting alone in the lounge awaiting my after-dinner coffee. This took some considerable time to arrive, and then I heard the waiter say behind me "Sir, the hippo", and between him and the back of my settee, mutely stood a fully grown pachyderm. Hippo are terrifying in attack, fiercely protective of their young, and with their enormous jaws can bite a man in half. In Africa they are responsible for killing more humans than lion and crocodile together, but here in the hotel they seem always to have observed a quiet decorum.

Towards the end of 1994, Martin Fowler, a former colleague in Vanuatu and now based in Windhoek the capital of Namibia, informed me that the EU was seeking a manager for their new project in the north of that country. I flew to Windhoek and drove up to the north for a preliminary reconnoitre. The project, whose aim was to improve the delivery of agricultural extension services to small farmers, would cover an area about 1,200 kilometres wide along Namibia's borders with Angola and Zambia, and some 100 kilometres deep towards the south. This area comprised most of 'black' Namibia, demarcated from the rest of the country by a quarantine fence built during apartheid times. As South West Africa, the country was ruled by South Africa, though ostensibly it was still a United Nations Trust Territory. The stated purpose of this barrier was to prevent cattle infected with Foot and Mouth, Rinderpest and other infectious diseases, possibly emanating from Angola and Zambia, infiltrating the almost exclusively white-owned properties south of the fence. But it also served to separate the smallholdings of black farmers, held under tribal law, from the large white-owned farms, averaging 5,000 hectares in size and occupied under freehold tenure. Once north of the barrier you were back among African villages, donkeys, goats and children on the road, and stalls on its verges selling wooden handicrafts, monkey oranges and fruit from the baobab;

NOWHERE NEAR GREENLAND

but south of it were roads empty of people, and lined with miles of cattle and game fencing with imposing estate entrances, one bearing the sign 'Trespassers And Poachers Will Not Be Prosecuted But Shot On Sight'.

As a legacy of the recent war between South Africa and the South West African Peoples Organisation, fighting for the independence of Namibia and strongly supported by Cubans operating across the Angolan border, there are magnificent, sealed roads linking the north with the south.

Estate Gate. Namibia, 1996

These run as straight as an arrow for hundreds of kilometres through the lightly wooded sand dunes of Kalahari semidesert, where the white farmers graze just one head of cattle on twenty hectares of land, or now more profitably raise game, such as antelope, buffalo and lion, for tourists to shoot. The main road north from the capital also passes through the 'golden triangle', a farming area at higher elevation attracting more rain, where white settlers grow good crops of maize and wheat, and keep herds of dairy and beef cattle.

During my initial visit of a few days, I was to choose where to live in northern

Sir, The Hippo

Namibia. The choice was essentially between Oshakati in the west, the largest African town outside of the capital and set on a near-featureless plain, and Rundu in the centre of the project area, overlooking the Okavango river which forms the border with Angola. The choice was, in popular vernacular another 'no brainer'. Oshakati, just one step removed from a sprawling shanty town, was chronically smothered in the smog of ill-maintained diesel buses and lorries, and the house proposed for me was on a main road between two large churches. I imagined how it would be on a Sunday morning, with the commotion of traffic combined with the dissonance of competing hymns and sermons in stereo. This town is also the main centre for the Ovambo people, who fought and bore the brunt of the war for independence. The memory was recent and still bitter, and every morning, government offices there began the day by raising the national flag and singing the Namibian anthem, led by former freedom fighters while the civil servants stood at attention, silent, respectful and immobile. However, not far beyond the town's wire fences, all heavily festooned with non-biodegradable plastic bags, and encircling a slew of broken bottles and old tyres, are the 'oshanas'. These are seasonal, shallow pools, hundreds of them, created every rainy season and which persist for several months. Spread across Ovamboland, and interspersed with farmers' fields of millet sprinkled with solitary Makalani palms, they provide mirage-like illusions and a limpid, shimmering quality of light.

Just west of Ovamboland, live the Himba people, whose women smear their entire bodies and the hair of their heads with a mixture of red clay and animal fat, and wear nothing but a skimpy leather apron fore and aft. These are principally cattle people, and my project did not extend into their territory, though for two days I sat between two of these statuesque ladies at a meeting in Oshakati, which was a notable, odoriferous experience for me.

Rundu, however, is a pleasant town perched high on a bluff above the Okavango river overlooking the flat and well-wooded savannah of southern Angola, stretching away to the northern horizon. To the west, upriver from Rundu, is a narrow floodplain where the river runs shallow between small islands, oxbow lagoons and patches of green reeds, that from the veranda of the Kavango River Lodge provide a serene prospect when the sun sinks down in the dusky browns and reds of southern Africa. Just across the river in Angola, was the largely abandoned town of Kalai, though since the death of Jonas Savimbi, who led a rebellion against the central government in Luanda, it is now being resettled.

NOWHERE NEAR GREENLAND

However, much of the area along the river is still heavily mined and there is little farming. The house proposed for me was newly built and spacious, within a walled garden which featured a bare expanse of pale sand and a large Camel Thorn acacia with inch-long thorns.

Livingstone was a step ahead of me
Victoria Falls, 1997

The eastern extremity of the project area was the far end of the Caprivi Strip, a four hundred kilometre-long arm of Namibian territory, only thirty kilometres wide, which terminates just beyond the town of Katima Mulilo on the banks of the Zambezi river. In the 19th century when Namibia was a German colony, Count von Caprivi laid claim to this strip of land, believing that access to the Zambezi would provide an important link for trade, possibly all the way to the Indian Ocean, but

Sir, The Hippo

apparently did not count on the barrier of the Victoria Falls. However, in recent years the strip has provided useful access to the falls and Zimbabwe, and is now much travelled by tourists. Only recently paved, the straight road through the strip provides good sighting of game, including the rare wild hunting dogs, recently decimated by distemper, and elephants whose presence is proclaimed by frequent road signs.

On the Okavango River, North Namibia, 1997

David Livingstone stayed here in the village of Linyanti on the edge of the great Okovango floodplain, where his wife gave birth to one of his children. And here, when the Chobe and Zambezi rivers are in seasonal flood around Easter time, the maize and millet fields are inundated and farmers are often taken by crocodile. As one of my project team was to be based in Katima Mulilo, I was delighted to have the excuse to motor many times along this colonial anomaly, and relax on the pontoon bar moored at the Zambezi River Lodge, watching the sun go down on the gliding waters of this iconic river, with a gin and tonic sparkling in a frosted glass.

After this brief introductory tour, I decided to base myself at Rundu, and from Malawi travelled back to Namibia the following month, this time by road through the length of Zambia, and arriving at the village of Sesheke on the opposite bank of the Zambezi facing Katima Mulilo. En route I had attempted to photograph a

NOWHERE NEAR GREENLAND

picturesque little bridge crossing a stream, in what to me closely resembled the middle of nowhere, but a zealous policeman came galloping and yelling down the road to stop me; so this was the lesson: do not attempt to photograph any bridge, no matter how small or insignificant, even deep in the bush, anywhere south of the Sahara. I was in my old Land Rover, crammed with my household effects from Malawi, my Alsatian dog Texas in a kennel, and as I had the flu, my great friend Jane Fraser, who had come up from her veterinary practice in Durban to assist my translocation, did most of the driving. However, I took over for the long stretch from Livingstone to Sesheke, which to travel at the speed dictated by the need to catch the last ferry of the day across the Zambezi, was one of the worst I have ever encountered. At times, we literally flew from one huge pothole to another, and the name of the village well described our febrile condition when we arrived there within a minute of the ferry departing. On the Namibian side, anxious to get home, immigration and customs officials gave us a most perfunctory reception, and my vehicle was never registered as having entered Namibia, which caused me some anxiety when some months later I had to obtain new licence plates.

One of my project tasks was to assist in the setting up of small farmer groups, through which the agricultural field staff would attempt to give technical advice to all the farmers in their area. Another was to promote the use of oxen for ploughing and the general preparation of land for planting millet, sorghum and maize. Though introduced in Mesopotamia about 6,000 years ago, this was a brand new technology here, and oxen had to be trained for this work, the right equipment obtained and the owners schooled in their handling and care. One of our expatriate staff, based in the Agricultural Bank of Namibia in Windhoek, which as a legacy of apartheid had never previously provided credit to black African farmers, would arrange loans to purchase the oxen and equipment, as well as for seed and fertilizer. I organised animal traction training courses, demonstrations for the farmers and workshops for staff. One senior lady from the ministry was to present a paper at one of these workshops, and, plainly ill, asked if she might do this sitting down, which she did. She died of Aids just days later. Another promising young Namibian for whom we had arranged a course in the UK also succumbed to this illness before he could leave. The incidence of HIV in Francistown, the second largest town in neighbouring Botswana, was at that time nearly 50% of the sexually active population, and Namibia was rapidly catching up, especially in those towns and villages along the main international lorry and bus routes, such as Katima Mulilo.
The wide and excellent main roads have a twenty-metre cleared verge on either

Sir, The Hippo

side to give wild game and drivers a chance of avoiding collisions. Kudu, a large antelope, are responsible for many accidents, especially at night when, confused by lights, they are mindful to leap and land on top of a vehicle, and over these long, straight distances on an excellent road, many drivers habitually travel at well over the official limit of 120 kilometres an hour, as I would have done had my old Land Rover been up to it. These roads are also the scene of many accidents due to drivers falling asleep over the extreme distances to be covered, often with scarcely a bend in a hundred kilometres. The instinctive and often fatal reaction of drivers, waking with a start as they veer off down a raised verge, is to turn the wheel abruptly to regain the road, which against the downward slope almost invariably overturns the vehicle. On his final working day in Namibia, this occurred to a British doctor friend, when nearing Rundu after the long drive from Katima Mulilo. His wife was killed and two passengers seriously injured. Mindful of this fatigue factor, the government has placed a rest stop, with a picnic table under shade, at intervals of about ten kilometres on all the main roads of the country.

Windhoek at about 5,000ft above sea level is a pleasant modern city, with whole neighbourhoods whose streets are all named after either composers, scientists or birds, and it is perhaps alone in southern Africa in lacking slums, which is appropriate, though by no means a given, for a sparsely populated country rich in uranium and diamonds Once when I was crossing Windhoek's wide Independence Avenue, head down in pelting rain and late for a meeting, having waited in vain for the storm to let up, I reached halfway when I was stopped in my tracks by a woman's piercing scream from the sidewalk behind me. Within inches of my toes a taxi whooshed by at speed, and without any doubt that scream saved my life.

The sea brings a great bounty of fish to Namibia, where the Benguela current sweeps near-freezing Antarctic water along its thousand mile, south Atlantic coastline. Cod, mackerel, tuna and numerous other species are trawled and long-lined on the ocean, while many local people come down to the coast for their annual holidays and catch fish from the shore with long rods, amid their clusters of tents and yammering portable generators keeping their catch cool until they return home. Here the great difference between the land and sea temperatures brings dense morning fog, which penetrates just a few hundred metres into the desert inland, providing life support for the strange, stranded octopus-like, thousand year old Welwitchia mirabilis plants, and those insects whose bodies slope down towards their head to direct beads of condensation to their mouths. Along the long waterless

NOWHERE NEAR GREENLAND

Skeleton Coast, shipwrecked sailors would have believed themselves saved once cast ashore, but died of thirst; and some may have died clutching the diamonds that strew the beach sands, now of prohibited access south of Walvis Bay.

Nearing one Easter, Vincent and Cecile, young French friends working in Rundu, asked me if I had any suggestions as to where they might spend a relaxing, long weekend, and they accepted my recommendation of one of the tourist lodges on the Zambezi below Katima Mulilo. They would have the choice of filling their time with fishing, boating, tennis or just watching this iconic river glide past from under one of the great spreading trees which line its banks. A local fisherman approached them as they sat on the bank, and asked them if they would like a ride in his dugout canoe. He paddled them out into the stream, which carried them round a bend downriver. Suddenly, with a crash and a jolt, they were thrown into the air as a hippo surfaced right beneath them. Massive, angry jaws gnashed down on the foot of the boatman, just catching his toes as he and his two passengers desperately thrashed the water to gain refuge on the bank. Then, while the hippo diverted its attention to smashing up the canoe, they scrambled ashore. They started off on a path that would lead them back to the lodge, but as it was flood-time on the river this soon sloped down into water, and as they waded deeper they realised they were in danger from crocodiles and went back the way they had come. After some time they were able to signal to a passing canoe to ferry them back, one by one to safety. So it was not so relaxing an Easter break.

While en route along the Caprivi Strip between Rundu and Katima Mulilo, I stayed several times at the Lianshulu Lodge on the bank of the Linyanti river, near that same village where Dr. David Livingstone and his family spent some months between 1851 and 1853 among the Makololo people. The lodge veranda runs along the edge of the water, and is a perfect setting from which to observe hippopotamus, and antelopes such as sitatunga and reed buck which inhabit this extensive swampy, and frequently flooded domain. Not long after I was there, a young German on the lodge staff celebrated his birthday, and after a few drinks and rousing songs with his colleagues, exuberantly dived off the veranda rail into the river and was immediately taken by a crocodile.

On my 800 km monthly runs between Rundu and Windhoek, I would sometimes overnight at one of the game lodges along the way, or make a short diversion to the Etosha National Park, remarkable for its five thousand square kilometres salt

Sir, The Hippo

pan. Tinted the palest shade of green by algae and minerals, the pan resembles a flat inland sea shimmering with mirages and empty to the horizon but for a few ostriches stalking into this wasteland, their jet black plumage wavering and distorted in the heat and glare. This silent, otherworldly emptiness contrasted sharply with the closely managed park around it, with its bustle of extensive camp sites, complete with supermarkets, and the clustering of cars and minibuses encircling supine lions and waterholes. The strict rules of this park decree that vehicles must stay on the roads and people in their vehicles, and none are allowed outside the official camps between sunset and sunrise. Good friends in Windhoek had their photo published in 'Private Eye', showing adjacent signs, one reading 'Toilet' and the other instructing 'Stay In Your Car'.

There are still scattered communities of San bushmen in the north east of Namibia. These small, wiry, copper-coloured people with their near-oriental eyes, are even today considerably discriminated against by the majority Bantu population, as they once were by white people who even hunted them for sport. They seldom come into the towns, preferring a life of hunting, and gleaning a basic existence from the Kalahari that surrounds their isolated villages. Some white families have taken in their young girls as servants, but also made sure of their schooling, and one in Rundu was looking forward to reading medicine at university. But, as with the aborigines in Australia, the San are desperately difficult to integrate into the modern life the state wills for the majority, and thus in neighbouring Botswana they have long been in conflict with the government which has sought to move them to reserves and curtail their traditional hunting rights - though the supreme court has recently reaffirmed these rights.

In mid-1997, the post of Director of Agriculture in St. Helena was advertised. My contract and the project in Namibia still had another year to run, but the romance of discovering and working on yet another small, isolated island beckoned, and I decided to apply. However, I had only just returned to Namibia after several weeks leave in Europe, so I informed the Overseas Development Administration I could spare only a few days to attend interviews at their administrative headquarters in Scotland, and would not attend a further interview scheduled for a week later in London. This was agreed, and I set off to drive down to Windhoek on the day of Princess Diana's death. Stopping for petrol 300 km down the road, there was a large crowd gathered around a television set breaking the news. She had gained particular respect here from her concern over land mines and her recent visit to

NOWHERE NEAR GREENLAND

Angola where these weapons had featured prominently in the recent cross-border war for the independence of Namibia from South Africa.

Dancing beneath granite arch on the Spitzkoppe
Namibia, Christmas, 1996

Following my interviews in Scotland, I was airily told, "See you in a week's time in London then". Somehow the news of my inability to remain for that had not got through, and straight away I travelled back by train to Heathrow, passing along the way Union Jacks and St. George's flags flying at half mast in the fields and atop church towers, and on the London underground I encountered crowds of young people bearing flowers. So I continued for another year in Namibia, during which, under standard European Union rules, the management of the project for an additional two years was put out to tender. This was not won by the consultancy company for which I worked, and at the end of October 1998 I returned to my house in France.

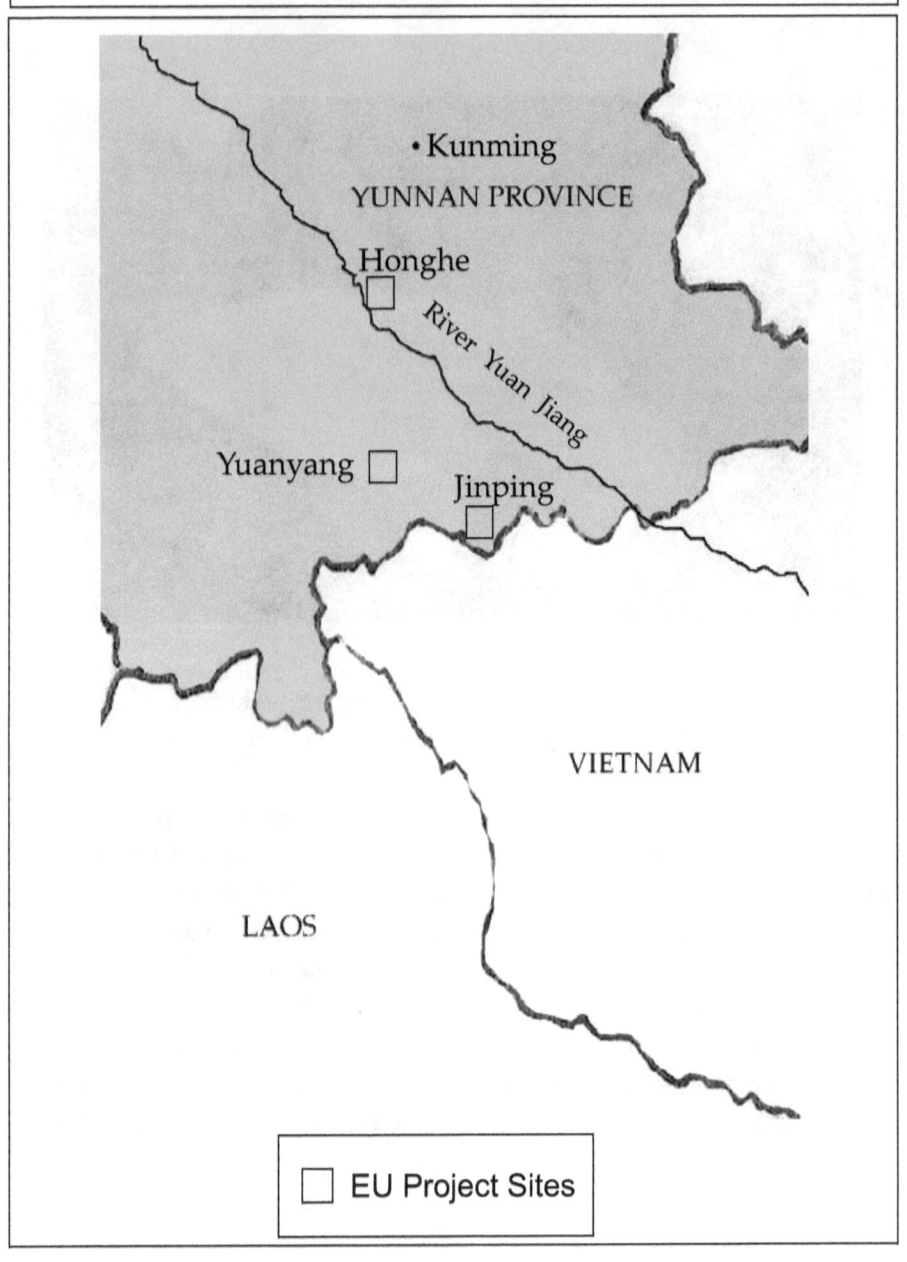

NOWHERE NEAR GREENLAND

TERRACES, TOAD SOUP AND ATOLL GODS

Not long after my return from Namibia, came the opportunity to review an EU project in the Central Cordillera of Luzon in the Philippines. Our team of three was based at Banawe, a small hill town at the centre of a World Heritage site, which in the Philippines is billed as the eighth wonder of the world. This comprises two thousand year old terraces that have transformed steep and otherwise useless mountain slopes into flourishing rice paddies, yielding two or more bountiful harvests a year. Once feared as head-hunters, fiercely resistant to Spanish and American colonialism and the more recent Japanese occupation, the introduction of roads, schools and missions have successfully integrated these mountain people as hard working farmers within the mainstream population. From high up on the steep slopes, these ancient, meticulously sculpted terraces march down in graded steps, gird the glittering ponds of flooded bunds where rice is yet unplanted, divide the plots of brilliant green young paddy from the yellow and beige of the ripening crop, and trace the contours to the distant foot of the mountain slope, curving away out of sight where the valley bends.

The concentrated cultivation of such difficult terrain demands routine, labour-intensive maintenance, but continuing migration of young people to the cities has caused a shortage of labour, resulting in the canals serving the terraces falling into

Terraces, Toad Soup and Atoll Gods

disrepair. The project was assisting with their rehabilitation, as well as promoting tree planting and agro-forestry to stabilise hill slopes and provide fuel-wood, as well as sponsoring micro-finance for small rural businesses The narrow mountain roads in this region are frequently cut by landslides, as a result of deforestation and the cultivation of steep slopes, combined with heavy rain and not infrequent earth tremors. Needless to say, our many visits to farmers' fields and villages covered considerably more vertical than horizontal distance - at least so it seemed to my legs and lungs.

Hay storage, Yunnan Highlands. China, 2000

The same year, I was invited to evaluate another EU-funded project, this time in Yunnan province in southern China. The project area included a number of villages south of the provincial capital Kunming, including some very close to the borders of Laos and Vietnam, in a restricted military area for which we had to obtain special permission to visit. This remote area of China is populated by over twenty minority ethnic groups, unlike in the majority of China where the Han predominate, and perhaps contribute a billion of the 1,400 million of the country's total population. Here, one encountered tribes such as the Red Hatted Yao, the Meow, the Honi and Kukong, the women of the first of these wearing a tall conical headdress, and of all

NOWHERE NEAR GREENLAND

them displaying intricately embroidered, many coloured jackets. Their menfolk, however, were undistinguished in the standard Mao-style uniform of a plain blue tunic and trousers.

This project, the only one funded by the EU in China, was of a pilot nature to test the result of devolving to farmers and their local authorities, all decisions concerning the kind, area and use of their crops. This reflected China's intention to move away from a command economy, and considerably reduce the number of communist cadres directing it throughout the country.

Blue hatted Meows, Yunnan province. China, 2000

Other components included forestry management, the provision of micro-finance for women-operated small business enterprises, and translocating impoverished farmers from the overcrowded, foggy highlands down to the malarial, low-lying, sub-tropical Yuan Jiang (Red River) valley, where they would need to learn to cultivate new crops such as sugar, mango and lychee.

I was accompanied by a German woman socio-economist, and together with two interpreters, and provincial representatives of the poverty alleviation bureau and the environmental protection agency, we travelled to the towns and villages of the area, where we met with local officials, the chief of which was always the magis-

Terraces, Toad Soup and Atoll Gods

trate. In the evenings at the small hotels where we stayed, there would usually be up to ten of us dining around a round table. My colleague and I experienced, and generally enjoyed, a possibly unique range of local dishes, which included the delicate, uncoiled tips of fern fronds (delicious) and toad soup (interesting). When a bowl of the latter swung round to me on the lazy Susan, I enquired as to the nature of the lumps of grey flesh floating in the liquid. Our interpreter from Beijing had no idea, and she asked the magistrate. Translating his reply, she said "You know frog? Well, not frog, more big, it walk not jump". "Ah, toad" I said. "Yes toad" she replied. It really was not so bad.

Red hatted Yaos, Yunnan province. China 2000

We visited two village primary schools that were in a very poor state of repair, and learned that few girls went on to complete their education, at even this basic level. And secondary education was so costly, way beyond the means of poor farmers, that one parent would have to leave home and work as migrant labour in a distant city in order to pay the fees. For a communist country, this came as a surprise to me, as did the overt nature of prostitution in Kunming, very much a vacation city for Chinese from the north, for I had expected attitudes in that regard to be more straight-laced. Another surprise was that unlike the Han, the Chinese minorities here are not limited to one child per family. In the hotel restaurants of Beijing and Kunming we had witnessed the tiresome behaviour of these spoilt 'little emperors'.

NOWHERE NEAR GREENLAND

I undertook two more consultancies in 2004 and 2005, I think possibly my last, on which I was accompanied by Dorosday Kenneth, the Director of Agriculture in Vanuatu. The first of these took us to Tanna, Malekula and Santo, very much home ground for me, to assess EU-assisted producer organisations, and the second to seven Pacific island countries, only three of which I had visited before, to evaluate an EU regional project to develop environmentally sustainable agriculture. I was intrigued to have the chance to visit Wallis & Futuna, a two small island French Overseas Territory, where the social benefits of still being tied to France were very evident, in terms of infrastructure and the general wealth and health of the local population. A high proportion of the indigenous people owns cars, and in an apparent time warp, white French gendarmes, in abbreviated tight shorts and kepis saunter out to meet arriving planes.

Hotel Malakai. Kiribati, 2005

In Kiribati, formally the Gilbert Islands, that long scattering of atolls straddling the equator, we left Tarawa, the capital, by fast speedboat to spend two days on the island of Malakai; the last plane to ferry visitors there broke down and they were there for several weeks. A typical atoll, with a twenty kilometres long narrow strip of land encircling a lagoon, its highest point is only some two or three metres above high water mark. The 'soil' comprises barely modified sand and coral, and the staple food crops of taro and sweet potato, augmented by coconuts and bananas, are largely grown in pits dug down to sea level and fed by decomposing plant material.

Terraces, Toad Soup and Atoll Gods

It is a strict custom, that all first-time visitors to Malakai should on arrival make an offering to the island gods at three separate places around the atoll; and the taste and expectation of these gods is for stick tobacco. (Manufactured in the Solomons and Papua New Guinea, stick tobacco has also been the preferred gift to offer when visiting those who still live in custom in Vanuatu, where it is crammed into the bowls of clay pipes – the latter, still made, at least until very recently, by a single company in Britain.)

At a Malakai Shrine. Kiribati, 2005.

Thus on our first circuit of the island, we stopped to make our offerings at the shrines. These proved to be waist high concrete plinths, atop which were poised the crudely fashioned head and shoulders of the deity, and halfway down the plinth was a niche in which to place the offering. No ceremony attended our observance, and, as far as I could ascertain, no prayers were offered up by the islanders accompanying us, though perhaps in the neighbouring villages some venerable gentlemen were already hunting out their clay pipes.

www.ingramcontent.com/pod-product-compliance
Lightning Source LLC
Chambersburg PA
CBHW020941230426
43666CB00005B/109